# BECOMING THE GOSPEL

# THE GOSPEL AND OUR CULTURE SERIES

A series to foster the missional encounter of the gospel
with North American culture

John R. Franke
*General Editor*

• •

## Volumes Published to Date

Lois Y. Barrett et al., *Treasure in Clay Jars: Patterns in Missional Faithfulness*

James V. Brownson, Inagrace T. Dietterich, Barry A. Harvey,
and Charles C. West, *StormFront: The Good News of God*

Michael J. Gorman, *Becoming the Gospel: Paul, Participation, and Mission*

Darrell L. Guder, *The Continuing Conversion of the Church*

Darrell L. Guder et al., *Missional Church: A Vision for the
Sending of the Church in North America*

George R. Hunsberger, *Bearing the Witness of the Spirit:
Lesslie Newbigin's Theology of Cultural Plurality*

George R. Hunsberger, *The Story That Chooses Us:
A Tapestry of Missional Vision*

George R. Hunsberger and Craig Van Gelder, editors, *The Church between
Gospel and Culture: The Emerging Mission in North America*

Craig Van Gelder, editor, *Confident Witness — Changing World:
Rediscovering the Gospel in North America*

# Becoming the Gospel

*Paul, Participation, and Mission*

Michael J. Gorman

WILLIAM B. EERDMANS PUBLISHING COMPANY

GRAND RAPIDS, MICHIGAN / CAMBRIDGE, U.K.

Wm. B. Eerdmans Publishing Co.

2140 Oak Industrial Drive N.E., Grand Rapids, Michigan 49505 /

P.O. Box 163, Cambridge CB3 9PU U.K.

www.eerdmans.com

Printed in the United States of America

21  20  19  18  17  16  15        7  6  5  4  3  2  1

**Library of Congress Cataloging-in-Publication Data**

Gorman, Michael J., 1955-

    Becoming the gospel: Paul, participation, and mission / Michael J. Gorman.

       pages      cm.      — (The Gospel and our culture series)

    Includes bibliographical references.

    ISBN 978-0-8028-6884-8 (pbk.: alk. paper)

    1. Bible. Epistles of Paul — Criticism, interpretation, etc.

    2. Missions — Biblical teaching.

    3. Mission of the church — Biblical teaching.

    I. Title.

BS2650.52.G67   2015

227'.06 — dc23

                                       2014043606

Dedicated to my wife Nancy,

our three adult children, Mark, Amy, and Brian,

and Rev. Mark A. Derby

for their ongoing participation in the *missio Dei*

# Contents

# Acknowledgments

This book owes much to many formal and informal conversations about Paul and about the mission of the church. I am grateful to those institutions and academic groups that invited me to present earlier versions of various chapters: St. Mary's Seminary & University, Notre Dame Seminary, North Park Theological Seminary, and Washington Adventist University (the chapter on 1 and 2 Corinthians); the Forum on Missional Hermeneutics of the Gospel and Our Culture Network, an affiliate member of the Society of Biblical Literature (the chapter on Philippians); and the Theological Hermeneutics of Christian Scripture (now Theological Interpretation of Scripture) unit of the Society of Biblical Literature (the chapter on Romans). In addition, I am grateful to the following journals and editors: the *Journal of Theological Interpretation (JTI)* and editor Joel Green for permission to publish a revised version of the Romans chapter, the original of which appeared in the Spring 2011 issue of *JTI*; and the *Journal for the Study of Paul and His Letters (JSPL)*, and then-editors Michael Bird and Nijay Gupta, for permission to publish a revised version of the 1 and 2 Corinthians chapter, the original of which appeared in the Fall 2011 issue of *JSPL*.

I am grateful as well to those who responded formally or informally to various earlier versions of these chapters in public fora, including especially Steve Fowl, Beverly Gaventa, Richard Hays, Bob Jewett, and Tom Wright. I am appreciative of Dean Flemming and Jim Miller, who provided helpful comments on a draft of the book. In addition, Michael Barram read the entire manuscript carefully and made numerous suggestions that improved both the style and the content; I am deeply in his debt. And as always I am indebted to Andy Johnson, who read and commented on parts of the book and shared his pre-publication commentary work on 1 Thessalonians with me.

In addition, I am also very grateful to my research assistants over the years who have helped with various parts of this book, especially Susan Jaeger, Kurt Pfund, Daniel Jackson, and Gary Staszak. Gary helped bring the book to completion with his fine eye for detail in proofreading and indexing. I appreciate as well my students in the 2014 Ecumenical Institute of Theology class "Paul and the Missional Church," who helped me think through the book one final time (and found a number of typos!). Ted Wiese of that class made some particularly insightful suggestions.

Finally, I express my gratitude to my wife Nancy, whose steadfast love for me, for others, for God, and for the gospel of God have inspired me for many years.

EASTER 2014

# Becoming the Gospel

In his insightful book *Living the Christian Story,* theologian John Colwell makes the following major assertion:

> The gospel story . . . defines the life of the Christian and the life of the Church, while the life of the Church and the life of the Christian is, correspondingly, a retelling and reinterpreting of that gospel story. The world has no access to the gospel story other than as it is narrated in the life, worship, and proclamation of the Church. . . . Through its service and being as witness, the Church is a rendering of the gospel to the world.[1]

A similar perspective was enunciated clearly by the important missiologist Lesslie Newbigin, who said,

> I have come to feel that the primary reality of which we have to take account in seeking for a Christian impact on public life is the Christian congregation. How is it possible that the gospel should be credible, that people should come to believe that the power which has the last word in human affairs is represented by a man hanging on a cross? I am suggesting that the only answer, the only hermeneutic [means of interpretation] of the gospel, is a congregation of men and women who believe it and live by it.[2]

1. John E. Colwell, *Living the Christian Story: The Distinctiveness of Christian Ethics* (New York: T. & T. Clark, 2001), p. 85.
2. Lesslie Newbigin, *The Gospel in a Pluralist Society* (Grand Rapids: Eerdmans, 1989), p. 27, in a chapter titled "The Congregation as Hermeneutic of the Gospel."

More recently, and echoing the work of two prominent theologians, John Howard Yoder and Stanley Hauerwas, Bryan Stone summarizes his book *Evangelism after Christendom* as follows:

> The thesis of this book is that the most evangelistic thing the church can do today is to be the church — to be formed imaginatively by the Holy Spirit through core practices such as worship, forgiveness, hospitality, and economic sharing into a distinctive people in the world, a new social option, the body of Christ.[3]

Many similar sentiments have been expressed in recent years by theologians, missiologists, and biblical scholars with deep commitments to the life of the church. "Christian ecclesial life," writes Kavin Rowe in his interpretation of Acts, is the "cultural explication of God's identity."[4]

I have expressed such sentiments myself on numerous occasions. The central claim of this book — *Becoming the Gospel: Paul, Participation, and Mission* — is that already in the first Christian century the apostle Paul wanted the communities he addressed not merely to *believe* the gospel but to *become* the gospel, and in so doing to participate in the very life and mission of God.[5]

This claim is really the central thesis of all of my writing about Paul. The present work is the sequel to a previous book, *Inhabiting the Cruciform God: Kenosis, Justification, and Theosis in Paul's Narrative Soteriology,* which in turn was the sequel to an earlier volume, *Cruciformity: Paul's Narrative Spirituality of the Cross.*[6] These three interrelated monographs constitute a trilogy on Paul.

That this trilogy exists is partly deliberate, partly accidental. It is deliberate in the sense that I have continually sought to deepen and extend my

---

3. Bryan P. Stone, *Evangelism after Christendom: The Theology and Practice of Christian Witness* (Grand Rapids: Brazos, 2006).

4. C. Kavin Rowe, *World Upside Down: Reading Acts in the Graeco-Roman Age* (New York: Oxford University Press, 2009), p. 8.

5. Writing from a slightly different, but complementary, perspective, N. T. Wright calls the church the "central symbol" of Paul's worldview and gospel, insisting that for Paul the church's unity and holiness, including especially its practice of reconciliation, are critical to the gospel's integrity. See his *Paul and the Faithfulness of God,* vol. 4 of Christian Origins and the Question of God (Minneapolis: Fortress, 2013).

6. *Cruciformity: Paul's Narrative Spirituality of the Cross* (Grand Rapids: Eerdmans, 2001); *Inhabiting the Cruciform God: Kenosis, Justification, and Theosis in Paul's Narrative Soteriology* (Grand Rapids: Eerdmans, 2009).

explorations of Paul's theology and spirituality, and these new explorations have led first to new conclusions and then to new publications, each building on earlier work. It is also deliberate in that I have attempted to focus these explorations on similar or related topics during various periods of my journey with the apostle Paul. The existence of the trilogy is accidental, however, in the sense that I did not originally intend to write three closely connected books on Paul that are best read one after the other.

Already in *Cruciformity* I spoke of the Pauline assemblies as communities and even "colonies" of cruciformity — specifically cruciform faith, love, power, and hope — that had an inherently "missionary character."[7] This third book unpacks that claim in more detail, while also connecting its theme of cruciform existence more specifically and fully to the emphasis on participation in Christ, and thereby in the life of God, that is central to *Inhabiting the Cruciform God.* But this book is more than a further development of *Cruciformity* and *Inhabiting.* It is also a prolonged response to a concern about the second book expressed by theologian David Congdon in a comment on my blog, which then became part of a conversation on the blog and, finally, a published review.[8] Congdon, who actually liked much about *Inhabiting,* thought that I had seriously underdeveloped the theme of mission in the unpacking of my thesis about Pauline theology as a theology of theosis — becoming like God by participating in the life of God.[9] He con-

---

7. *Cruciformity,* pp. 49-67, with the communities' missionary character discussed on pp. 363-66.

8. The conversation may be seen at http://www.michaeljgorman.net/2009/08/16/theosis-and-mission-the-conversation-continues/. Congdon's review was later published in *Koinonia* 21 (2009): 125-28, though in that review he does not bring up the missional concerns noted in the blog posts.

9. To be more specific about my definition of theosis: "Theosis is about divine intention and action, human transformation, and the *telos* of human existence — union with God" (*Inhabiting the Cruciform God,* p. 5). "Theosis is transformative participation in the kenotic, cruciform character of God through Spirit-enabled conformity to the incarnate, crucified, and resurrected/glorified Christ" (*Inhabiting the Cruciform God,* pp. 7, 162). The term and concept "theosis," or "deification," is not well known in many Western ecclesial circles, but it has come back onto the radar screen recently. There is no "official" definition of the term, but it is commonly expressed in phrases such as union with God, becoming like God, sharing (or participation) in the divine life, human transfiguration, restoration to full humanity in Christ, sharing in Christ the God-man, and even "Christification." In a helpful introduction to the topic, Norman Russell offers a comprehensive, synthetic working definition: "Theosis is our restoration as persons to integrity and wholeness by participation in Christ through the Holy Spirit, in a process which is initiated in this world through our life of ecclesial communion and moral striving and finds ultimate fulfillment in our union with the Father — all within

tended that my understanding of theosis implicitly separated being and act, union with God and mission, and that if God is a being-in-mission, so also is the church that participates in God's life. And he suggested, rightly, that I did not want to argue for separation of act and being but did want to argue for participation (or theosis) as requiring mission.[10] In several exchanges, he pointed out certain Pauline texts that are not considered in the book (a valid point, especially if the book is read apart from *Cruciformity*; the texts are now treated in this new book). Interestingly, another respondent to *Inhabiting*, in some now unrecoverable online review, seems to have read my book in the way Congdon feared it could be. The main point of this other review went something like this: "Theosis rules out the possibility of mission."

The thesis of the present book is precisely the opposite: theosis — Spirit-enabled transformative participation in the life and character of God revealed in the crucified and resurrected Messiah Jesus — is the starting point of mission and is, in fact, its proper theological framework. And I am not alone in making this sort of proposal.[11] David Congdon was right: being and

---

the broad context of the divine economy" (*Fellow Workers with God: Orthodox Thinking on Theosis* [Crestwood, NY: St. Vladimir's Seminary Press, 2009], p. 21). The fundamental theological axiom of theosis is the formulation by church fathers such as Irenaeus and Athanasius that God (or Christ) became what we are so that we might become what God (or Christ) is. This axiom is rooted in Pauline "interchange" texts such as Gal. 3:13; 2 Cor. 5:21; and 2 Cor. 8:9 (discussed in chapter seven). As a spiritual theology, theosis is predicated as well on the Pauline and Johannine experience of Christ's indwelling (see, e.g., Gal. 2:19-20; Eph. 3:17; Col. 1:27; Rom. 8:1-17; John 15; 17:20-23). For additional suggested reading on theosis, see note 20 in chapter eight (p. 269).

10. Congdon's most significant, but rather technical, sentences bear repeating here: "[T]he question is whether there is any 'gap' between being and act in your ecclesiology, which is then a question of whether there is a 'gap' between being and act in your doctrine of God. Missional theology defines God's being in terms of mission (act), and the same goes for ecclesiology. I feel like, in your book, you come up to the point of saying that the being of the church is in act, but you never actually say it. You say that the obedience of faith is 'inherently a participation in the being . . . of God' (review of Gorman, *Inhabiting the Cruciform God*, p. 93), but you don't make the crucial reverse move: that participation in God is inherently (and we ought to add, solely) our obedience of faith. Your account needs an actualistic ontology in order to be suitable for a missional hermeneutic. Otherwise there is a substance that participates in God apart from mission. I don't think you want that, but it isn't explicitly clear in the text."

11. See also Ross Hastings, *Missional God, Missional Church: Hope for Re-evangelizing the West* (Downers Grove, IL: InterVarsity, 2012), who makes basically the same claim through a theological/missional reading of the Gospel of John, particularly John 20:19-23, though the book is also peppered with apt discussions of Paul. Relying in part on Paul's witness, Hastings argues that churches, as missional bodies participating in the life of the missional God, are "communities of Christ's risen presence" (ch. 5) as well as "communities of Christ's crucified

act, life and mission, belong together both for God and for the church. As I said to him in the blog exchanges, *Inhabiting* was addressing certain issues that kept mission in the conversation, but it was not the focus. Neither, however, was it sidelined. To quote the conclusion of *Inhabiting the Cruciform God*, where this point is made clearly but relatively briefly:

> [T]he use of the term theosis does not remove salvation from the larger narrative and divine project to which the Scriptures of Israel and the Pauline letters bear witness. Rather, salvation in Paul is the fulfillment of Israel's story, the calling of a new people composed of both Gentiles and Jews, being made children of Abraham as they are formed into the image of the Jewish Messiah (Gal. 3:29, 6:16). Salvation in Paul is the remedy for humanity's predicament, the creation of a new humanity being re-made into the likeness of Christ the last Adam (1 Cor. 15:45-49). And human salvation in Paul is one dimension — the one that Paul stresses — of the cosmic drama of liberation (Rom. 8:18-25), reconciliation (Col. 1:19-20), and victory over all evil powers (1 Cor. 15:24-26, 54-57) that includes the universal acclamation of Jesus as Lord (Phil. 2:9-11) and the completion of the process of theosis (Rom. 8:29-30) before culminating finally in that mysterious reality when God will be "all in all" (1 Cor. 15:28). *In the meantime, by the power of the Spirit of Father and Son, the new people, the new humanity bears witness in word and deed to that glorious future by participating now in the life and mission of the triune cruciform God.*[12]

presence" (ch. 8). The result of the latter is communities focused on both "mission about the cross" and "mission under the cross," meaning shaped by the cross (ch. 8) — that is, communities of cruciformity. Similarly, Paul Collins suggests that "the element of missiological witness" in John 17:21-23 "reinforces the potential for the metaphor of deification to be re-received today in the collective context of the Church and to provide the basis for an enriched understanding of mission as well as a renewed understanding of the cosmic dimensions of the divine purposes" (Paul M. Collins, *Partaking in Divine Nature: Deification and Communion* [New York: T. & T. Clark, 2010], p. 47). See as well Morna D. Hooker and Frances M. Young, *Holiness and Mission: Learning from the Early Church about Mission in the City* (London: SCM, 2010). In the first two chapters of the book, New Testament scholar Hooker (though she does not use the word "theosis") argues that early Christian mission was predicated on the biblical mandate to be holy as God is holy, and that Christian proclamation and praxis were imitation of Emmanuel, God with us. See also her last sentence in the book (p. 107): "Mission is rooted in holiness — in becoming like Christ, who is the image of God."

12. *Inhabiting the Cruciform God*, pp. 172-73 (emphasis added). Unfortunately, Congdon does not refer to this paragraph either in the informal blog posts or in the published review. He might say, however, that the last sentence does not sufficiently address the issue of mission to overcome the relative inattention to it in the rest of the book. On the insepa-

This book, then, picks up where that quote, and that book, ends. I invite you to join me in the ongoing exploration and conversation.

## Paul, Participation, and Mission

According to Paul, God was in Christ reconciling the world to himself, and to do so God in Christ became what we are so that in Christ we might become what God is, as Paul puts it in 2 Corinthians 5:14-21. Commenting on the climax of this passage (v. 21) — "For our sake he [God] made him [Christ] to be sin who knew no sin, so that in him we might become the righteousness of God" — Morna Hooker writes that the "we"

> has particular significance for Paul's own understanding of discipleship and ministry, [and] becomes an invitation to others to share in the divine activity. What Christ is to us — righteousness, wisdom, sanctification, redemption — Christians must now be to the world.[13]

The goal of human existence, for Paul and for those who receive his words as Christian Scripture, is to participate now and forever, individually and corporately, in the very life and character of this cruciform, missional, world-redeeming God of righteousness and restorative justice *(dikaiosynē)*. As I have written elsewhere (re-presented here in slightly modified form):

---

rability of theosis from mission, see now my "Paul's Corporate, Cruciform, Missional Theosis in Second Corinthians," in *'In Christ' in Paul: Explorations in Paul's Theology of Union and Participation,* ed. Kevin J. Vanhoozer, Constantine R. Campbell, and Michael J. Thate, WUNT 2 series (Tübingen: Mohr Siebeck, 2014). Hastings, *Missional God,* has a chapter titled "Mission as Theosis" (pp. 268-92), and he describes his theology of the church as *"participational . . .* an organic consequence of union in and participation with the missional God" (p. 15). See also Collins, *Partaking in Divine Nature,* discussing theosis and liturgy (worship), and responding to the claim that theosis can sound self-serving: "The celebration of the sacraments in the collective context of the Church sets the process of deification in relation to the Church's participation in God's mission [*missio Dei*] in the world. The calling to deification, and the processes of being deified are not esoteric or elitist but are part of the Church's witness to the purpose and value of human life and of God's purpose in calling all things into existence so that God may become 'all in all' (1 Corinthians 15.28; Ephesians 1.23)" (pp. 185-86).

13. Morna D. Hooker, "On Becoming the Righteousness of God: Another Look at 2 Cor. 5:21," *Novum Testamentum* 50 (2008): 358-75 (here p. 375). Hooker alludes as well here to 1 Cor. 1:30.

Paul believed himself to be caught up in a divine mission — a mission not everyone appreciated — to spread a powerful word of good news (the "gospel") that would establish an international network of transformed, peaceable, multicultural communities worshiping, obeying, and bearing public witness to the one true God by conformity to his Son in the power of the Spirit.[14]

This divine mission was and is the "benevolent intervention of God into the history of Israel, human history more generally, and the entire cosmos to set right a world gone awry."[15] As such, the gospel was and is revelatory; it reveals God's faithfulness and mercy; God's love; God's peace, justice, and righteousness; even, we might say, God's hope, God's dream for the world, a dream that will one day be realized, beyond any shadow of doubt. These divine character traits (so to speak) all come to expression in and through Jesus' self-gift; to be in Christ is to also be caught up in God's mission and thus in God's own character — indeed, in God's very life. In my view, and apparently in the view of a growing number of others, this has immense practical implications for Christian mission.[16]

I believe that theosis and other terms (deification, Christification, Christosis[17]) adequately summarize this transformative reality of Spirit-enabled, Christlike participation in the life and mission of God. But I know that others (if they know the terms) may disagree, arguing either that the words are unbiblical or anachronistic, or that one can acknowledge participation in God without understanding it as what some parts of the church have called theosis or deification. I will not abandon these lesser-known terms in this book, using them and "participation" interchangeably but with more

14. Michael J. Gorman, *Reading Paul* (Eugene, OR: Cascade, 2008), p. 22. The modification is the addition of the phrase "bearing public witness."

15. Gorman, *Reading Paul*, p. 44 (original emphasis removed).

16. In addition to the book by Hastings mentioned in previous notes and the feedback I have received from pastors and others engaged in mission, I offer as support for this claim two additional items: (1) a scholarly article engaging *Inhabiting the Cruciform God* that is representative of the sentiments I have heard from other theologians: David R. Purves, "Relating Kenosis to Soteriology: Implications for Christian Ministry amongst Homeless People," *Horizons in Biblical Theology* 35 (2013): 70-90; and (2) a review of the present book planned by the Forum on Missional Hermeneutics of the Gospel and Our Culture Network (GOCN) for a future annual meeting of the Society of Biblical Literature. (GOCN is a network of scholars, pastors, and communities concerned about the church's mission in the post-Christendom West.)

17. Ben C. Blackwell, *Christosis: Pauline Soteriology in Light of Deification in Irenaeus and Cyril of Alexandria*, WUNT 2/314 (Tübingen: Mohr Siebeck, 2011).

frequent use of participation language. Those who find fault with this substitution of terms and/or abstain from the term theosis will at least, I hope, agree that transformative participation is central to Paul and to our appropriation of his spirituality and missional activity today. Those who like terms such as theosis and deification — which are gaining in currency in certain circles — will, I hope, understand that my less frequent use of the terms in most of this book is for pragmatic reasons of communication with a broad audience and does not reflect a retraction of my thesis in *Inhabiting the Cruciform God*.[18] In any event, the language of theosis and/or participation is not merely an individualistic idiom but especially an ecclesial one — a way of articulating the reality of communal, cruciform participation in the cross-shaped Trinity.[19]

Although I will draw on large portions of Paul's letters in the following pages, one might say that the book's "theme text" is 2 Corinthians 5:21: "For our sake he made him to be sin who knew no sin, so that in him we might become the righteousness [or justice] of God."[20] In fact, this book could be titled *Becoming the Justice of God*, for Paul's gospel is the announcement of the arrival and power of God's right-wising, transformative justice in Jesus Christ. In 2 Corinthians 5:14-21 (and in shorter summaries of the gospel, such as Rom. 1:16-17), justification as inclusive of transformation, participa-

---

18. For reasons that will become apparent, in the final substantive chapter of the book (on Romans), the term "theosis" will actually be prominent. Already a half-century ago Reformed theologian T. F. Torrance urged Western Christians not to "quarrel about the word *theosis*, offensive though it may be to us, but follow its intention" — "to partake of the living presence and saving acts of God the Creator and Redeemer" (*Theology in Reconstruction* [Grand Rapids: Eerdmans, 1965; repr. Eugene, OR: Wipf & Stock, 1996], pp. 243-44). That is, transformative participation in the life and mission of God. More recently, Constantine R. Campbell (*Paul and Union with Christ: An Exegetical and Theological Study* [Grand Rapids: Zondervan, 2012]) has argued for the use of four terms to express this pervasive aspect of Paul's theology: union, participation, identification, and incorporation (summaries on pp. 29, 406-20), though "union with Christ," he says, is a handy summary of these four dimensions (p. 414). Campbell is concerned about the possible misuse of the language of "divinization" (p. 63) but cautiously accepts my interpretation of theosis, i.e., that cruciformity, conformity to Christ crucified, is actually theoformity, conformity to God (pp. 57-58, 364-68). Unfortunately, Campbell does not develop the possible missional implications of Paul's participatory language.

19. I explore this claim in depth in *Inhabiting the Cruciform God*. See also Hastings, *Missional God, Missional Church*, esp. pp. 268-92; he says that theosis/participation means that both the inner and outer lives of the church will reflect the inner and outer life of the Trinity, i.e., it will be both communal and kenotic, or self-emptying (p. 265).

20. All Scripture quotations, unless otherwise indicated, are from the NRSV, with occasional alternatives in brackets, as here. Translations marked MJG are those of the author.

tion, and mission all find powerful expression.[21] *To understand justification less robustly is simply to misunderstand Paul.* At the same time, however, this book understands the "justice" of Paul's justification (more precisely, of *God's* justification) to be inextricably connected to such divine traits and practical human virtues (enabled by God's Spirit) as faithfulness, love, peace and reconciliation, and righteousness. These divine traits become the human, missional characteristics of those individuals and communities who inhabit the missional, cruciform God. *To put it simply: the cross of Christ reveals a missional, justifying, justice-making God and creates a missional, justified, justice-making people.*[22] Because the cross reveals a missional God, the church saved and shaped by the cross will be a missional people.[23] As the twentieth-century theologian Emil Brunner put it, "The Church exists by mission, just as a fire exists by burning. Where there is no mission there is no Church. . . ."[24]

21. The theme of justice has become increasingly central to my interpretation of Paul. Some readers, however, become nervous when they hear "justice" language associated with the apostle Paul. They fear that he is being turned into an advocate of nonpersonal, nonspiritual, progressive, or "liberal" theology that detracts from Paul's true intentions. As I have already argued in *Inhabiting the Cruciform God,* and as I intend to show especially in the chapter on justification and justice, such fears are misplaced. Paul's theology and spirituality are a legitimate and substantive continuation of the prophetic ministry and message of the Hebrew prophets and of Jesus. This does not make him "unspiritual" — or anything else one might fear — but rather interprets him properly as fully and covenantally spiritual: passionate about love of God and love of neighbor, filled with the Spirit of justice who filled Isaiah, Amos, Hosea, and Jesus. But Paul expresses this Spirit-filled prophetic reality in new ways in light of the incarnation, death, and resurrection of Jesus. In other words, cruciformity and justice are inseparable from each other. The same can be said of peacemaking and reconciliation, which are related in the Bible (and specifically in Paul) not only to justice but also to love — all components of the Bible's grand vision of *shalom.* These interrelated practices constitute the several sides, so to speak, of one coin, the missional identity of those who are in Christ. On Christ and peace in Paul, see not only the two chapters in this book, but also my article "The Lord of Peace: Christ Our Peace in Pauline Theology," *Journal for the Study of Paul and His Letters* 3 (2013): 219-53, as well as the portions of the chapters on peace (chs. 6 and 7) devoted to Paul in my *The Death of the Messiah and the Birth of the New Covenant: A (Not So) New Model of the Atonement* (Eugene, OR: Cascade, 2014).

22. See also my *Death of the Messiah* for the significance of this claim both in and beyond Paul. Again, it is necessary to stress that the word "justice" must be filled with biblical content, not the latest secular notions.

23. For a theological argument that God is a missional God, see Stephen R. Holmes, "Trinitarian Missiology: Towards a Theology of God as Missionary," *International Journal of Systematic Theology* 8 (2006): 72-90.

24. Emil Brunner, *The Word and the World* (London: SCM, 1931), p. 108.

## An Overview of the Book

This book lies at the intersection of three theological subdisciplines: Pauline studies, hermeneutics, and missiology. I intend it to be both for scholars and for pastors and other church leaders. One of the most important professional developments for me in recent years (even predating the writing of *Inhabiting*) has been my affiliation with the Forum on Missional Hermeneutics of the Gospel and Our Culture Network, which has met annually in conjunction with the Society of Biblical Literature. In the conversations generated by that Forum, scholarly and pastoral concerns meet, as do biblical specialists, missional theologians, and pastoral practitioners. Learning to read Paul missionally — not merely as the quintessential "missionary" but as a formator of missional communities — has been an exhilarating experience. Some of the fruit of this labor has been previously published in earlier books and articles, but in this book I obviously focus on this hermeneutical (interpretive) approach more fully, both implicitly throughout the book and explicitly at certain junctures.

Another word needs to be said about the title of this book. First, the word "becoming" clearly places emphasis on a process, for that is what participation in Christ — transformation into the image of God in Christ (or theosis) — truly is. It is possible that one could (mis-)interpret "inhabiting" in the title *Inhabiting the Cruciform God* to be a static state rather than a dynamic process. Such misinterpretation is impossible with "becoming."

A word also needs to be said about the origin and nature of these chapters. Some of them began as essays in their own right, though when I wrote them I had a larger missional-Paul project in mind and meant them to be complementary expressions of a Pauline missional hermeneutic.[25] (That is, I had this book in mind.) In editing and expanding the original essays, and in composing new essays specifically for this book, I have not set out to write the definitive, systematic, comprehensive word on participation and mission in Paul and its hermeneutical significance. Rather, this book is a series of integrated forays into this important field of theological study, reflection, and action. I hope that it will engender further reflection, discussion, and mission, not only in the academy, but also in the church.

25. Two of the five chapters are adapted from previously published articles: "Justification and Justice in Paul, with Special Reference to the Corinthians," *Journal for the Study of Paul and His Letters* 1 (2011): 23-40; and "Romans: The First Christian Treatise on Theosis," *Journal of Theological Interpretation* 5 (2011): 13-34. In addition, some of the main thoughts developed in this book were sketched out in "Missional Musings on Paul," *Catalyst* (Spring 2011), http://www.catalystresources.org/missional-musings-on-paul/.

That said, I think that even in this relatively brief treatment of participatory mission, or missional participation, in Paul, a rather comprehensive picture of what this means for the apostle and for us who read his letters as Scripture emerges. Specifically, we will find Paul advocating a witness to the gospel that is both embodied and narrated, one that simultaneously practices, in an integrated way, what we today might call virtue, evangelism, reconciliation, and justice, all as aspects of transformative participation in the glory of God revealed in the crucified and resurrected Jesus by the Spirit. These aspects of mission in Paul are addressed in the several chapters that follow an introductory overview about reading Paul missionally.

Following this introductory invitation, the book is organized as follows:

CHAPTER ONE
Paul and the Mission of God

CHAPTER TWO
Reading Paul Missionally

CHAPTER THREE
Becoming the Gospel of Faith(fulness), Love, and Hope:
1 Thessalonians

CHAPTER FOUR
Becoming and Telling the Story of Christ: Philippians

CHAPTER FIVE
Becoming the Gospel of Peace (I): Overview

CHAPTER SIX
Becoming the Gospel of Peace (II): Ephesians

CHAPTER SEVEN
Becoming the Justice of God: 1 & 2 Corinthians

CHAPTER EIGHT
Becoming the Gospel of God's Justice/Righteousness and Glory:
Missional Theosis in Romans

FINAL REFLECTIONS
Becoming the Gospel (Reprise)

The first chapter, "Paul and the Mission of God," considers what Paul thinks God is up to in the world (the *missio Dei*): in a word, salvation. It then relates God's salvation to participation in Christ before addressing the challenging question of if, and how, Paul expected his communities and individual believers (rather than just apostles and "missionaries") to participate in the mission of God. This chapter provides the basic Pauline framework for the rest of the book. The chapter argues that, for Paul, to participate in Christ is both to benefit from God's mission of liberation and reconciliation and to bear witness to this divine mission — thus furthering it — by becoming a faithful embodiment of it. Both communities and individuals bear public witness to the gospel and thus participate in the *missio Dei*.

The second chapter, "Reading Paul Missionally," sets the interpretive framework for the rest of the book. It first explores the idea of missional hermeneutics, or biblical interpretation done from the perspective of the church as a sent community, as it has been developing among certain recent biblical scholars, missiologists, and ecclesial leaders. We review several approaches to, or "streams" of, missional hermeneutics, and we suggest the kinds of questions that a missional hermeneutic will ask of Scripture, including Paul's letters. We then propose that the guiding question in a Pauline missional hermeneutic is, "How do we read Paul for what he says about the *missio Dei* and about our participation in it?" That is, we are interested not only in what Paul said to his churches, but also, and indeed most importantly, in how his invitation to them to participate in God's mission is also an invitation, indeed a summons, to us. Accordingly, as we read Paul's letters in the subsequent chapters, the "so what?" question will always be before us.

The third chapter, "Becoming the Gospel of Faith(fulness), Love, and Hope: 1 Thessalonians," explores the missional significance of the famous — and early — Pauline triad expressed in 1 Thessalonians 1:3 and 5:8 that later becomes known as the three theological virtues. The chapter shows how God through Christ, by the Spirit, makes people into a community of Godlike, Christlike faith (and faithfulness), love, and hope. As such, and only as such, does this community bear witness to its neighbors far and wide that the God of Israel is calling all people into a new way of life in which God is properly worshiped, people are appropriately loved, and the fear of wrath and death are conquered. Paul shows the Thessalonians, and us, how Christ, ministers, and the entire community share in the embodiment of the gospel.

The fourth chapter, "Becoming and Telling the Story of Christ: Philippians," investigates the rich poetic or hymnic text found in Philippians 2:6-11 — which I have called Paul's master story — from a missional perspective. This text has been the subject of many diverse investigations and interpretations. The chapter argues that the hymn/poem summarizes the gospel that Paul wants the Philippian assembly to (continue to) proclaim and (continue to) embody, in spite of opposition. Philippians 2:6-11 is thus a missional Christology for a missional people, a missional people who display a narrative and narrated witness. Participating in the *missio Dei*, the Philippians will both hold forth (in word and deed) and defend the basic Pauline claims about the crucified Jesus as the self-giving, life-giving Son of God and sovereign Lord, in fulfillment of Scripture and in contrast to Caesar. These claims have been vindicated by God in exalting Jesus, and they will soon be acknowledged by all creation. Paul's words speak to the contemporary church in several ways about the coherent form and content of its missional life and message. These can be summarized in the phrases "the great commission," "the great commandment," and "the great challenge." The letter to the Philippians also reminds us that suffering was and is a normal consequence of faithful witness.

The fifth and sixth chapters, on becoming the gospel of peace (shalom), argue for the importance of peace and reconciliation in the Pauline corpus generally and in Ephesians particularly. Chapter five, "Becoming the Gospel of Peace (I): Overview," surveys the language of peace and reconciliation in the Pauline letters to show how, for Paul, the biblical vision of *shalom* comes to fulfillment in Christ and is prominent in his letters, though often neglected by his interpreters. For Paul, in Christ the God of peace has brought the peace of God. Chapter six, "Becoming the Gospel of Peace (II): Ephesians," argues that although the authorship of Ephesians is disputed, it captures an essential element of Pauline missional theology. In Ephesians we see that the drama of salvation is the story of the divine peace initiative. Those who are reconciled to God through Christ are invited — even expected, as a natural part of their reconciliation — to participate in God's ongoing mission of making peace both inside and outside the church. Believers are, in a sense, to "wear God" — the God of peace.

Building on the discussions of *shalom,* chapter seven, "Becoming the Justice of God: 1 & 2 Corinthians," addresses a significant question that many have wondered about: whether Paul was apathetic about the central biblical theme of justice, especially as seen in the prophets. Despite some studies of this theme in Paul, it has not received the attention it deserves, and questions linger. This chapter argues that justice was central to Paul's theology, particularly his teaching on justification. It explores seven links between justification and justice in his writings, giving special attention to the connections the apostle draws in 1 and 2 Corinthians. For Paul, justice is both in continuity with and a new development of biblical justice; it is both prophetic and cruciform. The chapter concludes with theological reflections on the place of justice in the missional life of the contemporary Christian community.

The eighth chapter, following on the exploration of justification and justice, is called "Becoming the Gospel of God's Justice/Righteousness and Glory: Missional Theosis in Romans." It builds on renewed interest in theosis generally, and particularly with respect to Paul. As an extension of the general argument of *Inhabiting the Cruciform God,* this chapter argues specifically that Romans is an early Christian treatise on theosis, and specifically *missional* theosis. In *Inhabiting,* I argued that theosis, when used of Paul, means transformative participation in the kenotic, cruciform character of God through Spirit-enabled conformity to the incarnate, crucified, and resurrected/glorified Christ. This chapter traces Paul's soteriology of restoring human *dikaiosynē* and *doxa,* or justice/righteousness and glory — fundamental elements of theosis — in Romans. For Paul, this restoration is participation in God's own justice/righteousness and glory, and it is accomplished by participation in the death and resurrection of the obedient and faithful Son. It is manifested in "righteoused," multicultural, cruciform communities of Christlike Godlikeness in which Gentiles and Jews glorify God together as a foreshadowing of the final glory of God. Their corporate existence is, at least implicitly, a counterpoint to the pseudo-glory of Rome and a permanent model for the church in the face of normal expressions of political, especially empire-like, power. Their transformation, then, is a liturgical and missional participation in the life of the triune God that bears witness to God's desire to reconcile people in Christ so that they experience the righteousness and glory of God together.

In each of the main chapters, I briefly illustrate, with one or more contemporary examples, a few ways in which the trajectory of Paul's missional understanding of the church has reached the twenty-first century and is embodied in our own contexts. The last chapter, "Becoming the Gospel (Reprise)," recaps the other chapters and makes several concluding suggestions regarding the missional life of the church when it takes Paul seriously. Neither in this chapter nor throughout the book, however, will I try to impose concrete "requirements" on the church in mission. Such an approach would betray the fundamentally particular and contextual ways in which Paul addresses his congregations and in which contemporary missiologists urge churches to examine their own contexts carefully to discern specifically how they need to participate in the *missio Dei* where they are. Moreover, this book is primarily a theological interpretation of Paul's letters within a missional framework, not a handbook of missional practice or strategy per se. Imaginative, contextual reflection on Paul's letters is the best follow-up to a book such as this.[26] This work, then, is not a handbook for mission but a foundation and a stimulus for it. It is a sort of Pauline theology for the (already-existing) holistic mission of the church, as well as a means to expand and deepen that mission in light of Paul's theology and praxis, specifically the praxis he saw in, and expected of, the communities he "pastored."[27]

The absence of chapters on other Pauline letters should not be taken as a sign that they lack a missional dimension. Rather, the letters treated here are those with which I have been most fully engaged for many years and about which I think I have something concrete to offer.


## Becoming the Gospel: Anticipation, Participation, Mission

This book, like all of my work on Paul, is intended to interpret Paul both in his first-century context, addressing early Christian communities, and in his ongoing significance for us who read his letters as Christian Scripture. N. T. (Tom) Wright hints at the spirit of this book. He says that if "the very truth" of the gospel is "not to be fatally compromised,"

> [t]he gospel of God, today and tomorrow as in Paul's day . . . must become, as it did in Jesus, flesh and blood. That which was unveiled before an unprepared world in Jesus Christ must be unveiled again and again, as those who believe in Jesus Christ live by the Spirit and, in life as well as in word, announce the gospel to the world.[28]

Yes, the gospel must become flesh and blood in and as the church, which is to say as well that the church must become the gospel, embodying God's

26. I will confess that I simply lack the knowledge and experience to write about the implementation of Paul's missional theologizing in the way that, say, Elaine Enns and Ched Myers do. See their *Ambassadors of Reconciliation*, vol. 2: *Diverse Christian Practices of Restorative Justice and Peacemaking* (Maryknoll, NY: Orbis, 2009). See also Lois Y. Barrett et al., *Treasure in Clay Jars: Patterns in Missional Faithfulness* (Grand Rapids: Eerdmans, 2004) for brief descriptions of churches attempting to embody the missional spirit of Paul in various ways.

27. This sentence contains a deliberate allusion to Walter Rauschenbusch's classic *A Theology for the Social Gospel* (New York: Macmillan, 1917; repr. Louisville: Westminster John Knox, 1997), though I am not thereby putting my stamp of approval on everything the book said and every way it has been used.

28. N. T. Wright, *What Saint Paul Really Said: Was Paul of Tarsus the Real Founder of Christianity?* (Grand Rapids: Eerdmans, 1997), p. 165.

salvation. We will discuss "salvation" in chapter one, but the definition of salvation offered by John Wesley, heavily influenced by the Greek Fathers and their theology of participation and theosis, is worthy of citation here:

> By salvation I mean, not barely (according to the vulgar notion) deliverance from hell, or going to heaven, but a present deliverance from sin, a restoration of the soul to its primitive health, its original purity; a recovery of the divine nature; the renewal of our souls after the image of God in righteousness and true holiness, in justice, mercy, and truth.[29]

We may not use the same language today, but the spiritual renewal that Wesley describes, which brings about Godlike justice, mercy, and truth, does not suggest a community alone with God but one that lives in the world, embodying and witnessing to the justice, mercy, and truth of God in Christ.[30]

It has been suggested that Paul's understanding of salvation can be summarized in the two words *anticipation* and *participation*.[31] We might better combine these words and speak of *anticipatory participation*. Paul understands the coming, death, resurrection, and exaltation of Jesus as the inauguration of the prophetically promised age of peace, justice, and salvation — the age-to-come, or the new creation. Of course "*this* age" — the era of sin and death — persists, and will do so until the *parousia,* or return of Christ. Therefore, interpreters of Paul refer to this phenomenon as the "overlap" of the ages (see 1 Cor. 10:11). We may illustrate this graphically in the following way:[32]

---

29. Gerald R. Cragg, ed., *The Works of John Wesley,* Vol. 11: *The Appeals to Men of Reason and Religion and Certain Related Open Letters* (Nashville: Abingdon, 1987), p. 106, para. 1.3. Randy L. Maddox calls it Wesley's "characteristic definition of salvation" ("John Wesley and Eastern Orthodoxy: Influences, Convergences, and Differences," *Asbury Journal* 45 [1990]: 29-53; here p. 39).

30. The words of a Charles Wesley hymn begin to touch on this in terms of its full Christological import: "Jesus, we follow Thee,/in all Thy footsteps tread,/and pant for full conformity/to our exalted Head.//We in Thy birth are born,/sustain Thy grief and loss,/share in Thy want, and shame, and scorn,/and die upon Thy cross.//Baptized into Thy death/we sink into Thy grace,/till Thou the quickening Spirit breathe,/and to the utmost save.//Thou said'st, 'Where'er I am/there shall My servant be';/Master, the welcome word we claim/and die to live with Thee." (This is no. 130 of Wesley's Hymns on the Lord's Supper; I am grateful to Rev. Phil Hamner for drawing this hymn to my attention.)

31. Marianne Meye Thompson, *Colossians & Philemon,* Two Horizons New Testament Commentary (Grand Rapids: Eerdmans, 2005), p. 69, echoing Leander Keck.

32. The graphic is taken from Michael J. Gorman, *Reading Paul* (Eugene, OR: Cascade, 2008), p. 60.

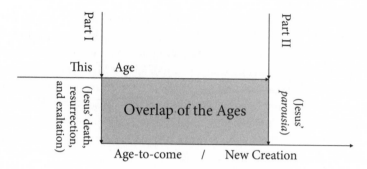

In Christ the new creation of God has begun in the power of the Spirit, and although it is not here in its fullness, salvation is in fact already a present reality in which we participate. Paul succinctly captures the heart of this reality in the claim "in hope we were saved" (Rom. 8:24).

Anticipatory participation means that the new creation of Christlike love, *shalom,* reconciliation with God and one another, and restorative justice will come to expression in the present among those who live in God's crucified and resurrected Messiah by the power of the Spirit. Peace, love, and justice are not merely to be hoped for, in other words, but embodied now: "the kingdom of God is . . . righteousness [or justice] and peace and joy in the Holy Spirit" (Rom. 14:17).[33] And by their very nature, these relational realities — love, peace/reconciliation, justice — are missional; they encourage the formation of a community that is not turned in on itself but is concerned both for its own life and for the life of the world — the life of those who are currently perishing, to use Pauline language.[34] For Paul, wrote J. Christiaan Beker, the "vocation of the church is not self-preservation for eternal life but service to the created world in the sure hope of the world's transformation

---

33. The context of Romans 14 places this claim within the framework of love (Rom. 14:15). N. T. Wright's *Kingdom New Testament: A Contemporary Translation* (New York: HarperOne, 2011) translates *dikaiosynē* in Rom. 14:17 with "justice" rather than "righteousness."

34. Elsewhere I have referred to the spirituality of Paul and the other New Testament writers as ultimately centrifugal rather than centripetal. See Michael J. Gorman, "The This-Worldliness of the New Testament's Other-Worldly Spirituality," in *The Bible and Spirituality: Exploratory Essays in Reading Scripture Spiritually,* ed. Andrew T. Lincoln, J. Gordon McConville, and Lloyd K. Pietersen (Eugene, OR: Cascade, 2013), pp. 151-70 (p. 154). As we will see below, Paul sees mission as inclusive of both centripetal and centrifugal activity. For the Pauline language of perishing, see, e.g., Rom. 2:12; 1 Cor. 1:18; 2 Cor. 2:15; 4:3; 2 Thess. 2:10. Even stronger than perishing is the language of deadness in Eph. 2:1, 5; 5:14.

at the time of God's final triumph." Otherwise, the church's "sighing for the redemption of the world (Rom. 8:19-21) is simply reduced to a faint ecclesial whisper."[35] The church is "the dawning of the new age" — the new age inaugurated by the death and resurrection of Jesus and proclaimed by Paul.[36] Similarly, N. T. Wright has said that Paul "saw the church as a *microcosmos*, a little world, not simply as an alternative to the present one, an escapist's country cottage for those tired of city life, but as the prototype of what was to come."[37] And what is to come, notes Wright, is new creation, the joining, or reconciliation, of heaven and earth.[38]

In other words, because Paul expects the church to embody the gospel, to become the gospel, its very identity is inherently missional. We explore various dimensions of that missional, anticipatory participation in the remainder of this book.

One of the primary contentions of this book is the inseparability of the church's life together and its activity, or witness, in the world. For Paul, they were clearly inseparable and were both part of God's mission, as Michael Barram in particular has convincingly argued.[39] Philosophically, this can be described as the inseparability of being and act. We acknowledge the truth of this principle in everyday life when we rightly doubt that a discredited person or entity, someone or some organization without integrity, can maintain any respectability or influence in the sphere of public opinion. Christians know its truth as well from the prayer of Jesus before he died. He prayed that his disciples would remain in unity both with himself and the Father and with one another. Why? So that their witness to the Father's saving mission enacted in the life and death of the Son would be received as such by the world (John 17:20-23).

---

35. J. Christiaan Beker, *Paul the Apostle: The Triumph of God in Life and Thought* (Philadelphia: Fortress, 1980), pp. 313, 327.

36. The phrase "the dawning of the new age" is Beker's (*Paul the Apostle,* pp. 303-27).

37. Wright, *Paul and the Faithfulness of God,* p. 1492.

38. In the same context (*Paul and the Faithfulness of God,* pp. 1493-94) Wright also says, "Paul's apostolic task was, so to speak, tabernacle-construction, temple-building. . . . In other words, he saw his vocation in terms of bringing into being 'places' — humans, one by one and collectively — in which heaven and earth would come together and be, yes, *reconciled.* 'God was reconciling the world to himself in the Messiah': the Messiah is the new temple where heaven and earth meet, reconciled through his sacrifice. Paul's vocation was to announce that this had happened . . . and so to extend this temple-shaped mission into the rest of the world. This was his equivalent of those sudden biblical glimpses of pagans flocking to Jerusalem to worship the true god."

39. See especially his *Mission and Moral Reflection in Paul,* Studies in Biblical Literature 75 (New York: Peter Lang, 2006).

Finding the right language for all of this is something of a challenge. "Pastoral" versus "missional" is inadequate because the formation of the church in Christ is part of God's mission. Even "pastoral care" or "spiritual care" versus "evangelism" or "evangelization" suggests more of a gap than Paul would want us to imagine. For one thing, he himself can speak of preaching the gospel to the Roman Christians — that is, evangelizing or "gospelizing" them — even though they are already believers (Rom. 1:15). Moreover, Paul suggests in Philippians that the spiritual life of the church, the unity of the community in love, is the way of life that is appropriate to the gospel and is simultaneously the essence of their corporate witness in the world (Phil. 1:27–2:16).

Something like "inward journey" and "outward journey" might be more helpful, except that this pair of terms implies the existence of two journeys, even if they are (ideally) connected. Abandoning all hope of finding the perfect language, I have chosen, when necessary, to distinguish between the "internal focus" and the "external focus" of the church. This suggests not two journeys, or two separate church "lives," but a unified existence. At the same time, this pair of terms suggests a real-life dynamic: sometimes a community must focus on the internal realities of its corporate life and sometimes on the external ones, without ever forgetting that the two are inseparable.

I think it is also appropriate, therefore, to use the terms "centripetal" (moving toward a center) and "centrifugal" (moving away from a center) to characterize this unified divine mission and the care of it by church leaders and communities.[40] Each term implies energy and activity, a dynamic rather

40. Although I am not a missiologist, I am aware that these terms have sometimes been used by missiologists and that they have also been subject to some critique. For a brief theological overview, see David W. Congdon, "Why I Think Missional Theology Is the Future of Theology, or, Why I Think Theology Must Become Missional or Perish," at http://theologyandpraxis.files.wordpress.com/2008/08/why-i-think-missional-theology5.pdf, p. 9. Congdon differentiates between worship (centripetal) and mission (centrifugal), whereas I would want to refer to both as participation in the mission of God and as being part of missional existence, while agreeing that worship is primarily, though not exclusively, centripetal. I concur strongly with Congdon when he says, "We need both movements [centripetal and centrifugal] together in our ecclesiology [understanding of the church]. Any priority of one over the other would result in a lopsided doctrine of the church and most likely reflects a misunderstanding about the relation between being and act.... Insofar ... as the 'center' is located in the earthly ecclesial community, then both centripetal and centrifugal forces will be transcended by and sublated into the center that is Christ. But even if our 'center' is Christ and his reign, we are still sent out in mission as his ambassadors, even as we come to him in worship and adoration." For use of the terms in connection with the biblical text, see,

than a static reality, while the two terms together imply a single center from which and to which this activity and energy flow. The continuous back and forth, the in and out, of this dynamic relationship, it seems to me, is the nature of the church as Paul perceives it. This ecclesial centripetal activity does not have the center as its final goal but is always unwinding, so to speak, and becoming centrifugal activity. Similarly, ecclesial centrifugal activity eventually regroups and redirects itself toward the center — in order that it can once again unwind and move outside the center. This is one way, I think, to read Paul at certain key points: he contends for the integrity of the church both in its internal life and in its public witness because each feeds the other and because, ultimately, the two are one, as we will see.

With these introductory perspectives in hand, we turn now to a fundamental question about Paul: What does he think about the mission of God, and how does he envision himself and others participating in God's project?

---

e.g., Robert L. Gallagher and Paul Hertig, "Introduction: Background to Acts," in *Mission in Acts: Ancient Narratives in Contemporary Context,* ed. Robert L. Gallagher and Paul Hertig, American Society of Missiology Series 34 (Maryknoll, NY: Orbis, 2004), pp. 2-17 (here pp. 9-10), who use the terms to characterize the narrative dynamic in Acts. I am using them as a convenient way (and one less problematic, in my view, than certain other options) of characterizing a dynamic I see in the letters of Paul without thereby either (1) claiming to use them in precisely the same way as any particular missiologist or (2) offering support for their uncritical use in all matters relating to Christian mission.

# CHAPTER 1

# Paul and the Mission of God

Willard Swartley credits some of the great New Testament scholars of the twentieth century with proposing that there is a "missional vision at the heart of Pauline thought."[1] If he and they are correct, as I believe they are, what might it mean for us to read Paul "missionally"? The question itself requires unpacking before it can be answered. There are at least two principal ways to understand the question.

First, we could interpret the question to mean, "What would we discover if we read Paul's letters, first and foremost, not for the fascinating historical and social windows they provide on early Christianity, not for their impressive literary and rhetorical features, not even for their substantive contributions to various aspects of Christian theology, but for their witness to Paul's vision of God's mission in the world (the *missio Dei*) and to the role he, his colleagues, and the churches were to play in that mission?" This way of understanding the question involves some significant assumptions: that Paul believed God had a mission in the world and, especially, that not only he and his colleagues, but also the churches he founded and/or "pastored," were supposed to participate in that mission. Granting these assumptions (perhaps after making an argument that they are at least plausible), one would then proceed to discern the explicit and implicit answers to the question. This would still be, nonetheless, primarily a historical, exegetical exercise, an inquiry into what Paul said, and perhaps also why, when, and to whom. It would not *necessarily* have implications for Christian mission today, though it might.

---

1. Willard M. Swartley, *Covenant of Peace: The Missing Peace in New Testament Theology and Ethics* (Grand Rapids: Eerdmans, 2006), p. 195. He mentions Johannes Munck, Oscar Cullmann, and Krister Stendahl.

Second, we could also interpret the question ("What might it mean to read Paul 'missionally'?") to mean, "For those of us who read Paul's letters as Christian Scripture, as divine address to the church, what would we discern about *our* role in the divine mission (the *missio Dei*) in *our* situation today?" This way of understanding the question also involves some significant assumptions: not only that Paul believed God had a mission in the world, but also that Paul was *right* in his understanding of that mission. Moreover, interpreting the question in this manner assumes that the church has a role in God's mission and that this role can somehow be discerned through the study of Paul's letters. While hopefully grounded in careful exegesis, this kind of inquiry would be much more of a hermeneutical, or interpretive, exercise.

These two interpretations of the question, and thus of the notion of reading Paul missionally, are not necessarily mutually exclusive. Yet it is certainly possible to separate them. In fact, one might pursue the first (historical, exegetical) line of questioning without ever getting to the second (the hermeneutical, or interpretive). One might also conclude that Paul's letters do not speak much at all of a role for the original, first-century churches in God's mission, limiting such a missional role to apostles and other ministers, but still assign a missional role to the church, meaning all Christians, today.

The claim of this book is that these two understandings of the question "What might it mean to read Paul 'missionally'?" can and should be complementary. In fact, it is my view that when we look for a witness to the *missio Dei* in Paul's letters, we are already beginning to ask a hermeneutical question; it is an inherently theological quest. This means two things of some significance. First, it means that the historical, exegetical questions and answers will automatically carry hermeneutical weight. We may not know exactly what the implications of the answers will be, but we do know that there are in fact implications. In other words, we may need time and space to hammer out those implications individually and in community, but we commit to such a hermeneutical process simply by raising the questions. In this book, I assume that the answers we discover will prompt more questions, will cry out for interpretation, for carefully discerned "application." This book will not, however, provide all the answers to those questions. It will not because it cannot.

Second, the complementarity of the exegetical and the hermeneutical approaches to reading Paul missionally also means that there will be appropriate interpretations of Paul's letters that go beyond his original vision and intentions. For instance, exegetically and historically we might discover a very limited, or only an implicit, missional role for the churches and for non-apostolic individuals in Paul's letters. Or we might recognize that the earliest Christians could not fully implement their implicit or explicit missional call because of their relatively marginalized and even hidden place in the society of their day. Please note: I am not offering these possibilities as conclusions. My point, rather, is that there may be legitimate theological reasons for enlarging whatever missional role the Pauline churches had (or did not have) when we contemplate Christian mission today. What is limited or implicit in one context (for example, peacemaking in first-century Corinth or Rome) can be appropriately expanded in another. We might refer to this very real possibility as a kind of missional trajectory, an implicit movement in the scope of the church's involvement in the *missio Dei*.

These rather theoretical issues lead us to pose four basic questions concerning Paul and the interpretation of Paul's letters missionally: (1) What was Paul's vision of the *missio Dei?* (2) What was Paul's overall understanding of the churches' part in that divine mission? Are they merely beneficiaries ("believers" in a rather passive sense), or are they also participants? (3) Does participation imply mission? (4) How might the developing theological discipline of missional hermeneutics (interpretation) help us think about how to read and appropriate Paul's letters for our own situation?

## The *Missio Dei*

What is God up to in the world? What is the *missio Dei*, the mission of God?

For Paul the answer to that question is clear: to bring salvation to the world.[2] "For I am not ashamed of the gospel; it is the power of God for salvation to everyone who has faith, to the Jew first and also to the Greek" (Rom. 1:16). The means of that salvation is the death and resurrection of Jesus Christ, God's Son, Israel's Messiah, and the world's true Lord. This is the gospel, the good news. The mode by which that salvation is *conveyed* to the world is the preaching of this good news both in word and in deed. And the mode by which that salvation is *received* is best described not as *faith* in the sense of intellectual assent but as faith in the sense of full *participation*, a comprehensive transformation of conviction, character, and communal affiliation. This is what it means to be "in Christ," Paul's most fundamental expression for this participatory life that is, in fact, salvation itself:

2. And, according to Romans 8, to the entire cosmos, as we will note shortly.

¹⁴For the love of Christ urges us on, because we are convinced that one has died for all; therefore all have died. ¹⁵And he died for all, so that those who live might live no longer for themselves, but for him who died and was raised for them. ¹⁶From now on, therefore, we regard no one from a human point of view; even though we once knew Christ from a human point of view, we know him no longer in that way. ¹⁷So if anyone is in Christ, there is a new creation: everything old has passed away; see, everything has become new! (2 Cor. 5:14-17)

We will return momentarily to this notion of salvation as renewal through participation, but first we need to examine a bit more closely the *missio Dei*. What is the nature of this salvation God seeks to bring to the world?

According to Paul, God is on a mission to liberate humanity — and indeed the entire cosmos — from the powers of Sin and Death: "For the law of the Spirit of life in Christ Jesus has set you free from the law of sin and of death" (Rom. 8:2). The fullness of this liberation is a future reality for which we may, and should, now confidently hope. It is nothing less than the prophetically promised new creation: "that the creation itself will be set free from its bondage to decay and will obtain the freedom of the glory of the children of God" (Rom. 8:21). In the present, however, God is already at work liberating humanity from Sin and Death, through the sin-defeating and life-giving death and resurrection of his Son, as a foretaste of the glorious future that is coming. It is the new creation reaching back from the future into the present.

It is important that we not read Paul with Western, individualistic lenses. What God is doing, God is doing ultimately for all of humanity and for the entire cosmos (Rom. 8:18-25). In the present, God's mission is about more than individuals. In the words of Beverly Gaventa, God's mission is the work of "rescuing the world from the powers of Sin and Death so that a newly created humanity — Jew and Gentile — is released for the praise of God in community."³ God is therefore at work creating an international network of multicultural, socio-economically diverse communities ("churches") that participate in this liberating, transformative reality *now* — even if incom-

---

3. Beverly Roberts Gaventa, "The Mission of God in Paul's Letter to the Romans," in *Paul as Missionary: Identity, Activity, Theology, and Practice*, ed. Trevor J. Burke and Brian S. Rosner, Library of New Testament Studies 420 (London: T. & T. Clark, 2011), pp. 65-75 (here pp. 65-66). Gaventa is referring to Romans, but the claim is true for Paul more broadly. On the relation between sin, death, and salvation for humans and for the cosmos, see Beverly Roberts Gaventa, ed., *Apocalyptic Paul: Cosmos and Anthropos in Romans 5–8* (Waco, TX: Baylor University Press, 2013).

pletely and imperfectly: "May the God of steadfastness and encouragement grant you to live in harmony with one another, in accordance with Christ Jesus, so that together you may with one voice glorify the God and Father of our Lord Jesus Christ" (Rom. 15:5-6). They worship the one true God; confess his Son Jesus as the one true Lord; live in conformity to the self-giving divine love displayed on the cross by means of the power of the Holy Spirit, who is the Spirit of the Father and of the Son; and bear witness to the present and future realities in which they participate. These communities constitute the people of the new covenant, which had been promised by the prophets (e.g., Jer. 31:31-34; cf. Ezek. 34:25; 37:26), was inaugurated by Jesus' death (1 Cor. 11:23-26), and is made effective by the Spirit (2 Cor. 3:6). This people participates in the new creation even now (Gal. 6:15; 2 Cor. 5:17), anticipating its eschatological fullness.

Paul uses numerous words and images to give voice to this comprehensive vision of salvation. In addition to salvation itself, liberation, transformation, and new creation, he speaks also of peace, reconciliation, and justification — all of which we will address in various ways later in the book. In addition, as mentioned in the Introduction ("Invitation"), there are terms and metaphors for salvation that Paul does not use explicitly but that are nonetheless appropriate ways of characterizing salvation according to the apostle. One of these — one that is of great importance as a kind of "umbrella term" — is participation.[4]

---

4. The renewed interest in participation was triggered by E. P. Sanders, *Paul and Palestinian Judaism* (Philadelphia: Fortress, 1977). For a good survey, see James D. G. Dunn, *The Theology of Paul the Apostle* (Grand Rapids: Eerdmans, 1998), pp. 390-441. See also especially Daniel G. Powers, *Salvation through Participation: An Examination of the Notion of the Believers' Corporate Unity with Christ in Early Christian Soteriology,* Contributions to Biblical Exegesis and Theology 29 (Leuven: Peeters, 2001); Richard B. Hays, *The Faith of Jesus Christ: The Narrative Substructure of Gal. 3:1-4:11,* 2nd ed. (Grand Rapids: Eerdmans, 2002 [orig. 1983]), esp. a section titled "Participation in Christ as the Key to Pauline Soteriology" (pp. xxix-xxxiii); S. A. Cummins, "Divine Life and Corporate Christology: God, Messiah Jesus, and the Covenant Community in Paul," in *The Messiah in the Old and New Testaments,* ed. Stanley E. Porter (Grand Rapids: Eerdmans, 2007), pp. 190-209; Robert C. Tannehill, "Participation in Christ," in *The Shape of the Gospel: New Testament Essays* (Eugene, OR: Cascade, 2007), pp. 223-37; Douglas A. Campbell, *The Quest for Paul's Gospel: A Suggested Strategy* (London/New York: T. & T. Clark, 2005); Douglas A. Campbell, *The Deliverance of God: An Apocalyptic Rereading of Justification in Paul* (Grand Rapids: Eerdmans, 2009); David L. Stubbs, "The Shape of Soteriology and the *Pistis Christou* [Faith of Christ] Debate," *Scottish Journal of Theology* 61 (2008): 137-57; Constantine R. Campbell, *Paul and Union with Christ: An Exegetical and Theological Study* (Grand Rapids: Zondervan, 2012); N. T. Wright, *Paul and the Faithfulness of God,* vol. 4 of Christian Origins and the Question of

## Paul, Salvation, and Participation

For Paul, salvation is obviously a great gift; Paul would not hesitate to speak of "Christ and his benefits."[5] But for Paul, the "benefits" of salvation are not something to be found at a distance, nor are they consigned only to the future ("heaven" or other eschatological rewards, including new creation). Rather, salvation involves participation. But what does it mean to speak of salvation in Paul as participation? There are at least seven interrelated linguistic and theological features of Paul's letters that help us understand the centrality of participation to his theology and spirituality.[6]

First, there is **the language of baptism** as dying and rising with Christ and as entering into Christ:

> [3]Do you not know that all of us who have been baptized *into* Christ Jesus were baptized *into* his death? [4]Therefore we have been buried *with* [co-buried with; *synetaphēmen*] him by baptism *into* death, so that, just as Christ was raised from the dead by the glory of the Father, so we too might walk *in* newness of life. [5]For if we have been united *with* him *in* a death like his, we will certainly be united *with* him *in* a resurrection like his. [6]We know that our old self was crucified *with* [co-crucified with; *synestaurōthē*] him so that the body of sin might be destroyed, and we might no longer be enslaved to sin. [7]For whoever has died is freed from sin. [8]But if we have died *with* Christ, we believe that we will also live *with* [co-live with; *syzēsomen*] him. (Rom. 6:3-8; emphasis added)

Both the image of baptism itself (i.e., being dipped into water) and the various English prepositions in this text help us grasp the participatory

---

God (Minneapolis: Fortress, 2013), ch. 10; and Kevin J. Vanhoozer, Constantine R. Campbell, and Michael J. Thate, eds., *'In Christ' in Paul: Explorations in Paul's Theology of Union and Participation*, WUNT 2 series (Tübingen: Mohr Siebeck, 2014).

5. As in Arland J. Hultgren, *Christ and His Benefits: Christology and Redemption in the New Testament* (Philadelphia: Fortress, 1987).

6. My approach here is different from, but complementary to, that of Richard Hays in his important article on this subject: "What Is 'Real Participation in Christ'? A Dialogue with E. P. Sanders on Pauline Soteriology," in *Redefining First-Century Jewish and Christian Identities: Essays in Honor of Ed Parish Sanders*, ed. Fabian E. Udoh et al. (Notre Dame: University of Notre Dame Press, 2008), pp. 336-51. Hays describes participation for Paul as consisting of four main elements: belonging to a family, political or military solidarity with Christ (as in Romans 6), participating in the *ekklēsia*, and living within the Christ story ("narrative participation") — what I refer to as Paul's narrative spirituality of cruciformity.

nature of baptism as the rite of initiation into the Christian church and into the story of Jesus — his ongoing, existential reality in the world. Those who have believed the gospel and decided to make that faith known in the public act of baptism are baptized (note the italicized prepositions) *into* him, *into* his death; they are buried *with* him *into* death in order to walk *in* newness of life; they have already been united *with* him *in* a death like his and will be united *with* him *in* a resurrection like his; their old self was crucified *with* him; they have died *with* him and will live *with* him.[7] The stress is repeatedly and emphatically on baptism, its present consequences, and its future hope as participation. Of particular interest to us is the emphasis in Romans 6 that baptism into Christ results in a new attachment — a "slavery" to God and to righteousness (6:13-23) that involves the presentation of the self, body and mind, to God (cf. Rom. 12:1-2), and of the bodily "members" to God as "weapons" of righteousness/justice: "No longer present your members to sin as weapons of injustice/unrighteousness, but present yourselves to God as those who have been brought from death to life, and present your members to God as weapons of justice/righteousness."[8] This all means that participation is ultimately about action — about being God's (cross-shaped, Christlike) weaponry and agents in the world.

Similarly to Romans 6, in Galatians 3:27 Paul says, "As many of you as were baptized into *(eis)* Christ have clothed yourselves with Christ." Note again the prepositions — baptized *into* Christ, clothed *with* Christ — as well as the images of being dipped and being dressed (see also point six below). If this is what happens to those who believe the gospel and are baptized, then the very meaning of belief, or faith, has implicitly shifted from a notion of assent or even trust to one of participation: of transferal from one realm to another. It is an understanding of faith as embrace — or better yet, of being embraced, even enveloped. The initial reality continues after the moment of baptism — believers are always in Christ, they always "wear" Christ, they are constantly in some sense dead with Christ and yet simultaneously, paradoxically, alive with Christ.

---

7. The Greek actually uses prepositions, prefixes, and grammatical-case-markers to express what the English prepositions translate. The importance of the prefix "co-" (Greek *syn*) will be discussed below, at point seven.

8. NRSV alt. The Greek word *hopla*, "weapons," appears twice in Rom. 6:13 but is usually translated "instruments," as the NRSV does, along with the NIV. But the CEB uses "weapons." For the correctness of the translation of *hopla* as "weapons," see the commentaries and Hays, "What Is 'Real Participation in Christ'?", pp. 341-43.

Second, there is in Paul **the parallel language about faith and justification** as dying and rising with Christ and as entering into Christ. We have already noted that the notion of dying and rising in baptism implies a new understanding of faith as a participatory experience, not a mere cognitive or even affective one. This implicit sense of faith is more explicit in Galatians 2, in Paul's discussion of justification, where Paul says that believers have "faithed" into Christ (Gal. 2:16) and that this experience of "justification by faith" is also an experience of co-crucifixion and co-resurrection with Christ:

> [16]. . . we know that a person is justified not by the works of the law but through faith in [or, "through the faithfulness of"[9]] Jesus Christ. And we have come to believe in [or "into"; Greek *eis*] Christ Jesus, so that we might be justified by faith in Christ [or, "by the faithfulness of Christ"], and not by doing the works of the law, because no one will be justified by the works of the law. [17]But if, in our effort to be justified in Christ. . . . [19]For through the law I died to the law, so that I might live to God. I have been crucified [co-crucified; *synestaurōmai*] with Christ; [20]and it is no longer I who live, but it is Christ who lives in me. And the life I now live in the flesh I live by faith in the Son of God [or, "by the faithfulness of the Son of God"], who loved me and gave himself for me. (Gal. 2:16-18a; 19-20)

In this text we learn that, as with baptism, faith effects a transfer "into" Christ (2:16); that justification (right covenant relations with God) is found "in," that is, "within" Christ (2:17); and that the process of justification by this kind of participatory faith, rather than by the law, can also be described in the language of co-crucifixion and, implicitly, co-resurrection (2:19-20).[10] Although these elements do not normally receive emphasis in traditional interpretations of this passage, they make complete sense as aspects of justification by faith (initiation in terms of personal response to the gospel) in parallel with baptism (initiation as public expression of the personal response).[11] Those who have believed the gospel have died and yet they live

9. This paragraph contains three Greek phrases (in vv. 16 and 20) that can be rendered as references either to faith in Christ or to the faith (faithfulness) of Christ. See the classic work of Richard Hays, *The Faith of Jesus Christ*, and summary arguments in my *Cruciformity: Paul's Narrative Spirituality of the Cross* (Grand Rapids: Eerdmans, 2001), pp. 96-121.

10. Co-resurrection is implied by the claims of Christ being alive and inhabiting the dead-but-now-living believer.

11. On these two passages (Romans 6 and Galatians 2) and their parallel elements, see

— they have been raised to new life. Galatians 2 tells us from the perspective of justification by faith what we have already seen from the perspective of baptism, for faith and baptism are two sides of one coin of participation.

Third, there is **the language of being "in Christ" and of Christ being within**. Both Romans 6 and Galatians 2 and 3 use the language of being "in" Christ, the result of faith/baptism. Moreover, as is well known, the language of being "in Christ" is characteristic of Paul's way of articulating the life of faith; it appears many times in his letters.[12] Three things about this language are important to note: it is deeply personal language, revealing an intimate union; it is also corporate language, referring to being part of the body of Christ; and it is covenantal language, implying membership in the people of God reconfigured around the crucified and resurrected Messiah. Thus the "in Christ" relationship is personal but not private, and it includes a set of covenantal responsibilities, rather than merely expressing a set of benefits.

Complementing Paul's "in Christ" language is his "Christ within" language. That is, the resurrected crucified Messiah lives within believers, both individually and, especially, corporately. The result is what we might refer to as "mutual indwelling" or "reciprocal residence." Paul can speak of this divine-human union using either Christ or the Spirit as the participant on the divine side:

> [1]There is therefore now no condemnation for *those who are in Christ Jesus.* . . . [9]But you are not in the flesh; *you are in the Spirit,* since *the Spirit of God dwells in you.* Anyone who does not have the Spirit of Christ does not belong to him. [10]But if *Christ is in you,* though the body is dead because of sin, the Spirit is life because of righteousness. [11]If *the Spirit* of him who raised Jesus from the dead *dwells in you,* he who raised Christ from the dead will give life to your mortal bodies also through *his Spirit that dwells in you.* (Rom. 8:1, 9-11; emphasis added)

Here Paul contends, among other things, that this relationship of mutual indwelling is an experience of life and righteousness rather than death and condemnation — that is, of salvation.

Fourth, there is **the language of being clothed with Christ** (or putting him on), as we have already seen in discussing Galatians 3:27. The baptismal

---

further my *Inhabiting the Cruciform God: Kenosis, Justification, and Theosis in Paul's Narrative Soteriology* (Grand Rapids: Eerdmans, 2009), ch. 2, esp. pp. 63-79.

12. For a thorough and generally helpful study see Campbell, *Paul and Union with Christ.*

indicative ("what is") in that text can also become an ongoing existential imperative ("what ought to be"), as in Romans 13:12-14:

> [12][T]he night is far gone, the day is near. Let us then lay aside the works of darkness and put on the armor of light; [13]let us live honorably as in the day, not in reveling and drunkenness, not in debauchery and licentiousness, not in quarreling and jealousy. [14]Instead, put on the Lord Jesus Christ, and make no provision for the flesh, to gratify its desires. (Rom. 13:12-14)[13]

Both this text in Romans and its parallel in 1 Thessalonians 5:8 suggest that salvation and its corollary life is a kind of apocalyptic battle — hardly a static understanding of what salvation entails.

Fifth, there is **the language of sharing, *koinōnia*.**[14] The intimacy of clothing language is echoed in the language of intimate sharing, of loyal and loving partnership. The *koin-* word group (the word *koinōnia* and related words), as Paul uses it, means more than what the English term "fellowship," often used to translate *koinōnia,* conveys. In 2 Corinthians and Philippians Paul speaks of a *koinōnia* in the Spirit, which clearly in context means intimate communion, life-sharing, with God and with one another (2 Cor. 13:13; Phil. 2:1). In 1 Corinthians, Paul speaks of *koinōnia* with Jesus as the purpose of God's call (1 Cor. 1:9).

Paul also speaks of the Lord's Supper as a *koinōnia* in the Lord Jesus and specifically in his body and blood — i.e., his death (1 Cor. 10:16) — which excludes *koinōnia* with any other deity or sacrifice (1 Cor. 10:18-22). In other words, the Supper gives expression to the individual and corporate reality of being the body of Christ that gives him (Christ) full and exclusive loyalty, and it does so in part by embodying the cross in its treatment of others at the Supper (11:17-34). The convergence of *koinōnia* with Jesus and *koinōnia* with one another in these texts from 1 Corinthians 10 and 11 is remarkable. Without reducing union with Christ to ecclesiology, Paul makes it clear that union with Christ apart from the community is impossible, and anything that destroys the community, the body of Christ, is an attack on Christ himself, the body of the Lord (esp. 11:29). If we wish to refer to the meal as a "sacrament" and/or as "communion," we must recognize that Jesus is

---

13. Cf. 1 Thess. 5:8. See also Col. 3:8-10 and Eph. 4:22-24, which merge the indicative and the imperative nicely.

14. On the importance of *koinōnia* in Paul, see also, among others, Wright, *Paul and the Faithfulness of God,* pp. 10-12, 16-21, 48.

present at the meal if and only if the identity of Jesus is embodied in practices that reflect his death; otherwise Jesus is absent and the meal is not the Lord's Supper (11:20). That is, partaking of the bread and the cup is indeed participation in Christ, but only when the partaking is an expression of the more fundamental *koinōnia* of being clothed with Christ and his self-giving, others-oriented love.[15]

Indeed, according to Philippians, Paul's life-goal is the *koinōnia* of Christ's sufferings (which are the fruit of his self-giving love), meaning sharing in and conformity to his death and thereby (paradoxically) intimate knowledge of the power of his resurrection (Phil. 3:10).[16] We must remember that whenever Paul makes autobiographical statements, he is offering himself as an example to be imitated — "Be imitators of me, as I am of Christ" (1 Cor. 11:1). He wants the Philippians, and all who hear or read the letter to them, to have this kind of *koinōnia* with Christ — participation in his death and resurrection — as their life goal.[17] Moreover, faith itself, Paul indicates, is a *koinōnia* with Jesus (Philem. 5-6).

*Koinōnia* can refer to partnership in ministry generally (2 Cor. 8:23; Gal. 2:9; Philem. 17), but it can also be inclusive of financial support and suffering (2 Cor. 8:4; Phil. 1:5, 7; 4:14-15). This sharing among believers can be "spiritual" (Phil. 2:1), or better "Spirit-ual," though that does not mean intangible, for the sharing is expressed in concrete practices of mutual love and harmony (Phil. 2:2-4). The sharing can also be monetary: "Contribute *(koinōnountes)* to the needs of the saints" (Rom. 12:13; cf. Rom. 15:16; 2 Cor. 8:4; 9:13; 1 Tim. 6:18; probably Gal. 6:6). In addition, the sharing can be *both* spiritual and monetary, one complementing the other in a relationship (e.g., Rom. 15:26-27). This mutuality among believers can extend to suffering, a complementary *koinōnia* of suffering and comfort (2 Cor. 1:7). And just as *koinōnia* with other deities is inappropriate, so also is *koinōnia* with those characterized as "unrighteousness" and "darkness" (2 Cor. 6:14).

To summarize: the Pauline language of *koinōnia* indicates a deep participation in Christ, especially in his death, that is shared with other believers and that comes to fruition in concrete practices of sacrificial, generous, self-giving love and even suffering.

---

15. See especially Rodrigo Morales, "A Liturgical Conversion of the Imagination: Worship and Ethics in 1 Corinthians," *Letter and Spirit* 5 (2009): 103-24.

16. Cf. Col. 1:24, though it lacks the *koin-* word-group.

17. On the specific subject of suffering, Paul writes: "For he [God] has graciously granted you the privilege not only of believing in Christ, but of suffering for him as well — since you are having the same struggle that you saw I had and now hear that I still have" (Phil. 1:29-30).

Sixth, there is **the language of the transformation of those in Christ**. In addition to Romans 6 and Romans 8 (discussed above in connection with other aspects of participation), three texts are especially important in this regard: 2 Corinthians 3:18; 2 Corinthians 5:21; and Romans 12:1-2. All speak of renewal through participation.

In 2 Corinthians 3, Paul makes it clear that to "turn" to the Lord (Jesus) results in both being in Christ and beholding him with "unveiled faces" (2 Cor. 3:14-16). From this "location" and in this "position," believers "are being transformed *(metamorphoumetha)* into the same image from one degree of glory to another," which "comes from the Lord, the Spirit" (2 Cor. 3:18). Moreover, this is an act of divine new creation: "[I]t is the God who said, 'Let light shine out of darkness,' who has shone in our hearts to give the light of the knowledge of the glory of God in the face of Jesus Christ" (2 Cor. 4:6; cf. Gen. 1:3), who is the image of God (2 Cor. 4:4). That is, there is a mutual indwelling of God/God's light in believers and of believers in God's image/Son/Spirit. The transformation noted in 2 Corinthians 3:18 is brought about by means of this intimate sharing in the divine life and is, in fact, an ongoing participation in that life, that "glory." This is a process of ongoing renewal *(anakainoutai),* even re-creation, in the face of suffering and death (2 Cor. 4:16). It is being remade into the image of God's son (cf. Rom. 8:29). The context in 2 Corinthians makes it clear that, paradoxically, "glory" in the present has a cruciform character.

Later in the same letter, Paul picks up the themes of participation, new creation, and transformation when he says "if anyone is in Christ, there is a new creation: everything old has passed away; see, everything has become new *(kaina)*!" (2 Cor. 5:17) and then specifies that "[f]or our sake he [God] made him to be sin who knew no sin, so that in him we might become the righteousness *(dikaiosynē)* of God" (2 Cor. 5:21). Participation in God's new creation means, once again, transformation — this time not into the glory of God but into the righteousness, or justice, of God.[18] Yet fundamentally, the glory of God and the righteousness/justice of God are parallel, even overlapping terms; each refers to Jesus, who is both God's glorious image (2 Cor. 4:4) and the incarnate expression of God's righteousness/justice (1 Cor. 1:30). To become the righteousness/justice of God is to be transformed into the image of God, which is to become *like* Christ by being *in* Christ.

So too in Romans, Paul speaks of "present[ing] your bodies as a [single] living sacrifice, holy and acceptable to God, which is your spiritual worship"

18. The Greek word *dikaiosynē* can have both senses.

and of "not be[ing] conformed to this world, but be[ing] transformed *(meta-morphousthe)* by the renewing *(anakainōsei)* of your minds, so that you may discern what is the will of God — what is good and acceptable and perfect" (Rom. 12:1-2). Although "in Christ" language is not explicitly present in these two verses, the sense of the text is not a summons to individuals as individuals, but to a community of embodied persons who together constitute a single "living sacrifice." That this is the sense of the passage is confirmed by the rest of chapter 12, which, in a summary of 1 Corinthians 12–14, speaks about the practices of using gifts and loving others as "one body in Christ" (Rom. 12:5). This is the shape of the community that has died and risen with and into Christ (Romans 6), that dies and rises with and in Christ daily, constantly presenting its members to God in service to the Lord and to righteousness/justice (cf. the verb "present" [forms of *paristēmi*] in Rom. 6:13, 16, 19; 12:1).

All of this is highly, if implicitly, missional: to be transformed into the image of God revealed in Christ; to participate in God's new creation and to become God's righteousness; to discern and do God's will; to present bodies to God, both as a sacrifice and, probably, as "weapons" in an apocalyptic battle (so Rom. 6:13, translating the Greek *hopla* as "weapons" rather than "instruments," as noted above; cf. Rom. 13:12) — these are all indications of action in service to what God is up to in the world.

Seventh, and finally, there is **the language of sharing in various aspects of Christ's story that are expressed in the Greek prefix** *syn-* (English "co-").[19] We have already seen some of these in previously mentioned texts. Among the others in Paul's letters, perhaps the most dramatic and revealing is a cluster in Romans 8. Paul expresses the intimacy of believers' identification with Christ and the Spirit in a series of words that begin with the prefix "co-" (Greek *syg-, sym-, syn-, sys-;* often rendered as "with" in English):

- *symmartyrei* (8:16; lit. "co-witness")
- *sygklēronomoi* (8:17; lit. "co-heirs")
- *sympaschomen* (8:17; lit. "co-suffer")
- *syndoxasthōmen* (8:17; lit. "be co-glorified")
- *systenazei* (8:22; lit. "co-groan")
- *synantilambanetai* (8:26; "co-take hold of"; e.g., "help")
- *synergei* (8:28; lit. "co-works")
- *symmorphous* (8:29; lit. "co-formed"; cf. Phil. 3:10, 21).[20]

19. In actual usage as a prefix, the spelling of *syn* can change.
20. In addition, there is the phrase "with him [Christ]" in 8:32.

This cluster of "co-" terms suggests that life in Christ is one of Spirit-enabled, intimate identification with the story of Jesus that can be summarized in the term "co-formed" or "conformed" to Christ, especially to his suffering and death in the present and to his resurrection glory in the future.[21] As we will see in various ways throughout this book, a life-story of suffering and glory is itself inherently missional, and, conversely, Christian mission is fundamentally about participation in suffering and glory, as the subtitle of missiologist Scott Sunquist's theology of Christian mission rightly asserts.[22] This summary of Pauline participation in terms of suffering and glory is rather general, like that of dying and rising with Christ in Romans 6, and yet its structure is sufficiently clear so that concrete Christlike practices — of humility, generosity, self-sacrifice for the good of others, etc. — can be easily included within this overall framework. Paul discusses such practices in Romans 12–15 and, of course, elsewhere.

So what should we conclude from this discussion of participation in Paul?

1. Justification by faith and baptism into Christ are themselves participatory events of initiation.
2. Those who believe the gospel and are baptized enter into a life of participation in Christ and with others who have also been incorporated into Christ's body.
3. Christian existence is one of intimate and exclusive communion with Christ, both individually and corporately, in which believers live in Christ/the Spirit and he/the Spirit lives in and among them.
4. To be in Christ is to be in a constant process of transformation into his image, vividly expressed in the image of putting Christ on like clothing.
5. This participation in Christ is characterized especially by ongoing participation in his cross, meaning especially self-giving, sacrificial love as the faithful embodiment of the gospel and even the likelihood of suffering as a result of this faithful witness.
6. To be in Christ is therefore to be part of God's mission as both beneficiaries of it and participants in it; in fact, benefiting and participating are inseparable, even synonymous, realities.

21. This claim is worked out in detail in my *Cruciformity.*
22. Scott W. Sunquist, *Understanding Christian Mission: Participation in Suffering and Glory* (Grand Rapids: Baker Academic, 2013). Sunquist divides his book into three parts: "Suffering and Glory in History: The Mission Movement"; "The Suffering and Glory of the Triune God: Trinitarian Mission in Scripture"; and "The Suffering and Glory of the Church: The Church in Mission Today."

7. Renewal in Christ is not an end in itself, but is part of a larger divine agenda — to form a people that participates in the new creation by becoming the righteousness of God and by presenting itself to God to do God's will in the world.

So far, these points are not terribly controversial conclusions about Paul.[23] But the next two implications of our discussion thus far are both critical and potentially controversial:

8. Although "ministers" like Paul and his colleagues have distinctive gifts and roles in God's mission, inasmuch as their lives are paradigmatic, it is expected that all who participate in Christ demonstrate a similar loving, faithful witness to the gospel in their particular contexts. That is, all believers are witnesses, all are in some sense apostolic; all participate in the new creation, and all participate in the apocalyptic battle; they share in Christ by sharing in faithful witness to the gospel, even if that means suffering. The church, for Paul, is inherently missional.

9. To participate in Christ is not merely to exist within a closed circle of fellow believers but also to bear witness in the world. This is implicit in several ways, including the requirement that participation in Christ be exclusive, which would entail forsaking idolatry and thus social situations where idolatry is practiced. Additionally, the expectation that his communities will suffer for the gospel, found throughout most of Paul's letters, assumes some sort of faithful public witness that generates harassment or worse. "Participation" does not mean a "holy huddle."

That is, to be *in* Christ is not to be *insulated from* the world, but to be *involved in* the world. Or, as Morna Hooker has put it, for Paul holiness, or Godlikeness, has lost its meaning as separation from others and has become "triangular," meaning believers loving God *and* neighbor.[24]

---

23. For three insightful works (another "accidental" trilogy?) that stress corporate transformative participation in Christ as the key to Paul's understanding of the church and of ministry, see the work of James W. Thompson: *Pastoral Ministry according to Paul: A Biblical Vision* (Grand Rapids: Baker Academic, 2006); *Moral Formation according to Paul: The Context and Coherence of Pauline Ethics* (Grand Rapids: Baker Academic, 2011); and *The Church according to Paul: Rediscovering the Community Conformed to Christ* (Grand Rapids: Baker Academic, 2014). Mission has not been central to Thompson's work, though it appears in one chapter (ch. 6) of his latest book, *The Church according to Paul*.

24. Morna D. Hooker, "Be Holy as I Am Holy," in Morna D. Hooker and Frances M. Young,

We may synthesize these various summary points as follows: *To partic-ipate in Christ is both to benefit from God's mission of liberation and recon-ciliation and to bear witness to this divine mission — thus furthering it — by becoming a faithful embodiment of it.*

The problem with this conclusion, some will argue, is that Paul himself does not call his churches or individuals in them to "preach the gospel." That, some would say, is a task for apostles. Despite the apparently logical implications of his participationist language, Paul's own directives might argue against the ultimate conclusions offered above.

Is this in fact the case?

## Participation and Mission: Missional Individuals and Communities?

One of the many scholarly debates in the study of Paul is the question of whether Paul intended his communities, and the individuals within them, to actively evangelize others — to spread the *euangelion,* the good news, as Paul did.[25] This is a legitimate question, since Paul only appears to issue such an imperative once — in Philippians 2:16 — if at all, since the translation of that verse is debated: "holding fast to the word of life" (NRSV) versus "holding forth the word of life" (KJV).[26]

---

*Holiness and Mission: Learning from the Early Church about Mission in the City* (London: SCM, 2010), pp. 4-19 (here p. 17).

25. I do not intend to formally review the scholarly debate at great length since this book is, in essence, my response to and participation in the discussion. For a very brief but helpful overview of the issues, plus an important constructive proposal, see Michael Barram, "Pauline Mission as Salvific Intentionality: Fostering a Missional Consciousness in 1 Corinthians 9:19-23 and 10:31–11:1," in *Paul as Missionary: Identity, Activity, Theology, and Practice,* ed. Trevor J. Burke and Brian S. Rosner, Library of New Testament Studies 420 (London: T. & T. Clark, 2011), pp. 234-46. For a longer review of the scholarly debate, divided into pre-1950 and post-1950 discussions, see Robert L. Plummer, *Paul's Understanding of the Church's Mission: Did the Apostle Paul Expect the Early Christian Communities to Evangelize?,* Paternoster Biblical Monographs (Milton Keynes, UK: Paternoster, 2006), pp. 1-42. For a longer treatment of the entire subject of Paul and mission more broadly, see Michael Barram, *Mission and Moral Reflection in Paul,* Studies in Biblical Literature 75 (New York: Peter Lang, 2006).

26. There is a longstanding debate among scholars about this verse, to which we will return in chapter four on Philippians. Most published translations side with the NRSV, which followed the RSV, in translating the phrase as something like "hold firmly" (NIV, NLT) or "hold on" (NAB, CEB), or even "clinging" (*Kingdom NT* by N. T. Wright; similarly, *The Voice*). The original NIV had "hold out," with a footnote offering the alternative "hold on to." The Good

It seems quite clear, however, that Paul *assumes* that his communities will be joyfully sharing the gospel of salvation with others, as 1 Corinthians demonstrates, at least with respect to family members. Paul tells the married Corinthians with unbelieving spouses not to seek a divorce (1 Cor. 7:12-13), in part because their witness may convert the unbelieving partner: "Wife, for all you know, you might save your husband. Husband, for all you know, you might save your wife" (1 Cor. 7:16).[27]

The verb "save" *(sōzō)* that Paul uses twice in 1 Corinthians 7:16 is the same verb he uses two chapters later to identify the goal of his own flexible and enculturated, but consistently cruciform, mode of apostolic existence. He uses it interchangeably with "win" (or "gain"; *kerdainō*):

> [19]For though I am free with respect to all, I have made myself a slave to all, so that I might *win* more of them. [20]To the Jews I became as a Jew, in order to *win* Jews. To those under the law I became as one under the law (though I myself am not under the law) so that I might *win* those under the law. [21]To those outside the law I became as one outside the law (though I am not free from God's law but am under Christ's law) so that I might *win* those outside the law. [22]To the weak I became weak, so that I might *win* the weak. I have become all things to all people, that I might by all means *save* some. (1 Cor. 9:19-22; emphasis added)

As always, Paul writes autobiographically not merely to describe himself but to offer himself as an example. In the context of 1 Corinthians 8:1–11:1, Paul has both internal and external concerns in mind for which he offers himself paradigmatically. On the one hand, he wants to prevent the Corinthians from doing anything that might cause someone in their community to leave Christ and return to idolatry (esp. 8:1-13), and, on the other hand, he also wants to prevent them from doing anything that might give someone reason not to leave idolatry behind in order to enter Christ and the church (esp. 10:23–11:1). His missional praxis is, in other words, both centripetal (focused in on the existing community) and centrifugal (focused outwards), and he wants the Corinthians to act similarly. Both kinds of activity are part

---

News has "as you offer them the message of life," and *The Message* has "Carry the light-giving Message into the night."

27. There is exegetical debate about the "tone" of Paul's words here, whether optimistic or pessimistic; the latter tone would render the questions something like "How do you know whether you will save . . . ?" I favor the optimistic interpretation; in either case, however, the text assumes that personal witness is the norm.

of a fully missional approach to Christian practices and decision making.[28] Here is Paul's summary of the missional dimension of his concerns:

> [23]"All things are lawful," but not all things are beneficial. "All things are lawful," but not all things build up. [24]Do not seek your own advantage, but that of the other. [25]Eat whatever is sold in the meat market without raising any question on the ground of conscience, [26]for "the earth and its fullness are the Lord's." [27]If an unbeliever invites you to a meal and you are disposed to go, eat whatever is set before you without raising any question on the ground of conscience. [28]But if someone says to you, "This has been offered in sacrifice," then do not eat it, out of consideration for the one who informed you, and for the sake of conscience — [29]I mean the other's conscience, not your own. For why should my liberty be subject to the judgment of someone else's conscience? [30]If I partake with thankfulness, why should I be denounced because of that for which I give thanks? [31]So, whether you eat or drink, or whatever you do, do everything for the glory of God. [32]Give no offense to Jews or to Greeks or to the church of God, [33]just as I try to please everyone in everything I do, not seeking my own advantage, but that of many, so that they may be saved. [1]Be imitators of me, as I am of Christ. (1 Cor. 10:23–11:1)

There are a number of challenging interpretive issues in this text. Essentially, however, the centrifugal missional mindset and praxis Paul describes here means allowing the well-being of others to take precedence over one's own interests and even rights (1 Cor. 10:23-24, 32-33), which means to become an imitator not only of Paul but also, and more importantly, of Christ (1 Cor. 10:33–11:1; cf. Phil. 2:1-8). In Michael Barram's words, Paul wants the Corinthian believers to "develop what we may call a 'missional consciousness' in every aspect of their individual and corporate lives. . . . To cultivate a purposive, missional posture — a *'salvific intentionality.'* . . . It is this salvific intentionality that links Paul's comprehensive mission to that of the Corinthian church."[29] We see Paul urging that this salvific intentionality be at work among the Corinthians not only in the home and in social interaction with others in their homes, but also within the assembly at worship. Paul

28. See Barram, *Mission and Moral Reflection.*

29. Barram, "Pauline Mission as Salvific Intentionality," pp. 236-37; emphasis added. Morna Hooker, commenting on 1 Corinthians 9 in connection with 2 Cor. 4:10-12, argues that Paul's pattern of "death" working through him to produce life in others is "the pattern, not for apostles alone, but for *all* Christian disciples (Hooker, "Be Holy as I Am Holy," p. 15).

wants to check the tendency among certain Corinthians to exercise the gift of speaking in tongues indiscriminately:

> [23]If, therefore, the whole church comes together and all speak in tongues, and outsiders or unbelievers enter, will they not say that you are out of your mind? [24]But if all prophesy, an unbeliever or outsider who enters is reproved by all and called to account by all. [25]After the secrets of the unbeliever's heart are disclosed, that person will bow down before God and worship him, declaring, "God is really among you." (1 Cor. 14:23-25)

This is a plea to control the self-centered desire to express one's spiritual gift, no matter the possible negative witness, in favor of self-restraint out of concern for the welfare, even the salvation, of others. It should be noted here that although it is possible that unbelievers would just wander into a meeting of the assembly (perhaps friends or clients of the church's patron/host), it is far more likely that the norm was that they came by invitation of others, which of course implies some kind of "faith-sharing" on the part of those who are in the church at Corinth, and elsewhere.

It would be more precise, therefore, to say that what Paul wants in Corinth and in all his churches is a "salvific intentionality" *that expresses the mind, or mindset, of Christ.* This Christlike mindset, inseparable from Christlike action, is depicted in Philippians 2:5-8 with great clarity:

> [5]Let this same mindset be operative in your community, which is indeed a community in Christ Jesus, [6]who, though he was in the form of God, did not regard equality with God as something to be exploited, [7]but emptied himself, taking the form of a slave, being born in human likeness. And being found in human form, [8]he humbled himself and became obedient to the point of death — even death on a cross. (Phil. 2:5-8 alt.[30])

This is to be the fundamental similarity between Paul and all those in Christ: a mindset that issues inevitably in loving, cruciform inward-focused

---

30. I have altered the NRSV text of verse 5 in order to indicate the dynamic sense of the verb "to have" and to express the parallelism between the Greek phrases *en hymin* ("in/among you [plural]") and *en Christō Iēsou* (in Christ Jesus). Steve Fowl interprets the Greek word family *phron-* (here yielding "mind" or "mindset") as not merely suggesting an attitude but connoting a pattern of perceiving/thinking, feeling, judging, and acting. See Stephen E. Fowl, *Philippians,* Two Horizons New Testament Commentary (Grand Rapids: Eerdmans, 2005), pp. 28-29, 36-37, 89-90, et passim.

(i.e., community-focused, or centripetal) and outward-focused (i.e., centrifugal) praxis.[31] Both express and further the *missio Dei*. The one mind of Christ — that is, his fundamental dispositions and corollary practices — is to shape the way Paul and all believers interact with others both inside and outside the *ekklēsia*. In fact, although Paul employs Philippians 2:5-8 in order to further internal unity at Philippi, it is stating the obvious to say that the first purpose of Christ's self-humbling, self-giving incarnation and death narrated in those verses was missional in a centrifugal sense: to save humanity. Indeed, if "salvation," broadly understood, is the context and goal of all Christian activity, then in a fundamental sense the normal distinction between "pastoral" and "missional" action (and between "pastoral" and "evangelistic") collapses, since the ultimate good of the other is the focus of all action: entrance into or growth in the reality of God's project to save humanity. That is, for Paul *all Christian praxis is inherently missional.* And it is rooted, as Morna Hooker points out in connecting 1 Corinthians 9 with Philippians 2, in Christlike empathy. "Here is the pattern for all mission: empathy — getting alongside those in need — in order to share with them the blessings of the gospel."[32]

This cruciform missional praxis, which is given its Christological grounding in Philippians, is central to 1 Corinthians. This empathetic praxis of salvific intentionality can be characterized, negatively, as not giving offense and also, positively, as pleasing, or seeking the advantage (that is, the good, the welfare) of, others — meaning especially their salvation (10:32-33). In his own words quoted above, Paul orders his life in such a way that it will consistently contribute to the "winning" and "saving" (see also 1 Cor. 10:33) of all kinds of people. Since Paul explicitly exhorts the Corinthians not to give offense (10:32) to Jews (Jewish non-Christians), Greeks (Gentile non-Christians), or the church of God (Christians) and clearly implies that they should, instead, seek the salvation of all, we may rightly infer that Paul invites and expects the Corinthians to share his apostolic ministry of "winning" unbelievers to faith in Jesus as Messiah

---

31. Barram ultimately echoes this sentiment when, in discussing the fundamental issue at stake in 1 Cor. 8:1–11:1, he summarizes Paul's point to be "whatever the situation, salvific intentionality represents enacted love" ("Pauline Mission as Salvific Intentionality," p. 242). Paul's most basic understanding of love appears in the pair of contrasting Greek idioms that mean "seeking the [interests/welfare] of the other/others" and "not seeking one's own [interests/welfare]." Versions of this idiomatic pair, or of one of its elements, appear in 1 Cor. 13:5 (Paul's description of love); 1 Cor. 10:24, 33; and Phil. 2:4, 21.

32. Hooker, in Hooker and Young, *Holiness and Mission,* p. 91.

and Lord and therefore into the community of the washed, justified, and sanctified (1 Cor. 6:11).

In other words, the Corinthians — and we can assume, in fact, all of Paul's addressees — *have a missional role that is fundamentally similar to Paul's even if it is manifested in different circumstances and in different concrete modes of expression.*[33] Both Paul and his communities are called to participate in the saving mission of God, indeed to embody it. Foregoing rights to safeguard or encourage the salvation of others is a form of evangelism. In fact, it is a form of becoming the gospel.[34]

Perhaps the surest sign that the early Pauline communities did in fact evangelize, at least in the sense of embodying the gospel and being "caught in the act," so to speak, is the regularity with which these communities were harassed and persecuted in some form.[35] In other words, when they did in fact offend others — not by virtue of *failing* to embody the cross (the offense against which Paul writes in 1 Corinthians) but precisely by embodying the word of the cross, the gospel of God, in all of its ramifications. After all, if the "word of the cross" is itself offensive (1 Cor. 1:18-25), how is it possible for a community that embodies that word not to offend someone(s) at some point? The Corinthians may, in fact, be unique in their apparent immunity from persecution. But is that "normal" or desirable in Pauline perspective? Or is it the fruit of immaturity and lack of faithfulness?

When we read Paul's letters to the Thessalonians and the Philippians, and probably also those to the Galatians and even the Romans, we learn that believers in these churches shared in the fate of the apostle, which was also the fate of their Lord:

> [6]And you became imitators of us and of the Lord, for in spite of persecution you received the word with joy inspired by the Holy Spirit, [7]so that you became an example to all the believers in Macedonia and in Achaia. (1 Thess. 1:6-7)

---

33. Thompson (*The Church according to Paul*, ch. 6) comes to similar conclusions, arguing that individual believers and communities gave witness to Christ in their associations with family members and others, in their corporate worship, and by virtue of their different lifestyles.

34. On the imitation of Paul as participation in the ministry of the gospel, see Morna D. Hooker, "On Becoming the Righteousness of God: Another Look at 2 Corinthians 5:21," *Novum Testamentum* 50 (2008): 358-75.

35. See the discussion in Plummer, *Paul's Understanding of the Church's Mission*, pp. 107-39.

[14]For you, brothers and sisters, became imitators of the churches of God in Christ Jesus that are in Judea, for you suffered the same things from your own compatriots as they did from those Jews [15]who killed both the Lord Jesus and the prophets, and drove us out; they displease God and oppose everyone. . . . (1 Thess. 2:14-15 alt.)[36]

[7]It is right for me to think this way [with gratitude] about all of you, because you hold me in your heart, for all of you share *(synkoinōnous)* in God's grace with me, both in my imprisonment and in the defense and confirmation of the gospel. . . . [27]Only, live your [plural; i.e., "communal"] life in a manner worthy of the gospel of Christ, so that, whether I come and see you or am absent and hear about you, I will know that you are standing firm in one spirit, striving side by side with one mind for the faith of the gospel, [28]and are in no way intimidated by your opponents. For them this is evidence of their destruction, but of your salvation. And this is God's doing. [29]For he has graciously granted you the privilege ["has graced you"; *echaristhē*] not only of believing in Christ, but of suffering for him as well — [30]since you are having the same struggle that you saw I had and now hear that I still have. (Phil. 1:7, 27-30)[37]

Paul's sentiments expressed to the Philippians capture the attitude he has about the reality of his churches' suffering: God has graced you with the privilege not only of benefiting from Christ but also of participating in Christ. Suffering for, with, and in the Messiah Jesus is normal, the fruit of living worthily of the gospel by becoming the gospel. Why? Because some people will dislike, at the very least, other people who stop going to normal social functions that incorporate rituals of devotion to the pagan deities, including the emperor. Some will dislike, at the very least, those who treat their slaves — or their masters — with a newfound respect. Some will dislike, at the very

---

36. I have altered the NRSV translation of the very end of verse 14 and the beginning of verse 15 (NRSV: "the Jews, who killed both the Lord Jesus and the prophets") to better reflect the actual grammar and message of the text.

37. See also Gal. 3:4, "Did you experience [lit. 'suffer'; *epathete*] so much for nothing? — if it really was for nothing," and Rom. 5:3 ("we also boast in our sufferings"); 8:17-39; 12:12 ("be patient in suffering"). For Gal. 3:4 as a reference to suffering, see John Anthony Dunne, "Suffering in Vain: A Study of the Interpretation of ΠΑΣΧΩ in *Galatians* 3.4," *Journal for the Study of the New Testament* 36 (2013): 3-16; Alexander V. Prokhorov, "Taking the Jews out of the Equation: Galatians 6.12-17 as a Summons to Cease Evading Persecution," *Journal for the Study of the New Testament* 36 (2013): 172-88.

least, those who show a very un-Roman concern for the weakest members of a community. And so on.

When we consider these texts about witness and/or suffering from 1 Corinthians, 1 Thessalonians, Philippians, and elsewhere, as well as others from various letters that we will discuss in the subsequent chapters of this book, we are driven to the conclusion that Paul does, in fact, bear witness to the reality that his communities were — and, from his perspective, were called to be — missional, including (but not limited to) seeking the conversion and thus the salvation of others.[38] In other words, the real question before us is not *if* Paul wanted his communities to be missional (in the centrifugal sense) and evangelical (in the sense of sharing the evangel, the gospel), but *how* that mission was to occur. What does "missional" or "evangelical" mean when we speak of the churches Paul founded and nurtured?

The answer this book proposes at some length is, in brief, that for Paul the church is a *living exegesis* of the gospel of God. The church "performs the gospel as a living commentary on it. . . . It lives the story, embodies the story, tells the story."[39] And it does so because, and inasmuch as, it participates in the life of the God — Father, Son, and Spirit — who is the source and the content of that gospel. In other words, although Paul did not believe that all participants in Christ, all members of the *ekklēsia,* should become *euangelistai* (evangelists in the sense of traveling missionaries or public preachers), he firmly believed that they should all become the *euangelion* (the evangel, the gospel).[40] Summarizing Paul's expectations of his first-century communities and of us, Morna Hooker says that mission "is not a task to be assigned to a few chosen representatives, but a task for the whole Church, since the Church, as the body of Christ in the world, represents to the world what Christ is."[41]

---

38. Barram is absolutely right to insist that we must understand mission in Paul "more comprehensively," "broadly," and "holistically" ("Pauline Mission as Salvific Intentionality," pp. 236, 241, 244, et passim). Thus, while I tend to side with the conclusions of Robert Plummer (and those on whom he builds) — that Paul wanted continuity between his own mission and that of his churches, and suffering is one strong indication that such continuity existed — I find Plummer's understanding of "witness" and "missionary activity" (his common phrases) too narrow both exegetically and hermeneutically.

39. *Cruciformity,* pp. 366-67 (quote from p. 367).

40. The term "evangelist" *(euangelistēs)* appears in the New Testament only in Acts 21:8; Eph. 4:11; 2 Tim. 4:5.

41. Hooker, "Be Holy as I Am Holy," p. 18.

## Witness in Word as Well as Deed

All of this is *not* to say that Paul was uninterested in verbal witness. As we saw in looking at 1 Corinthians, Paul is quite interested in the churches' verbal witness, including the individual witness of each member in his or her own particular situation, even if that interest does not rise to the surface in many letters.[42] Rather, as Dean Flemming has convincingly argued, Paul's notion of congregational and individual mission has three interrelated dimensions — being, doing, and telling — that constitute a unified and holistic understanding of mission.[43] In this book we stress the being and doing ("becoming"), because that, I think, is Paul's emphasis, but this emphasis only makes sense, as we will see, in the context of a people that speaks about its identity and correlates its way of life with its message.

When persecuted, for instance — whether by verbal harassment or something worse — someone frequently would have asked for an explanation for this new anti-social and anti-religious behavior, and someone — some Pauline Christian(s) — would have provided at least a rudimentary answer, such as "Only Jesus is Lord, he is our Lord, and he could/should be your Lord, too. Are you interested in hearing more of the story and seeing it in action?" Reflecting on the New Testament, including Paul, Flemming contends that evangelization, or evangelism (his term), "means the invitation, through word, deed, and example, for people to follow Christ with their whole lives, as part of the Christian community."[44] Flemming's contention is faithful to Paul; to "gospel-ize" (evangelize) requires a community that is itself in an ongoing process of being gospel-ized, and such a community that is being gospel-ized will be a witness; it will naturally be missional.

Paul himself seems to have understood himself explicitly in this sort of way, and his communities implicitly in similar ways. In Romans 15, he describes his ministry for the Roman believers, probably in the hope of gaining their support, financial or otherwise, as he plans to go to Spain. He claims to have a legitimate boast, in Christ, about his ministry, but only inasmuch as what he has said and *done* proclaims the gospel:

---

42. For a survey of the relevant texts, see Plummer, *Paul's Understanding of the Church's Mission*, pp. 71-139.

43. Dean Flemming, *Recovering the Full Mission of God* (Downers Grove, IL: InterVarsity, 2013). He also uses the terms presence, practice, and proclamation.

44. Flemming, *Recovering the Full Mission of God,* p. 18.

[18]For I will not venture to speak of anything except what Christ has accomplished through me to win obedience from the Gentiles, *by word and deed,* [19]by the power of signs and wonders, by the power of the Spirit of God, so that from Jerusalem and as far around as Illyricum I have fully proclaimed the good news of Christ. (Rom. 15:18-19; emphasis added)

The phrase "word and deed" in verse 18 is critical. It would be a mistake to limit the deeds to the signs and wonders Paul mentions in verse 19. Rather, Paul claims, Christ has lived and worked in him, giving him his mind and empowering him to speak and to live the gospel fully. *This is what the indwelling and empowering Spirit does to people.* If Paul's goal is that the communities he founded and/or addressed have the mind of Christ (Phil. 2:5), as he and his colleagues do (1 Cor. 2:16), and if he desires that Christ be formed in them (Gal. 4:19), then it is only fair to conclude — in fact it would be wrong not to conclude — that Paul wants his communities to proclaim the good news in word and deed, not as apostles per se, but simply as those who live in Christ and in whom Christ lives. As they *become* the gospel, they will have opportunities to *speak* the gospel.

If Paul does not, or does not frequently, explicitly tell his communities to speak the gospel, it is because, like a dog, a community in Christ cannot help but bark. Dogs bark by virtue of being dogs; they do not need to be instructed to do so. Sometimes they bark on their own, sometimes when prompted or disturbed, sometimes hesitatingly, and sometimes aggressively. But bark they do. Paul simply wants his communities' barking to be appropriate to the communicative task at hand, rather than annoying. Moreover, as Robert Plummer points out, Paul believes that ultimately the gospel as divine power (see Rom. 1:16-17) — we might even say as the power behind the barking — ensures that a community filled with the gospel and thus with the Spirit of God will in fact bear witness.[45]

The line of argumentation I have been pursuing is a contested one. As noted earlier, there has been significant debate about the role of the Pauline communities in mission. John Dickson, for instance, has argued strongly

---

45. "While Paul does speak of the missionary task entrusted to him as an *obligation,* it is more comprehensively described as a natural overflow of the dynamic gospel's presence in his life. The church also, because it is created and characterized by that same gospel, must be [I would say *will be*] an active missionary community" (Plummer, *Paul's Understanding of the Church's Mission,* p. 145). Commenting on Paul, his churches, and mission, Morna Hooker says, "Mission is not an optional extra, but is part of a Christian's DNA" (Hooker, "Be Holy as I Am Holy," p. 17).

that their role was expressed in certain less direct (my term) missional activities:

- financial assistance, in the form of maintaining and sending missionaries, as well as providing occasional gifts to them;
- prayer, specifically for unbelievers and for Paul's mission;
- social integration, i.e., maintaining relationships with nonbelievers and participating in certain activities with them (especially banquets);
- ethical apologetic, including maintaining a "good appearance" (such as fulfilling normal life-responsibilities), "displaying 'graciousness,'" and generally "walking wisely" toward outsiders;
- public worship; and
- verbal apologetic (which he finds only in Colossians 4:6 in the Pauline letters).[46]

I, too, find all of these activities prescribed and/or described in Paul's letters; some of them (e.g., "social integration" and "public worship") have already been noted. Dickson, however, does not say enough about the significance of the churches' interaction with "the world" — how such interaction would itself be missional, sometimes benevolently so, sometimes confrontationally so — in a more direct way. N. T. Wright, though he is not convinced that there is sufficient evidence to side completely with James Ware (who argues that Philippians 2:16 can *only* mean "holding forth the word of life"[47]) in the debate, helps us see how, theologically, interaction with outsiders is more directly missional:

> As we saw in looking at the central worldview-symbol, the *ekklēsia* itself, one of the ways in which Paul describes it is as the Temple. And this may indicate quite a different mode of "mission." Paul seems to have believed that the individual churches, little groups of baptized believers coming together in communities of worship and love, dotted here and there around the north-east Mediterranean world, were each a living Temple in which the creator God, the God who had dwelt in the Temple in Jerusalem, was now dwelling. They were, in other words, the advance signs of that time

---

46. John P. Dickson, *Mission Commitment in Ancient Judaism and in the Pauline Communities,* WUNT 2/159 (Tübingen: Mohr Siebeck, 2003).

47. James P. Ware, *Paul and the Mission of the Church: Philippians in Ancient Jewish Context* (Grand Rapids: Baker Academic, 2011), esp. pp. 256-70.

when the whole world would be filled with the divine glory. Each lamp that was lit, in Colosse or Philippi or wherever, was a point of light, of divine presence, as a sign of the dawn that would come when the whole world would be so illuminated. That, I think, is part of what he means in Colossians 1.27: the Messiah in you, the hope of glory. The indwelling Messiah, living in his Temple in Colosse, was the sign that "the hope of glory" was starting to come true — the hope, that is, that YHWH would return in glory to his Temple, and that he would thereby fill the whole earth with his knowledge and glory, with his justice, peace and joy. Paul sees each *ekklēsia* as a sign of that future reality. To that extent, and in that sense, we can already say that "mission" was indeed part of the symbolic reality (together with unity and holiness) by which Paul understood his communities to be defined.[48]

Even Wright, in my view, does not go far enough. Advance signs — yes. Points of light — yes. But, even more — spaces of anticipatory participation. Communities of "justice, peace and joy" are more than just signs; they are, like the Spirit, a form of down payment, a guarantee that the age of justice, peace, and joy is not a pipe dream but a future reality that can be known, imperfectly and incompletely but really, in the present. That is what it means for the churches to become the gospel and to "gospelize" — and thereby to participate in the *missio Dei*.

I think that Wright actually agrees with this:

They [the people of God] were called to be, in some sense or other, the renewed human race, the genuine humans, the people who would embody what the creator God had had in mind all along when he first made this strange creature in his own image. Since Paul believed that this purpose had been fulfilled in and through the Messiah and his people, he regarded the signs of renewed human life as among the key elements of symbolic praxis within his worldview.[49]

48. Wright, *Paul and the Faithfulness of God*, p. 437.
49. Wright, *Paul and the Faithfulness of God*, p. 438. Cf. these lines as well: "[P]art of the whole point of Paul's message (and part of the reason for its complexity) is the urgent imperative to anticipate in the present, *through the presence, power and personality of the spirit,* that which we are promised in the future" (p. 440). "Paul is not leaving the cosmos without images to mediate the presence of the one true God. On the contrary. The world, the cosmos, is already presented with the one true Image, the Messiah himself; and the symbolic praxis of the Messiah's people is thus grounded, by the Spirit, in the vocation to be imagebearers, to be

Yes — renewed human life, according to the crucified and resurrected Messiah. Becoming the gospel! Again, Wright:

> Paul insisted on the praxis which was to become, not just a miscellaneous or from-time-to-time lifestyle choice, but part of the assumed mental furniture of the *ekklēsia:* the praxis of being "new humanity," reflecting to the world, through its unity and holiness, the image of the one God which had been reflected fully and for ever "in the face of Jesus the Messiah."[50]

Precisely. A reframing of the question about Paul and mission (including evangelism/evangelization) in the churches, as I am proposing, around the verb "becoming" will inevitably carry with it a broadening of our understanding of salvation.[51] If Paul does in fact want his congregations to act purposively for the salvation of all, what does that salvation look like in real life, "on the ground," so to speak? The contention of this book is that, biblically speaking, and particularly for Paul, salvation incorporates the breadth of God's desires for humans individually and corporately. It includes a life of faith, hope, and love; of Christlike self-giving for the good of others; of peace and reconciliation with God and one another; of prophetic, restorative justice; of righteousness and, ultimately, of full participation in the glory of God.[52] It is something believers talk about, yes, but above all it is something they do, something indeed they *are.* And when people actually *are* something — something that stands in some sense in contrast to normal living — they will provoke reactions: sometimes quite positive, sometimes more negative, sometimes *very* negative — even fatal, as (it would seem) at Thessalonica.

This way of understanding mission may not be formal "evangelism" by some modern or even postmodern definition, but it is nonetheless preach-

---

the means of participating in and reflecting the true divine life into a world whose iconography had been giving off either a radically distorted vision or a downright lying one" (p. 442).

50. Wright, *Paul and the Faithfulness of God,* p. 450.

51. For an overview of salvation in the Bible, stressing the breadth of its meaning, see Michael J. Gorman and Richard Middleton, "Salvation," *New Interpreter's Dictionary of the Bible* 5:45-61 (Nashville: Abingdon, 2009).

52. As noted in the Introduction, John Wesley, under the influence of the Greek Fathers, defined salvation as "a present deliverance from sin, a restoration of the soul to its primitive health, its original purity; a recovery of the divine nature; the renewal of our souls after the image of God in righteousness and true holiness, in justice, mercy, and truth" (*The Works of John Wesley,* Vol. 11: *The Appeals to Men of Reason and Religion and Certain Related Open Letters,* ed. Gerald R. Cragg [Nashville: Abingdon, 1987], p. 106, para. 1.3).

ing the gospel (see 1 Cor. 12:3; Phil. 2:6-11; etc.). The answer to the question mentioned earlier — did Paul expect his communities to preach the gospel? — is not dependent on one exegetical/translational issue that is frequently debated: Does Paul want the Philippians to "hold forth" the word of life or "hold fast to" the word of life (Phil. 2:16)? Nevertheless, the theological answer to that question from Paul, I would submit, is a resounding "yes" — that is, both to hold fast to, and to hold forth, the gospel: to "gospel-ize" in faithful, creative, embodied word and deed.

# CHAPTER 2

# Reading Paul Missionally

We have addressed, at least in a preliminary way, one of the two ways of interpreting the question "What does it mean to read Paul missionally?" raised at the beginning of chapter one: "What would we discover if we read Paul's letters, first and foremost . . . for their witness to Paul's vision of God's mission in the world (the *missio Dei*) and to the role he, his colleagues, and the churches were to play in that mission?" We turn in this chapter, rather more briefly, to the second way to interpret that question: "For those of us who read Paul's letters as Christian Scripture, as divine address to the church, what would we discern about *our* role in the divine mission (the *missio Dei*) in *our* situation today?" What does contemporary mission in the "spirit" of Paul, so to speak, look like?

Our emphasis here will not be on a direct answer to that question — for such an answer would require consideration of the main chapters of this book and of the context in which the question is asked — but rather on some of the resources available to help us ask and answer the question responsibly and productively. At the same time, as noted earlier, for those who do read Paul's letters as Christian Scripture, the exegetical and historical work we have begun, and will continue in subsequent chapters, already provides perspectives, frameworks, and even implicit answers to the hermeneutical question of what Paul says to us about Christian mission today.

We are in the midst of exciting, fervent times with respect to the two theological disciplines that come together in this book: Pauline studies and missional hermeneutics. The former is perhaps the oldest subdiscipline in theology (see 2 Pet. 3:15-16!), while the latter is quite new, at least as a formal area of study.[1] Missional hermeneutics is neither the same as missiology

---

1. According to George Hunsberger, the term "missional hermeneutic" was likely coined

nor the same as hermeneutics as it has been normally practiced. Rather, missional hermeneutics is what happens when missiologists, biblical scholars, and ecclesial leaders intentionally work together to probe the biblical text for what it says about the *missio Dei* and about our participation in it.[2] Missional hermeneutics should be seen as a subset, or perhaps an extension, of theological interpretation — the approach to biblical studies that is appropriate to the church in its quest to know, love, and serve God and neighbor, and therefore to bring Scripture and all aspects of theology into constructive conversation.[3]

## What Is a Missional Hermeneutic?

Missiologist George Hunsberger raises the fundamental question of a missional hermeneutic, or interpretive strategy: "What difference does it make if the Bible is approached from the perspective of the mission of God and the

---

by James Brownson in 1992. See George R. Hunsberger, "Proposals for a Missional Hermeneutic: Mapping a Conversation," *Missiology: An International Review* 39 (2011): 309-21 (here p. 316).

2. For overviews, see Michael Barram, "The Bible, Mission, and Social Location: Toward a Missional Hermeneutic," *Interpretation* 61 (2007): 42-58; James V. Brownson, *Speaking the Truth in Love: New Testament Resources for a Missional Hermeneutic* (Harrisburg, PA: Trinity Press International, 1998); Hunsberger, "Proposals for a Missional Hermeneutic," with an earlier version also at http://www.gocn.org/resources/articles/proposals-missional-hermeneutic-mapping-conversation); and Michael J. Gorman, *Elements of Biblical Exegesis: A Basic Guide for Students and Ministers,* revised and expanded edition (Grand Rapids: Baker Academic, 2009), pp. 155-58. See also Richard Bauckham, *Bible and Mission: Christian Witness in a Post-modern World* (Grand Rapids: Baker, 2003); Christopher J. H. Wright, *The Mission of God: Unlocking the Bible's Grand Narrative* (Downers Grove, IL: InterVarsity, 2006); Michael W. Goheen, *A Light to the Nations: The Missional Church and the Biblical Story* (Grand Rapids: Baker Academic, 2011); James C. Miller; *Reading Scripture Missionally* (Eugene, OR: Cascade, forthcoming); and Dean Flemming, *Why Mission? A New Testament Exploration* (Nashville: Abingdon, forthcoming).

3. The recent reinvigoration of theological interpretation is represented by important publishing developments like the *Journal of Theological Interpretation,* edited by Joel Green, and several commentary series from publishers such as Brazos (Brazos Theological Commentary on the Bible), Eerdmans (Two Horizons New Testament Commentary; Two Horizons Old Testament Commentary), and Westminster John Knox (Belief: A Theological Commentary on the Bible). For brief overviews of theological interpretation, see Gorman, *Elements of Biblical Exegesis,* pp. 144-55; Richard B. Hays, "Reading the Bible with Eyes of Faith: The Practice of Theological Exegesis," *Journal of Theological Interpretation* 1 (2007): 5-21.

missionary nature of the church?"[4] Practitioners of a missional hermeneutic deliberately read the biblical text as witness to God's purposes in the world and as invitation — even as summons — to participate in that divine activity. In the words of New Testament scholar Michael Barram, a leading voice in missional hermeneutics, missional interpretation is "biblical interpretation conducted from the hermeneutical perspective of the church's location as a sent community."[5] Indeed, Barram argues that this sense of "the missional 'sent-ness' of the interpretive community of faith has become pretty close to a *sine qua non* for ecclesial hermeneutics."[6] This, Barram argues, makes missional interpretation somewhat distinct from theological interpretation, at least as it has been most recently described and practiced:

> In short, I wonder if missional hermeneutics, given its core assumptions and affirmations, does not end up at least implicitly claiming that the "sent-ness" of the interpretive community *must* be an explicit and guiding component of any interpretative enterprise seeking to do full justice to the biblical text. Given that I find no significant disagreement on the broad principles and assumptions affirmed by both "theological interpretation" and "missional hermeneutics," perhaps the one difference I do perceive is, in fact, a point of disagreement, at least from the perspective of missional hermeneutics. To frame the issue fairly sharply, for "missional hermeneutics" the "sent-ness" of the interpretive community is not merely one of a number of worthwhile hermeneutical considerations; rather, in some very real sense it seems to function as *the* fundamental consideration. Missional hermeneutics may be a necessary enterprise, therefore, precisely because its focus on the "sent-ness" of the interpretive community may, in some cases, enable it to go beyond forms of "theological interpretation" that lack this emphasis.[7]

Barram's sharp comments are helpful in reminding us of the church's fundamental missional identity, from which its approach to Scripture springs, or should spring. I agree completely with the basic thrust of Barram's argument about mission and scriptural interpretation. Although I more often use the word "participation" than "sent-ness," they are complementary rather

---

4. Hunsberger, "Proposals for a Missional Hermeneutic," p. 309.

5. Michael Barram, "Reflections on the Practice of Missional Hermeneutics: 'Streaming' Philippians 1:20-30" (unpublished paper delivered at the GOCN Forum on Missional Hermeneutics, November 21, 2009), p. 9.

6. Barram, "Reflections," p. 10.

7. Barram, "Reflections," pp. 10-11.

than competing biblical and theological concepts. I would, however, still maintain that missional hermeneutics is a form of theological interpretation, even while granting Barram's claim that theological interpretation as a whole needs to make the missional identity of the church a more explicit and central feature of its approach to scriptural interpretation.[8]

To summarize the working definition that is emerging, I refer to something I have written elsewhere:

> [A missional hermeneutic] is grounded in the theological principle of the *missio Dei,* or mission of God. This term summarizes the conviction that the Scriptures of both Testaments bear witness to a God who, as creator and redeemer of the world, is already on a mission. Indeed, God is by nature a missional God, who is seeking not just to save "souls" to take to heaven some day, but to restore and save the created order: individuals, communities, nations, the environment, the world, the cosmos. This God calls the people of God assembled in the name of Christ — who was the incarnation of the divine mission — to participate in this *missio Dei,* to discern what God is up to in the world, and to join in.[9]

Some of the implications of this approach to biblical interpretation follow:[10]

- Mission is not a *part* of the church's life (represented locally by a small line item in the budget) but the *whole,* the *essence* of the church's existence; mission is *comprehensive.*
- Mission is not the church's initiative but its response, its participation in God's mission; mission is *derivative.*
- Mission is not an extension of Western (or any other) power, culture, and values; rather, it is specifically participation in the coming of the kingdom of God. It is therefore critical of all attempts to coerce Christian mission for implicit or explicit political purposes other than the "politics" of the reign of God — the realities of new life, peace, and justice *(shalom)* promised by the prophets, inaugurated by Jesus, and

---

8. I would note here that the *Journal of Theological Interpretation* has published the work of some scholars who self-identify as operating with a missional hermeneutic. See, e.g., Michael A. Rynkiewich, "Mission, Hermeneutics, and the Local Church," *Journal of Theological Interpretation* 1 (2007): 47-60; Dean Flemming, "Revelation and the *Missio Dei:* Toward a Missional Reading of the Apocalypse," *Journal of Theological Interpretation* 6 (2012): 161-78.

9. Gorman, *Elements of Biblical Exegesis,* p. 155.

10. These are in Gorman, *Elements of Biblical Exegesis,* p. 156.

first spread to the world by the apostles. For Christians in the West, it is crucial that they recognize the failure of Christendom as something to be welcomed, and that they see the church appropriately and biblically as a distinctive subculture within a larger, non-Christian culture. Mission is *theo- and Christocentric.*

- Mission is not unidirectional (e.g., West to East) but *reciprocal.*
- Mission must become the governing framework within which all biblical interpretation takes place; mission is *hermeneutical.*

George Hunsberger has studied the contributions of those at the forefront of the emerging field of missional hermeneutics and has identified four "streams" of emphasis, or basic approaches, to missional hermeneutics.[11] The first two of these, I would suggest, stress the biblical text itself, while the other two focus more deliberately on interpreters and their contexts. These are not at all mutually exclusive, but they do represent different perspectives:

1. *The missional direction of the story.* This text-centered approach emphasizes the framework for interpretation as "the story it [the Bible] tells of the mission of God and the formation of a community sent to participate in it."[12] The working assumption is that, despite its diversity, the Bible is to be read as a single narrative of salvation from Genesis to Revelation. It is a hermeneutic of biblical theology, the Bible as a whole.[13]

2. *The missional purpose of the writings.* This second text-centered approach asserts that the goal of interpretation is "to fulfill the equipping purpose of the biblical writings" themselves. More specifically, the purpose of the New Testament writings was (then) and is (now) the ongoing formation and equipping of missional communities. It is a hermeneutic of the canonical documents themselves, particularly those in the New Testament.[14]

---

11. Hunsberger, "Proposals for a Missional Hermeneutic." The study is based on presentations and writings of missiologists and biblical scholars who have been part of the GOCN (Gospel and Our Culture Network) Forum on Missional Hermeneutics since 2005. The Forum meets annually in conjunction with the meetings of the Society of Biblical Literature.

12. Hunsberger, "Proposals for a Missional Hermeneutic," p. 310.

13. For discussion and critique, see Hunsberger, "Proposals for a Missional Hermeneutic," pp. 310-13. Two major names associated with this approach are Christopher Wright and Michael Goheen.

14. For discussion and critique, see Hunsberger, "Proposals for a Missional Hermeneutic," pp. 313-14. The major name associated with this approach is Darrell Guder, with James Brownson having some similar interests.

3. *The missional location of the Christian community.* This more reader-centered approach does not directly challenge the previous two approaches but shifts the focus to the social location of the interpreters, highlighting the importance of particular contexts for asking and answering the question of how, in reading Scripture, are its readers caught up into God's purposes in their particular corner of the world today.[15]

4. *The missional engagement with cultures.* In this somewhat similar contextual approach, "the gospel functions as the interpretive *matrix* within which the received biblical tradition is brought into critical conversation with a particular human context."[16] As the New Testament writers reread the Scriptures of Israel to engage their culture with the new gospel of Christ, so also Christian believers today reread the New Testament, in particular, guided by its fundamental motifs, to engage contemporary cultures imaginatively and faithfully with the gospel.

To these four "streams," James Brownson adds a reminder, if not an additional stream. It is related especially to the third stream, with its emphasis on context: "that missional encounters between people are, almost by definition, *cross-cultural* encounters."[17] This is because, especially (he says) in the postmodern era, "*difference* is fundamental, absolute." Thus, "if a missional hermeneutic is going to avoid becoming either a totalizing narrative that suppresses difference, or a pastiche that simply satisfies for the moment, a missional hermeneutic must take the reality of *difference* with utmost seriousness. And this brings us back to . . . the centrality of cross-cultural encounter for a missional hermeneutic." Brownson rightly points out that this dynamic is already at work in Paul's ministry and letters, as the apostle tries to bring about "reconciliation without uniformity." Our challenge is to understand God's mission, and read Scripture, with that sort of lens.

15. For discussion and critique, see Hunsberger, "Proposals for a Missional Hermeneutic," pp. 314-16. Two major names associated with this approach are Michael Barram and James Miller. For an attempt at missional hermeneutics in this vein, though not an interpretation of Paul, see my *Reading Revelation Responsibly: Uncivil Worship and Witness; Following the Lamb into the New Creation* (Eugene, OR: Cascade, 2011).

16. Hunsberger, "Proposals for a Missional Hermeneutic," p. 316. For discussion and critique of this approach, see pp. 316-18. The major name associated with this approach is James Brownson.

17. James V. Brownson, "A Response at SBL to Hunsberger's 'Proposals . . .' Essay," delivered at the annual meeting of the GOCN Forum on Missional Hermeneutics in November 2008: http://www.gocn.org/resources/articles/response-sbl-hunsbergers-proposals-essay. All quotations in this paragraph are from the website version of the essay.

So which of these four, or five, approaches will guide us in the following chapters?

As noted above, these streams are not mutually exclusive. However, as we discussed in the Introduction ("Invitation"), the focus of this book is not primarily on the specific questions of direct missional engagement in specific contexts. Thus, although the third and fourth (and perhaps fifth) approaches represent the ultimate goal of a missional hermeneutic, in this book it is the first two, more text-centered, approaches that will be our primary concern. The additional streams provide, then, the lenses with which, and the contexts within which, this book, as well as the scriptural texts, can be read with missional profit.

These diverse approaches, it must be emphasized yet again, are not "merely" exegetical and historical in orientation. They are themselves hermeneutical; even to approach the Bible in this missional way is to assume that there is a continuity in the biblical narrative; that there is in fact a *missio Dei;* that the biblical writings exist, at least in part, to invite and summon us to participation in that divine mission; and so on.

There are perhaps five key questions that readers operating with a missional hermeneutic will want to ask of the biblical texts (in this case, the Pauline writings) and themselves:[18]

- What do these texts say, implicitly or explicitly, about the polyvalent (complex and comprehensive) *missio Dei* and the missional character of God?
- What do these texts reveal about humanity and the world?
- What do these texts say about the nature and mission of God's people in the world, that is, about the church understood as an agent of divine mission (rather than as an institution, club, civic organization, or guardian of Christendom)?
- How do these texts relate to the larger scriptural witness, in both Testaments, to the *missio Dei* and the mission of God's people?
- In what concrete ways, in our specific context, might we deliberately read this text as God's call to us as the people of God to participate in the *missio Dei* to which it bears witness?

In the chapters that follow, we will be focusing explicitly and primarily on Paul's perspective on these sorts of questions, especially the first four. Be-

18. These are adapted from Gorman, *Elements of Biblical Exegesis,* p. 156.

cause I believe in great continuity between the first four questions and the fifth, that fifth question will always be with us; in fact, it will be the largely implicit but actually most significant question this book raises, from start to finish. That is, the question within, behind, and in front of the analyses of Paul's letters in this book is an interpretive one, a missional one. This is because Paul's letters are, in an important sense, missional writings, as our earlier discussion about the question concerning Paul and mission in the churches suggested. This brings us to the work of Pauline scholars who are beginning to think about Paul deliberately as a missional writer and about readers of Paul's letters as missional interpreters.

## Paul, His Mission, and Missional Hermeneutics

In 2005 the Gospel and Our Culture Network (GOCN) began a Forum on Missional Hermeneutics that meets annually at the same time as the Society of Biblical Literature (SBL). Three of the biblical scholars on the Forum's steering committee, as well as other regular and occasional participants in the Forum, are Pauline scholars.[19] Connecting Paul and mission is, of course, a natural and time-honored interpretive step.[20] But our understanding of Paul as missionary and of the contemporary implications of that understanding is moving in new directions.

In his very readable published dissertation, *Mission and Moral Reflection in Paul,* Michael Barram argues that "mission" is not a discrete aspect of Paul's work, such as evangelism and initial community formation, but a principal rubric for understanding the apostle's entire vocation, including moral reflection and ongoing community nurturing.[21] Paul's letters are therefore "mission documents." If Barram is right, as I think he is, then we need to

19. The Pauline scholars who have been members of the steering committee include Michael Barram, James Miller, and myself. Additional Pauline scholars have been regular participants, including Matthew Lowe. Invited participants have included Stephen Fowl, Richard Hays, and Sylvia Keesmaat, plus a session on the missional hermeneutic operating in the work of N. T. Wright (with a major presentation by him) in 2014.

20. A classic work is Johannes Munck, *Paul and the Salvation of Mankind,* trans. Frank Clarke (London: SCM, 1959). For recent works see, e.g., Eckhard J. Schnabel, *Paul the Missionary: Realities, Strategies and Methods* (Downers Grove, IL: InterVarsity, 2008); and Trevor J. Burke and Brian S. Rosner, eds., *Paul as Missionary: Identity, Activity, Theology, and Practice,* Library of New Testament Studies 420 (London: T. & T. Clark, 2011).

21. Michael Barram, *Mission and Moral Reflection in Paul,* Studies in Biblical Literature 75 (New York: Peter Lang, 2006).

read Paul's letters in two ways: first, as witnesses to Paul's understanding of God's mission, his role in it, and the place of his congregations in it; and, second, as scriptural texts for our own missional identity, our contemporary vocational and ecclesial self-understanding and practices. Thus is born a Pauline missional hermeneutic, one that addresses both questions raised in chapter one and again at the beginning of this chapter.

In a Pauline missional hermeneutic, the guiding question is a variant of the fifth question listed above: "How do we read Paul for what he says about the *missio Dei* and about our participation in it?" In other words, although the *topic* before us may be, say, Paul's instructions to the Corin-thians, or Paul and justice, or Paul and reconciliation, the *issue* before us is not primarily exegetical or historical, but hermeneutical. We answer certain basic questions in a particular way. What is a Pauline letter? (A missional document.) To whom is it addressed? (To us in our particular contexts.) How are we to read it appropriately? (Missionally.) Older his-torical and exegetical questions — e.g., about how and whom Paul evan-gelized, and whether he expected his communities to do the same — are still relevant, but they will not be our primary concerns, and they are not ends in themselves. Rather, they are part of a larger discussion about Paul and mission, a conversation that assumes that mission is absolutely integral to ecclesial identity, both in the first century and in the twenty-first. Thus we are now obliged to reformulate the old question, "Did Paul expect his congregations to evangelize others?" for it is, in one sense, the wrong question. The better question is "How did Paul expect his commu-nities to participate in the *missio Dei*?," with the corollary fundamental hermeneutical question, "How does God expect us who read Paul's letters to participate in the *missio Dei*?"

New questions always generate new possibilities and still more ques-tions. We have already seen that a missional hermeneutic will force us to think carefully about basic questions of ecclesiology and ethics. In fact, a missional hermeneutic will bind those two fields so closely together that retaining two different theological labels ("ecclesiology"; "ethics") will no longer be sustainable. The contention of Richard Hays in his *Moral Vision of the New Testament* — that theology and ethics are inseparable in Paul — is now strengthened by a missional reading.[22] As Barram writes, "Theology

22. See Richard B. Hays, *The Moral Vision of the New Testament: Community, Cross, New Creation; A Contemporary Introduction to New Testament Ethics* (San Francisco: HarperCol-lins, 1996), p. 18.

and ethics come together in Paul's mission."[23] So also do centripetal and centrifugal concerns.

Still more new perspectives and questions will naturally arise, especially if we, like Paul, take our specific contexts seriously. Paul did not treat the Corinthians and the Philippians, for instance, in precisely the same way. A missional hermeneutic is a contextual hermeneutic, and we will therefore ask different concrete questions depending on our specific location in space and time.

For example, unlike Luke or James, Paul has never been the "go-to" guy for those interested in various aspects of "social justice." But a close reading of 1 and 2 Corinthians, for instance, reveals that justice concerns were on Paul's mind (e.g., 1 Cor. 6:1-11; 1 Cor. 11:17-34; and 2 Corinthians 8 in connection with 2 Cor. 5:21), and that they grow directly out of his core convictions about Jesus and about justification/salvation in him.[24] Noticing these concerns and their theological underpinnings will prompt us to ask a question such as "What do Paul's admonitions about justice reveal about his understanding of Christ and the Christian community as the embodiment of God's justice in the world?" And then we will need to follow that question up with yet another: "What does that revelation mean for our life in and as the church today?" Similarly, Paul has seldom been interpreted as a peacemaker or advocate of nonviolence, but that too is changing and being connected to mission.[25] Additionally, recent theological concerns about ecological issues have driven Pauline scholars to passages like Romans 8 and Colossians 1 in search of ways to read those texts that can address the ecological issues of our day.[26] Such forays, from the perspective of missional hermeneutics, are not merely

23. Barram, *Mission and Moral Reflection,* p. 142.

24. See e.g., A. Katherine Grieb, " 'So That in Him We Might Become the Righteousness of God' (2 Cor. 5:21): Some Theological Reflections on the Church Becoming Justice," *Ex Auditu* 22 (2006): 58-80.

25. The apostle receives significant attention in two recent works on New Testament theology and peace by Mennonite Willard Swartley: *Send Forth Your Light: A Vision for Peace, Mission, and Worship* (Scottdale, PA: Herald, 2007) and the more academic *Covenant of Peace: The Missing Peace in New Testament Theology and Ethics* (Grand Rapids: Eerdmans, 2006). See also my *Inhabiting the Cruciform God: Kenosis, Justification, and Theosis in Paul's Narrative Soteriology* (Grand Rapids: Eerdmans, 2009), especially chs. 2 and 4; and my *The Death of the Messiah and the Birth of the New Covenant: A (Not So) New Model of the Atonement* (Eugene, OR: Cascade, 2014), chs. 6 and 7, and the bibliography there.

26. See, among other works, David Horrell, Cherryl Hunt, and Christopher Southgate, eds., *Greening Paul: Reading the Apostle in a Time of Ecological Crisis* (Waco, TX: Baylor University Press, 2010); Presian Smyers Burroughs, "Liberation in the Midst of Futility and

attempts to engage "hot topics" or even to practice responsible Christian stewardship. Rather, they are means of probing once again that fundamental question: "What is the *missio Dei* to which Paul bears witness, sometimes explicitly and sometimes implicitly, and how are we called to participate in it?"

At the same time, Paul will never allow us to separate social justice (or peacemaking or ecological concerns) from the gospel, or make the latter a subsidiary (at best) of the former. What George Hunsinger has said of Karl Barth's Christocentric soteriology, if turned into a message about something called "social justice" (or whatever), is even more true of the apostle Paul:

> Insofar as what needs to become actual in (or among) us is conceived as some independent good or gift (e.g., a virtuous disposition, social justice, eternal blessedness), then salvation itself becomes externalized as "something different from him, some general gift mediated by him," rather than being identical with himself. Thus "at the last moment, we ignore him as though he were only a means or instrument or channel" (IV/1, 116).[27]

For Paul, as for Barth, the gift of Christ is salvation itself, and all that it entails can never be separated from him.

*[handwritten margin note: virtuous disposition; social justice; eternal blessedness]*

Do these new developments in Pauline studies and missional hermeneutics mean the demise of evangelism or faith-sharing in the sense of attempting to gain new converts? As Paul would certainly say, *mē genoito* (may it never be)! What they do indicate, however, is that evangelism must be understood more holistically, and that the connection between Paul and mission generally must be understood more broadly, and appropriated more creatively, than we have often done in the past. It means, in fact, to understand the gospel, the *euangelion* (the root of the word "evangelism"), much more broadly and biblically. If, as Paul tells us, the good news will one day come to its ultimate fulfillment in the liberation of the entire creation (Rom. 8:18-25), then N. T. Wright is right to say that "acts of justice, mercy, and peace in the present are proper, albeit inevitably partial, fitful and puzzling anticipations of God's eventual design."[28] That is anticipatory participation, and it is both centripetal and centrifugal.

---

Destruction: Romans 8 and the Christian Vocation of Nourishing Life" (Th.D. diss., Duke Divinity School, 2014).

27. George Hunsinger, *How to Read Karl Barth: The Shape of His Theology* (New York: Oxford University Press, 1991), p. 144.

28. N. T. Wright, *What Saint Paul Really Said: Was Paul of Tarsus the Real Founder of Christianity?* (Grand Rapids: Eerdmans, 1997), p. 164.

To read Paul missionally is to read him as a participant in, advocate for, and interpreter of the *missio Dei,* the mission of God first revealed in the story and Scriptures of Israel and now manifested in its fullness in the reality and story of Christ. It is to read his letters as witnesses to that *missio Dei* and as invitations to be part of it, indeed to participate in the very life of God. Once the church starts to read Paul that way more deliberately and more consistently, it will be thrilling, I believe, to see what transpires.[29]


## Conclusion

The thesis of chapter one, and one major claim of this book, in a nutshell, was this: that Paul expected the salvation of God to spread throughout the world not only by means of his own gospel ministry (and that of his close colleagues), but also by means of the participation of his converts in the various house churches. *They were, in essence, to become the gospel, not merely playing a supportive role by praying for and underwriting Paul's work, but participating in the advance of the gospel through proclamation, praxis, and persecution (i.e., suffering).* In a word, through *witness:* witness in word, in deed, and in the unpleasant consequences that often attend faithful witness.

But my goal in this book is not principally a historical argument. In fact, if that were the primary goal it would have a quite different shape. Rather, my goal is theological and indeed missional. The thesis of this chapter, and the burden of the book, is that those of us who read Paul's letters as Christian Scripture need also to participate in the advance of the gospel by becoming the gospel, in word, in deed, and — if we are faithful and it becomes necessary — in suffering.

Participation, in other words, is essential not only to salvation, ethics,

29. One initial attempt to do this is Eddie Gibbs, *The Rebirth of the Church: Applying Paul's Vision for Ministry in Our Post-Christian World* (Grand Rapids: Baker Academic, 2013). Echoing other voices, including N. T. Wright's, Gibbs suggests that there are significant parallels between Paul's pre-Christendom and our post-Christendom contexts. Gibbs is especially helpful in stressing the urban context of Paul's churches; the significance of community, ongoing pastoral care and transformation, and networks in and among those churches; and the challenge to Western individualism and privatism that those characteristics offer. However, although Gibbs speaks of mission in participatory terms, his primary emphasis is on centripetal rather than centrifugal practices, and his understanding of the church's mission (or at least its primary missional activity, or "ministry" — the word in the book's subtitle) is narrower than the one proposed in this book.

and eschatology, as many students of Paul have noted, but also to mission. Indeed, to separate these aspects of Pauline theology and spirituality is to commit an egregious act of misinterpretation of the apostle, for all of these are inseparably knit together for him. To be in Christ is to be in mission; to participate in the gospel is to participate in the advance of the gospel.

In expecting that his churches become the gospel, Paul was not asking them to do something different from what he himself practiced. Just as Christ had been revealed "in" Paul (Gal. 1:16[30]), so also Christ was being revealed *through* him. Paul understood his apostolic identity as a life-narrative that substantively corresponded to and thus re-presented the life-narrative of Christ, especially as that narrative was articulated in texts like Philippians 2:6-11. This was Paul's master story, not only the most fundamental and significant telling of the Christ-story itself, but also the controlling narrative of his own existence, as the earliest preserved reflection on his ministry clearly indicates (1 Thessalonians 2), and as other texts (e.g., 1 Corinthians 9) corroborate.[31]

This master story is also the controlling narrative for life in Christ for all believers, both individually and corporately, and it is such both for their internal life together and for their external, public life in the world (see, e.g., Phil. 1:27–2:16). In fact, to a large degree it is their life together that *is* their life in the world. Their "fellowship" is their witness; their practices of acclaiming Jesus as Lord and living in harmony with that act of adoration and allegiance constitute their public testimony as well as their *koinōnia*. Centripetal activity is naturally also centrifugal.

In fact, if we understand the word *koinōnia* properly, we will see it much more as participation, expressed in concrete practices, than merely as friendly socializing or even shared ("common") interests. When this *koinōnia* goes well, as it did in Philippi, Paul is quite pleased. When it goes poorly, as it did in several ways in Corinth, Paul becomes distressed. Fixing the internal situation to align with the cross and the work of the Spirit is simultaneously repairing the community's corporate witness to and in the world.

In the chapters to come, we explore various aspects of this participatory witness in the Pauline communities. And we do so always with the "so what?" question before us.

---

30. NRSV has "to me," but the Greek *en emoi* is probably better translated "in me."

31. On Phil. 2:6-11 as Paul's master story, see my *Cruciformity: Paul's Narrative Spirituality of the Cross* (Grand Rapids: Eerdmans, 2001), pp. 23, 88-94, 164-74, 366-67, 383-85, 400-401, et passim.

# CHAPTER 3

# Becoming the Gospel of Faith(fulness), Love, and Hope: 1 Thessalonians

Few things are more fundamental to Christianity than faith, hope, and love. This chapter explores the role of this triad (in a slightly different order) in Paul's first letter to the believers in Thessalonica. The chapter claims that faith, or faithfulness, love, and hope were essential components of the public life and witness of these early Christians. And it considers what Paul says about the centrality of faith(fulness), love, and hope to the mission of God, and thus also to Paul's mission and to the mission of the church then and now.

## Three Missional Virtues

The Christian tradition refers to faith, hope, and love as the three theological virtues. They can also be called the three theological graces or marks (that is, identity markers). These three theological marks appear together in Paul's first letter to the Thessalonians, which is also probably the earliest Christian writing that has been preserved.[1] They exist together as a triad, in other words, from the very beginning of the Christian faith. In fact, this Pauline triad appears twice in 1 Thessalonians, at the beginning and at the end of the letter:[2]

1. 1 Thessalonians was probably written in the year 50 or 51. Some would argue that Galatians predates 1 Thessalonians. If they are correct, then the triad would still appear in the earliest preserved Christian document, for it appears also (though less succinctly) in Gal. 5:5-6: "For through the Spirit, by faith, we eagerly wait for the hope of righteousness. For in Christ Jesus neither circumcision nor uncircumcision counts for anything; the only thing that counts is faith working through love."

2. All Scripture references in this chapter that do not explicitly identify the book (e.g., 5:1 rather than 1 Thess. 5:1 or Rom. 5:1) indicate texts in 1 Thessalonians.

> [2]We always give thanks to God for all of you and mention you in our prayers, constantly [3]remembering before our God and Father your work of faith and labor of love and steadfastness of hope in our Lord Jesus Christ. (1:2-3)

> [8]But since we belong to the day, let us be sober, and put on the breastplate of faith and love, and for a helmet the hope of salvation. (5:8)

Three things are immediately worth noting about these texts from 1 Thessalonians. First, in each case, the ordering of the triad is different from what we normally hear: faith, love, and hope, rather than faith, hope, and, love, which is the sequence in the well-known text of 1 Corinthians 13 (v. 13). In 1 Thessalonians, hope is last, receiving the greatest emphasis in the letter.[3] Second, these virtues are not merely inner attitudes but attitudes with corollary practices; they work, labor, and remain steadfast (1:2-3), and they are elements of a kind of spiritual, apocalyptic battle (5:8). Third, the passage from the beginning of the letter (1:2-3) is *descriptive,* while the one from the end of the letter is *prescriptive,* an exhortation (5:8; "let us . . ."). Taken together, these three ways of speaking of the triad indicate how essential faith, love, and hope are to life in Christ; they are at the heart of Christian identity and praxis, both past and present.[4]

In the context of 1 Thessalonians, this triad of marks of Christian identity is connected to the main theme of the letter, which is holiness (sanctification).[5] This theme is itself summarized in two texts, one at the end of the first part of the letter, and one near the very end of the document:

> And may he [God/the Lord] so strengthen your hearts in holiness that you may be blameless before our God and Father at the coming of our Lord Jesus with all his saints. (1 Thess. 3:13)

3. See the discussion of 1 Thessalonians in Michael J. Gorman, *Apostle of the Crucified Lord: A Theological Introduction to Paul and His Letters* (Grand Rapids: Eerdmans, 2004), pp. 146-66.

4. Andy Johnson says about the triad of faith, love, and hope, when first announced in 1 Thess. 1:2-3, that "[w]hile it would be forced to argue that this triad actually structures the rest of the letter, it clearly does give the audience a 'preview of the letter's coming attractions'" (*1-2 Thessalonians,* Two Horizons New Testament Commentary [Grand Rapids: Eerdmans, forthcoming]).

5. These two terms reflect the two possible English translations of the *hag-* group of words in Greek, one translation from Old English (holiness, holy, etc.) and one from Latin (sanctification, sanctify, saint, etc.). In English, "sanctification" generally indicates a process, while "holiness" suggests the result of the process.

May the God of peace himself sanctify you entirely; and may your spirit and soul and body be kept sound and blameless at the coming of our Lord Jesus Christ. (1 Thess. 5:23)

But what is holiness? As we will see in more detail below, it is not withdrawal from the world, as some might think. Rather, it is a kind of participation in God that means participation in the world in a radically new and different way. Thus faith, love, and hope have to do with the distinctive form of Christian participation in the world; they are not merely centripetal activities but centrifugal ones. In other words, they have to do with witness, with mission. It is appropriate therefore to refer to them as the *missional* marks or the *missional* virtues.

Furthermore, in light of 1 Thessalonians as a whole and especially in light of the larger context of all of Paul's letters, these missional virtues correspond to aspects of the gospel itself — a message of faith, love, and hope. This gospel, in turn, is rooted in the very character and purpose of God, who is, in Paul's experience and theology, a God of faith (Greek *pistis;* i.e., faithfulness), love, and hope.[6] Indeed, for Paul God is a missional God, the one whose goal is to impart this faithfulness, love, and hope to humanity so that human beings come to share in the life and character of God. In a profound way, then, for Paul these missional virtues are indeed theological virtues.

In this chapter, we will explore this Pauline triad of missional virtues rooted in the gospel, and in the God, of faith, love, and hope. We will see that the faithfulness, love, and hope of the missional God are manifested in the death, resurrection, and parousia of Jesus the Messiah and Lord. They are proclaimed in the gospel and communicated — in the fullest sense of that word — to those who receive the gospel by the Holy Spirit. The result is a community of people whose lives are marked by the missional God's missional virtues. Christian identity, in other words, is missional at its core because Christian existence is a participation in the missional character of God. The God who acts faithfully, lovingly, and

---

6. Ascribing these virtues, other than love, to God may at first seem counterintuitive. As we will see below, the translation of the Greek noun *pistis* ("faith," "faithfulness") and its related words into English, whether in reference to God or to humans, is challenging in several respects. At the very least, for now, we must keep in mind that, depending on context, the *pistis* family of words can denote faithfulness as well as faith. As for the word *elpis,* hope, we will see below that with reference to God it primarily means oriented to the future and generating hopefulness in others.

eschatologically in Christ and the Spirit generates a people of faithfulness, love, and hope.[7]

We begin our investigation with a look at the specific situation in Thessalonica as it is reflected in 1 Thessalonians. As we proceed, we should constantly keep in mind, as already noted, that this letter is most likely the earliest Christian document that has been preserved; what we discover is foundational, and it is both ancient and modern.

## The Gospel at Thessalonica and the Believers' Public Witness[8]

The capital of the Roman province of Macedonia in northern Greece, Thessalonica was a natural port city — the only one on the famous highway called the Via Egnatia — of considerable size and economic and political importance. Although Thessalonica was a free city, not a Roman colony (as was Philippi), it was still a center of the imperial cult, of devotion to the emperor and the empire. And it was also the site of many temples to a wide variety of other deities. Moreover, on a clear day one could (and can) see Mt. Olympus, the abode of the gods, rising high into the heavens across the harbor. Reminders of the idols from which the Thessalonians would be called to turn (cf. 1:9) were everywhere.

According to Acts 17, Paul, Silas (Silvanus), and Timothy founded the Thessalonian church during what is usually called Paul's second missionary journey. The visit followed a very difficult experience at Philippi that included flogging and imprisonment (Acts 16:11-40; 1 Thess. 2:2). The brief account in Acts is fascinating in several ways. It depicts Paul as preaching in the synagogue at Thessalonica but finding most of his converts among non-Jews: "a great many of the devout Greeks [god-fearers?] and not a few of the leading women" (Acts 17:4). Paul's preaching of a Jewish Messiah who had to suffer and rise from the dead, identified as Jesus, was interpreted as "turning the world upside down . . . acting contrary to the decrees of the emperor,

---

7. For an entire commentary on 1 Thessalonians that is missional in its hermeneutical approach, see the forthcoming Two Horizons New Testament Commentary on 1-2 Thessalonians by Andy Johnson.

8. This section draws on the chapter on 1 Thessalonians in my book *Apostle of the Crucified Lord,* pp. 146-66. For other helpful overviews, see Todd D. Still, "Paul's Thessalonian Mission," *Southwestern Journal of Theology* 42 (1999): 4-16 and C. Kavin Rowe, *World Upside Down: Reading Acts in the Graeco-Roman Age* (New York: Oxford University Press, 2009), pp. 24-27, 91-137, with (obviously) emphasis on Acts.

saying that there is another king [meaning 'emperor'] named Jesus" (Acts 17:6b-7).[9] It led first to mob action instigated by fellow Jews (beginning in the *agora,* the forum/marketplace) and then to official proceedings against some of the believers (Acts 17:6-7). Clearly, according to Acts, the gospel of this Jewish apostle and his Jewish Messiah was perceived as an assault on the religious, economic, and political status quo. And that perception was, in an important sense, correct. During Paul's short visit, someone had rightly made the connection between crucified Messiah and reigning Lord, a Lord whose lordship challenged every aspect of life.

First Thessalonians itself echoes elements of this narrative. Paul and his team were opposed (2:2; 3:4) but nonetheless preached the word with conviction and power — probably meaning that their preaching was accompanied by miraculous signs of some sort (1:5). The Thessalonians were apparently mostly non-Jews who turned from their idols (1:9) and joyfully received the gospel despite persecution (1:6; 2:14). This persecution almost certainly stemmed from the Thessalonian believers' withdrawal from normal religious activities: they stopped participating in the city's vast variety of cults; they no longer took part in the religious activities of their trade guilds (collegia), which functioned also as social clubs, each with a patron deity; and they refused to call Caesar "lord" or honor him as such at public events. In addition, by virtue of their new life in Christ, these early Christians refrained from other kinds of "normal" cultural activities. As N. T. Wright puts it,

> [We] may suppose that part of the reason why Christians were unpopular (they seemed to have, as Tacitus put it, *odium humani generis,* "a hatred of the human race") was that they dissociated themselves from so much that was taken for granted as bringing colour and fun into the normal drab, and sometimes dangerous, drudgery of life. This was bound to be difficult. . . . There were all sorts of areas where navigating an appropriate course might be difficult, with social honour and shame at stake, and working on a different scale of values to the Christian one, in various directions. Paul must have known all this, but was concerned to tread that fine line between compromise and withdrawal over which, *mutatis mutandis,* Christians have continued to puzzle to this day.[10]

---

9. Kavin Rowe has recently identified this verse as the theme text of Acts by titling his important book on Acts *World Upside Down,* as the previous note indicates.

10. N. T. Wright, *Paul and the Faithfulness of God,* vol. 4 of Christian Origins and the Question of God (Minneapolis: Fortress, 2013), p. 379.

Thus, for both political and social reasons (both of which were ultimately "religious"), the Thessalonians had become an irritant to their pagan peers, but an inspiring example of faith, love, and hope to believers throughout Greece and beyond:

> [2]We always give thanks to God for all of you and mention you in our prayers, constantly [3]remembering before our God and Father your work of faith and labor of love and steadfastness of hope in our Lord Jesus Christ. [4]For we know, brothers and sisters beloved by God, that he has chosen you, [5]because our message of the gospel came to you not in word only, but also in power and in the Holy Spirit and with full conviction; just as you know what kind of persons we proved to be among you for your sake. [6]And you became imitators of us and of the Lord, for in spite of persecution you received the word with joy inspired by the Holy Spirit, [7]so that you became an example to all the believers in Macedonia and in Achaia. [8]For the word of the Lord has sounded forth from you not only in Macedonia and Achaia, but in every place your faith in God has become known, so that we have no need to speak about it. [9]For the people of those regions report about us what kind of welcome we had among you, and how you turned to God from idols, to serve a living and true God, [10]and to wait for his Son from heaven, whom he raised from the dead — Jesus, who rescues us from the wrath that is coming. (1 Thess. 1:2-10)

In fact, it was at least part of this Pauline triad — the Thessalonians' faith, or faithfulness, that was the source of irritation. Their turning from the many gods of Thessalonica to the one God of Israel, who was supposedly the only God, earned them a good reputation in Christian circles but was deeply problematic in the eyes of their unbelieving fellow Thessalonians.

## The Gospel Message

What can we say about the nature of the gospel message itself that Paul and his companions brought to Thessalonica? We should assume that even if Paul tailored his message in some way to the specific Thessalonian situation, his gospel was fundamentally the same message he preached elsewhere.[11]

---

11. Paul uses the word "gospel" six times in the letter (1:5; 2:2, 4, 8, 9; 3:2). As in other letters, "gospel" can stand by itself or be called "the gospel of God" or "the gospel of Christ."

The evidence of various summaries of the gospel that we find in Paul's letters[12] suggests that Paul would have spoken to the Thessalonians about the faithful (i.e., faithful to his promises) yet surprising (i.e., apocalyptic, or revelatory), loving, saving action of the one true God. This action took place in the coming, crucifixion, and resurrection of Jesus, the one who is the Messiah of Israel and Lord of all and who is coming again as God's future agent of final salvation and judgment/wrath. Paul would have told them that all who accept this news as God's powerful word of salvation are to be baptized as a sign of their entrance into the new community of Jews and Gentiles, men and women, slave and free. This community exists as a family of brothers and sisters, beloved children of the one God, "in" this Messiah and Lord Jesus; they are thereby also recipients of God's promised Holy Spirit.

Furthermore, Paul would have made it clear that entrance into this Lord and his family means embracing a new, exclusive allegiance to the one God and one Lord (over against all other supposed gods and lords, including the emperor); faith, indeed, should be understood as "believing allegiance."[13] It also means beginning a new life empowered by this Holy Spirit that is characterized by conformity to the Lord Jesus' own teaching about, and example of, faithfulness and love.[14] And finally, Paul would have attempted to embody the gospel in his own life, and to make that gospel-shaped life not the focus of, but certainly a witness to, his verbal proclamation.[15]

As we look at the first letter to the Thessalonians, we find many hints that this outline of Paul's gospel message constructed from other sources corresponds quite fully to what Paul likely proclaimed to the Thessalonians.

---

12. E.g., Rom. 1:3-4, 16-17; 3:21-31; 5:1-11; 1 Cor. 1:18-25; 12:3; 15:3-7; Gal. 2:15-21; 3:26-28; 4:4-6; and Phil. 2:6-11.

13. The term has been used by N. T. Wright (e.g., *Justification: God's Plan and Paul's Vision* [Downers Grove, IL: InterVarsity, 2009], p. 181). The language of faithful allegiance permeates his *Paul and the Faithfulness of God;* Wright correctly argues that Paul's notion is grounded in the Old Testament vision of love for God as loyalty to YHWH. "Believing allegiance" is also used by Andy Johnson in *1-2 Thessalonians* (forthcoming). See also the discussion of faith in my *Cruciformity: Paul's Narrative Spirituality of the Cross* (Grand Rapids: Eerdmans, 2001), pp. 95-154. Cf. "the obedience of faith" in Rom. 1:5; 16:26.

14. I refer to Jesus' teaching and example because I have come to believe that although Paul focused primarily on Jesus' death, he proclaimed an essential continuity between Jesus' life and teaching and his death. See esp. Rom. 12:14-21; 15:1-3.

15. This theme of apostolic integrity is not explicit in the various summaries of the gospel, but it appears regularly in Paul's letters; see, e.g., 1 Corinthians 9 and nearly all of 2 Corinthians, esp. chapters 1–7 and 10–13.

In addition, the brief narrative of Paul at Thessalonica in Acts 17:1-8 is largely in sync with the hints we find in the letter.

In 1 Thessalonians 1:1-8 we see that Paul reminds the Thessalonians that their life together as a family of brothers and sisters is a relationship with God the Father, Jesus the Messiah (Christ) and Lord, and the Holy Spirit. This life is a result of the transforming power of the gospel that Paul and his companions both proclaimed and embodied. It is a life that has been characterized since its beginning at Thessalonica by faith(fulness), love, and hope, but also by Spirit-inspired joy — specifically, joy in the face of persecution (1:6).[16] Of particular note is Paul's characterization of the Thessalonians' persecution as a form of imitating Christ (as well as Paul and company), though it was not voluntary imitation (1:6-7; 2:13-16; 3:3-4). What *was* voluntary, however, was their reaction to the persecution, which was their Christlike faithfulness (3:6-10).

All of this is grounded for Paul in the reality of the Thessalonians' conversion, of which he gives a compact account in 1:9-10. Their turning from idols implies that they are a church composed (at least largely) of Gentiles.[17] They have turned from idolatry to do two things: to serve the one true, living God, and to wait for his Son Jesus. This turning, or conversion, was more than a change of mind or the possession of a new religious feeling; it also involved "actions that would have been publicly visible."[18] In fact, as we have noted, it would have meant the cessation of previously performed public activities that would invite criticism and persecution:

> [N]o longer offering sacrifices to the emperor or the goddess Roma would signal their [the Thessalonian believers'] disloyalty to the empire. Refusing to celebrate the various festivals in honor of city gods, thereby invoking their wrath on the city, would indicate disloyalty to their city. Any artisans in the *ekklēsia* [assembly; church] who refused to honor the patron god/goddess of their trade guild would have risked economic hardship. In addition, if the patriarch of their extended household was not a member of

---

16. Though most translations have the word "faith" in 1:8, CEB has "faithfulness": "The news about your faithfulness to God has spread so that we don't even need to mention it."

17. A generalized statement about the community's turning from idols would not exclude a minority group of Jews, which is what Acts 17:4 implies to be the case.

18. Andy Johnson, "The Sanctification of the Imagination," in *Holiness and Ecclesiology in the New Testament*, ed. Kent E. Brower and Andy Johnson (Grand Rapids: Eerdmans, 2007), pp. 275-92 (here p. 279).

the *ekklēsia,* refusing to honor one's household gods would cause domestic tensions in the household.[19]

In 1:9-10 we also see the basic theology and Christology of Paul's gospel: he proclaims the one God of Israel who is both living and life-giving, the one who raised Jesus from the dead, and the one worthy of worship and service.[20] This God is the rightful judge of all, whose coming wrath is certain. His "Son" Jesus is the Jewish Messiah. Paul communicated at least three aspects of Jesus' messiahship to the Thessalonians: his death, his resurrection by God, and his future parousia (coming/presence). Moreover, as Messiah Jesus is also Savior, specifically the savior from God's coming wrath — for those who believe.

Serving and waiting thus characterize the Thessalonians' new life in Christ and God (1:1), post-idolatry. The former verb [serving] has to do with faithfulness, the latter [waiting] with hope.

## A Missional Church: Faith as Faithfulness in the Public Sphere

Paul's message, then, was not only about faith as intellectual assent (belief) or even heartfelt conviction (trust), though he clearly expected, and witnessed, both a cognitive and an emotive response as part of the Thessalonians' reception of the gospel.[21] Paul's message, however, was above all about faith

---

19. Johnson, "The Sanctification of the Imagination," pp. 279-80. For a thorough discussion of the causes of persecution/opposition, see Todd D. Still, *Conflict at Thessalonica: A Pauline Church and Its Neighbours,* Journal for the Study of the New Testament: Supplement Series 183 (Sheffield: Sheffield University Press, 1999), pp. 208-67. Still argues that the Thessalonian believers were seen as socially exclusive and offensive, and as subversive to family, religion, and government. He also contends (pp. 268-86) that the conflict helped to shore up the Thessalonians' faith, love, and hope. This appears, ultimately, to be true, as Paul tells us in breathing a sigh of relief (3:1-13). But my contention is that intense practices of faith(fulness), love, and hope are more the *causes* than the *results* of conflict, though of course the Thessalonians' opponents would not characterize those practices in the same way.

20. On the "living God" in Jewish and Pauline theology, see Mark J. Goodwin, *Paul: Apostle of the Living God* (Harrisburg, PA: Trinity, 2001).

21. On one occasion in the letter Paul specifically speaks of the content of belief (4:14; "since we believe that [*pisteuomen hoti*] Jesus died and rose again"), and it is assumed or implied elsewhere, but this is not the main use of the *pist-* word-group in the letter. Gordon Zerbe argues that the "cognitive, convictional aspect to *pistis* in 1 Thessalonians . . . is oriented precisely to ground the readers' abiding loyalty in the context of competing claims for loyalty

expressed as service to the one true God, as faithful living before this God, *and this faithful living was to be done in the public sphere, not just "at home" or "in church."* Similarly, Paul's message about waiting for the Lord's parousia was obviously not about a passive form of waiting but about an active hope, a certainty about the future that enabled a certain kind of life in the present, a life in contrast to the Thessalonians' former way of living and that of their unconverted family members, friends, and associates (see 4:5, 13).

The Thessalonians seem to have heard Paul loudly and clearly that his gospel was a summons to exclusive allegiance to the one God and his Son Jesus, and that such an exclusive kind of faith/faithfulness might have serious consequences — a kind of imitation of, or even participation in, the sufferings of Jesus. We cannot of course be sure of this — perhaps Paul is just interpreting their suffering after the fact — but the "we" in the following text seems to include the Thessalonians:

> [2][A]nd we sent Timothy, our brother and co-worker for God in proclaiming the gospel of Christ, to strengthen and encourage you for the sake of your faith, [3]so that no one would be shaken by these persecutions. Indeed, you yourselves know that this is what we are destined for. [4]In fact, when we were with you, we told you beforehand that we were to suffer persecution; so it turned out, as you know. (1 Thess. 3:2-4)

It is difficult to imagine that Paul would have predicted and experienced suffering for himself and, it appears, for the Thessalonian believers without interpreting it, and interpreting it specifically as a consequence of his and their own Christlike devotion to the true God, the true Lord. The story of Jesus is, in part, a story of persecution, and the good news cannot avoid that part of the story. Thus when Paul told the story of Jesus' death, it seems, he did not fail to communicate its causes — and its likely consequences for those associated with Jesus.

What seems to be the case is that the Thessalonian believers not only *believed* but also *embodied* and *shared* the gospel. They did so not merely in their tight-knit community, but in their world: among their friends, relatives, associates, and so on — perhaps including their masters or patrons (on the assumption that most of the believers were not among the elite). Maybe their witness began as a simple decision to refrain from certain cultic activities,

---

(to Caesar), not to establish precise doctrinal norms in themselves" (Gordon Mark Zerbe, *Citizenship: Paul on Peace and Politics* [Winnipeg, MB: CMU Press, 2012], p. 42).

but for persecution to occur, whatever specific form it took, there had to be action that provoked reaction. And there was likely a counter-reaction of explanation (apologia) in response to any initial and ongoing opposition.[22]

Paul's fear of the Thessalonians' failure implies an ongoing dynamic of action (witness-bearing), followed by reaction (critique? questioning? pressure? harassment? arrest?), followed again by action. Only this time (and "this time" could be repeated on multiple occasions as the back-and-forth dynamic played itself out again and again), the Thessalonians' action could be either faithfulness to God or acquiescence to the powers of persecution. It seems highly likely, then, that the Thessalonian believers bore public witness to their faith, love, and hope — by what they did and did not do, and how they interpreted what they did and did not do — in various venues. Perhaps, as well, they invited others to come and see their faith, love, and hope in action at their community gatherings — even as their words of witness and invitation were rebuffed, one suspects, more often than not.[23]

Paul's deep affection for this community, which began in the initial visit, permeates the letter (in which he calls the readers "brothers [and sisters]" once every half-dozen verses). He and his team worked "night and day" so as not to burden the church (2:9). With pure motives, Paul claims, they selflessly devoted themselves to the Thessalonians, like a mother and father (2:1-12). Upon leaving for Beroea and then Athens, Paul desperately wanted to visit his "crown of boasting" again but was blocked by Satan (2:17-20). Meanwhile, apparently, the persecutions in Thessalonica had continued and

---

22. Discussing the ongoing debate about whether the Thessalonians "preached the gospel/ evangelized" or "simply lived the gospel" and thus were a pattern of faithful living in the midst of persecution, Andy Johnson wisely says, "Both [embodying and proclaiming the good news] go hand in hand, and the most natural reading of the language here indicates that the audience was engaged in doing both. . . . However, this need not mean that the audience was engaged in the same sort of public preaching as was Paul. . . . Narrating the gospel orally might take other forms, e.g., discussing the reason for their change of public behavior with unbelievers in their household or with those visiting their household from other locales, prophetically calling into question the idolatry of their culture in their daily routine and conversations with others. In any case, it was [according to Paul] God's power at work in their words giving those words the power to reverberate in all directions as they narrated the gospel" (*1-2 Thessalonians*, forthcoming).

23. I am not inclined to see the situation as if the Thessalonians are "fire and brimstone" preachers offering their families and friends only a message of apocalyptic judgment on their idolatry and immorality, as some do. This aspect of the Pauline gospel was no doubt a part of their thinking and speaking, but it was more likely than not surpassed by the virtues and practices of faithfulness, love, and hope that Paul lauds.

worsened (3:3). The concerns of 4:13-18 suggest that some of the believers may have been martyred.[24] Eventually Paul therefore sent Timothy from Athens to check on the Thessalonian believers. Had the persecution proven too much for them? Had they been unfaithful to their new Lord? Had they stopped loving their new brothers and sisters, or perhaps retaliated against their persecutors? Had they lost hope?

What Timothy discovered was good news: the believers were enduring the persecution with such steadfast faith and love that they were an encouragement to Paul in his own sufferings (3:6-10). The Thessalonians also loved and missed their spiritual parent (3:6), though the tone of chapter two suggests that some had likely grown critical of the apostle, perhaps for apparently abandoning them in their time of trouble. Now Paul himself wanted to see them face to face to strengthen their faith still further (3:10). Until that time, however, Paul could do but two things: pray for them (3:10-13) and send a letter as a substitute for his visit. Having settled in Corinth for a while (Acts 18:1), Paul probably wrote 1 Thessalonians from there, most likely in 50 or 51.[25] The purpose of the letter was, in fact, to be an answer to Paul's own prayer — to strengthen the Thessalonian believers with reassurance and instruction, and specifically to reaffirm and further solidify their life of faith(fulness), love, and hope together.[26]

That is, *Paul is writing a missional exhortation to a missional community.*[27]

24. This seems to be the minority view today, though I persist in believing that it makes the most sense of the data: (1) intense and ongoing persecution; (2) grave concern on Paul's part; and (3) Thessalonian concern about the deceased (plural) *possibly within just months (and certainly within a year or so)* of the church's founding. While it is true that there is no *explicit* evidence of martyrdom, neither is there *explicit* evidence of charges of political subversion, disdain for the emperor, hatred of humanity, withdrawal from social contact, or "atheism" (disbelief in the gods) aimed at the Thessalonian believers, and yet one or more of these is regularly (and probably rightly) offered to explain the persecution. Todd Still (*Conflict at Thessalonica,* pp. 215-17) cautiously suggests that there may have been very rare instances of actual martyrdom.

25. There is some scholarly discussion suggesting a later date for 1 Thessalonians as a follow-up to a later visit to Thessalonica (Acts 20:1-2 has Paul in Macedonia for some time), but this is a minority view.

26. We will explore each of these more fully below.

27. Thus I cannot agree with Witherington (Ben Witherington III, *1 and 2 Thessalonians: A Socio-Rhetorical Commentary* [Grand Rapids: Eerdmans, 2006], pp. 21-29) and others that the letter is primarily a specimen of epideictic rhetoric (praise) rather than deliberative rhetoric or parenesis (exhortation), though there are certainly epideictic elements. Its function is to encourage the Thessalonians to "keep on keeping on" and even to attend to the areas of their common life and witness still in need of maturation.

We can affirm this without also affirming that the Thessalonians engaged in what some would call "evangelism," such as door-to-door "witnessing," as some have imagined in reading 1:6-10. But the scenario I have just outlined not only makes sense historically; it also makes sense in terms of the letter itself. If Paul is not concerned about their public witness — their faithfulness in that sense — why does he worry about them? Paul's anxiety for the churches (cf. 2 Cor. 11:28) assumes that they are living in ways, or *should* be living in ways, that get them into trouble. It is often said that Paul's primary concern in the first half of the letter is the Thessalonians' perseverance, but this is true only inasmuch as the question of their perseverance is raised by their public presence and embodied testimony. Significantly, Paul is far less concerned about their safety per se than he is about their faithful witness, and their reputation for such faithfulness (3:1-10).[28]

The Thessalonians' reputation (and the substance behind it) appears to have started out in good shape and spread quite widely, definitely among other believers (probably very new believers) in Macedonia and Achaia, and possibly also among others (1:6-10). The Thessalonians' believing allegiance may have been shaken a bit by the persecutions, but Paul's intervention in the form of a proxy-visit by Timothy (3:1-4), intended to prevent their failure of faith, was apparently not necessary (at least for that purpose), as the Thessalonians were still full of faithfulness and love (3:6). Their reputation (and, again, the substance behind it) remained intact. Still, Paul wants to visit them in person to further strengthen them for the stress of persecution (3:10).

How would the Thessalonians have found themselves in this kind of situation unless they had been and done something to "deserve" it? The report of their "faithfulness and love" (3:6), I would suggest, corresponds not only to the demands of the gospel, but also to two of the principal charges that family members, "friends," and others would bring against the Thessalonian believers: disloyalty to the state (lack of *fides* [Latin] or *pistis* [Greek], faithfulness) and hatred of humanity (lack of love). Thus, their reputation throughout Greece did not stem from their spreading the "word of the Lord" in an evangelistic campaign per se, but in an uncanny display of faithfulness — which for some who heard about it (i.e., their nonbelieving critics) would have been not loyalty but irrational stubbornness and even treason. But in doubting the existence of an evangelistic campaign, or even a more generalized sense of evangelistic activity in terms of widespread "recruitment," we

---

28. The word *pistis* (faith, faithfulness) occurs five times in 3:1-10.

cannot minimize the significance of 1:6-10.[29] The church at Thessalonica is still a church in mission, a church that embodies the gospel of faithfulness, love, and hope publicly. This is what it means to be a church in God and in Christ (1:1).

## The Missional God of Faithfulness, Love, and Hope (Promise)

In a unique phrase in the Pauline correspondence, the apostle tells the Thessalonians that they exist, not merely "in Christ" or "in the Messiah," which is common Pauline idiom, but "in God the Father and the Lord Jesus Christ" (1:1). That is, they live in God, sharing in the divine life. This is a claim that immediately raises a rather obvious question: "What does that mean?" If being in Christ means, at least in part, to be shaped or molded by the one in whom believers live, then being in God implies something similar: a life shaped by God (the Father). This is not surprising, since becoming like God is the fundamental meaning of holiness in the biblical tradition (e.g., Lev. 11:44-45; 1 Pet. 1:16), and this letter's primary theme, as we have already seen, is holiness.

But the phrase "in God the Father" also raises the question, "What is this God like whose life believers share?" A brief examination of this question

29. Richard S. Ascough ("Redescribing the Thessalonians' 'Mission' in Light of Graeco-Roman Associations," *New Testament Studies* 60 [2014]: 61-82) rejects the common interpretation of 1 Thess. 1:6-10 that has the Thessalonians, as a group, involved in active missionary (recruitment) activity. He argues that the Thessalonians are known for promoting their deity and the community's founders/benefactors, as members of any ancient association would do. Ascough is probably right to doubt the standard reading of 1 Thess. 1:6-10. But Paul does not even hint that any promotion of him and his team took place. Furthermore, even if the Thessalonians were following the cultural convention of promoting their cult, deity, and founder, for Paul this would be a legitimate form of verbal witness to this distinctive — that is, crucified and resurrected — deity. The focus of my argument is on the evangelistic character of the community and its members simply by virtue of their transformed lives and normal social interactions — with all their consequences. Even Ascough says that in order to show their new devotion to the one God, the Thessalonians would likely "narrate to themselves and others the story of how they came to know of this God . . . and why they chose to appropriate this God above all others" (p. 68). Is this not evangelization? Ascough contends that whatever the Thessalonians said, "self-promotion and claims of preeminence," not recruitment, were the "primary aim," with evangelism being a possible "by-product" (p. 69), and that such claims may have caused the negative responses (p. 69, n. 29). Ascough's points actually reinforce my interpretation, except that he assumes (without proof) that ecclesial motives and practices would have been precisely the same as those of associations.

with respect to 1 Thessalonians, plus a few glances elsewhere in the Pauline correspondence, will be instructive.

## God the Father in 1 Thessalonians

First of all, the God of 1 Thessalonians is named both God and Father (1:1, 3). Moreover, this God is called the "living and true God" (1:9), a common Jewish designation for YHWH over against all idols, who are not gods at all.[30] Thus it is totally appropriate for people to turn from their devotion to false gods in order to "serve" (1:9) the true God, as the Thessalonians have done. As the only true deity, God alone is worthy of devotion and allegiance, that is, of both faith and faithfulness. Paul refers to this proper devotion as the Thessalonians' "faith in [or faithfulness to] God" (1:8).

Second, this God is a missional God, one who actively calls and chooses people to bring them into relationship with himself and into the coming kingdom of God (1:4; 2:12; 4:7; 5:24). Paul uses the standard language of election found in the Scriptures of Israel and now freshly applied to Gentiles as well as Jews who have responded to the gospel. Furthermore, the electing God is also the peacemaking and sanctifying God: "May the God of peace himself sanctify you entirely; and may your spirit and soul and body be kept sound and blameless at the coming of our Lord Jesus Christ. The one who calls you is faithful, and he will do this" (5:23-24; cf. 4:7). Extremely critical for our purposes is the second verse in this passage: the God of peace and holiness is the faithful *(pistos)* God.[31]

Faithfulness is at the heart of the biblical depiction of God. According to Walter Brueggemann, among all of the Old Testament's depictions of God, "Israel's most elemental and most recurring practice is to speak about Yahweh's reliability and trustworthiness," a "confessional inclination" that "can hardly be overvalued."[32] This "primary propensity of Israel . . . to focus on fidelity," Walter Brueggemann writes, is revealed in terms like "merciful, gracious, abounding in steadfast love, and faithfulness," which "saturate Israel's speech about Yahweh and Israel's imagination."[33]

30. See Goodwin, *Paul: Apostle of the Living God.*
31. The most comprehensive and significant treatment of God's fidelity in Paul is Wright, *Paul and the Faithfulness of God.*
32. Walter E. Brueggemann, *Theology of the Old Testament: Testimony, Dispute, Advocacy* (Minneapolis: Fortress, 1997), p. 226.
33. Brueggemann, *Theology of the Old Testament,* p. 226.

According to Paul, God's purpose is to call a people into existence from both Jews and Gentiles, and to make them fully into the kind of peaceable, holy, and faithful community the people of God were always intended to be. That purpose cannot and will not be thwarted, because God is faithful. We should note here what should be obvious but is easily overlooked: that for Paul God's work of calling and forming a people is not over but is continuing; it is God's desire to transfer yet more people out of the realm of the perishing and into the realm of those being saved.[34] Those who belong to God in Jesus will persist in God's love and grace, and will be delivered from the coming wrath of God (1:10; 5:9).

Third, this missional, faithful God is a loving God. Already in the first chapter of 1 Thessalonians Paul refers to his audience as "brothers and sisters beloved by God" (1:4). Moreover, in the biblical tradition, election itself (as in 1:4, etc., noted above) is an act of divine love. As Brueggemann notes, Israel's very existence is due to God's "originary love," characteristically expressed in the verbs "love," "choose," and "set one's heart on," all attributed to Yahweh.[35] Furthermore, according to Paul this electing, loving God teaches others to love (4:9); it is integral to the divine mission. This mission of love was expressed most definitively — even if it is stated only implicitly in this letter — in the death of Jesus (5:9-10).[36]

So far, then, we see that the living, missional God to whom Paul bears witness in 1 Thessalonians is characterized in several ways, which can be summarized as follows: the God who, in faithfulness and love, calls a people into existence, making peace with them, sanctifying them so that they can become a peaceful and holy people marked by faithfulness and love. This missional God does this in and through the death and resurrection of the Son (1:10; 4:14; 5:10) and the initial and ongoing work of the Spirit (1:5; 4:8).

But what about hope? If hope is part of the triad, an essential component

34. This divine desire is what lies behind Paul's desire for others' salvation; we see one or both aspects in texts such as Rom. 1:16-17; 3:21-31; 9:1-5; 10:1, 12-13, 21; 11:13-15, 32; 15:7-21; 1 Cor. 7:12-16; 9:19-23; 10:33; cf. 1 Tim. 1:15; 2:4.

35. Brueggemann, *Theology of the Old Testament*, pp. 414-17 (p. 414). Of these three, the last is used only twice (Deut. 7:7; 10:15) while "love" and "choose" appear frequently. See, e.g., Deut. 4:37.

36. 1 Thess. 5:9-10 does not mention either God's or Christ's love per se, but when Paul writes at greater length about the death of Jesus, it is often associated explicitly with God's and/or Christ's love (e.g., Rom. 5:8; 8:31-39; 2 Cor. 5:14; Gal. 2:19-20; cf. Eph. 5:1-2, 25). Moreover, deliverance from wrath (5:9) is associated with God's love in Rom. 5:1-11.

of life "in God," in what sense is God not only faithful and loving, but also hopeful?

In some respects, this question seems rather odd and counterintuitive. But the idea of God being hopeful has some biblical and, in fact, Pauline, precedent. In 1 Timothy 2:3-6, for instance, we see "God our Savior" described as the one who "desires everyone to be saved and to come to the knowledge of the truth" (v. 4) and who acted missionally so that universal salvation could occur: "For there is one God; there is also one mediator between God and humankind, Christ Jesus, himself human, who gave himself a ransom for all — this was attested at the right time" (vv. 5-6). God's desire, God's hope, so to speak, is not forced on humans, but it is embodied in action, in mission. God acts on the divinely hoped-for future. God is, we might say, future-oriented.

Elsewhere in Scripture, and specifically in Paul, we learn that God makes and keeps promises, another aspect of God's future, or eschatological, orientation.[37] In fact, a close relationship exists between God's faithfulness and God's future orientation, God's promises. Because God has acted faithfully in the past, we can trust that God will faithfully keep any promises about the future; we see this in Paul's words to the Thessalonians cited above: "The one who calls you is faithful, and he will do this" (5:24). These words are meant to engender hope in a faithful God.

Thus for Paul there is a close relationship between faith and hope in the triad of faith, love, and hope.[38] One way of describing hope, as I have suggested elsewhere, is as the future tense of faith.[39] So too we can describe God's "hope" — God's desires and promises — as the future tense of God's

---

37. For Paul the most obvious example of God as promise-maker and promise-keeper is the story of Abraham, as narrated in Genesis and re-narrated by Paul, especially in Galatians 3 and Romans 4.

38. See especially the example of Abraham in Romans 4, including these words (4:18-21):

> [18]Hoping against hope, he [Abraham] believed that he would become "the father of many nations," according to what was said, "So numerous shall your descendants be." [19]He did not weaken in faith when he considered his own body, which was already as good as dead (for he was about a hundred years old), or when he considered the barrenness of Sarah's womb. [20]No distrust made him waver concerning the promise of God, but he grew strong in his faith as he gave glory to God, [21]being fully convinced that God was able to do what he had promised.

39. For this characterization of hope, see my *Reading Paul* (Eugene, OR: Cascade, 2008), pp. 160-63. For a fuller discussion of hope in terms of the complementary notion of the "future of cruciformity," see my *Cruciformity*, pp. 304-48.

faithfulness. The analogy is not theologically perfect, but it is helpful. To say that God is a God of hope (Rom. 15:13) is to say that God gives hope because God keeps promises, and we know that God keeps promises when we look back on what God has already done (God's faithfulness). This is the great biblical theme of remembering, of not forgetting, of recalling God's past saving actions, especially in times of trouble:

> [21]But this I call to mind, and therefore I have hope: [22]The steadfast love of the Lord never ceases, his mercies never come to an end; [23]they are new every morning; great is your faithfulness. [24]"The Lord is my portion," says my soul, "therefore I will hope in him." [25]The Lord is good to those who wait for him, to the soul that seeks him. [26]It is good that one should wait quietly for the salvation of the Lord. (Lam. 3:21-26)

> [10]I have not hidden your saving help within my heart, I have spoken of your faithfulness and your salvation; I have not concealed your steadfast love and your faithfulness from the great congregation. [11]Do not, O Lord, withhold your mercy from me; let your steadfast love and your faithfulness keep me safe forever. (Ps. 40:10-11)[40]

Walter Brueggemann reminds us that "Israel's testimony to Yahweh as a promise-maker presents Yahweh as both powerful and reliable enough to turn life in the world, for Israel and for all peoples, beyond present circumstance to new life-giving possibility. Yahweh's promises keep the world open toward well-being, even in the face of deathly circumstance."[41]

This does not mean that God has turned a blind eye to evil and injustice, as 1 Thessalonians makes clear. The coming (and perhaps already-present) wrath of God (1:10; 2:16; 5:9) is real, but it is not God's intention or preference for people.[42] The reality of divine wrath is, in fact, the "flip side" of divine righteousness, in the sense of God's saving, restorative activity (see Rom. 1:16-18). God's desire and action to save, expressed in the death of Jesus, is in part God's desire to keep humanity from his own justifiable wrath (reading 1 Thess. 1:10 and 5:9 together).

We see the connection between God's faithfulness and God's promised

---

40. See also, e.g., Psalm 136, with its refrain, "for [the Lord's] steadfast love endures forever."

41. Brueggemann, *Theology of the Old Testament,* p. 164.

42. On divine wrath in Paul, see Rom. 1:18; 2:5, 8; 3:5; 4:15; 5:9; 9:22; 12:19; 13:4; cf. Col. 3:6; Eph. 5:6. Rom. 1:18, like 1 Thess. 2:16, suggests a present experience of wrath for the disobedient.

future (i.e., future salvation) in Paul's theology of the resurrection in 1 Thessalonians. God is not only the *living* God, but also the *life-giving* God, as demonstrated in the raising of Jesus from the dead (1:10). The resurrection of Jesus is the definitive demonstration of God's desire and decision to give life the final word over death, to give people a future and a hope. The resurrection assures believers of future salvation, meaning both deliverance from the coming wrath (1:10; 5:9) and a future life with God and Christ:

> For since we believe that Jesus died and rose again, even so, through Jesus, God will bring with him those who have died . . . and so we will be with the Lord forever. (4:14, 17b)

> [9]For God has destined us not for wrath but for obtaining salvation through our Lord Jesus Christ, [10]who died for us, so that whether we are awake or asleep we may live with him. (5:9-10)

So, is God not only a faith-er and a lover but also a hoper?[43] Not precisely. But God is a promise-maker, the God of salvation whose future faithfulness, grounded in his past faithfulness, generates hope among the faithful. And this God's activity is manifested in the activity of his Son Jesus, the Messiah.

## The Messiah's Faithfulness, Love, and Hope

Throughout his letters, Paul stresses the obedience and fidelity of Jesus the Messiah. As I and others have argued elsewhere, Paul believes that the basis of justification is first of all not human faith or faithfulness but the faithfulness of the Messiah, expressed in the Greek phrase *pistis Christou* — "the faith of Christ."[44] Although there are still some who dispute this interpretation, it has gained significant support and continues to do so.[45] For Paul,

---

43. I owe this way of wording the question to Andy Johnson.

44. See *Cruciformity,* pp. 110-21, and the bibliography cited there, including especially Richard B. Hays, *The Faith of Jesus Christ: The Narrative Substructure of Gal. 3:1–4:11,* 2nd ed. (Grand Rapids: Eerdmans, 2002 [orig. 1983]).

45. One of the most persistent opponents of this view is James D. G. Dunn. See, e.g., his article "ΕΚ ΠΙΣΤΕΩΣ: A Key to the Meaning of ΠΙΣΤΙΣ ΧΡΙΣΤΟΥ," in *The Word Leaps the Gap: Essays on Scripture and Theology in Honor of Richard B. Hays,* ed. J. Ross Wagner, C. Kavin Rowe, and A. Katherine Grieb (Grand Rapids: Eerdmans, 2008), pp. 351-66.

the faithfulness of the Messiah is where his humanity and his divinity (to use later theological categories) intersect. On the one hand, as N. T. Wright says in commenting on Romans 3, "[t]he Messiah's faithfulness is the living embodiment of the divine covenant faithfulness."[46] On the other hand, his faithfulness is also the living embodiment, we might say, of Israel's and humanity's call to be in proper relationship to God.

It is the latter dimension that is stressed in 1 Thessalonians. In this letter, Paul does not use the phrase *pistis Christou* or a variation of it, but he does nonetheless refer to Christ's fidelity, specifically his fidelity during persecution. The Lord Jesus, in fact, is the primary prototype of faithfulness to God in the midst of persecution, with Paul and colleagues, other churches, and the prophets being additional examples of such fidelity:

> [Y]ou became imitators of us and of the Lord, for in spite of persecution you received the word with joy inspired by the Holy Spirit. . . . (1:6)

> [14]For you, brothers and sisters, became imitators of the churches of God in Christ Jesus that are in Judea, for you suffered the same things from your own compatriots as they did from those Jews [15]who killed both the Lord Jesus and the prophets, and drove us out. . . . (2:14-15a alt.)

Accordingly, the Thessalonians' faithfulness *(pistis)* that has resonated throughout the region (1:8) is a derivative faithfulness, one based on the *pistis Christou*. In fact, Paul may have the story of Christ's faithfulness specifically in mind when he says that "the word of the Lord [the narrative about Jesus] has sounded forth from you not only in Macedonia and Achaia, but in every place your faith in God [i.e., your faithfulness to God in the midst of persecution] has become known, so that we have no need to speak about it" (1:8).[47]

Far less controversial in Pauline theology, of course, is the notion of the love of Christ, which no one disputes. As with Christ's faith, however, specific references to Christ's love are absent from 1 Thessalonians. But at least four texts imply Christ's love. First, he is the one who "rescues us from the wrath that is coming" (1:10); as eschatological deliverer, obviously Jesus acts

---

46. Wright, *Paul and the Faithfulness of God*, p. 1470.

47. The close, virtually parallel relationship between the phrases "the word of [or 'about' — so CEB] the Lord" *(ho logos tou kyriou)* and the phrase "your faith" *(hē pistis hymōn)* may imply that what the Thessalonians had become known for was their Christlike fidelity. Cf. CEB: "The news about your faithfulness to God. . . ."

for the good of his people, which is certainly a "labor of love" (1:3). Christ is not here depicted as the means of appeasing an angry God, but as God's own agent of deliverance from wrath, as 5:9 makes clear. Second, Paul offers a prayer-wish that "the Lord make you increase and abound in love" (3:12), with "the Lord" identified in context as Jesus (3:11). Only a loving Lord can effect love in others. Third, as we will see below, when Paul depicts his apostolic, parental love for the Thessalonians (2:5-12), he does so by comparing himself to Christ's self-giving love on the cross. Once again, Christ's love is implicit, if not explicit. Fourth, and perhaps most importantly, Paul tells us that Christ "died for us, so that whether we are awake or asleep we may live with him" (5:10). This is the ultimate gift of love.

This brief text in 1 Thessalonians 5 is no doubt a summary of the heart of what Paul actually said to the Thessalonians when he proclaimed the gospel to them. As noted above in the discussion of God's love, for Paul the death of Jesus is an act of love, both God's and Christ's.[48] Even here in this brief reference that altruism comes through: Jesus' death is a life-giving death for the benefit of others, delivering people from wrath and into salvation (5:9), defined as being in the presence of Jesus the Lord, both now and after death (5:10). Thus, although there is not a specific reference to the faithfulness or love of Jesus in 1 Thessalonians, we can presume both that Paul communicated these to the Thessalonians when he first preached the gospel and that he had them in mind as he wrote his letter.[49]

But what about hope? Our answer has been anticipated in the discussion of God the Father: Jesus is "hopeful" in the sense of being oriented toward the future; he is the one who will deliver from the coming wrath (1:10; cf. 3:13; 4:15; 5:9), and he is the one who, even in the more immediate future, directs the church toward better times (3:11). In each case (see 3:11; 5:9), the Lord Jesus does so in conjunction with the Father. Together, the Father and the Son create a hopeful people by virtue of their promises with respect to the future — and their power to make good on those promises. For this reason, Paul can say, especially of those who have faithfully endured persecution, that Jesus is the source and focus of their hope and that this hope is in the presence of "God our Father" (1:3).

48. Once again, see, e.g., Rom. 5:8; 8:31-39; 2 Cor. 5:14; Gal. 2:19-20; cf. Eph. 5:1-2, 25.

49. What I have argued elsewhere is that for Paul, Christ's faith and love are inseparable, and that on the cross Christ's faithfulness to God and love for humanity simultaneously reached their quintessential expression. See, e.g., *Cruciformity*, pp. 113-15, 162-63; *Inhabiting the Cruciform God: Kenosis, Justification, and Theosis in Paul's Narrative Soteriology* (Grand Rapids: Eerdmans, 2009), pp. 57-62.

## *The Spirit of Faithfulness, Love, and Hope*

We have focused thus far in describing the missional God of 1 Thessalonians on the Father and the Son. But what about the Spirit? Although Paul does not develop his understanding of the Spirit at length in this letter (in contrast to Romans, 1 Corinthians, and Galatians, for example), the Spirit is nonetheless present and active, both explicitly and implicitly. Indeed, the Spirit, we might say, provides the divine energy that makes faithfulness, love, and hope possible.

Paul credits the activity of the Spirit with both the apostolic proclamation of the gospel and the Thessalonians' reception of it (1:5-6). The Spirit was, and is, ultimately behind the Thessalonians' joyful and faithful response to the gospel in spite of its cost: "And you became imitators of us and of the Lord, for in spite of persecution you received the word with joy inspired by the Holy Spirit" (1:6). Furthermore, when Paul refers to the Thessalonians as those "taught by God to love one another" (4:9), he does so right after referring to God's gift of the Holy Spirit (4:8). This reference, in turn, points to the Thessalonians' need for sexual holiness as a manifestation of brotherly and sisterly love, and as a witness to the world (4:1-8). And finally, although Paul does not directly link the Spirit to hope, he does exhort the Thessalonian believers not to "quench" the Spirit, meaning especially the prophetic voice in the community (5:19-22). At least one key aspect of the function of that prophetic voice is to preserve believers so that they will attain their hope at the parousia (5:23-24). In other words, it is the Spirit of the missional God revealed in Jesus' death and resurrection who makes the divinely willed faithfulness, love, and hope available to and effective in the Thessalonian community.

To conclude this section: A faithful, loving, and promise-making, promise-keeping God; that is the God we find in 1 Thessalonians, revealed dramatically in the activity of the Son and made effective among the Thessalonians by the Spirit. This is not a static God, but one who has acted, and will act, in saving ways. To be "in this God" is to benefit from, and to participate in, a divine mission. In other words, for Paul's God, being and act are inseparable; being, or identity, is known only in faithful, loving, and hope-giving, promise-keeping activity. For Paul, this truth came to fullest expression in the death and resurrection of Jesus, and it comes to expression once again in individuals and communities of Godlike, Christlike, faithful, loving, and hope-giving, promise-keeping activity — the labor of those who are "in the Messiah" and, therein, empowered by the Spirit. Among these missional individuals and groups are both Paul and the Thessalonians.

## The Apostle of Faithfulness, Love, and Hope

It is rather self-evident that Paul, as an apostle, was a missional person, one devoted to the mission of God in Christ. In 1 Thessalonians this reality emerges throughout the letter, but especially in the first three chapters, and most particularly in 2:1-12, which Andy Johnson refers to as Paul offering himself and his team as a "model for participation in the *Missio Dei*."[50]

Like the God who called and sent him, Paul was faithful, loving, and hopeful, as were his colleagues. Throughout the letter Paul's affection for and devotion to the Thessalonians is on display. On numerous occasions he calls them "brothers [and sisters]" *(adelphoi)*.[51] Paul also calls the Thessalonians "beloved" (2:8; *agapētoi;* NRSV "dear to us"). It is not entirely clear that "beloved" here refers only to the fact that Paul (with his colleagues) loves the Thessalonians, since "beloved" is an echo of "beloved by God" (1:4; *ēgapēmenoi*). This lack of clarity about the identity of the lover(s) may not be deliberate, but it is likely significant, for Paul's love is a derivative love, a participatory love, a love that comes ultimately from God and is shaped concretely by the faithfulness and love of Christ displayed on the cross.

We see this first of all in Paul's narrative of the initial mission that he and his colleagues undertook in Thessalonica (2:1-12). He reminds the Thessalonians that they preached the gospel of God to them with "courage" in spite of the recent persecution in Philippi and opposition in Thessalonica itself (2:1-2). This was first of all an act of faithfulness to God in stewardship of the gospel, and not done for any other reason: "just as we have been approved by God to be entrusted with the message of the gospel, even so we speak, not to please mortals, but to please God who tests our hearts" (2:4).

Preaching the gospel to the Thessalonians was also an act of love, not only in its motivation, but also in its concrete shape. In 2:5-12 Paul uses three metaphors to portray the apostolic mission. Two are obvious: the maternal image of a nurse tenderly nursing her own children (2:7) and the paternal image of a father giving his children moral guidance and encouragement (2:11-12). In between is a third metaphor, less obvious than the other two, in which Paul characterizes the apostolic mission in Christlike, indeed cruciform language (2:7-9). He says that the deep love he and his colleagues had for the Thessalonians led them to share not only the gospel,

---

50. Johnson, *1-2 Thessalonians* (forthcoming).

51. 1 Thess. 1:4; 2:1, 9, 14, 17; 3:7; 4:1, 10 (twice); 5:1, 4, 12, 14, 25, 26, 27.

but also their own selves (2:8; *psychas;* "souls"; "lives"; "very beings"), an echo of early Christian language for Jesus' own self-donation in death.[52] Moreover, in order not to burden their hearers financially, Paul and his team did not throw their apostolic weight around demanding money,[53] but they worked night and day with their hands to support themselves. Since early Christian apostles and teachers were deemed worthy of financial support (see, e.g., 1 Cor. 9:1-14; 1 Tim. 5:17), Paul's denial of this basic apostolic right was, for him, a way of imitating Christ, indeed of participating in Christ, who had given up his status and rights (Phil. 2:6-11; 2 Cor. 8:9). In fact, Paul even narrates the shape of the apostolic mission in language that is reminiscent of Christ's own status-renouncing and self-giving love.[54] Elsewhere I have referred to this as an x-y-z pattern that has the following shape:[55]

### Although [x] status, not [y] selfishness
### but [z] self-renunciation and self-giving

| The Narrative Pattern | Christ (Phil. 2:6-8) | Paul and his colleagues (1 Thess. 2:5-9) |
|---|---|---|
| Although [x] status | though he was in the form of God (2:6a) | . . . though we might have made demands/thrown our weight around as apostles of Christ. (2:7a) |
| not [y] selfishness | [he] did not regard equality with God as something to be exploited (2:6b) | As you know and as God is our witness, we never came with words of flattery or with a pretext for greed; nor did we seek praise from mortals, whether from you or from others. . . . (2:5-6) |

52. 1 Thess. 2:8 has "share with you . . . our own selves" *(metadounai hymin . . . tas heautōn psychas).* See, e.g., the words of Jesus in Mark 10:45 (= Matt. 20:28), "For the Son of Man came not to be served but to serve, and to give his life *(dounai tēn psychēn autou)* a ransom for many"; John 10:15b, "I lay down my life *(tēn psychēn mou tithēmi)* for the sheep" (see also 10:11, 17). For the connection of Jesus' self-giving (using *psychē*) to that of his disciples, see John 15:13; 1 John 3:16.

53. This is the sense of the Greek *en barei einai* (so also CEB, NAB, NET). NRSV has "might have made demands."

54. See further Gorman, *Cruciformity,* pp. 192-95.

55. See *Cruciformity,* pp. 89-91, 164-69, et passim.

| The Narrative Pattern | Christ (Phil. 2:6-8) | Paul and his colleagues (1 Thess. 2:5-9) |
|---|---|---|
| but [z] self-renunciation and self-giving | but emptied himself, taking the form of a slave, being born in human likeness. And being found in human form, he humbled himself and became obedient to the point of death — even death on a cross. (2:7-8) | But we were gentle among you, like a nurse tenderly caring for her own children. So deeply do we care for you that we are determined to share with you not only the gospel of God but also our own selves, because you have become very dear to us. You remember our labor and toil, brothers and sisters; we worked night and day, so that we might not burden any of you while we proclaimed to you the gospel of God. (2:7b-9) |

In 1 Corinthians 9, where Paul narrates a similar decision and form of apostolic mission, he specifically refers to this pattern of missional ministry as a freely chosen form of self-enslavement to others, even more explicitly echoing Christ's self-imposed slavery from Philippians 2:

> [4]Do we not have the right to our food and drink? [5]Do we not have the right to be accompanied by a believing wife, as do the other apostles and the brothers of the Lord and Cephas? . . . [12]If others share this rightful claim on you, do not we still more? Nevertheless, we have not made use of this right, but we endure anything rather than put an obstacle in the way of the gospel of Christ. . . . [15]But I have made no use of any of these rights, nor am I writing this so that they may be applied in my case. . . . Indeed, I would rather die than that — no one will deprive me of my ground for boasting! [16]If I proclaim the gospel, this gives me no ground for boasting, for an obligation is laid on me, and woe to me if I do not proclaim the gospel! [17]For if I do this of my own will, I have a reward; but if not of my own will, I am entrusted with a commission. [18]What then is my reward? Just this: that in my proclamation I may make the gospel free of charge, so as not to make full use of my rights in the gospel. [19]For though I am free with respect to all, I have made myself a slave to all, so that I might win more of them. (1 Cor. 9:4-19)

That is, although [x] Paul had the right to be financially supported and to take a wife with him on his journeys, he [y] made no use of these rights but instead [z] "enslaved" himself by performing his gospel ministry free of charge (and, implicitly, doing so without a wife).

It is clear from both 1 Thessalonians and 1 Corinthians that Paul sees this missional existence not only as his imitation of Christ's love, but also as his imitation of Christ's obedience, Christ's faithfulness to God (see especially 1 Cor. 9:17). Thus Paul's self-giving love for others in faithfulness to God and in conformity to the very content of the gospel is constitutive of his apostolic identity. His concrete apostolic practices of Christlike, maternal, and paternal love are his way of participating in the missional love of God that is seen preeminently in the self-giving, loving, reconciling death of Christ on the cross (Rom. 5:6-8; 8:31-39; 2 Cor. 5:14-21; Gal. 2:19-20).

The apostolic narrative continues in the remainder of the first half of 1 Thessalonians. One could hardly ask for a more vivid example of Paul's loving "anxiety for all the churches" (2 Cor. 11:28) than his heart-wrenching narrative of worry and relief about the fate of the Thessalonians in the midst of their persecution (2:13–3:10). Paul's loving concern about the Thessalonians' faithfulness to God is clearly also a manifestation of his faithfulness to them; indeed, faithfulness and love are inseparable in Paul, as they are in God the Father and in Christ. Paul concludes the narrative with a prayer-wish (3:11-13) in which he reaffirms his love for the Thessalonians even as he urges them to love one another and to extend that love outside the community: "And may the Lord make you increase and abound in love for one another and for all [i.e., nonbelievers], just as we abound in love for you" (1 Thess. 3:12). To be "in God" and "in Christ [the Lord]" is to be "in" love.

At the same time as Paul is faithfully and lovingly anxious, he is hopeful, even when he is fearful. The mixture of emotions is apparent as Paul narrates his concern for the Thessalonians and his decision to send Timothy to them (2:17–3:10). His fears and hopes are expressed, that is, in mission, in the act of sending Timothy. But even in remembering and narrating the situation, Paul's primary sense of hope comes through: he calls the Thessalonians "our hope" (2:19), and he sends Timothy not merely in a state of fear, "to find out about your faith[fulness]" (3:5), but also in a state of missional hope, "to strengthen and encourage you for the sake of your faith, so that no one would be shaken by these persecutions" (3:2b-3). Paul's fears and hopes are answered with news of the Thessalonians' faithfulness and love (3:6-7).

Thus in Paul's response to the crisis in Thessalonica, we see a unified pastoral act of faithfulness, love, and hope that reflects the God of the gospel and the gospel of God, and it does so because Paul is participating in the life and mission of this God. But what about the *ekklēsia* at Thessalonica? Are its members also participants in this divine life and mission?

## The Thessalonians as a Missional Community of Faithfulness, Love, and Hope

From the very start of his letter, as we noted at the beginning of the chapter, Paul mentions to the Thessalonians that he always thanks God for their "work of faith and labor of love and steadfastness of hope in our Lord Jesus Christ" (1:3). This triad of virtues, put into practice, is evidence of God's choice of the Thessalonian believers and of the Spirit's work among them.

When we examine this triad closely in Paul's writings, and particularly here in 1 Thessalonians, we discover how central to Paul's ethics and ecclesiology — we might better say his spirituality — they are.[56] The reason faith, love, and hope are so central, this chapter has been suggesting, is that they reflect the missional character of God, the missional narrative of Christ, and the apostolic message and missional identity. That is, these three "virtues" reflect the gospel in its origins ("the gospel of God"), in its manifestation in Jesus, and in its proclamation, and therefore also in its effects. The trio "faith, love, and hope" is not an arbitrary group of virtues but a natural consequence of the gospel of God.

In fact, as we also noted at the start of the chapter, these virtues are not merely internal attitudes. They are virtues that include concrete practices, and it is the practices — the "work . . . labor . . . steadfastness" — that interests Paul. Indeed, like any virtue, these three virtues are known as such only when they are displayed in daily life. They are therefore better called "missional virtues" or "missional practices." Why missional? Faith, love, and hope are missional first of all because they are the fruit of God's mission manifested in Christ and proclaimed by the apostle. Furthermore, they are missional because they are practices that are meant to embody the gospel and thus to proclaim it. That is, faith, love, and hope are "evangelistic" (witnesses to the gospel) by their very nature; they express a particular way of being that is an incarnation, in the lives of real communities and individuals, of a transformative message, the good news.

*For this reason, then, the argument about whether Paul wants his commu-*

---

56. For a fuller exposition, see my *Cruciformity*.

*nities to spread the good news based on the occurrences of exhortations to do so (or the lack thereof), is fundamentally misguided.* Paul wants his communities, including the one at Thessalonica, to embody the gospel of faithfulness, love, and hope. This does not mean that they will act precisely like God or like Jesus (which is impossible for all sorts of reasons), or even exactly like Paul and his colleagues. Rather, the Thessalonians will be expected to engage in what some have called "non-identical repetition," that is, practices that are analogous to those of God, Christ, and the apostles but appropriate to the social locations and vocations of those who embody them.[57] Moreover, the missional impulse that drove God and Christ, and that drives Paul and his team, will also be manifested in the Thessalonians' Spirit-guided life together, including their external, or public, life.[58] This is not to say that the Thessalonians are merely to calculate their faithfulness, love, and hope in terms of the impact of their practices on others. Rather, depending on the situation and the practice in question, this triad of practices will bear witness to others concerning the gospel of God.

We turn, then, to each of these three missional practices to see how they do, or can, bear witness to the gospel in and through the Thessalonians.

### Faithfulness

As we have already indicated, the Greek word-family usually translated into English with some form of the word "faith" (Greek *pistis* as a noun, *pistos* as an adjective) or its associated verb (in English) "believe" (Greek *pisteuō*) means much more than simple belief in the sense of "intellectual assent." We need to read Paul with a thick, rather than a thin, understanding of faith in mind. In Paul's world the *pist-* word-family usually indicates faithfulness, and it has been suggested by a number of scholars that although this word-family is difficult to render into English, especially with one word, a phrase

57. On the notion of nonidentical repetition, see, among others, Stephen E. Fowl, "Christology and Ethics in Philippians 2:5-11," in *Where Christology Began: Essays on Philippians 2*, ed. Ralph P. Martin and Brian J. Dodd (Louisville: Westminster John Knox, 1998), pp. 140-53 (esp. p. 148); and Stephen E. Fowl, *Philippians*, Two Horizons New Testament Commentary (Grand Rapids: Eerdmans, 2005), p. 168.

58. It would be an error to assume that because the Thessalonians almost certainly believe in Paul's teaching that there is a coming divine wrath, they therefore have antipathy toward their unbelieving family members, friends, and associates. Quite the opposite seems to be the case, as they are reminded to treat outsiders well, even those who persecute them (5:15).

like "believing allegiance," "faithful allegiance," or "trusting loyalty" comes close to conveying its core meaning in many instances.[59]

Gordon Zerbe rightly notes that the participial noun *pisteuontes,* which Paul uses to designate those in Christ (often translated "believers"), simultaneously connotes several ideas: "'those who are convinced, submit in trust, and declare loyalty.'"[60] He has argued, therefore, that the Greek noun *pisteuontes,* "believers," should be rendered "loyalists" in the Pauline context if we want to express its significance appropriately in one word.[61] To be sure, as a Jew Paul would have understood the relationship God's people are to have with God in terms of trust and love, but also in terms of faithfulness and obedience. Famously, Paul seems unable to disjoin faith and obedience when he thinks of the proclamation of the gospel, as the bookends that open and close Romans indicate:

> . . . through whom [Christ] we have received grace and apostleship to bring about the obedience of faith among all the Gentiles for the sake of his name. . . . (Rom. 1:5)

> [25]Now to God who is able to strengthen you according to my gospel and the proclamation of Jesus Christ, according to the revelation of the mystery that was kept secret for long ages [26]but is now disclosed, and through the prophetic writings is made known to all the Gentiles, according to the command of the eternal God, to bring about the obedience of faith. . . . (Rom. 16:25-26)

Similarly, Paul uses faith and obedience interchangeably in the middle of Romans: "But not all have obeyed the good news; for Isaiah says, 'Lord, who has believed our message?'" (Rom. 10:16).

The connection between "belief" and "obedience" suggests that, for Paul, faith is a posture of both heartfelt devotion and concrete commitment, as was the case for Israel in relation to YHWH. Indeed, Paul seems to prefer the "faith" or *pist-* word-family to describe what the Old Testament refers to as love for God, which meant both a deeply felt affective relationship with

---

59. See n. 13 above.

60. Zerbe, *Citizenship,* p. 26. He summarizes these three dimensions as conviction, trust, and loyalty. As Zerbe notes and we will see in the chapter on justification and justice, we find a similar problem in interpreting Paul's use of the noun *dikaiosynē,* meaning "justice" or "righteousness," and its linguistic relatives.

61. Zerbe, *Citizenship,* pp. 26-46.

YHWH and covenant loyalty to YHWH (i.e., fidelity, obedience).[62] And since for Paul faith is not only the initial response of a person to the gospel message, but also a person's ongoing posture of devotion and commitment, the word "faithfulness" — meaning "trusting faithfulness" or "believing allegiance" — is a better rendering of *pistis* and its cognates than is "faith," as we have already suggested.[63] (In the subsequent discussion, however, we will sometimes leave the *pistis* family of words untranslated.)

That this is the case in 1 Thessalonians is evident from a survey of the occurrences of the *pist-* family in the letter. In the first chapter Paul documents the Thessalonians' *pistis*, stressing its origin and its nature, with special emphasis on the situation of persecution in which it arose and its exemplary character for other Christ-communities:[64]

- their *pistis* is not "in God" (NRSV) but "toward God" *(pros ton theon)* (1:8), indicating a change in orientation and thus of loyalty: "your faithfulness to God" (CEB);[65]
- this *pistis* consisted of "turn[ing] to God [or 'toward': *pros ton theon*] from idols, to serve [*douleuein;* 'to be enslaved to'[66]] a living and true God, and to wait for his Son from heaven" (1:9b-10);
- their *pistis* came in response to the Spirit-empowered and Spirit-confirmed apostolic proclamation of the gospel (1:5; cf. 2:13);

62. See Brueggemann, *Theology of the Old Testament,* pp. 417-34, esp. pp. 417-21; Gorman, *Cruciformity,* pp. 99-100. Perhaps the most fundamental feature of this obedience/loyalty, Brueggemann rightly contends, is the doing of justice (pp. 421-25). See also the chapter on justification and justice in this book.

63. Elsewhere, I have argued that *pistis* in Paul can be described as "an initial and ongoing cruciformity, grounded in the faithfulness of Jesus the Messiah" (*Cruciformity,* p. 95).

64. Abraham J. Malherbe (*The Letters to the Thessalonians,* AB 32b [New York: Doubleday, 2000], pp. 116-18, 124) understands the *pistis* and the Thessalonians' reputation in this section of the letter primarily as a reference to their evangelistic efforts, but the entire tone of the first half of the letter suggests primarily *pistis* as faithfulness and the reputation as the news of their endurance (so also, e.g., Witherington, *1 and 2 Thessalonians,* pp. 72-73). Malherbe also subscribes to a self-admittedly minority position in interpreting the Thessalonians' distress (1:6; Greek *thlipsis;* NRSV "persecution") primarily as the spiritual anxiety produced by the message of divine wrath that was part of Paul's gospel, rather than their persecution, even though he acknowledges their subsequent persecution (*Letters,* pp. 127-29). This view is rightly rejected by Witherington (*1 and 2 Thessalonians,* p. 72).

65. So also Zerbe, *Citizenship,* p. 42: the Thessalonians made a "decision of loyalty [pledge] toward God." He adds, "*Pistis* is specified as a 'pledge' that involves a complete turn around *(epistrephein)* of life and loyalty."

66. Johnson, "The Sanctification of the Imagination," p. 280.

- their *pistis* was met immediately with persecution, which Paul interprets as imitation of him and his colleagues and of the Lord (1:6; cf. 2:1-2, 14-16);
- their *pistis* issued in concrete "work" (1:3); and
- their *pistis* and its fruit (the "work") became known in, and an example for, other communities of *pisteuontes* (1:7-10).[67]

In the second and third chapters, we learn something of the Thessalonians' ongoing persecution: that it was at the hand of Gentiles (2:14); that it continued after Paul's departure (2:17–3:5); and that it greatly concerned Paul (3:1-5), as we have discussed above, until his delegate Timothy returned with good news (3:6-10). We also learn that Paul had warned the Thessalonians that persecution was normal for those in Christ (3:3b-4). But persecution also means a crisis, a test of the *pistis* of the *pisteuontes*.

Thus Timothy's mission and his report back to Paul focused on the Thessalonians' *pistis* during the persecution. First, the mission:

> [2]and we sent Timothy, our brother and co-worker for God in proclaiming the gospel of Christ, to strengthen and encourage you for the sake of your <u>faith</u>, [3]so that no one would be shaken by these persecutions. . . . [5]For this reason [i.e., the inevitability of persecution], when I could bear it no longer, I sent to find out about your <u>faith</u>; I was afraid that somehow the tempter had tempted you and that our labor had been in vain. (3:2-3a, 5)

Second, the report:

> [6]But Timothy has just now come to us from you, and has brought us the good news of your <u>faith</u> and love. He has told us also that you always remember us kindly and long to see us — just as we long to see you. [7]For this reason, brothers and sisters, during all our distress and persecution we have been encouraged about you through your <u>faith</u>. (3:6-7)

And after the report, Paul's response:

> [8]For we now live, if you <u>continue to stand firm in the Lord</u>. [9]How can we thank God enough for you in return for all the joy that we feel before our

---

67. Andy Johnson rightly notes that the Thessalonians as a whole, as a body, were one corporate example of *pistis* ("The Sanctification of the Imagination," p. 279).

God because of you? [10]Night and day we pray most earnestly that we may see you face to face and restore whatever is lacking in your <u>faith</u>. (3:8-10)

Paul is clearly not concerned here about the Thessalonians' intellectual assent to an early Christian creed, but about their faithfulness, their public witness as the tangible sign of the reality of their *pistis*, their "firm[ness] in the Lord." "Paul's overriding concern in the letter is for their [the Thessalonians'] continued 'loyalty.'"[68] The CEB, therefore, rightly translates *pistis* as "faithfulness" throughout chapter 3.[69] The Thessalonians' *pistis* refers to the "whole range of human life, active and passive, attitudinal and bodily, inner and outer, personal, social, and political."[70] Could the Thessalonian *ekklēsia* withstand the tempter's temptations (3:5),[71] that is, the pressure to recant the good news of Christ (3:2)? Recanting would mean, practically speaking, returning to the idols the Thessalonians had left behind when they first came to faith.

The tempter's temptations could have come from multiple sources: family members, friends, colleagues, fellow workers and members of associations, patrons, slaves, masters, local officials, and so on. Both recanting and resisting would have to take the form of public witness and corroborating action. Recanters would be known by their forsaking the Jesus-cult and returning to the cult(s) they had abandoned, evidenced in making sacrifices, participating in rituals, offering prayers, vowing allegiance to the emperor, and so on. Resisters would be known by their refusing to forsake the Jesus-cult, their continuing to name Jesus as Lord and the God of Israel as the only god and divine father, their refusing to participate in any other cultic activity, and their stubbornness (i.e., faithfulness — *pistis*) in this mode of resistance despite the threat and the reality of ongoing persecution.

In other words, the Thessalonians were bearing witness simply by virtue of being faithful. The gospel of the faithful God and his faithful Messiah generates faith in people and generates people who remain faithful. This se-

68. Zerbe, *Citizenship*, p. 42.

69. Except, oddly, in 3:10.

70. Douglas Harink, *Paul among the Postliberals: Pauline Theology beyond Christendom and Modernity* (Grand Rapids: Brazos, 2003), p. 35.

71. Cf. 1 Pet. 5:8-9: "Discipline yourselves, keep alert. Like a roaring lion your adversary the devil prowls around, looking for someone to devour. Resist him, steadfast in your faith, for you know that your brothers and sisters in all the world are undergoing the same kinds of suffering."

quence of God's faithfulness expecting and generating faithfulness in return is a pattern derived from the Scriptures of Israel and from the fundamental Jewish worldview.[72]

That the Thessalonians are "faithful" does not mean that as *pisteuontes* they are perfect, or that there is no danger that their faithfulness could become faithlessness; just the opposite is the case (as was certainly true of Israel in the Old Testament). Thus Paul acted pastorally vis-à-vis their *pistis* in two ways: prospectively, by sending Timothy in order to strengthen them and prevent their faithlessness (3:2-3); and then retrospectively, by going himself in order to "restore whatever is lacking" in their *pistis* after their surviving the persecution (3:10). The description of the latter action, the visit, suggests a kind of post-traumatic healing process.[73]

All of this tells us that the Thessalonians' conversion — their identity transformation — was inherently, if unintentionally, both missional and dangerous as soon as they decided to "go public" with their faith, which would have happened, almost by necessity, from the very first moment of faith. Indeed, because *pistis* involved a change of allegiance and of cult(s), it could never be anything but public, and never anything but witness-bearing, or missional — and hence risky.

Does this mean that the Thessalonian *pisteuontes* were asked to try to "convert" their family members, friends, colleagues, and so on, or that they tried to do so? We cannot know the answer to this precise question, but we can certainly speculate with a high degree of certainty that when the Thessalonians abandoned the cultic activities of their family, friends, and fellow beneficiaries of their city and empire, when they went off to meetings with fellow *pisteountes* in a new cult, and when some of their most fundamental attitudes and behaviors radically changed, they were asked to explain and defend their new behaviors. It was almost certainly the perception of impious and unpatriotic behavior, and of unsatisfactory explanations for that behavior, that fueled the persecution. *Pistis* as "belief" was also inevitably *pistis* as faithful witness and faithful endurance (the "steadfastness of hope"; 1:3).

It is therefore nearly impossible, if one reads 1 Thessalonians carefully and contextually, to imagine this group of young converts, full of joy in their

---

72. Zerbe (*Citizenship*, p. 33) notes the similarity between Josephus and Paul on the relationship between divine and human fidelity.

73. The Greek verb (*katartisai;* NRSV "restore") in 3:10 may refer to restoration or completion. The context suggests that what is lacking, if anything, is due to the persecution, and hence the process will be one of repair.

new cult (1:6), not spreading the good news to others, including even their persecutors — whom they were taught not to harm but to love (5:15).

## Love

One poignant description of the Thessalonian community is as those taught by God to love (4:9).[74] To participate in the divine life is to be instructed in divine love. Thus the Thessalonians are also called to love, as we have already noted on several occasions. As God's and Paul's beloved, they are to "increase and abound in love for one another," but they are also to love others, to "increase and abound in love . . . for all" (3:12). The entire context of the letter suggests that this kind of love consists of "self-giving *practices*"[75] in imitation of Paul (2:6-12; 3:12) and ultimately, as we saw earlier, in imitation of Jesus. Because it was God who taught the Thessalonians to love one another, they must do so "more and more" (4:10).

This effusive, overflowing love directed toward others can properly be called missional love. "Missional" here does not mean that this love has as its primary goal the conversion of the other, though that should not be ruled out as part of what love is when directed toward those outside the *ekklēsia*. But the primary mission of love in 1 Thessalonians is simply to participate appropriately in the love of God (i.e., the love received from God) by loving others. Love is, by definition, others-focused, as Paul makes clear in such passages as 1 Corinthians 13.[76] These practical expressions of love are performed not just by individuals, and not just for fellow believers. As Andy Johnson puts it, "these are actions done: by the *ekklēsia* as a whole; by persons within the *ekklēsia* for the sake of others within it; by individuals within the *ekklēsia* for the sake of others outside it."[77]

That this love is rooted in the gospel of God's reconciling love for enemies (cf. Rom. 5:6-8) is evident in the additional injunction Paul includes in the letter to do good (that is, to practice love), not only to one another, but even to those who inflict evil: "See that none of you repays evil for evil, but always seek to do good to one another and to all" (5:15; cf. Rom. 12:17). This exhortation is an extension of the general admonition in 3:12 ("increase

---

74. As noted above, "taught by God" is likely an implicit reference to the work of the Spirit (cf. Gal. 5:22).

75. Johnson, "The Sanctification of the Imagination," p. 283.

76. Esp. 1 Cor. 13:5; cf. 1 Cor. 8:1; 10:24, 33; Rom. 15:1-3; Gal. 5:13-14; Phil. 2:1-4.

77. Johnson, "The Sanctification of the Imagination," p. 284 n. 46.

and abound in love for one another and for all").[78] The scope of this non-retaliatory, loving goodness certainly includes the Thessalonians' harassers and persecutors; in fact, in the context of the letter, these people are quite possibly the primary group Paul has in view when he uses the word "all," at least in 5:15. Indirectly, as Romans 12:17-21 also suggests, such Christlike non-retaliation is a form of evangelism.

Thus to "increase and abound in love . . . for all," to "seek to do good . . . to all," without repaying evil for evil, constitutes an essential aspect of the public life and witness of the *ekklēsia* and of each individual within it. The verbs "increase," "abound," and "seek" *(pleonasai; perisseusai; diōkete)* in 3:12 and 5:15 suggest a deliberate, imaginative, proactive kind of love — a missional love. Like the positive injunction we call the "Golden Rule" (Matt. 7:12a; "In everything do to others as you would have them do to you"), this is not merely a passive or reactive love, but one that is always looking for opportunities to do good for others, outside the community as well as within it. Such love for those outside will be consistent with the love of God revealed in the cross of Jesus, embodied imaginatively in Paul's own missional activity, and taught now by the Spirit. Its specific manifestations will depend on the communities and individuals involved, and on the situations in which they find themselves. But at the very least, in light of the biblical ethos as a whole, we can expect missional cruciform love to include generosity, especially to the most vulnerable; hospitality of various sorts, especially (again) to the most vulnerable; and non-retaliation. This, the Thessalonians might say, is simply our sharing with others what has been shared with us: the unmerited, overflowing love of God.

In the conflicted area of sexuality, Paul also speaks to the Thessalonians about both love and witness as part of his general exhortation to holiness, or countercultural identity (4:1-12). Located at the beginning of the second main part of the letter, the hortatory section, Paul's admonition to holiness (4:3, 7-8) includes these strong words:

> [3] . . . that you abstain from fornication [Greek *porneias,* better translated "sexual immorality"]; [4]that each one of you know how to control your own body [Greek *skeuos,* vessel] in holiness and honor, [5]not with lustful passion, like the Gentiles who do not know God; [6]that no one wrong or

---

78. Some might be inclined to interpret the "all" of 5:15 as a reference only, or primarily, to all in the community. But the phrase is an exact replica of the one in 3:12, which clearly indicates "insiders" ("one another") and "outsiders" ("all").

exploit a brother or sister in this matter, because the Lord is an avenger in all these things, just as we have already told you beforehand and solemnly warned you. (4:3b-6)

While there is debate about the precise meaning of parts of this passage,[79] the overall message is clear: as a sanctified people who are still in the process of being sanctified, the faithful are to turn away from sexual immorality just as they turned away from idolatry (1:9-10), for sexual immorality is one of the basic "marks" of those who do not know the one, true, living God.[80] Those in Christ will not engage in such exploitative behavior, for it is a violation of the way brothers and sisters should treat one another; it is hardly an example of self-giving love.

The context links Paul's concern about sexual morality to the greater concerns of love and witness. Formally, Paul seems to begin a new section at 4:9 ("Now concerning . . ."), but materially he still has brotherly and sisterly relations on his mind, as he urges an increase of *philadelphia*, or, *agapē* within the family (4:9-10): "⁹Now concerning love of the brothers and sisters [*philadelphias*], you do not need to have anyone write to you, for you yourselves have been taught by God to love [*agapan*] one another; ¹⁰and indeed you do love all the brothers and sisters throughout Macedonia" (4:9-10a). Paul seems to be especially concerned that the Thessalonians not shirk their responsibility to continue working, specifically with their hands (4:11-12), just as Paul worked as an act of love for them (2:5-12). The refusal of some to work might be a result of their overzealous apocalyptic hope (as when followers of the late Harold Camping sold everything to wait for the parousia), but most scholars today see the decision not to work as implying participation in the culture's client-patron system, as a client of someone either inside or outside the church. In either case, not to work would be a burden on others, which would be both a failure to love those in the community and a poor witness to "those outside." Rather, all the Thessalonians should be

79. Especially debated is the translation of the phrase in verse 4, "control . . . body," since the Greek word *skeuos* ("vessel") could refer to a bodily organ or to a woman/wife as a vessel for the man's seed. Thus the phrase could be a reference to self-control of one's sexual urges/genitalia, which is more likely in my view, or to getting married (in which case the phrase would mean "obtain a vessel").

80. These two generic sins, idolatry and sexual immorality, are frequently linked in Second Temple Jewish literature, predicated normally of Gentiles. Cf. Paul in Rom. 1:18-32. See also 1 Cor. 6:18 and 10:14, in which he tells the Corinthians to "flee" from sexual immorality *(porneia)* and idolatry, respectively.

responsible (financially "self-sufficient") and thereby also "behave [Greek *peripatēte*, 'walk'] properly toward outsiders" (4:12).[81] The language of 4:9-12 should not be read as apostolic counsel to refrain from all public life or to "keep a low profile." Rather, as Andy Johnson argues, Paul is trying to prevent the Thessalonians from engaging the world "*on its own terms* (i.e., as structured by the patronage system)," for they are to embody "the way of thinking produced by the cross (1 Cor. 1:18) rather than the 'commonsense' assumptions of the patronage system"; this would mean a "reconfiguration of public life in cruciform, and therefore holy, terms, not a withdrawal into the sphere of the private."[82]

In light of 4:9-12, it does not take much literary or historical imagination to conclude that Paul also saw proper sexual behavior both as an expression of Christian love and as a witness to outsiders *precisely because* it is an expression of love, a "labor of love" (1:3). Accordingly, Paul's plea for a countercultural sexual ethic and behavior within the community is not just a call for difference for the sake of difference, but a plea for life that pleases God, with an eye on the missional effect of such a God-centered approach to sex (as well as work) within the context of cruciform love for fellow believers and for the world.

## Hope

In considering the passages on hope especially in 1 Thessalonians and Romans, Reinhard Feldmeier and Hermann Spieckermann make the provocative claim that "[h]ope is not anticipation of the future, but participation in God."[83] They base this claim on the present experience of those in Christ, who already know God as Abba (Father) and are assured of salvation even

---

81. On the whole passage, see the discussion in Malherbe, *Letters*, pp. 242-60. Witherington (*1 and 2 Thessalonians*, pp. 121-23) points out that the exhortation to a "quiet" life does not mean isolationism, but keeping a low profile might be especially prudent in a situation of conflict. This strategy, however, would not mean a withdrawal from witness. Rather, Witherington suggests, following Bruce Winter, the withdrawal Paul desires is not from people in general but from the patron-client system. Thus by their work (specifically, their manual labor) and their nonparticipation in the system of honor-seeking, reciprocity, and so on, the Thessalonians would be able to do good to others as an expression of their faith and love, avoiding the cultural norms of being either parasites or sycophants within the patron-client system (p. 123).

82. Johnson, *1-2 Thessalonians*, forthcoming.

83. Reinhard Feldmeier and Hermann Spieckermann, *God of the Living: A Biblical Theology*, trans. Mark E. Biddle (Waco, TX: Baylor University Press, 2011), pp. 12-13.

in the midst of spiritual struggle and suffering. They find similar, indeed stronger, evidence for their claim in other New Testament texts.

Although Feldmeier and Spieckermann probably go too far in saying that hope is not "anticipation of the future," a modified version of their claim is true: that for Paul hope is not *merely* anticipation of the future but a present, anticipatory *participation* in the future, specifically in God's eschatological promise of glory (e.g., Rom. 8:17-39; 2 Cor. 3:18; 4:17-18; 1 Thess. 2:12).[84] Feldmeier and Spieckermann are quite right, however, to insist that hope *(elpis),* with *pistis* (and I would add *agapē*), "constitutes Christian being" in Paul and elsewhere.[85] As we have already noted, Paul mentions hope (with *pistis* and *agapē,* as a triad) in 1:3 and 5:8; it is a mark of in-Christ identity. And as he also says to the Thessalonians, lacking hope is a mark of not being part of the *ekklēsia:*

> But we do not want you to be uninformed, brothers and sisters, about those who have died, so that you may not grieve as others do who have no hope. (4:13; cf. Eph. 2:12)

This text raises the important question of whether hope is in some sense missional. We have already seen that hope, according to Paul in 1 Thessalonians, is more than an attitude; it is a practice, a virtue that issues in concrete behaviors. In and around 4:13 Paul makes the following implicit or explicit claims:

- some Thessalonian believers have died (4:13);
- some Thessalonian believers have mourned, or are mourning, these deaths, and perhaps other deaths (4:14);
- mourning in and of itself is not inappropriate for the *ekklēsia;*[86]
- there is, however, a kind of mourning that is characteristic of those outside the *ekklēsia,* who have no hope (i.e., do not share the hope of the gospel), and a kind of mourning that is appropriate for those in the *ekklēsia,* who have the hope of the gospel (4:13); and
- there are both a private and a public dimension to appropriate mourning and hopefulness for those in the *ekklēsia* (4:18).

---

84. See the discussion of anticipatory participation in chapter one.

85. Feldmeier and Spieckermann, *God of the Living,* p. 513.

86. The exhortation to "encourage" or "comfort" one another (4:18) presumes that mourning is to be addressed, not discouraged or dismissed.

In other words, we should take the phrase "so that you may not grieve as others do," not as a *prohibition* of grief (as if that were possible) but as a *reconfiguration* of grief in light of the gospel, particularly its promise of resurrection. It is similar, in other words, to the admonition about sex in 4:3-7; Paul prohibits neither sex nor grief, but he reconfigures the practice of each in light of the gospel practices of love (for sex) and hope (for grief).

What does this mean for the question of grief and mission? Like sexual behavior, the practice of grief is a public behavior. To be sure, like lust, grief can be attitudinal, but especially in the Greco-Roman culture (as in many cultures), grief was something people displayed — publicly. Accordingly, for the *ekklēsia* in Thessalonica, how they grieved and how they hoped — specifically how they hoped in the midst of grief — was a form of bearing witness to family members, friends, associates, and so on. The church's hope was, and is, missional — again, not first of all by virtue of an intention to convert but simply by virtue of the countercultural nature of the hope of the gospel. As Andy Johnson remarks, "Neither a grief borne out of a sense of hopelessness nor a grief thinly masked by various forms of gnostic speculations of disembodied bliss — often seen at 'Christian' funerals! — is the kind of grief that enables the Church to give public witness to the particular hope that animates it."[87]

More broadly still, we should think of hope for Paul as something that permits and enables risk-taking and thereby generates creative practices.[88] Those who have a firm hope about the future will prepare for it and anticipate it in their daily lives (5:1-11). Those who hope can remain faithful to the Lord Jesus when the imperial lord, or his friends and representatives, make demands or threats. Those who hope can accept their status as a "new social identity of no-power" and not fear the powers-that-be or clamor for worldly power.[89] Those who hope can avoid seeking retaliation (5:15), knowing that God is the judge. In fact, it is as a space marked off by hope that the believing community is also a community of peace and of peacemaking.[90] Finally,

---

87. Johnson, *1-2 Thessalonians*, forthcoming.

88. For a theopolitical reading of 1 Thessalonians along these lines, see Nestor O. Míguez, *The Practice of Hope: Ideology and Intention in 1 Thessalonians*, trans. Aquíles Martínez, Paul in Critical Contexts (Minneapolis: Fortress, 2012). While I do not concur fully with his approach or conclusions, he makes insightful concrete connections between the virtue of hope and counterimperial Christian practices.

89. The term in quotes is from Míguez, *The Practice of Hope*, pp. 41-45, 84, 115, 133, 147-48, 153, 161, 167.

90. On this, see especially my chapters on peace as the practice of hope in *The Death of the*

those who hope have the privilege, and the possibility, of constantly rejoicing and giving thanks when they pray (5:16-18), since their present life and future fate are in the hands of a loving, faithful, rescuing God.

## Conclusion

Quite simply, the Thessalonians had become, and were continuing to become, the gospel. The good news of God's faithfulness, love, and eschatological promise embodied in Jesus for the salvation of all is now embodied by the power of the Holy Spirit, in analogous ways, in the *ekklēsia* and for the good of "all." As a community of faithfulness, love, and hope, the *ekklēsia* is set apart — sanctified — to be God's holy people *in a public way*. But it can be that holy people only as it participates in God's holiness and thus in God's own life of faithfulness, love, and salvation, and thereby in God's corresponding missional activity of generating human faithfulness, love, and hope.

Such a corporate and individual lifestyle, because it is "holy," is at once countercultural and missional, confrontational and inviting. Nestor Míguez calls it "conduct that anticipates the kingdom," meaning especially the faith, love, and hope about which Paul has written.[91] Míguez writes,

> [A]s long as the community lives, in its conduct and in vigilance (the elements that announce the reign of God), the reign begins making itself present. When this community arms itself with the elements that permit its testimony to go out [faith, love, hope — 5:8], it confronts the false gods and the policies that promise a false peace and security, and the modes of dominions and motivations of the surrounding world. In such a confrontation, the church expresses the existence of another government for the life of its members, of another *kyrios,* and of another Kingdom and, therefore, the actuality of another understanding of reality. This, then, becomes an alternative option, a counterhegemonic one.

An alternative option. That is the church, says Paul: public, holy, and full of faithfulness, love, and hope.

---

*Messiah and the Birth of the New Covenant: A (Not So) New Model of the Atonement* (Eugene, OR: Cascade, 2014). See also chapters five and six below.

91. Míguez, *The Practice of Hope,* pp. 151-52.

## The Church Today: Communities of Faithfulness, Love, and Hope

In principle, and in some sense also in reality, every church, each Christian community, is a place of faithfulness, love, and hope. From the most mundane of tasks like cooking meals for the infirm, the shut-in, or those who mourn, to "mission trips" that aim at rebuilding houses and lives, Christian people and churches aim to practice the virtues of faithfulness, love, and hope.

But it might be helpful for a moment to consider a somewhat unusual Christian entity, a community of believers that is not a church per se, in order to think creatively about Christian identity and witness today. I say "somewhat unusual" rather than "nontraditional" since, as we will see shortly, there is something quite traditional about this community.

Rutba House in Durham, North Carolina is a small intentional Christian community consisting of several families — and many guests who come and go, or come and stay — in two houses within easy walking distance of each other.[92] Located in the largely African American Walltown section of this small southern city and university town, it is also only steps away from a small Baptist church, which has become more interracial since Rutba House was founded in 2003. Rutba House co-founder Jonathan Wilson-Hartgrove is on the church's ministerial staff.

Jonathan and his wife Leah founded Rutba House as a house of hospitality, naming it after a town in Iraq where their Christian Peacemaker Team was shown hospitality and given medical care while witnessing to Christ's peace at the start of the Iraq War.[93] Rutba House is part of a movement (for lack of a better term) called "the new monasticism," a network of churches and other Christian communities that have intentionally relocated to the "edges of empire," to the places that have been left behind economically, socially, and so on.[94]

The new monasticism is a varied network of communities, yet it has a set of defining marks including relocation, resource-sharing, hospitality, racial reconciliation, intentional discipleship, stewardship of the earth, peacemaking, and contemplation.[95] To the best of my knowledge, nowhere do these

92. See http://emerging-communities.com/tag/rutba-house/ and http://jonathanwilson hartgrove.com/.

93. For more on Christian Peacemaker Teams, see the discussion at the end of chapter six.

94. See, e.g., Jonathan Wilson-Hartgrove, *New Monasticism: What It Has to Say to Today's Church* (Grand Rapids: Brazos, 2008); Rutba House, ed., *School(s) for Conversion: 12 Marks of a New Monasticism* (Eugene, OR: Wipf & Stock, 2005).

95. For the full list of marks and discussion, see Rutba House, *School(s) for Conversion*.

communities formally call themselves communities of cruciform faithfulness, love, and hope, but they could. "Hospitality" is certainly an excellent summary of life at Rutba House, and the stories that Jonathan tells about their life of faithful, loving, hopeful hospitality could fill a book — and they have (actually, more than one). Indeed one of Jonathan's books is called *The Awakening of Hope*.[96] Like the Thessalonians, the Rutba House is a small Christian community that has a far-reaching reputation. And what is most striking about their life together is their refusal to separate their passion for Jesus and their passion for justice.

The point of mentioning Rutba House here in the first chapter of interpreting a specific Pauline letter and community missionally is not to promote this specific community or to suggest that all Christians must immediately relocate and pool their resources to serve the poor and one another in faithfulness, love, and hope. But Rutba House is an icon of what God is doing in the world, and how. Like the Thessalonians, Rutba House is an alter-culture, a challenge to the dominant idolatries and ideologies of its southern American host culture. Like that first-century church, the members of Rutba House pray together (even following a modified traditional monastic approach to prayer) and focus on knowing Jesus as Lord and one another as brothers and sisters. They take care of one another, but above all they welcome others and try to look out for "all" in their community, and beyond. They share with others, not only the gospel, but also their very lives. They attempt to live at peace with their neighbors and the greater community.

But the members of Rutba House know that Christian witness is inherently a public reality. Therefore they also willingly risk rebuke and rejection from their peers, not to mention authorities, when they challenge the idolatries of their culture, whether in literal temples or in the halls of municipal buildings or state legislatures that are occasionally still trapped in practices of racism or economic injustice. And they gain respect from fellow believers when they welcome the homeless, rise to the defense of the widow, visit the imprisoned, and so on.

Are these practices of peacemaking and justice-making? Of course, and

---

96. Jonathan Wilson-Hartgrove, *The Awakening of Hope: Why We Practice a Common Faith* (Grand Rapids: Zondervan, 2012), an explanation of communal practices at Rutba House and elsewhere in light of the mission of God and the desire to "live faithfully" through both reflection and action. His other books include *The Wisdom of Stability: Rooting Faith in a Mobile Culture* (Brewster, MA: Paraclete, 2010) and *Strangers at My Door: A True Story of Finding Jesus in Unexpected Guests* (New York: Convergent/Random House, 2013), which is full of compelling narratives.

Rutba House could therefore have been pigeonholed into one of those chapters later in the book. But what Rutba House says to the Christian community more broadly is not, "Start another Rutba House," but, "Intentionally practice cruciform faithfulness, love, and hope wherever you are — and maybe in places where thus far you have been afraid to go."

Thus reading 1 Thessalonians as Scripture, and specifically as witness both to the *missio Dei* and to God's call to participate in that mission, is enhanced by reading this Pauline letter in conversation with contemporary practitioners of missional virtue. Those practitioners can be located in North Carolina or in any other part of God's world that is now and always the object of God's faithfulness, love, and hope.

# CHAPTER 4

# Becoming and Telling the Story of Christ: Philippians

Paul's letter to the Philippians is centered on its most famous passage, the "hymn" or poem in Philippians 2:6-11. In this chapter we explore the missional significance of that passage, calling it Paul's master story, a story — not surprisingly — of faith, love, and hope, a story of sharing in the mission of Jesus the Servant of God. But it is also a story preserved in a letter that bears witness to the privilege and challenge of participating in that story, and of proclaiming Jesus the Servant-Lord in word and deed, even if those activities result in opposition and suffering. Since we have investigated the somewhat similar Thessalonian situation in some detail, in this chapter we can be briefer in our discussion of the Philippians themselves and pay more attention to the text's challenge and promise to the contemporary Christian community, including some consideration of the persecuted church around the world.

## Master Story and Mission

Like Thessalonica, Philippi was a city of the province of Macedonia, though smaller than the provincial capital. And like the Thessalonian church, the community of believers at Philippi seems to have begun its life surrounded by opposition, opposition that did not go away as time went on. As with the Thessalonians, Paul wrote in part because of the problem of persecution, but he did so this time from prison.[1]

---

1. For details on the situation, see, e.g., my *Apostle of the Crucified Lord: A Theological Introduction to Paul and His Letters* (Grand Rapids: Eerdmans, 2004), pp. 412-18. For Paul's conflict with authorities and other suffering at the founding of the community, see Acts 16:16-

Philippians is a short but powerful Pauline letter. In spite of the church's challenging circumstances that are reflected in the letter, scholars have often referred to it as a letter of friendship, though it might be better classified as a family letter.[2] Popular interpreters, for good reason, often call it Paul's letter of joy.[3] Some scholars have claimed, in contrast, that its governing theme is suffering.[4] While these kinds of rhetorical and thematic characterizations are not inaccurate, they are nonetheless inadequate. Philippians is above all an extended commentary on one portion of the letter, the famous text in Philippians 2:6-11.[5] It describes Christ Jesus as the one

> [6]who, though [and/or "because"[6]] he was in the form of God, did not regard equality with God as something to be exploited, [7]but emptied himself, taking the form of a slave, being born in human likeness. And being

---

39; 1 Thess. 2:1-2; Phil. 1:29-30. On the Philippians' suffering, see Phil. 1:28-30; 2 Cor. 8:2. On Paul's imprisonment while writing, see Philippians 1. There is debate about the location and date of Paul's imprisonment; he could be in Rome, Ephesus, Caesarea, or elsewhere, and the letter could be from the early 50s to early 60s.

2. Those who consider it a friendship letter include Gordon D. Fee, *Paul's Letter to the Philippians*, NICNT (Grand Rapids: Eerdmans, 1995), pp. 2-7 and Stephen E. Fowl, *Philippians*, Two Horizons New Testament Commentary (Grand Rapids: Eerdmans, 2005), pp. 8-9, as well as many others. Ben Witherington III, in *Paul's Letter to the Philippians: A Socio-Rhetorical Commentary* (Grand Rapids: Eerdmans, 2011), pp. 14, 17-21, however, makes the case for calling it a family letter.

3. On joy, see Phil. 1:4, 18, 25; 2:2, 17-18, 28-29; 3:1; 4:1, 4, 10.

4. See the brief discussion of such interpreters, and the fine extended treatment of suffering at Philippi and in the letter, in Peter Oakes, *Philippians: From People to Letter*, SNTS Monograph Series 110 (Cambridge: Cambridge University Press, 2001), pp. 77-102. Suffering is clearly a critical concern in Philippians, but it should be seen in conjunction with the larger theme of cruciform witness discussed in this chapter.

5. See especially my *Apostle of the Crucified Lord*, pp. 419-23, where there is a table of the verbal and thematic echoes of 2:6-11 throughout the letter. See also, e.g., Dean Flemming, *Philippians: A Commentary in the Wesleyan Tradition*, New Beacon Bible Commentary (Kansas City, MO: Beacon Hill, 2009), pp. 34-37. J. Ross Wagner connects this passage to 2:12 and traces the connection throughout the letter ("Working Out Salvation: Holiness and Community in Philippians," in *Holiness and Ecclesiology in the New Testament*, ed. Kent E. Brower and Andy Johnson [Grand Rapids: Eerdmans, 2007], pp. 257-74).

6. For the translation question in verse 6 — "though" and/or "because" — see my *Inhabiting the Cruciform God: Kenosis, Justification, and Theosis in Paul's Narrative Soteriology* (Grand Rapids: Eerdmans, 2009), pp. 9-39. In that chapter I argue for both translations: "although he was in the form of God" (that is, Christ acted differently than "normal" gods act) and also "because he was in the form of God" (that is, Christ acted as he did because that is the character of true divinity).

found in human form, [8]he humbled himself and became obedient to the point of death — even death on a cross. [9]Therefore God also highly exalted him and gave him the name that is above every name, [10]so that at the name of Jesus every knee should bend, in heaven and on earth and under the earth, [11]and every tongue should confess that Jesus Christ is Lord, to the glory of God the Father.

This text is the "theological and christological centerpiece,"[7] or "beating heart,"[8] of the letter.[9] Often identified as an early Christian hymn or poem, this brief passage has had more ink spilled (and words processed) over its interpretation than most other passages in the New Testament. And rightfully so, for it is more than just the centerpiece of a letter; it is, perhaps, the origin of Christology and even, at least in my view, Paul's "master story."[10]

Given the amount of attention this text has received over the centuries and in recent years, it seems almost impossible to think that there is anything left to say about it that has not already been said.[11] But there is; Philippians 2:6-11 can always be approached from new angles, and it is, I believe, more

7. Markus Bockmuehl, *The Epistle to the Philippians*, Black's New Testament Commentary (Peabody, MA: Hendrickson, 1998), p. 148; similarly, Flemming, *Philippians*, 36; Gorman, *Apostle of the Crucified Lord*, pp. 419-22; and Gorman, *Cruciformity: Paul's Narrative Spirituality of the Cross* (Grand Rapids: Eerdmans, 2001), pp. 39, 88, 253.

8. Ralph P. Martin and Gerald F. Hawthorne, *Philippians*, Word Biblical Commentary 43, rev. ed. (Nashville: Thomas Nelson, 2004), p. lxxii.

9. Bockmuehl adds that "the christological argument of 2:6-11 provides the spiritual focus, assurance and incentive for the letter's various instructions" (*Philippians*, p. 55) and that it "underwrite[s] the argument of every other part" of the letter (p. 41). And Fowl adds that everything before and after 2:5-11 "draws its coherence from this passage" (*Philippians*, p. 88).

10. On the possible origins of Christology in this text, see Ralph P. Martin and Brian J. Dodd, eds., *Where Christology Began: Essays on Philippians 2* (Louisville: Westminster John Knox, 1998). On this text as Paul's master story, see my *Cruciformity*, pp. 88-92, 164-72, 278-80, 316-19, 357-58, et passim. See also Thomas Stegman, " 'Run That You May Obtain the Prize' (1 Cor. 9:24): St. Paul and the Spiritual Exercises," *Studies in the Spirituality of the Jesuits* 44 (2012): 16-19.

11. In fact, when I wrote an article on Phil. 2:6-11 (" 'Although/Because He Was in the Form of God': The Theological Significance of Paul's Master Story [Philippians 2:6-11]," *Journal of Theological Interpretation* 1 [2007]: 147-69) that later became the first chapter of *Inhabiting the Cruciform God*, I thought that I myself was done. Nonetheless, I do believe that there is, and always will be, more to say about this rich text. I wrote my first essay on it more than thirty years ago, as a first-year seminarian, for the late Bruce Metzger, in a class on New Testament Christology. The paper became the basis of my Ph.D. dissertation, which in turn became the basis of most of my subsequent work on Paul. And another essay is in process.

inherently polyvalent — full of various shades of meaning — than the average Pauline text.

In this chapter we will explore this narrative poem, Paul's master story, in search of its implications for the church's missional life and message. Specifically, we will be looking at what may be called the apologetic and missional impulse of Philippians 2:6-11 in the context of the letter — and as a model for the contemporary church. We will see that Paul's master story is both a narrative about Christ and a narrative about the church. It summarizes the gospel that Paul wants the *ekklēsia* at Philippi to (continue to) embrace and (continue to) proclaim and (continue to) embody, in spite of opposition.

That is, *Philippians 2:6-11 is a missional Christology for a missional people.* The church is to become the gospel by participating in it. Those who participate in the reality to which Philippians 2:6-11 bears witness will both hold forth (in word and action) and defend the basic claims of the gospel as Paul proclaimed it: that the crucified Jesus is the self-giving, life-giving Son of God and sovereign Lord, in fulfillment of Scripture and in contrast to Caesar. These claims have been vindicated by God in exalting Jesus, who will soon be acknowledged as Lord by all creation. Participating in this story, therefore, means participating not only in the humiliation and exaltation of the Messiah, but also in the mission of God (the *missio Dei*). Paul's words, we will see, speak to the contemporary church in several ways about the coherent form and content of its missional life and message.[12]

We begin with a brief consideration of the situations of Paul and those to whom he writes at Philippi.

## Paul and the Philippians: Partners in the Gospel

Paul writes this letter, this commentary on the story of the suffering but now exalted Messiah and Lord, while in chains and suffering himself. Furthermore, he writes to a community that is (1) suffering for the gospel, almost certainly at the hands of nonbelievers; (2) dealing with "teachers," similar to those in Galatia, who wish (or might wish, if they are not yet on the scene) to cause the Gentiles in the community to "Judaize" (as Philippians 3 implies); and, at the same time, (3) experiencing at least some internal dissension (4:2-3).

---

12. For a reading of Philippians that is quite consonant with this chapter, see especially Dean Flemming, "Exploring a Missional Reading of Scripture: Philippians as a Case Study," *Evangelical Quarterly* 83 (2011): 3-18.

The Philippians are suffering, like Paul, "on behalf of the gospel" (1:29-30), and they are doing so, it would seem, in a certain similarity to their Lord, whom the Romans had crucified (Phil. 2:8). Philippi was a *very* Roman colony, and there was a "particular Philippian penchant to the Emperor Cult."[13] Thus, as Dean Flemming (among others) has suggested, the most likely reason for this persecution is that the Philippians appeared to be a threat to the Roman colony in which they lived but whose sovereign lord — the emperor — they no longer honored as such.[14] In this respect, at least, the Philippian believers were much like the Thessalonian faithful. (Paul himself, according to Acts 16:20-24, was thought to pose a similar anti-Roman threat at Philippi — and of course elsewhere, as Kavin Rowe has carefully shown in his book *World Upside Down*.[15]) These believers "could have experienced harassment from their neighbors and various forms of economic suffering":[16]

> We might imagine that Christian tradespeople would lose their customers. Pagan owners might punish Christian slaves. Patrons could withdraw financial support from Christian clients. Magistrates might drag believers to court. In short, Christians in Philippi might experience the kind of ostracism, discrimination, or even violence that has accompanied loyalty to Christ in many times and places.[17]

Thus the Philippians share in Paul's struggle for the gospel and sufferings similar to Paul's:

> [29]For he has graciously granted you the privilege not only of believing in Christ, but of suffering for him as well — [30]since you are having the same struggle that you saw I had and now hear that I still have. (Phil. 1:29-30)

This means, Paul says, that they are his partners in the gospel (see *koinōnia*, 1:5; *synkoinōnous*, 1:7), not merely in financial support of his ministry, or

---

13. Bockmuehl, *Philippians*, p. 6. Witherington (*Paul's Letter*, pp. 5-6) rightly cautions about overinterpreting the evidence to the point of claiming that the emperor cult dominated the city.

14. Flemming, *Philippians*, p. 28. See also Bockmuehl, *Philippians*, pp. 19, 100-101.

15. C. Kavin Rowe, *World Upside Down: Reading Acts in the Graeco-Roman Age* (New York: Oxford University Press, 2009). The "elsewhere," as we have just seen in chapter three, included Thessalonica.

16. Flemming, *Philippians*, p. 28, based on Oakes, *Philippians*, pp. 89-99. Fowl, *Philippians*, pp. 64-65, also following Oakes, concurs.

17. Flemming, *Philippians*, p. 28.

simply in emotional and tangible support during his imprisonment, but in  the actual "defense and confirmation of the gospel" (1:7):[18]

> [3]I thank my God every time I remember you, [4]constantly praying with joy in every one of my prayers for all of you, [5]because of your sharing [*koinōnia*] in the gospel from the first day until now. [6]I am confident of this, that the one who began a good work among you will bring it to completion by the day of Jesus Christ. [7]It is right for me to think this way about all of you, because you hold me in your heart, for all of you share in [*synkoinōnous*] God's grace with me, both in my imprisonment and in the defense [*apologia;* cf. 1:16[19]] and confirmation [*bebaiōsei*] of the gospel. [8]For God is my witness, how I long for all of you with the compassion of Christ Jesus. (Phil. 1:3-8)

They — all of the Philippian believers (1:7) — are part of the living witness to and *apologia* for the gospel. As Markus Bockmuehl puts it, the Philippians are partners with Paul and his team in the "public advocacy and corroboration of the gospel's truth and credibility."[20] For the Philippians as well as for Paul, the gospel's grace brings both salvation and suffering, both joy and challenge, but it also requires *pistis,* which means, as we saw in the previous chapter, both faith and faithfulness.[21] In the dynamic of this back-and-forth of challenge/suffering and trust/faithfulness lies the Philippians' public missional and apologetic identity.

Paul is convinced that his suffering will not derail the progress of the gospel — in fact it will help advance it (1:12) — and he seems to want to be sure that the Philippians know this about their situation, too. He informs the Philippian believers that "most of the brothers and sisters, having been made confident in the Lord by my imprisonment, dare to speak the word with greater boldness and without fear" (1:14). This sentence is highly signif-

---

18. So also Bockmuehl, *Philippians,* pp. 60, 64; Fowl, *Philippians,* pp. 23-25, 30-31; Flemming, *Philippians,* pp. 55-56. This is not to eliminate or minimize other aspects of the Philippians' partnership in the gospel, which include practical support of Paul in the form of finances and personal representatives (e.g., Epaphroditus [2:25-30]), intercessory prayer for Paul, living in conformity with the gospel, and suffering, in addition to verbal witness (so Flemming, "Exploring a Missional Reading," p. 10).

19. "I [Paul] have been put here [in prison] for the defense [*apologia*] of the gospel."

20. Bockmuehl, *Philippians,* p. 64.

21. Similarly, Fowl, *Philippians,* p. 30; John Reumann, *Philippians,* AB 33b (New Haven: Yale University Press, 2008), p. 291.

icant in at least three ways. First, it reveals that normal, everyday believers have been "speak[ing] the word" — sharing the gospel with family, friends, and associates — and are, for the most part, continuing to do so, with even greater fervor, despite Paul's imprisonment.[22] Second, then, the clear implication is that from Paul's perspective, evangelization is not just for apostles. "Speaking the word" — bearing witness to Christ, telling his story — is a normal activity for all Christians and all Christian communities. Paul will call this word the "word of life," or life-giving word, in Philippians 2:16. Third, the example of other believers remaining faithful and fervent in spite of the persecution of their apostle is meant to encourage the Philippians also to remain faithful and fervent, even in their own difficult circumstances.[23]

In fact, Paul says, the Philippians' suffering is a grace, a divine gift: "For he [God] has graciously granted you the privilege [*echaristhē*, related to *charis*, "grace"] not only of believing in Christ, but of suffering for him as well" (1:29). Accordingly, Paul offers the following admonition:

> [27]Only, live your life [or, better, "live out your citizenship as God's colony"; *politeuesthe*] in a manner worthy of the gospel of Christ, so that, whether

22. "Speaking [occasionally 'proclaiming' and once 'teaching'] the word" is a phrase more characteristic of Acts than of Paul's letters (Acts 4:29, 31; 8:4; 11:19; 13:5; 14:25; 15:35; 16:32; 17:13; 18:5, 11). In Acts it often refers to the activity of the apostles, but it is not restricted to them (see 8:4 and 11:19, each referring to the activity of those scattered by persecution). In Phil. 1:14 Paul uses his common terminology for all those in Christ, "brothers [and sisters]" *(adelphoi)*. There is therefore no reason, as most commentators recognize (e.g., Reumann, *Philippians*, p. 173; Flemming, *Philippians*, pp. 66-67; Bockmuehl, *Philippians*, p. 76), to restrict his reference in 1:14 to fellow apostles or missionary colleagues of Paul (contra John P. Dickson, *Mission Commitment in Ancient Judaism and in the Pauline Communities*, WUNT 2/159 [Tübingen: Mohr Siebeck, 2003], pp. 144-50), who argues that the presence of the definite article ["the"] before brothers here and elsewhere designates a class of official missionaries). The reference may, indeed, be implicitly restrictive, referring either to all those located near Paul's place of imprisonment (whether Rome, Ephesus, Caesarea, or wherever; so Reumann, *Philippians*, p. 197) or to all who are aware of his imprisonment. The qualifying phrase "most of" in 1:14 suggests reticence on the part of some, which is something more likely to be said of a (relatively) large body of believers rather than a small group of traveling evangelists. The references to "brothers [NRSV 'friends'] who are with me" and "[a]ll the saints" in 4:21-22 do not distinguish between a formal group of missionaries who are in solidarity with Paul and believers more broadly (so Dickson, *Mission Commitment*, pp. 148-49), but rather between believers who are with or near Paul in his imprisonment (e.g., visitors, including a scribe) and all those in the region of Paul's imprisonment.

23. As Bockmuehl notes, "it would have been a socially risky and costly business to identify publicly with a prisoner" (*Philippians*, p. 76).

I come and see you or am absent and hear about you, I will know that you are standing firm in one spirit, striving side by side with one mind for the faith of the gospel, [28]and are in no way intimidated by your opponents. (Phil. 1:27-28a)[24]

This short passage reveals several hopes that Paul has for the community of believers at Philippi:

- that their life together be worthy of the gospel;
- that they stand firm and united in their proclamation of the gospel; and
- that they not be intimidated by opposition.

In other words, Paul wants them to continue to proclaim the gospel with their lives and their lips, to continue becoming and telling the story of Christ despite persecution. "This is a 'mission statement,' if there ever were one."[25]

There is more than a hint early in the letter that Paul fears that the Philippians may give in to pressure and *not* fulfill his expectations, *not* strive for the faith of the gospel, *not* live worthily of the gospel.[26] He implies as well that they should share in his attitude, even if their situation is not yet as serious as his:

It is my eager expectation and hope that I will not be put to shame in any way, but that by my speaking with all boldness, Christ will be exalted now as always in my body, whether by life or by death. (Phil. 1:20)

The language Paul uses here and elsewhere in Philippians 1 about suffering for faithful witness to the gospel is quite similar to the language used in Mark's Gospel (and parallels) to report what Jesus himself said about suffering for the gospel and how he said it. In both Mark 8, for instance, and Philippians 1 we find mention of

---

24. See below for discussion of the translation of this verse.

25. Flemming, "Exploring a Missional Reading," p. 12.

26. So also James P. Ware, *Paul and the Mission of the Church: Philippians in Ancient Jewish Context* (Grand Rapids: Baker Academic, 2011), pp. 222-23, who thinks that this is why Paul stresses active missionizing by the congregation in this letter (esp. in 2:16) but not elsewhere. This is another aspect of the Philippian church that is similar to the Thessalonian situation — Paul's concern about his converts' endurance and faithfulness.

- openness and boldness (*parrēsia* in both Mark 8:32 [NRSV "openly"] and Phil. 1:20 [NRSV "boldness"]; cf. Phil. 1:14);
- suffering (*paschein* and cognates in both Mark 8:31 and Phil. 1:17, 29, as well as 3:10);
- avoiding shame (*epaischynomai* in Mark 8:38; *aischynomai* in Phil. 1:20);
- and gaining [life, salvation] (*kerdainō* in Mark 8:36 as well as Phil. 3:8; and *kerdos* in Phil. 1:21; 3:7).

Moreover, these are all in reference to

- the gospel (*euangelion* in Mark 8:35; Phil. 1:5, 7, 12, 16, 27) and
- the coming of the Son of Man/day of Christ (Mark 8:38; Phil. 1:6, 10; cf. 2:16).[27]

This similarity in language raises interesting questions about the relationship between these texts (possible common influences or sources, or one borrowing from the other) that cannot be addressed here. What does seem clear, however, is that Paul is using language that is common in the so-called Jesus tradition. Is Paul reminding them of what he knows they have already heard about Jesus' own teaching, which was perhaps part of what he himself had taught them when he founded the church?

That this question should be answered in the affirmative seems highly likely, and the implications are, once again, quite significant. For one thing, learning about Jesus' teaching and the demands of discipleship would not be restricted to so-called "missionaries" but would be for all believers. Furthermore, if the Philippians were taught that following Jesus included bold witness with the possibility of suffering for *all* disciples, then Paul's reminders about the cost of discipleship are just that — reminders: reminders about the call to faithful witness, the need to accept shame and suffering, and the consequences both of remaining faithful and of failing to do so. Paul agrees with Jesus that some form of faithful public witness in life and words is the norm for all Jesus' followers. It is not restricted to "missionaries."[28]

Perhaps Paul worries that the Philippians will stop confessing that Jesus, rather than Caesar, is Lord and therefore return to public behaviors that

---

27. See further my *The Death of the Messiah and the Birth of the New Covenant: A (Not So) New Model of the Atonement* (Eugene, OR: Cascade, 2014), ch. 4 (pp. 77-105).

28. Perhaps the clearest summary of this in the New Testament writings in the Pauline tradition is 2 Tim. 3:12: "Indeed, all who want to live a godly life in Christ Jesus will be persecuted."

demonstrate their loyalty to Rome and their acceptance of Roman values and ideologies — the Roman "gospel," the Roman master narrative.[29] For this reason he turns to *his* master story — which is really not his, but God's — in order to encourage their faithfulness, unity, gospel-living, and gospel-telling.

## Paul's Gospel/Master Story: An Overview

In his commentary on Philippians, John Reumann claims that Philippians 2:6-11 is in fact the gospel the Philippians preached, the gospel for which they suffered and of which their lives must be worthily lived. He writes, "Paul employs in vv 6-11 an encomium [speech in praise of someone or something] the Philippians had worked out to use in mission proclamation about Christ and God in their Greco-Roman world."[30] This suggestion differs from my own view that 2:6-11 contains *Paul's* master story, which is not particular to this letter or community, but Reumann and I agree that it is indeed the narrative that Paul wants the Philippian assembly to embrace, proclaim, and embody, in spite of some internal dissension and significant external opposition. Thus its very presence in the letter reveals the text's missional character in two senses.

First, the Philippians 2:6-11 text tells the story of the *missio Dei*, of God's activity with respect to humanity and indeed the entire cosmos. In 2:16, as we have already noted, Paul calls this "the word of life," the word that effects salvation and thus true life, "the power of God for salvation," as Paul says in Romans (Rom. 1:16). More specifically, this divine mission is carried out, obviously, through the mission of Christ. Richard Bauckham has persuasively argued that Philippians 2:6-11 is an early Christian reinterpretation of Isaiah

---

29. It is now widely recognized that Rome had a sort of gospel, an ideology enshrined in narratives about the emperor(s) and the empire, that could even use the language of "good news." One famous example is the calendrical inscription of 9 BCE found at Priene and elsewhere celebrating the good news *(euangelia)* of the birth of Augustus, the savior and bringer of peace. N. T. Wright speaks of a Roman *Heilsgeschichte*, or salvation history *(Paul and the Faithfulness of God,* vol. 4 of Christian Origins and the Question of God [Minneapolis: Fortress, 2013], p. xv), which even has its own "climax" — Augustus and his golden age (pp. 298-311).

30. Reumann, *Philippians,* p. 333. Reumann thinks it was a "tool for missionary outreach, to evangelize in Roman culture by people who lived in it, and so advance the gospel (1:5, 12, 27), reworking what they had learned from Paul in idioms of their own" (p. 363). On the form as "encomium" (about Christ and God), see his pp. 364-77. Reumann's main point is that the text is deliberately very Roman, both to echo and to subvert Roman theologies and ideologies. Reumann thinks Paul took the Philippians' missional encomium and applied it to their internal life and to their public witness (p. 365).

40–55, especially Isaiah 53 (Isa. 52:13–53:12), with Christ understood as the missional Servant of YHWH.[31] Similarly, Gregory Bloomquist has argued that the text is not about a Christology of humiliation and exaltation per se but "a depiction of the suffering of God's servant *in the light of the servant's mission*."[32] And James Ware has shown that the Isaianic servant songs (Isa. 42:1-4; 49:1-6; 50:4-9; 52:13–53:12) shaped Second Temple Jewish thought about an eschatological witness to the nations, a servant-mission that shapes Paul's own missional theology, especially in Philippians.[33]

Second, Philippians 2:6-11 presents to its auditors, or perhaps recalls for them, a story that, once believed, can and indeed must be both told to others and lived for others. It is a narrative to be both proclaimed and performed, or, perhaps better, proclaimed in deed as well as in word. Paul and the Philippians share in the servant-mission of Christ the Lord. Writes Bloomquist: "Paul depicts not only Jesus' experience in terms of the Isaian suffering servant, but also his own experience, the experiences of his co-workers, and those of the Philippians in terms of the same figure."[34] More specifically, James Ware argues persuasively that for Paul (and early Christians more generally) the death and especially the exaltation of the Servant Jesus as Lord was the inauguration of the eschatological age that would mean the conversion of the Gentiles to YHWH. Thus the church — meaning all believers — proclaims submission to the lordship of Jesus to all people in the present in anticipation of the final universal proclamation of his sovereignty.[35]

*That is to say, Philippians 2:6-11 is a missional Christology for a missional people.*

We will return to this claim below with some detailed exegetical com-

---

31. Richard Bauckham, *Jesus and the God of Israel: God Crucified and Other Studies on the New Testament's Christology of Divine Identity* (Grand Rapids: Eerdmans, 2009), esp. pp. 197-210; Wright, *Paul and the Faithfulness of God*, p. 683. See also Ware, *Paul and the Mission*, pp. 224-33. Cf. Bockmuehl, *Philippians*, pp. 135-36; Fowl, *Philippians*, p. 117. I actually argued this same thesis in my first paper on Philippians noted above; see also my *Cruciformity*, pp. 90, 316-19; and my *Apostle of the Crucified Lord*, pp. 422-23, 434-38.

32. L. Gregory Bloomquist, *The Function of Suffering in Philippians*, Journal for the Study of the New Testament: Supplement Series 78 (Sheffield: JSOT, 1993), p. 167 (emphasis added). Bloomquist goes too far in prefacing this insightful remark with the claim that the context and function of the passage demonstrate that "2.6-11 is not a presentation of Christology — that is, reflection on the abasement of the Lord and his exaltation after death." This is a false dichotomy; the text is both Christological and missional.

33. Ware, *Paul and the Mission*, 93-155.

34. Bloomquist, *Function of Suffering*, p. 167.

35. Ware, *Paul and the Mission*, pp. 224-33.

ments that will, I hope, demonstrate the truth of this characterization of our text. First, however, we need to take a step back and consider some basic but essential aspects of this rich poetic passage. We begin with an interpretive translation of 2:6-11 and its introductory sentence (2:5, linking it to what precedes) that will highlight some of its key features, which we will then discuss briefly.

## The Translation of Philippians 2:5-11

I offer the following translation of Paul's master story and its brief preface:

⁵Cultivate this mindset — this way of thinking, acting, and feeling[36] — in your community, which is in fact a community in Christ Jesus,

⁶who, *although* being in the form of God,
and indeed *because of* being in the form of God,

did not consider this equality with God as something to be exploited for
     his own advantage,

⁷but rather emptied himself,
    by taking the form of a slave,
       that is, by being born in the likeness of human beings.

And being found in human form,
⁸he humbled himself
    by becoming obedient to death —
       even death on a Roman cross.

―――――――――――――――――――

⁹Therefore God has highly exalted him
    and bestowed on him the name that is above every name,

¹⁰so that at the mention/name of Jesus
    every knee should bend, yes,
       in heaven and
       on earth and
       under the earth,
¹¹and every tongue acclaim,

36. See Fowl, *Philippians*, pp. 88-90; cf. pp. 28-29.

"Jesus the Jewish Messiah is the universal Lord and bearer of the
divine name,"

to the glory of God the Father.[37]

## Some Exegetical Comments[38]

### 1. Preface

The story is introduced by a line (2:5) that connects the story of Christ to the
story of the community, and about which translators have argued for a very
long time. Two basic options have been proposed: "Have the mind that was
in Christ" or "that Christ had" (e.g., NRSV, CEB, NET, NIV) or "Have the
mind which is yours in Christ" (e.g., NAB, RSV). I have argued numerous
times, however, that the correct translation depends on seeing the Greek
phrase *ho kai* — meaning "which also" or "which indeed" — as linking two
parallel prepositional phrases *(en hymin* and *en Christō Iēsou)* and is something like the following:

> "Cultivate this mindset
> within your community *(en hymin),*
>     which is in fact *(ho kai)*
> a community in Christ Jesus *(en Christō Iēsou),*
> who. . . ."

(I am still hoping that an actual Bible translation will adopt this.[39])

### 2. Background

Many "backgrounds" have been proposed for our text; I would argue that
allusions to at least three other important narratives are present: those of

37. A similar chiastic arrangement of verses 9-11 was presented by Erik Waaler in a paper called "Israel's Scripture in Phil. 2:5-11," delivered at the annual meeting of the Society of
Biblical Literature in New Orleans on November 23, 2009.

38. More detailed development of these points may be found in "'Although/Because he
was in the Form of God': The Theological Significance of Paul's Master Story (Phil. 2:6-11)," ch.
1 of my *Inhabiting the Cruciform God*; in *Cruciformity*, pp. 88-92, 164-69, et passim; and in the
chapter on Philippians in *Apostle of the Crucified Lord* (pp. 412-53). For a very similar overall
interpretation, see Wright, *Paul and the Faithfulness of God*, pp. 680-89.

39. For further discussion, see esp. *Cruciformity*, pp. 39-44.

Adam, the Suffering Servant, and the Roman emperor. The text depicts Christ simultaneously as the new Adam (or perhaps Adam's antitype), God's Suffering Servant, and the true lord of the cosmos — the last in contrast to false claims of and about the emperor.

### 3. Starting Point

As already noted,[40] I have also argued that the opening participle (*hyparchōn*, "being") should be understood both concessively ("although") and causally ("because"). The former, "although being" or "although he was," is what we might call the text's *surface* structure, while the latter, "because of being" or "because he was," is its *deep* structure. Both are significant.

### 4. Structure

As many have recognized, the story has two main parts, verses 6-8 and verses 9-11, narrating first Christ's freely chosen humiliation and then God's subsequent exaltation of him; they are linked by the "therefore" of 2:9. Furthermore, the structure of 2:6-8, as we suggested in the previous chapter,[41] may be described as "Although/because [x] not [y] but [z]," where [x], [y], and [z] refer to [x] status, [y] selfish exploitation (which is negated), and [z] self-renunciation and self-giving, meaning (positively) other-centeredness and obedience. Within this chain, the [z] is further divided into two parts, referring to Christ's incarnation and then crucifixion. The whole sequence is kenotic, or self-emptying, and downwardly oriented in stages. It is an un-Roman c.v. of shame, we might say, or *cursus pudorum* — a course of ignominies.[42] This can be portrayed as follows:

| Although/because of | [x] | being in the form of God |
|---|---|---|
| [he] did not | [y] | consider this equality with God as something to be exploited for his own advantage, |

40. See n. 6 above.

41. In the previous chapter we looked only at the surface structure, "although . . . ," of the beginning of the text.

42. See Joseph H. Hellerman, *Reconstructing Honor in Roman Philippi: Carmen Christi as Cursus Pudorum,* SNTS Monograph Series 132 (Cambridge: Cambridge University Press, 2005).

but rather          [$z_1$] emptied himself
                              by taking the form of a slave,
                              that is, by being born in the likeness of
                              human beings.

And                       being found in human form,

he                      [$z_2$] humbled himself by becoming obedient to
                              death — even death on a Roman cross.

### 5. Christology

The text begins by acknowledging Christ's preexisting equality with God. It then explicitly depicts Christ's freely chosen incarnation and crucifixion as, paradoxically, his faithful obedience (i.e., to God the Father; v. 8) and implicitly, in the immediate context of 2:1-4,[43] as his act of self-giving and life-giving love for others that reveals both the character of God and the will of God for creation. This is why we should refer to this text's Christology as a *missional Christology.* God's vindication of Christ in his exaltation as Lord and receipt of the divine name (*kyrios,* or perhaps even, implicitly, YHWH) does not reduce but enhances the glory of God the Father as creation acknowledges its proper sovereign. Jesus shares in the divine name (identity) and thus in the divine worship (see Isa. 45:23).

### 6. Worship

The divinely willed result of Christ's lordship is the acclamation of that lordship by all creation. The question of whether that universal acclamation is present or future poses something of a false dichotomy. Although the universal acclamation *in toto* is of course future, it is anticipated by the church's present acclamation, an acclamation that is ever-expansive and ever-more universal as the gospel progresses throughout the world in spite of attempts

43. Paul prefaces the poem/master story with its application to the Philippians and, in so doing, guides our interpretation of the poem itself as a story of love, humility, and regard for others: "[1]If then there is any encouragement in Christ, any consolation from love, any sharing in the Spirit, any compassion and sympathy, [2]make my joy complete: be of the same mind, having the same love, being in full accord and of one mind. [3]Do nothing from selfish ambition or conceit, but in humility regard others as better than yourselves. [4]Let each of you look not to your own interests, but to the interests of others."

to arrest it by arresting its leaders and persecuting at least some of the faithful. Christ is the alternative Lord who rules as God's Servant over this alternative world-empire.

## The Function of the Text in Its Immediate Context and in the Philippian Community

It is important to recognize that 2:6-11 is linked back to 2:1-4 by 2:5, and that 2:1-4 is linked back in turn to 1:27-30 by the phrase "If therefore" *(oun)* in 2:1 (NRSV "If then"). The narrative sequence in the letter is mission → community life → Christology, but the theo-logic of the text is the reverse: Christology → community life → mission. It is in this way that *Philippians 2:6-11 is, once again, a missional Christology for a missional people. Paul's master story is inextricably connected to the missional and apologetic concerns of Paul in writing to the Philippians that emerge in chapter one of the letter.* This poetic text — whether heard as part of Paul's letter or recited, perhaps even sung, in worship — serves at least three missional and formational functions, corresponding to faith, love, and hope — the same triad we examined in considering 1 Thessalonians.

First, faith, or *pistis.* This text in 2:6-11 provides the content of the gospel for the Philippians. This is what Paul, the Philippians, and (I would argue) all other Pauline congregations believe.[44] If conversion is *"the conscious adoption of a new . . . master stor[y] in the commitment to reshape one's life in a new community of interpretation and action,"*[45] then this is the master story to which the Philippians have been converted, having left behind one or more of the other master stories on offer in Roman Philippi. It is for this message that they suffer, and they do so with the same kind of *pistis,* or faithful obedience, that they see in the Christ of the text.[46] The text helps the Philippians

44. There are, of course, other summaries of the gospel in Paul (e.g., 1 Cor. 15:3ff.), and they would, in my estimation, be complementary to this one. If Reumann is correct, Phil. 2:6-11 is the Philippians' adaptation of Paul's gospel to their specific, very Roman missional context. But in my view, the structure and content of 2:6-11 so thoroughly permeate Paul's letters (as I have argued in multiple places) that the text is much more likely Paul's own, and indeed his master story.

45. See James S. Fowler, *Stages of Faith: The Psychology of Human Development and the Quest for Meaning* (San Francisco: HarperSanFrancisco, 1982), p. 282. I have altered Fowler's original wording, which is *"adoption of a new set of master stories."*

46. We should equate the obedience of Christ with the faith(fulness) of Christ men-

*moral calling*

know that to which they bear witness and prepares them for faithful witness, even perhaps martyrdom. It "functions, within the full paraenetic context of 1:12–2:18, as an exhortation to courageous partnership with Paul for the extension of the gospel of Christ."[47]

Second, the story reveals the nature of love. Although the word "love" does not appear explicitly in the story, the immediate context of 2:1-4 uses the word love (2:2; *agapē*) as well as other words and phrases (2:3-4) that echo Paul's description of love elsewhere, most especially the exhortation not to seek one's own interests:[48]

> Do nothing from selfish ambition or conceit, but in humility regard others as better than yourselves. Let each of you look not to your own interests *(ta heautōn),* but to the interests of others *(ta heterōn).* (Phil. 2:3-4)

> [Love] does not seek its own interests *(ta heautēs).* . . . (1 Cor. 13:5 MJG; NRSV "insist on its own way")

> Do not seek your own advantage *(to heautou),* but that of the other *(tou heterou).* (1 Cor. 10:24)

> . . . just as I [Paul] try to please everyone in everything I do, not seeking my own advantage *(to emautou symphoron),* but that of many, so that they may be saved. (1 Cor. 10:33)

The community's internal life of unity through *agapē* is to be a Spirit-empowered, Christ-shaped, living exegesis of the master story. The syntactical and semantic correspondences between 2:6-8 and 2:1-4 are re-

---

tioned in 3:9 *(pistis Christou),* which is best rendered "faith of Christ" rather than "faith in Christ" (NRSV). If this translation is accepted, then Christ's faith(fulness) is equated with his obedience, referring principally to his death, also in Romans (Rom. 3:22, 26 [faith] = Rom. 5:19 [obedience]). As we noted in the previous chapter, this connection explains Paul's characterization of his evangelistic goal as "the obedience of faith" (Rom. 1:5; 16:26), or faithful obedience/obedient faith.

47. Ware, *Paul and the Mission,* p. 232. For an overall position similar to Ware's treatment of Philippians 1–2, see Mark J. Keown, *Congregational Evangelism in Philippians: The Centrality of an Appeal for Gospel Proclamation to the Fabric of Philippians* (Milton Keynes, UK: Paternoster, 2008; Eugene, OR: Cascade, 2009). Keown argues that "proactive ecclesiological evangelistic mission" is "essential to the fabric of Philippians" (p. 273).

48. See also the reference to "the compassion of Christ Jesus" (Bockmuehl, *Philippians,* p. 65: "affectionate love") in 1:8.

markable.[49] Yet even the exhortations to unity in the community are not intended merely to create internal harmony; they serve to ensure the community's public witness to the gospel "in one Spirit" (1:27; MJG).[50] Paul's exhortations to Christlike regard for the welfare of others is spoken with the same urgency and in the same idiom whether he is speaking about internal harmony in the community of believers (Phil. 2:1-4; 1 Cor. 13:5) or about believers' external witness to others (1 Cor. 10:24, 33).[51] As Steve Fowl comments in reflecting on Western individualism:

> If we are to unlearn our commitments to individualism and to begin to embody the sort of common life to which Paul and the Philippians call us, we must come to share with them the sense of being caught up into the movement of God's economy of salvation. . . . Unless and until we see our lives as having been incorporated into that larger drama of redemption, we will never be able to see the necessity for the sort of ecclesial common life Paul urges on the Philippians.[52]

Thus there can be no dichotomy between the community's inner life and its external life. It is "in Christ" (2:5) all of the time, marked (Paul hopes) by unity and love. It is this same life-story that is embodied in the public square (cf. 1:27).[53] To live *worthily* of the gospel (Phil. 1:27) is simply to *live* the gospel, the story of self-giving love, in the world. Markus Bockmuehl, like many other interpreters, reminds us that the political and public overtones of the verb *politeuesthai* in 1:27 (despite NRSV's pale "live your life") need to be recognized: the word in Jewish sources means "walk" or "live" only if understood as "the adoption of a Jewish lifestyle . . . conceived as a deliberate, publicly visible,

---

49. See Gorman, *Cruciformity,* pp. 254-58.

50. Curiously, the NRSV, like most other translations, has "one spirit," missing the connection to 2:1. (But see the NIV: "in the one Spirit.")

51. In fact, 1 Cor. 10:24 and 33 apply, in the context of 1 Cor. 8:1–11:1, both to treatment of others in the community (cf. 1 Cor. 8:1-13) and to treatment of nonbelievers (1 Cor. 10:27-31). This is especially clear in 1 Cor. 10:32-33, where Jews, Greeks, and the church are distinguished as three separate "entities" but unified in being worthy of the same kind of loving, missional treatment: "Give no offense to Jews or to Greeks or to the church of God, just as I try to please everyone in everything I do, not seeking my own advantage, but that of many, so that they may be saved."

52. Fowl, *Philippians,* p. 88.

53. Reumann (*Philippians,* p. 284) says rightly that 1:27-30 "calls Philippian believers to express in *politeia* (public space) and relationships with one another *(ekklēsia)* what being 'in Christ' means."

and (at least in the broad sense) *politically relevant* act which in the context is distinguished from alternative lifestyles that might have been chosen instead."[54]

This ("Christian") lifestyle is one of servant-love, whether in the church or in the public square — no matter how that activity is understood or misunderstood by outsiders. Fowl therefore rightly translates the beginning of Philippians 1:27 as "Order your common life in a manner worthy of the gospel of Christ";[55] even more to the point might be something like "Conduct your common life as God's colony in the public square of Rome's colony in a manner worthy of the gospel of Christ" (MJG).[56] This is, truly, "God's politics." Which means, of course, that the church is called to be a faithful public performance, in word and deed, of the Christ-story in 2:6-11.[57]

As with the Thessalonians, it is the proclamation and embodiment of the Christ-story that has gotten the Philippians into trouble. Now they must continue to actualize or embody their corporate salvation,[58] holding forth, and holding fast to, the word of life (see further below). This is of course an act of Christlike faithfulness, but it is also fundamentally an act of love. Admittedly, Paul does not say this explicitly, any more than he here explicitly calls Christ's incarnation and death an act of love. But the context requires the interpretation of both Christ's story and the community's story in terms

---

54. Bockmuehl, *Philippians*, p. 97.

55. Fowl, *Philippians*, p. 59.

56. Cf. Bockmuehl: "live as worthy citizens of the gospel of Christ" (*Philippians*, p. 96). Ross Wagner ("Working Out Salvation," p. 258) similarly stresses the "public, communal life."

57. So also Bockmuehl, *Philippians*, 98. See as well especially Fowl's commentary and his *The Story of Christ in the Ethics of Paul*, Journal for the Study of the New Testament: Supplement Series 36 (Sheffield: Sheffield Academic Press, 1990), pp. 77-101. Ware (*Paul and the Mission*, p. 216), commenting on 1:27, argues that the phrase "the gospel of Christ" in Paul always refers to "missionizing proclamation" (with p. 216 n. 51 referring to Rom. 15:19; 1 Cor. 9:12; 2 Cor. 2:12; 9:13; 10:14; Gal. 1:7; 1 Thess. 3:2) rather than catechesis. He concludes that the "opening imperative of the letter [1:27] thus accents Paul's interest in a missional purpose of the life and conduct of the community at Philippi *as a means of attracting outsiders* to the message of Christ" (p. 26, emphasis added). I think Ware confuses the possible result of faithfulness to the Christ-story (conversion of others) with its alleged purpose, but that may be picking nits.

58. The imperatives and pronouns are plural in 2:12-16. Ware (*Paul and the Mission*, p. 241, summarizing his argument in the following pages) goes too far in claiming that 2:12-18 is "an exhortation to suffer for the spread of the gospel" (cf. p. 247 et passim). Suffering is always for Paul a result of faithfulness, not an end in itself, and faithfulness means more than just evangelistic activity. Brian K. Peterson, in "Being the Church in Philippi," *Horizons in Biblical Theology* 30 (2008): 163-78, also justly accuses Ware of overemphasizing faithfulness as proclamation (p. 169), but then he in turn goes too far, throughout the article, in rejecting proclamation as part of faithful embodiment. See further below.

of love. A life worthy of the gospel is a life of cruciform love, not only in the community but also in the public square. Just as love compelled Christ to become human and to be faithfully obedient even to death at the hands of Romans, so also the community in Christ will remain faithful to preaching the gospel in word and deed because it is compelled by love to do so. Just as Paul loved and loves the Philippians (1:1-8, 24), so also the Philippians can live worthily of the gospel only if they love the world sufficiently to bear witness to it. Just as John 3:16 — "God so loved the world" — has missional implications for the church to love the world, so also "Christ emptied himself and humbled himself in love" has missional implications for the church to love the world in incarnational and cruciform ways. In any way to limit the Christ-story to one of salvation for me or us is to rip the first half of the poem from its missional context in both the poem itself and the letter.

Third, and finally, the master story gives hope, and it does so in at least two ways. For one thing, the story will reassure the Philippian believers that their message of Jesus' Lordship really is true and cannot be stopped; in fact, it will one day be acknowledged everywhere and by every creature (2:10-11). No matter what the current opposition, "the truth will out." Furthermore, the story will reassure those who hear and believe it that just as God vindicated their obedient and loving Lord, the one who suffered at the hands of Roman authorities, God will also vindicate them when they are faithful and loving in the midst of Roman hostility. Paul makes this vindication explicit later in the letter (3:20-21). Faithfulness and love require hope to sustain them, and the story of Christ in Philippians 2:6-11 offers such hope.

## An Evangelistic Community?

I have been suggesting that Paul's master story not only expresses the *missio Dei,* the mission of God, but also encourages the Philippians to remain steadfast and loving in bearing witness to that story, thus participating in and extending the *missio Dei.* But of course there has been debate about what the Philippians are supposed to do with the master story, i.e., what does Paul mean when he uses the verb *epechō* in 2:16: "_____ing the word of life"? I want to suggest that the debate about "holding fast" (i.e., continuing to believe)[59] or

---

59. E.g., Bockmuehl, *Philippians,* pp. 158-59, because he finds no early Christian use of the verb for evangelistic activity. See also NRSV, ESV, RSV: "holding fast [to]"; NAB, CEB, NET: "hold[ing] on to"; NIV, NLT "hold firmly to."

"holding forth" (i.e., proclaiming)[60] may be a legitimate linguistic issue, but theologically and practically it is a false dichotomy. One does not need to hold fast — the preferred translation of *epechontes* for most scholars — unless one has first held forth (whether or not that is the specific meaning of *epechontes*). Only the reality of pushback to a public witness (public in the sense of outside the believing community, even if in a private setting), and the corollary temptation to capitulate, makes sense of Paul's exhortation in Philippians 2:16 in light of the events to which he refers in chapter 1.

But the exhortation in 2:16 still needs attention. James Ware, especially in his book *Paul and the Mission of the Church,* has been the most vocal scholarly proponent of the translation "holding forth." Brian Peterson has taken on Ware and other advocates of that view, arguing that Paul did not encourage the Philippians (or any other congregation) to actively evangelize others.[61] Rather, Peterson argues, Paul wants them just to be like Jesus, embodying the master story in their inner communal life and doing good to outsiders, living out "their identity in Christ as God's new creation in the face of empire," their life itself being the church's "calling and its mission."[62] Peterson assumes that "evangelism" means something like delivering tracts door-to-door with the goal of growing the church numerically.[63] If that is what evangelism is, then I would agree that Paul probably did not encourage his congregations to do that. (If for no other reason, the cost of papyrus and scribal services would have been beyond the Philippians' meager budget!)

Peterson, I suggest, is right in what he affirms and wrong in what he denies. He is right to insist that Paul's preoccupation is with faithful communal cruciform existence, not numerical growth, especially not by something like door-to-door evangelism. But he is wrong to suggest that verbal witness and expansion of the church are not part of Paul's goal for his churches.

First, as Peterson himself states, Paul wants the church to spread throughout the Roman empire as an alternative dominion with an alterna-

---

60. Ware (*Paul and the Mission,* p. 269, summarizing pp. 256-70) argues that "hold forth" is "the only possible meaning" for *epechō* in 2:16. I am inclined to agree, but the points I will make here do not depend on the correctness of Ware's argument. The GNT had "offer them," but the CEV changed to "hold firmly to" and put the GNT rendering in a note. See also earlier editions of the NIV: "hold out."

61. Peterson, "Being the Church," pp. 163-78.

62. Peterson, "Being the Church," p. 163.

63. For Peterson's argument against a Pauline fixation on numerical increase, over against the assumption of most modern "evangelism committees" (p. 165), see "Being the Church," pp. 165, 170.

tive emperor.[64] Second, there is evidence that certain churches in the Pauline regions collaborated and affected one another, including in their evangelizing efforts (especially Colossae, Laodicea, and Hierapolis, but also perhaps Corinth and Cenchreae).[65] Finally, and most importantly, it is counterintuitive, and indeed it stretches the limits of credulity, to imagine that the early Pauline communities simply did good to their neighbors and assembled to worship Jesus as Lord, practicing communal cruciformity in a kind of holy huddle, even a publicly visible holy huddle, without ever explaining either kind of behavior to their friends or inviting them to participate. If such silence was the norm in the Pauline communities, specifically at Philippi, why did they co-suffer for the gospel with their community founder and their community Lord?

*This is what we do*

Such suffering can only be explained if verbal witness — with or without the goal of conversion, but probably with that goal — was an integral and indeed routine aspect of the life of those in these Pauline communities. Thus to "hold fast" would mean, in part, to "hold forth" — i.e., not to cower but to *keep* holding forth. Holding forth, in fact, is the public evidence (again defining "public" as "outside the believing community") of holding fast. Otherwise, if "holding fast" meant only "keeping an internal conviction" or "sharing your faith in secret with fellow believers," there would be no need for Paul to tell the church that suffering is a grace and to reassure the church that the Christological narrative of servant-suffering followed by exaltation is also their narrative.

As John Howard Yoder often said, and Brian Peterson implies, the first task of the church is simply to be the church. In a sense, then, Ross Wagner is completely right that Paul "does not need to exhort the Philippians to engage in mission" because "they themselves *are* a proclamation of the rectifying power of God."[66] But that kind of "being" is inseparable from verbal witness, or evangelism (even if it is "soft" evangelism, i.e., responsive to inquiry rather than proactive), for at least three reasons:

---

64. Peterson, "Being the Church," pp. 173-78.

65. See Col. 4:7-18, where churches in Laodicea and Hierapolis are mentioned to the Colossians, and Rom. 16:1-3, where Phoebe of Cenchreae and Prisca (Priscilla) and Aquila, associated with nearby Corinth (Acts 18:2; 1 Cor. 16:19), are mentioned together. Although Paul did not found the church at Colossae (Col. 1:7 indicating that Epaphras did), and probably not at Laodicea or Hierapolis, Colossians reveals that they are interconnected because of Paul and his associates (or perhaps later "disciples").

66. Wagner, "Working Out Salvation," pp. 271-72; similarly, *inter alia,* Flemming, *Philippians,* p. 43.

1. because human existence is inherently relational and therefore communicative;

2. because opposition to behavior requires interpretation of that behavior and, normally, defense of it — successful or not — by the accused party;[67] and

3. the master story of Jesus is not simply about a self-giving prophet who inspires self-giving, but a claim about the nature of deity and lordship that exposes all other claims to deity and lordship as the false rivals that they are.[68] The Philippians' story is, in other words, inherently polemical, a kind of benevolent subversion, or apocalypse, or even "sabotage." As C. S. Lewis wrote:

> One of the things that surprised me when I first read the New Testament seriously was that it talked so much about a Dark Power in the universe — a mighty evil spirit who was held to be the Power behind death and disease, and sin. The difference is that Christianity thinks this Dark Power was created by God, and was good when he was created, and went wrong. Christianity agrees with Dualism that this universe is at war. But it does not think this is a war between independent powers. It thinks it is a civil war, a rebellion, and that we are living in a part of the universe occupied by the rebel. Enemy-occupied territory — that is what this world is. Christianity is the story of how the rightful king has landed, you might say landed in disguise, and is calling us all to take part in a great campaign of sabotage.[69]

Such a divine invasion of human history is only benevolent sabotage when its subversive activity is consistent with the loving servant-form of its Lord narrated in the master story. (Of course those being subverted will not normally perceive it, apart from grace, as benevolent sabotage.) At the same time, its servant activity only makes ultimate theological and practical sense, and only survives persecution, when it is connected to the acclamation that this crucified Jesus really is the revelation of God's identity and mission and really is the Lord of the world. And, to recall N. T. Wright's oft-heard phrase, "If Jesus is Lord, Caesar is not"; neither is Zeus or Apollo or Serapis or any other pseudo-deity. At some point, at many points, the Philippian believers

---

67. See also the discussion of the situation in Thessalonica in the previous chapter.

68. I owe the precise wording of this point to Andy Johnson.

69. C. S. Lewis, *Mere Christianity* (New York: HarperCollins, 2001 [orig. 1952]), pp. 46-47 (end of chap. 2).

must have made that claim to others in some way, shape, or form. In other words, the (alleged) dictum of Francis of Assisi, "Preach the gospel at all times; when necessary, use words," does not quite mesh with Paul's understanding of becoming the gospel; witness-bearing calls for interpretation.[70] "Walking little old ladies across the street" may be appropriate Christian behavior, but it does not lead to persecution. It only leads to persecution when one explains such behavior as a manifestation of true power, or when one excuses oneself from attending an event honoring the emperor, the empire, or other cultural deities — like youth soccer or professional football or a Fourth of July parade — in order to walk those little old ladies across the street, or to worship as Lord the one who essentially did the same thing when he willingly became humanity's slave.

## Life Together: Reading Philippians 2:6-11 Missionally Today

The last comment in the previous section may sound rather less like historical analysis than a hermeneutical jab. But it leads us naturally to reflect more directly, theologically and missionally, on our own context for reading Philippians 2:6-11. We turn, then, to the hermeneutical question, the "so what" of our study. What does it mean to read the Christ-poem and the letter in which it appears missionally?

### Fellowship and Worship as Preparation for Mission

I have suggested that Philippians 2:6-11 is, for Paul, the church's master story that it recites in some form, as creed or poem or hymn, when it gathers for worship. The text's immediate context suggests that the story it tells is inextricably connected both to the church's life together as *koinōnia* in the Spirit (2:1-4) and to its mission in the world (2:12-16), a mission of action accompanied by interpretive speech, a simultaneous becoming and interpreting.

Thus to recite the story of the Messiah Jesus liturgically is to remember the narrative shape of the One who, by the power of the Spirit, lives among us (and within whom we live) to form and re-form us into his image such that our individual and corporate narratives more faithfully resemble his.

---

70. It is highly unlikely that Francis said this or anything like it. Moreover, he was as much a preacher as a doer.

This brings glory to the Father. Worship of this God as Father, Son, and Spirit is therefore an exercise in spiritual formation for faithful living — for centripetal and centrifugal activity.

Part of that worship — its high point if we follow the trajectory of the story — is confessing "Jesus is Lord." To confess Jesus as Lord, to the glory of God the Father, in the fellowship of the Spirit is relatively easy to do in the safety of a community of the like-minded. But as a group of Christians makes this confession week in and week out, or (better) day in and day out, and as it keeps that confession connected to the larger story, it becomes empowered to live and proclaim that story faithfully outside of its own walls.

Here the insights of Aristotle and Thomas on virtue are worth considering. We become what we practice. Our liturgical habits make it possible, or not, to live and tell the story faithfully, even naturally, over time — or not. Churches that dispense with the telling of the story, perhaps in the interest of sensitivity to "seekers," will eventually have nothing identifiably Christian to say, either to themselves or to those seekers. But since everyone, and every community, needs a master story, a new one will fill the void, and the new master story will carry with it a new, and most likely alien, way of being in the world. The final consequence of this creedal amnesia will be that the church has nothing left to live for or, if necessary, to die for, that faithfully embodies the story of Jesus. (Parenthetically, this same consequence is likely for those with sacramental amnesia, though we learn that from the Corinthians [1 Cor. 11:17-34] rather than the Philippians.) The church will, instead, call on its children to live and die (and even kill) for some allegedly noble cause, almost certainly one that is ethnic or nationalistic in nature. It will have come, thereby, full circle, reaping the whirlwind of its fear of confession. By neglecting the story and confession of Jesus as universal Lord, the Lord who rules as Suffering Servant, the church will substitute the universal Lord for a tribal deity and the Suffering Servant for a conquering king. Sadly, this has too often been the pattern of the church throughout its history, *especially in its centrifugal activity.*

I would submit that the intrusion of an alien master story, and the ongoing re-conversion of the church to that pseudo-gospel, is the greatest and most persistent sin of the church, at least in the United States, today.[71] From presidential claims, both Democrat and Republican, that the United States is the light of the world and the hope for human freedom, to the language of "mission" that permeates military discourse, to talk of "redemptive violence,"

---

71. From my (limited) experience of the church in Europe and Africa, this problem is not unique to the U.S.

to the incorporation of nationalistic holidays and devotion into the liturgical life of the church, the church is constantly bombarded with temptations to honor an alien Lord with an alien mission in the world.

By telling and retelling the church's true master story, however, the church is empowered to cast off this alien, Rome-like master story and is prepared to live the true story missionally and faithfully, participating in the self-emptying, self-giving servanthood of Jesus. This is the case even though the church, when it is both faithful and attentive to its master story, knows that its participatory service may take it to the point of suffering and (potential) death, as was the experience of (some of) the Philippians.[72]

I have also suggested in this chapter that the mission of the church in Philippians consists of both word and deed. We can now be a bit more concrete about that in our own situation. I want to consider briefly the great commandment, the great commission, the great challenge, and the great consequences (asking readers to forgive the deliberate alliteration).

## The Great Commandment

As noted above, the narrative shape of the faithful community can be summarized in the word *love,* specifically the self-giving, others-centered *agapē* displayed in Jesus' incarnation and death. It is clear from Philippians that Paul especially wants that kind of love to be the hallmark of intra-fellowship (centripetal) relations and activities. But if we were to conclude that Paul limits such love to believers, we would be mistaken, as I have also already argued. But I think it bears repeating and elaborating.

For one thing, elsewhere in Paul's letters the apostle specifically exhorts his communities to do good to, that is to love, outsiders (e.g., the "all" of Rom. 12:17-18; Gal. 6:10; 1 Thess. 5:15; and the persecutors of Rom. 12:14; cf. 1 Cor. 4:12). For another, and more importantly, an individual or community in Christ is in Christ all the time. Its life is shaped by the narrative of the gospel 24/7. This is necessitated not merely by some principle of integrity, but by virtue of the substance of the gospel itself: the incarnation and death of Jesus were undertaken as an act of love toward "outsiders," to those hostile

---

72. I do not mean to imply that any Philippians had actually been killed, though that is not impossible. For an interpretation of another biblical book along these same lines, see my *Reading Revelation Responsibly: Uncivil Worship and Witness; Following the Lamb into the New Creation* (Eugene, OR: Cascade, 2011).

to God and in need of reconciliation, as Paul's letters elsewhere make more explicit (e.g., Rom. 5:6-8; 2 Cor. 5:12-21). The church's mission is to love "the world," to borrow Johannine terminology, even when that world is hostile, as it was in Philippi. In the spirit of conformity to Jesus, the church in the power of the Spirit must look again and again for new ways to love the world incarnationally and cruciformly in the interest of the world's salvation. To be missional requires immense imagination.

For example, David Purves in England has recently taken the interpretation of Philippians 2:6-11 offered in the larger work underlying this chapter *(Inhabiting the Cruciform God)* and applied it constructively and creatively to the church's ministry with the homeless.[73] He summarizes his own contentions about Philippians 2, participation, and ministry as follows:

> Christian ministry amongst homeless people is often characterised by division between the ministry itself as social action by independent voluntary organisations, and congregational life. This is arguably the result of sociological forces, but is also compounded by the prevalence in mainline churches of ethically lacking popular versions of penal substitution that privatise spirituality. We argue that in addition to strengthening the ethical content of such teaching, it is important to offer alternative theological tools that challenge Christian self-understanding. Kenosis [Christ's self-emptying] is just such a tool. In a brief historical sketch of biblical and theological approaches, we suggest that it is the ethical, narrative understanding of kenosis, rather than preoccupation with philosophically-orientated Christological debates about the locus of the apparent "emptying" of divine attributes, that is central to understanding kenosis. What we label the necessary ethically kenotic dimension to salvation is then explored, an area in which we are influenced by current biblical scholarship on "justification" in Paul by participationist-inclined scholars. . . . Kenosis as a "selfishness emptying" that leads to co-resurrection is an integral and ongoing part of the soteriological process of theosis. Relating kenosis to soteriology in this way has implications for church work amongst homeless people, and we suggest that when also taking into account current social work research, churches receive an imperative to offer ministry that is community orientated, relational, self-giving and absorptive.[74]

73. David R. Purves, "Relating Kenosis to Soteriology: Implications for Christian Ministry amongst Homeless People," *Horizons in Biblical Theology* 35 (2013): 70-90.

74. The text is from the author's own abstract (p. 70).

## *The Great Commission*[75]

Earlier I argued that the Philippian believers must have been engaging in some form of proclamation, even if it is best described as "soft" evangelism. Their cruciform neighbor-love, not to mention their likely abstention from social occasions that could be perceived as hatred of humanity and/or disrespect for the gods and the empire, either required (from the believers' perspective) an explanation or else prompted a request for such an explanation from the offended party.

Brian Peterson is right to say that the church's "love toward the outsider is not a strategy for the church's mission in order to arrive at some more ultimate goal," i.e., "more converts."[76] But when Peterson claims that "apparently such love IS the church's mission"[77] — he fails to take with sufficient seriousness his own excellent argument[78] that the church at Philippi — and today, in parallel fashion[79] — is an alternative to "Rome's dominion across the earth, as an extension of Rome's culture and influence."[80] Of course we should "give up hoping for Christianizing the world" if that means substituting Caesar's sword with Christ's cross.[81] But the answer to *bad* evangelism is not *no* evangelism — to stop telling the story — but rather to *tell the true story truly.*

The church that tells the master story of Jesus cannot choose between living a life of cruciform love and proclaiming Jesus as Lord. The church's cruciform life is grounded in its proclamation, and its proclamation is expressed in its cruciform life. The church does not live or tell two stories, one about love and another about Jesus as Lord, but one seamless story. At the same time, it does not tell a fractured story about a loving Jesus who gave himself in incarnation and death but now rules powerfully as conquering Lord, demanding obeisance and thus "lording it over" humanity. His is the rule of cruciform love, and the church calls the whole world to enter that reign of love.

Thus the church believes that the universal lordship of Jesus is a reality

---

75. I am of course borrowing a common way of summarizing the command of Jesus to make new disciples from among the nations (Matt. 28:18-20).

76. Peterson, "Being the Church," pp. 170-71.

77. Peterson, "Being the Church," p. 171.

78. Peterson, "Being the Church," pp. 173-78.

79. Peterson, "Being the Church," p. 176.

80. Peterson, "Being the Church," p. 173.

81. Peterson, "Being the Church," p. 177.

that everyone should know and in which everyone should participate, and this for two reasons. First, humanity was created to worship the one God, and this one God has exalted Jesus as Lord such that our recognizing his Lordship brings the glory to God that we were created to offer in devotion and love. Second, humanity was created to live as the image of God, and Jesus Christ the Second Adam and the self-giving, Suffering Servant of God shows us concretely what that means. Humanity has fallen short of both of those dimensions of God's intention, as the early chapters of Romans make abundantly clear and as Paul summarizes in Philippians in the words a "crooked and perverse generation" (Phil. 2:15). In anticipation of the universal proclamation of Jesus' lordship, we invite others to acknowledge and live that now, both for the glory of God and for their own fulfillment — their salvation, their life — as human beings. In so doing, we embody the mission of God given to Israel (Isa. 42:6; 49:6; cf. Dan. 12:3) and of Jesus given to his disciples (Matt. 5:14-16): to *be* and thus to *bring* light in the world. Paul expects nothing less of the Philippians or of us (Phil. 2:15).[82] That is, we are called not merely to *believe* that Jesus is Lord but to *embody* his Lordship, and to invite others to do the same.

One cannot speak of the "good news" of Jesus as "Lord" without focusing on the countercultural religious and political claims of this story. Once again, "If Jesus is Lord, Caesar is not." The church is tempted in every age to identify with secular power, with empire, and usually to call that power divine. When that happens, the mission of the church, even its evangelism, becomes so skewed that it is no longer a faithful commentary on its master story. Indeed, we could and should go so far as to say that it no longer preaches the gospel but a pseudo-gospel that is not a gospel at all. The counterintuitive, counter-imperial, kenotic God revealed in the story of Christ deconstructs that tempting pseudo-master story. Yet this pseudo-master story seems to be a cat with at least nine (or perhaps ninety times nine) lives, reemerging in new ways in each new culture and each new generation. Only with vigilance — and prayer and fasting — can this demon be cast out again and again and again.

## The Great Challenge

The great commandment and the great commission, interpreted through the lens of Philippians 2, lead also to a third dimension of Christian mission for

82. Cf. Acts 13:47.

our contemporary situation. It is what some have called "the third mission of the church" — the care of creation.[83] I prefer to call it the great challenge.

That the Lordship of Jesus has a cosmic dimension is clear in this passage (2:10-11). Thus a missional church grounded in this text cannot neglect the reality of humanity's connection to a larger universe. In what sense can the cosmic expression of Jesus' lordship be expressed, or furthered, by the church in its missional life?

In two ways, I would suggest. First of all, the Scriptures of Israel make it abundantly clear that human sin and human salvation are both connected to the cosmos, and Paul knew this well (e.g., Gen. 3:17-19; Hos. 4:1-3; cf. Rom. 8:18-25; Col. 1:15-20).[84] I bristled when I first saw that the Evangelical Environmental Network cites Philippians 2:4-8 as one of its Scripture texts for ecological responsibility. But it does so under the heading of texts about "The Relationship between Environmental Problems and Christian Love and Justice."[85] To the degree that the church's mission is to love others, we will need to consider more fully how our use of the world's resources contributes either to justice or to injustice for others. And in doing so, the church should not be afraid to connect its witness in word and deed to its following Jesus.

Second, if humanity is called and enabled in Christ to be what Adam as the image of God was intended to be but was not, then we now are the heirs of Adam's task: to care for God's garden as God's servant-lords, God's stewards (Gen. 2:15 serving as a commentary on Gen. 1:27-28). The mission of the church, as a foretaste of the coming new creation, is charged with creation-care now, not as an optional part of the church's mission for those politically left of center, but for the church simply as the church. Otherwise it will not be living in the public square worthily of the gospel.[86]

83. See, e.g., Norman C. Habel, "The Third Mission of the Church: Good News for the Earth," *Trinity Occasional Papers* 16 (1998): 31-43.

84. Hosea 4:1-3, perhaps the least known of these texts, reads as follows: "Hear the word of the Lord, O people of Israel; for the Lord has an indictment against the inhabitants of the land. There is no faithfulness or loyalty, and no knowledge of God in the land. Swearing, lying, and murder, and stealing and adultery break out; bloodshed follows bloodshed. Therefore the land mourns, and all who live in it languish; together with the wild animals and the birds of the air, even the fish of the sea are perishing." See also Laurie J. Braaten, "All Creation Groans: Romans 8:22 in Light of the Biblical Sources," *Horizons in Biblical Theology* 28 (2006): 131-59.

85. See "Creation Care: An Introduction for Busy Pastors; Evangelicals and Scientists United to Protect Creation," p. 4, at http://www.chgeharvard.org/sites/default/files/CreationCare_1_06_2012.pdf. The organization's web site is www.creationcare.org.

86. For more on Paul and the "third mission of the church," see, for starters, David Horrell, "A New Perspective on Paul? Rereading Paul in an Age of Ecological Crisis," *Journal*

## *The Great Consequences: The Servant Church and the Suffering Church Today*

Just as every Christian community is a place of faith, love, and hope, as we discussed at the end of the previous chapter, so also every Christian community is, by definition, a place of servanthood. The Pauline poem in Philippians 2:6-11 may appear, from its most immediate context (2:1-4), to stress the internal focus of that service in the Spirit due to the external pressures and internal conflicts the Philippians faced. But looking just a few lines earlier, and immediately after the poem, we see clearly that this service was also extended outside the believing community into the wider *polis,* which of course did not perceive it as service but as something like treason and disdain for humanity.

The letter to the Philippians may be an extended meditation on 2:6-11, but Philippians 2:6-11 is itself perhaps best understood as an expansion of the word of Jesus recorded in Mark 10:45 — "For the Son of Man came not to be served but to serve, and to give his life a ransom for many" — and a summary of the footwashing narrative in John 13, culminating in the words, "So if I, your Lord and Teacher, have washed your feet, you also ought to wash one another's feet" (John 13:14). Again, the focus in John 13 may be primarily the community of disciples, but the self-giving love of God in Christ is clearly for the whole world (e.g., John 3:16), even when that world hates the disciples and their Lord (e.g., John 15:18-23).

Documenting the ways in which local churches have been and continue to be servant communities would fill more pages than any book can hold. It suffices, perhaps, to say that specific, contextually imaginative forms of servanthood are what every Christian community needs to embody in order to become the gospel where they are situated.[87] What needs some specific attention, however, is the suffering church, the many persecuted Christians

---

*for the Study of the New Testament* 33 (2010): 3-30; David Horrell, Cherryl Hunt, and Christopher Southgate, eds., *Greening Paul: Reading the Apostle in a Time of Ecological Crisis* (Waco, TX: Baylor University Press, 2010); and Presian Smyers Burroughs, "Liberation in the Midst of Futility and Destruction: Romans 8 and the Christian Vocation of Nourishing Life" (Th.D. diss., Duke Divinity School, 2014).

87. Of scores of books that could be mentioned that narrate examples of such creative contextuality, I list just two: Lois Y. Barrett et al., eds., *Treasure in Clay Jars: Patterns in Missional Faithfulness* (Grand Rapids: Eerdmans, 2004), and Ronald J. Sider, Philip N. Olson, and Heidi Rolland Unruh, *Churches That Make a Difference: Reaching Your Community with Good News and Good Works* (Grand Rapids: Baker, 2002).

throughout the world, many of whom are largely, if not completely, unknown to most North American Christians.

Dean Flemming writes that "[t]he story of a crucified Savior, who rules, not by universal domination, but by self-emptying love, confronts Rome's entire vision of the world. Living the story of Jesus in Caesar's colony is a risky business."[88] This leads him to reflect on listening to the text of Philippians "from both a local and a global perspective."[89] Philippians is a highly contextualized interpretation of the church's role in God's *missio,* and the realities of alter-cultural existence (as a "contrast community") and the consequences of that existence will vary significantly today from place to place. The suffering, persecuted church in regions of the Middle East, Africa, and Asia has much to teach the (generally) unpersecuted Western/Northern church about faithfulness and integrity, and about joy in the midst of suffering — not unlike the Philippians.

Accordingly, the unpersecuted church needs to study, to learn about the persecuted church around the world, and to pray with and for fellow Christians whose faith and faithfulness are on the line every day. This would contribute to the spiritual unity of the church, and perhaps also to the wider church's integrity and courage in its own contexts. The unpersecuted church needs also, therefore, to engage in self-examination. No one wants to suffer, to be persecuted. But the elephant-in-the-room question for the comfortable church is, of course, "*Why* are you so comfortable?" What have you done — what have *we* done — to make Christian faith so bland as to be frequently worthy of neither serious embrace nor serious opposition?[90]

The letter to the Philippians and, in fact, nearly every other New Testament writing make it abundantly clear that just as suffering was the fate of the church's servant-Lord, so also will the faithful servant-church suffer. Suffering is, Paul says to the Philippians and to all Christians, a graced sharing in the sufferings of Paul and of Jesus himself, God's Suffering Servant, as we have seen (esp. Phil. 1:29). Paul believed that Jesus brought the peace of God and summoned his followers to be peacemakers (1 Thess. 5:12-24; Phil. 4:7-9; cf. Matt. 5:9), but Paul also knew from experience that Jesus could just as easily bring division (as Jesus himself also said [Matt. 10:34-36; Luke 12:51-53]). Ac-

88. Flemming, "Exploring a Missional Reading," p. 14.

89. Flemming, "Exploring a Missional Reading," pp. 16-17.

90. On the relationship among evangelism, ecclesial virtues and practices, and martyrdom, see William T. Cavanaugh, *Torture and Eucharist: Theology, Politics, and the Body of Christ* (Malden, MA: Blackwell, 1998); Bryan P. Stone, *Evangelism after Christendom: The Theology and Practice of Christian Witness* (Grand Rapids: Brazos, 2006), pp. 277-312.

cording to Luke, Paul and his companions were "turning the world upside down" by "acting contrary to the decrees of the emperor, saying that there is another king named Jesus" (Acts 17:6-7). The beatitude that extols peacemaking is immediately followed by two others that promise persecution (Matt. 5:10-12). Perhaps Jesus should have just said, "Blessed are the troublemakers."

The church only suffers when, by its participation in Jesus' servanthood, it challenges the political, social, economic, intellectual, ethical, and/or religious status quo. When it *is* the status quo, it poses no threat and receives no opposition. When the church is a contrast society, an alternative polis of an alternative empire, it will suffer; it does not need to look for trouble, for trouble will find it. Trouble, or "persecution," can take many forms, from relatively mild social harassment by family members, friends, or associates to mob- or state-sponsored campaigns of murder.

As I was writing this book, U.S. missionary Kenneth Bae, who was also a tour guide, was arrested in North Korea, charged with "hostile acts against the state," and sentenced to fifteen years of hard labor (though he was released on November 8, 2014). That sounds much like Acts or the situation of imprisonment that generated Paul's letter to the Philippians. Sometime later in North Korea, an Australian missionary based in Hong Kong was taken into custody for distributing religious writings; John Short was seventy-five. A few days later, several Christians in Tripoli (Libya) were kidnapped and executed. These are but snapshots (specifically the kind that make the news) of the many currents of persecution around the world.[91] Lest it appear, or be assumed, that such "troublemaking" is made only by conservative evangelical missionaries who might be insensitive to the political and cultural realities of foreign countries, it is good to remember that Christians like the late Rev. Dr. Martin Luther King Jr. and even the former Archbishop of Canterbury, Rowan Williams, have been arrested for practicing their Christian faith in the public arena of their own nations.[92]

My point is not primarily to endorse the actions of these particular individuals or (in the case of some) the churches or mission agencies they may represent; I know only one of them personally. Nor is my point to sug-

91. For contemporary descriptions and analyses of the worldwide situation by prize-winning journalists, see Rupert Shortt, *Christianophobia: A Faith Under Attack* (Grand Rapids: Eerdmans, 2012) and John L. Allen Jr., *The Global War on Christians: Dispatches from the Front Lines of Anti-Christian Persecution* (New York: Image/Random House, 2013).

92. In 1984, long before becoming Archbishop of Canterbury in 2002, Rowan Williams was arrested outside an air base in Suffolk, England while reading the Psalms as an act of protest against nuclear weapons.

gest that people acting in the name of Christianity, or simply being Christians, have always faithfully represented their servant-Lord and his gospel; of course they have not. But without ignoring the legitimate concerns about colonialism, cultural oppression, and the like, both past and present, we need to recognize the realities facing many ordinary Christians and their leaders around the world. Their human rights are often violated, and campaigns to stop such injustice are valid. But more importantly, theologically speaking, the persecuted church reminds all of us of the cost of discipleship, of the political character of the gospel, and of the need to discern in our own contexts what faithful discipleship means. The goal is not to challenge the status quo but to be the faithful church, the church that serves God in Christ instead of earthly powers — and that will always pose a challenge, and sometimes a threat, to the status quo, even as it seeks to be a servant community. This is the political paradox of faithful Christian existence.

## Word, Deed, and Integrity: The Church as Apologia for the Gospel

Finally, we come briefly to a word from Philippians that has been briefly mentioned yet has been largely hovering in the background: *apologia*, translated as "defense" by the NRSV: "for all of you share in God's grace with me, both in my imprisonment and in the defense and confirmation of the gospel" (Phil. 1:7). More specifically, we come to the apologetic character of the Philippians 2:6-11–shaped church. What I mean by this is that the church that embodies its master story is one that may indeed warrant suffering and even death, as Paul and the Philippians knew well, but in that suffering and death it will be bearing faithful witness to its Lord. It will not be *suffering* for the wrong reasons (e.g., failing to be concerned about injustice or the destruction of the environment, or mistreating people in the name of Christian faith), and it will not be *avoiding suffering* for the wrong reasons (e.g., practicing a civil religion that functionally acknowledges an alternative lord even as it talks of "God" and "the Lord Jesus").

Rather, the church will strive to be what it is, and to be shaped by its story, through the power of the Spirit, so that its life and the lives of all Christians will be a reasonable facsimile of what God intends for humanity to be. In this way, it will simultaneously embody the divine mission and be a credible commentary on — and thus *apologia* for — the story that narrates that mission. Only as such will the church be able to "striv[e] side by side with one mind for the faith of the gospel" (1:27). Simultaneously, its existence will be a "confirmation" of the gospel, as Philippians 1:7 also says, an indication that what Christians sing about is really the true story of God, of humanity, and of humanity's place in the cosmos.

## Conclusion

Philippians 2:6-11 is, surprisingly, a radically missional text. By missional, I mean that the poem, which is Paul's master story, summarizes the gospel that Paul wants the Philippian assembly both to proclaim and to embody, in spite of opposition, and thereby both to hold forth and to defend. What they, and we, are called to proclaim and perform is the Pauline narrative about the crucified Jesus as the self-giving, life-giving Son of God and sovereign Lord.

That Philippians 2:6-11 is a poem, a psalm of sorts, written from and for a painful situation (imprisonment and persecution) but part of a letter baptized in joy, may explain why these reflections by N. T. Wright on the Book of Psalms (and specifically the motif of time in the Psalms) resonate so deeply with our consideration of Paul's letter to the Philippians:

> We are called, then, to stretch out the arms of our minds and hearts, and to find ourselves, Christ shaped, cross shaped, at the intersection of the past, present, and future of God's time and our own time. This is a place of intense pain and intense joy, the sort that perhaps only music and poetry can express or embody. The Psalms are gifts that help us not only to think wisely about the overlaps and paradoxes of time, but to live within them, to reach out in the day of trouble and remind ourselves — and not only ourselves, but also the mysterious one whom the Psalms call "you" — of the story in which we live. Past, present, and future belong to him. We are called to live, joyfully and painfully, in the story that is both his and ours. Our times are in his hand.[93]

As we live in that story we will be a missional people, each of us allowing our time to be at God's disposal. To become the gospel is to allow Christ's story to become our story, and our time — as well as our energy and other resources — to become his in the service of that gospel. In doing so, we take risks — Paul calls it living worthily of the gospel — that we would not

---

93. N. T. Wright, *The Case for the Psalms: Why They Are Essential* (New York: Harper-Collins, 2013), p. 75.

ordinarily take. Why? We will let Paul have the final word or two. First, a word of purpose, of mission:

> It is my eager expectation and hope that I will not be put to shame [or do anything shameful vis-à-vis the gospel] in any way, but that by my speaking with all boldness, Christ will be exalted now as always in my body, whether by life or by death. (Phil. 1:20)

Then, as well, a word of joy and trust for a missional people telling and living the story of their crucified and resurrected Lord:

> ⁴Rejoice in the Lord always; again I will say, Rejoice. ⁵Let your gentleness be known to everyone. The Lord is near. ⁶Do not worry about anything, but in everything by prayer and supplication with thanksgiving let your requests be made known to God. ⁷And the peace of God, which surpasses all understanding, will guard your hearts and your minds in Christ Jesus. . . . ⁹Keep on doing the things that you have learned and received and heard and seen in me, and the God of peace will be with you. (Phil. 4:4-7, 9)

The God of peace and the peace of God guard the missional, cruciform people of God, those who partner with Paul, and with the Spirit, in the *missio Dei.*

With those words we turn next, naturally, to Paul and peace, the subject of the following two chapters.

# CHAPTER 5

# Becoming the Gospel of Peace (I): Overview

Some Christians are quite fond of the phrases about peace from the end of Paul's letter to the Philippians and quoted in the conclusion to the previous chapter: "the peace of God" and "the God of peace" (Phil. 4:7, 9). These and similar texts raise the question, What does the Christian gospel have to do with peace, or with peacemaking? According to some Christians, the answer would be captured primarily, perhaps even exclusively, in the title of a bestselling 1950s book by Billy Graham called *Peace with God: The Secret of Happiness*.[1] For them, the peace that the gospel brings is a "vertical" peace: reconciliation with God, with little or no inherent "horizontal" implications for relationships among humans. This peace is a personal and private affair, not a public matter, and it is a centrifugal peace — a peace that requires peacemaking — only in a limited, evangelistic way: bringing the gospel of personal peace to others so that they too may have peace with God.

The notion of peace with God is of course very Pauline (e.g., Rom. 5:1). Mennonite New Testament scholar Willard Swartley claims, in fact, that "Paul, more than any other writer in the New Testament canon, makes peace, peacemaking, and peace-building central to his theological reflection and moral admonition."[2] Swartley's claim, if correct, suggests that the peace that Paul

1. Billy Graham, *Peace with God: The Secret of Happiness* (Garden City, NY: Doubleday, 1953). I do not mean to impugn either the book or the author, only to suggest that the title is an inadequate summary of the meaning of peace in the Christian gospel. Interestingly, although Graham's focus in the book is on "authentic personal peace" (preface to revised 1984 edition [Nashville: Thomas Nelson], p. x), at least in the 1984 revision he has a chapter called "Am I My Brother's Keeper?" in which he briefly applies the Christian "antidote" to sin, fear, and hatred to such issues as labor relations, race relations, and human suffering.

2. Willard M. Swartley, *Covenant of Peace: The Missing Peace in New Testament Theology and Ethics* (Grand Rapids: Eerdmans, 2006), p. 190.

preached and embodied was not a narrow peace confined to the quest for personal tranquility or happiness. Rather, as we will see in this chapter, for Paul peace — *shalom* — is the fullness of life promised by God in the Scriptures, manifest in Jesus the Messiah, and actualized for human beings by the ongoing power of the Spirit. *Shalom* means healing and wholeness, including peace both with God and with others, and even with the rest of the created order.

For Paul, then, the church is a community of peace and of peacemaking, and it is such because it has been brought into being by "the gospel of peace" (Eph. 6:15). That is, the church is — and is to become — a living embodiment of God's peacemaking good news in Christ. Peace, for Paul, is a fundamental part of his theology and spirituality, specifically his theology and spirituality of missional participation in the life of the triune God.

In this chapter we briefly consider the significance of *shalom* in biblical theology before turning to peace in Paul.[3] We will look first at his letters as a whole before turning briefly to Romans. In the next chapter, we examine peace in the letter to the Ephesians and consider some examples of contemporary Christian peacemaking. But before we attend to all of this, we begin with a brief word about the overall neglect of peace in New Testament studies generally, and the study of Paul specifically.

## The Missing Peace/Piece

If ordinary Christian people and churches have a narrow understanding of peace in the Pauline letters, and in the New Testament more generally, it is probably not their fault. Many biblical scholars and theologians have paid scant attention to peace and peacemaking in the New Testament, including the writings of the apostle who spoke in the same breath about the peace of God and the God of peace (Phil. 4:7, 9).[4] This gap in New Testament studies is what led Willard Swartley to write his important 2006 book *Covenant of Peace: The Missing Peace in New Testament Theology and Ethics* as a corrective.[5] The book identifies the general absence of peace from New

3. As we will see in chapter seven, the peace, or *shalom,* of God is closely connected to the justice of God, both as divine trait and as ecclesial practice.

4. See the documentation of this lacuna in Swartley, *Covenant of Peace,* pp. 431-71, and (much more briefly) in Pieter G. R. de Villiers, "Peace in the Pauline Letters: A Perspective on Biblical Spirituality," *Neotestamentica* 43 (2009): 1-26, esp. p. 6. As Swartley demonstrates, there are some notable exceptions to the oversight.

5. See the note above for full bibliographical information.

Testament studies (especially from the major, influential treatments of New Testament theology and ethics), explores the theme in Jesus and in the various New Testament writers, and considers the significance of New Testament peacemaking for contemporary Christian existence. It is perhaps the only single-author book ever written that comprehensively addresses peace and peacemaking in the New Testament.[6]

This is not to say that *no* New Testament scholars have paid attention to peace and its ethical cousins (enemy love, nonviolence, etc.) in Jesus, Paul, and the New Testament writings. In fact, there has been a growing awareness among scholars and theologians that both Jesus and Paul, and perhaps other key figures of the New Testament as well, taught and lived their message in the context of the famed *Pax Romana,* and indeed offered a compelling alternative to Rome's ideology and practices of "peace."[7] Nonetheless, Swartley's principal point stands: peace and peacemaking are significant dimensions of the New Testament that are seriously underrepresented in the literature. The consequences for the life and mission of the Christian church, I would suggest, have been devastating.

6. Earlier attempts to rectify the situation include John Howard Yoder, *The Politics of Jesus: Behold the Man! Our Victorious Lamb,* 2nd ed. (Grand Rapids: Eerdmans, 1994 [orig. 1972]); John Howard Yoder, *He Came Preaching Peace* (Eugene, OR: Wipf & Stock, 1998 [orig. Herald Press, 1985]); Klaus Wengst, *Pax Romana and the Peace of Jesus Christ,* trans. John Bowden (Philadelphia: Fortress, 1987); and Michael Desjardins, *Peace, Violence and the New Testament* (Sheffield: Sheffield Academic Press, 1991). After Swartley's work appeared, Ched Myers (who, though not an academic but a practitioner, has published widely in biblical studies) and his colleague Elaine Enns (also a practitioner) wrote two volumes called *Ambassadors of Reconciliation,* vol. 1: *New Testament Reflections on Restorative Justice and Peacemaking* (Maryknoll, NY: Orbis, 2009) and *Ambassadors of Reconciliation,* vol. 2: *Diverse Christian Practices of Restorative Justice and Peacemaking* (Maryknoll, NY: Orbis, 2009). (I am grateful to Sylvia Keesmaat for drawing these two volumes to my attention.) For a multi-author collection of essays on peace in both Testaments, written by biblical scholars, see Laura L. Brenneman and Brad D. Schantz, eds., *Struggles for Shalom: Peace and Violence Across the Testaments* (Eugene, OR: Pickwick, 2014), a volume in honor of Swartley and Perry Yoder. Swartley's article in that volume ("Peace and Violence in the New Testament: Definition and Methodology," pp. 141-54) is helpful for bibliography, methodology for study, and definitions. In writing this chapter, I developed my analyses and arguments independently of these and other scholars, after which I consulted their works with profit — and with happy surprise that we had come to similar conclusions. See also my article "The Lord of Peace: Christ Our Peace in Pauline Theology," *Journal for the Study of Paul and His Letters* 3 (2013): 219-53, which was expanded to include the theology of Luke and published as ch. 6 in my *The Death of the Messiah and the Birth of the New Covenant: A (Not So) New Model of the Atonement* (Eugene, OR: Cascade, 2014).

7. Swartley himself recognizes this (e.g., *Covenant of Peace,* p. 5 n. 8), and he mentions with appreciation those scholars' works that have paid attention to peace in the New Testament.

We will have several reasons to refer to Swartley's book throughout this chapter. For now, however, we follow his lead and begin with the context for peace studies in the New Testament (including Paul): the visions of *shalom* in the biblical prophets and other scriptural writings.

## Shalom

It is beyond the scope of this chapter to look in depth at *shalom* in the Scriptures of Israel, the Christian Old Testament. Ironically, it may well be the case that both Christian scholars and Christian laypeople have paid more attention to peace in the Old Testament than in the New. The irony is especially poignant if Swartley is correct — and I think he is — in claiming that the New Testament should be seen as the fulfillment of Ezekiel's promised "covenant of peace" (Ezek. 34:25; 37:26).[8]

There has been significant recent work on *shalom*/*eirēnē*/peace in the Bible.[9] The Bible itself does not offer a systematic definition of the word, whose meaning, especially in the Scriptures of Israel, is heavily context-dependent.[10] For our purposes, we will define *shalom* — a word that appears 238 times in the Bible (Old Testament)[11] — rather generally.[12] First, negatively, *shalom* is the resolution and cessation — and henceforth the absence — of chaos, conflict,

---

8. Swartley, *Covenant of Peace*, p. xiii. More generally, we may say that the New Testament writers attest to the inauguration of God's eschatological *shalom* in the life, death, and resurrection of Jesus, and in the subsequent communities of his disciples.

9. See, e.g., Perry B. Yoder, *Shalom: The Bible's Word for Salvation, Justice, and Peace* (Nappanee, IN: Evangel, 1987); Ulrich Mauser, *The Gospel of Peace: A Scriptural Message for Today's World,* Studies in Peace and Scripture 1 (Louisville: Westminster John Knox, 1992); Shemaryahu Talmon, "The Signification of שלום and Its Semantic Field in the Hebrew Bible," in *The Quest for Context and Meaning: Studies in Biblical Intertextuality in Honor of James A. Sanders,* ed. Craig A. Evans and Shemaryahu Talmon (Leiden: Brill, 1997), pp. 75-115; Swartley, *Covenant of Peace;* Willard M. Swartley, "Peace in the NT," in *The New Interpreter's Dictionary of the Bible* 4:422-23 (Nashville: Abingdon, 2009); Daniel L. Smith-Christopher, "Peace in the OT," in *The New Interpreter's Dictionary of the Bible* 4:423-25 (Nashville: Abingdon, 2009); Brenneman and Schantz, *Struggles for Shalom.*

10. See the words of caution in Talmon, "Signification," pp. 75-78, even as he pursues a "synoptic or holistic approach" (p. 78).

11. Talmon, "Signification," p. 80.

12. As Pieter de Villiers rightly emphasizes, *shalom*/peace is more than a word, and peace is expressed in the Bible through a variety of words and images ("Peace in the Pauline Letters," pp. 5-6). Nevertheless, to keep the discussion manageable, in this and the following chapter we will focus primarily on the key Greek and Hebrew terms *shalom* and *eirēnē*.

oppression, and broken relations. Second, positively, *shalom* is the establishment, and henceforth the presence, of wholeness, reconciliation, goodness, justice, and the flourishing of creation — "physical and spiritual wellbeing."[13]

*Shalom,* therefore, is clearly a thick theological term (and reality), a kind of semantic magnet that draws other terms (and realities) into its field.[14] Swartley contends that *shalom* in the Christian OT is semantically and theologically related to righteousness and justice, salvation, eschatology, the kingdom of God, covenant, and grace. *Eirēnē,* in the New Testament, is related to nearly everything: love of God, neighbor, and enemy (including non-retaliation); faith, hope, holiness, and harmony in the corporate body; blessing and wholeness; reconciliation and new covenant; salvation and grace; and kingdom of God, righteousness, justice, and justification.[15] And throughout the biblical writings, peace is first of all a divine gift that calls forth human response and participation.

In both Testaments, however, peace in the present is always a concrete reality, a solution, so to speak, to a real, specific problem.[16] Depending on the context, peace includes (1) personal well-being and calm, prosperity, and/or freedom from danger; (2) interpersonal harmony, social welfare, and prosperity; (3) and inter-group cessation of discord or hostility, including war.[17] In general, then, terms like "well-being" (including wholeness and health) and "friendship/goodwill" express the significance of *shalom*.[18] It is the antithesis of conflict, whether between humans and God, between humans and other humans, or within the individual person. The transition from the absence of peace — which is the "default" human predicament — to its presence requires transformation, sometimes including the defeat of the earthly or spiritual powers causing the chaos, conflict, oppression, and broken relations.

We see Israel's hope for *shalom* in the sense of a lasting, permanent peace in various texts, especially in the prophets. Of several that could be cited, the

13. Talmon, "Signification," p. 81.

14. Talmon ("Signification," p. 81) reminds us that the rich texture of the word *shalom* is scarcely well translated by words such as "peace" or even *eirēnē*.

15. See Swartley, *Covenant of Peace,* p. 30 and p. 41, where he supplies helpful graphics to illustrate these semantic connections.

16. See Talmon, "Signification," and William Klassen, "Pursue Peace: A Concrete Ethical Mandate (Romans 12:18-21)," in *Ja und Nein: Christliche Theologie im Angesicht Israels,* FS Wolfgang Schrage, ed. Klaus Wengst and Gerhard Saß (Neukirchen-Vluyn: Neukirchener, 1998), pp. 195-207.

17. Talmon, "Signification," pp. 82-89.

18. Talmon, "Signification," pp. 89-91.

beginning of Isaiah 2 is noteworthy — and has captured the imagination of many over the centuries:

> [1]The word that Isaiah son of Amoz saw concerning Judah and Jerusalem. [2]In days to come the mountain of the Lord's house shall be established as the highest of the mountains, and shall be raised above the hills; all the nations shall stream to it. [3]Many peoples shall come and say, "Come, let us go up to the mountain of the Lord, to the house of the God of Jacob; that he may teach us his ways and that we may walk in his paths." For out of Zion shall go forth instruction, and the word of the Lord from Jerusalem. [4]He shall judge between the nations, and shall arbitrate for many peoples; they shall beat their swords into plowshares, and their spears into pruning hooks; nation shall not lift up sword against nation, neither shall they learn war any more. (Isa. 2:1-4)

Here Isaiah recounts the audition/vision he received of a coming day in which Jerusalem ("Zion") will be a place where not only the people of Israel, but "many peoples" will be taught by God and will live together in a place of divine justice and peace. The psalmist's vision of justice and peace embracing (Ps. 85:10) will have come to pass. Later in Isaiah, we hear these words:

> [17]. . . I will appoint <u>Peace</u> as your overseer and <u>Righteousness</u> [or Justice] as your taskmaster. [18]<u>Violence shall no more be heard</u> in your land, devastation or destruction within your borders; you shall call your walls Salvation, and your gates Praise. (Isa. 60:17b-18)

In these beautiful texts, rich in imagery, we see that *shalom* is relational and specifically covenantal, a situation in which humans are in proper relation to one another, God, and the whole creation.[19] This is a time for which God's people long, experiencing it only partially and proleptically in the present, having an eschatological hope for *shalom* in its fullness.

At the same time, a distinguishing mark of New Testament theology, from Matthew to Revelation, is that the eschatological reality of peace has broken into the present through God's gifts of the Son and the Spirit. This does

---

19. Talmon, "Signification," pp. 102, 107-15, says that the (Hebrew) Bible's vision of a future age of peace consists of "three ever-widening concentric circles: (1) Israel at peace; (2) the world at peace; and (3) cosmic peace" (p. 107). Interestingly, the texts that embody this vision normally do not contain the word *shalom* (p. 114), which Talmon sees as connected with specific historical realities.

not mean, however, that peace in the New Testament is monolithic. Swartley notes six referents for peace in the New Testament, all Christocentric:

- as reconciliation between humans and God;
- as reconciliation among humans;
- as the new creation and alternative community to the *Pax Romana;*
- as sociopolitical reality;
- as present and future cosmic harmony; and
- as inner tranquility in the midst of adversity.[20]

There is, nonetheless, a unity to this diversity: the conviction that God's promised *shalom* has arrived. As Stephen Fowl and others have noted, in the early centuries of the Christian church, diverse theologians pointed to the church as the fulfillment of Isaiah 2.[21] Here were communities practicing, or at least attempting to practice, the truthfulness, faithfulness, justice, and peace of God that had come to humanity in Christ.

Although Paul may not specifically quote Isaiah 2, his vision of the church as a peace fellowship coheres well with the specific articulations of this in later Christian writers. Thus to Paul himself we now turn, to look at the concrete ways in which the arrival of God's eschatological peace is manifested in his writings.

## Peace in Paul: A Brief Survey

If the Old Testament writers, particularly the prophets, were so enthralled with a robust understanding of peace, what happened to Paul?[22] Furthermore, though Jesus does not seem to use the word "peace" frequently, at least one of the most famous sentences he ever uttered refers to it: "Blessed are the peacemakers" (Matt. 5:9).[23] Paul and peace, on the other hand, are not a natural pair, apart from the "peace with God" line from Romans 5:1.

Yet, ironically, Christians regularly sing a Pauline line about Jesus the peacemaker:

20. Swartley, "Peace and Violence."

21. See, e.g., Stephen Fowl, *God's Beautiful City: Christian Mission after Christendom,* The Ekklesia Project Pamphlet #4 (Eugene, OR: Wipf & Stock, 2011), pp. 10-15.

22. We will pose the same kind of question in the chapter on justice.

23. Actually, the "peace" word-family appears 28 times in the four gospels, of which almost half (13) are in Luke, followed by John and Matthew (6 each) and then Mark (3).

Crown him the Lord of peace,
whose power a scepter sways
from pole to pole, that wars may cease,
and all be prayer and praise.
His reign shall know no end,
and round his pierced feet
fair flowers of paradise extend
their fragrance ever sweet.[24]

Though the book of Revelation (e.g., Rev. 19:2) is the primary inspiration for the hymn's theme, the phrase "the Lord of peace" is Pauline. It appears, in fact, only once in the entire Bible, in 2 Thessalonians 3:16. The hymn-writer is almost certainly exegetically correct; that is, "the Lord of peace" refers specifically to Jesus, not to God the Father. Yet even from much Pauline scholarship one would hardly know that a fundamental Christological claim of the Pauline corpus is that Jesus is the Lord of peace. It is not a prominent theme in Pauline studies except, as we would expect, among Anabaptist scholars.

But therefore to assume that Paul is unconcerned about peace would be a serious mistake. The peace word-family (*eirēnē* and cognates) occurs forty-seven times in the Pauline correspondence, of which twenty-nine are in the undisputed letters of Paul. Across all thirteen letters, Romans (eleven occurrences) and Ephesians (eight) lead the pack and will therefore be discussed most fully in this chapter and the next, as already noted.[25] We need also to expand our vision of peace in Paul beyond the "peace" word family to include the related word-family of "reconciliation" *(katallagē),* which appears thirteen times in the Pauline corpus, overlapping significantly (and expectedly) in letters containing the "peace" word-family: Romans (four occurrences, including three in Rom. 5:10-11) and Ephesians (once; 2:16), plus its cousin Colossians (twice; 1:20, 22). But the most occurrences are in 2 Corinthians (five occurrences, all in 2 Cor. 5:18-20), to which we will pay careful, if brief, attention.[26]

These statistics are significant, but they alone do not tell the whole story. In fact, as Swartley rightly emphasizes,

24. The hymn was published by Matthew Bridges, an Anglican turned Catholic, in 1852.

25. In canonical order, the occurrences are as follows: Romans (11), 1 Corinthians (4), 2 Corinthians (3), Galatians (3), Ephesians (8), Philippians (3), Colossians (3), 1 Thessalonians (4), 2 Thessalonians (3), 1 Timothy (2), 2 Timothy (2), Titus (1), Philemon (1).

26. Noteworthy is the occurrence of the "reconciliation" word-family in clusters in Romans 5, Colossians 1, and 2 Corinthians 5.

[t]he case for Paul's major emphasis on peacemaking is based not on vocabulary count alone. Rather, the notion of making peace between humans and God and between formerly alienated humans is so central to the core of Pauline doctrinal and ethical thought that it is impossible to develop a faithful construal of Pauline thought without peacemaking and/or reconciliation at the core.[27]

Nevertheless, to begin our discussion, a few observations about Paul's usage of peace-talk will be instructive. We find peace in Paul both as divine gift, or grace, and as ecclesial task, or practice.

### The God of Peace and the Peace of God: Peace as Divine Gift

First of all, not surprisingly, "peace" is a consistent component of the opening greeting in Paul's letters, always combined with, and following, "grace."[28] This pair appears in all thirteen of the letters; in eleven of them the wish is simply for grace and peace,[29] while in two it is expanded to include "mercy" between grace and peace (1 Tim. 1:2; 2 Tim. 1:2). Equally important to note is that in nearly every case these greetings explicitly identify the source of peace (as well as grace and mercy) as God and Christ.[30] That is, these greetings are not mere formalities; "peace" is not here the equivalent of using *"shalom"* to

27. Swartley, *Covenant of Peace*, p. 190. Ralph P. Martin (*Reconciliation: A Study of Paul's Theology* [Atlanta: John Knox, 1981]) proposed reconciliation as the core of Paul's theology. So also, e.g., Stanley E. Porter, "Reconciliation as the Heart of Paul's Missionary Theology," in *Paul as Missionary: Identity, Activity, Theology, and Practice*, ed. Trevor J. Burke and Brian S. Rosner, Library of New Testament Studies 420 (London: T. & T. Clark, 2011), pp. 169-79.

28. It is found in certain non-Pauline letters, too: 1 Pet. 1:2; 2 Pet. 1:2 (both "grace and peace"); 2 John 3 ("Grace, mercy, and peace"); Jude 2 ("mercy, peace, and love"); Rev. 1:4 ("Grace . . . and peace").

29. Rom. 1:7; 1 Cor. 1:3; 2 Cor. 1:2; Gal. 1:3; Eph. 1:2; Phil. 1:2; Col. 1:2; 1 Thess. 1:1; 2 Thess. 1:2; Titus 1:4; Philem. 3.

30. The only exceptions are Colossians and 1 Thessalonians, in which the recipients' theological location — being "in Christ" (Colossians) or in "God the Father and the Lord Jesus" (1 Thessalonians) — immediately precedes the grace-peace word: "To the saints and faithful brothers and sisters in Christ in Colossae: Grace to you and peace from God our Father"; "To the church of the Thessalonians in God the Father and the Lord Jesus Christ: Grace to you and peace." There is no need to mention Christ in Colossians, nor either God or Christ in 1 Thessalonians, because the recipients' theological location (indicated by "in") is precisely the source of their peace. (This does not mean that Paul *couldn't* have repeated himself, as Ephesians, Philippians, and 2 Thessalonians show.)

say "hello." Rather, these are theologically rich opening words. Indeed, they are essentially prayers that identify peace as a gift, and God and Christ as the giver of that gift. Moreover, there are not two different sources of peace, but only one; the single giver of peace is God/Christ, or perhaps better said, God in Christ, or God in and through Jesus the Messiah and Lord.[31]

By pronouncing a word of peace on the recipients of his letters, then, Paul is making certain theological claims. First, he is saying that the God revealed in Christ is the same peacemaking and peace-granting God known in the Scriptures of Israel; this is not a different deity.[32] God is, in fact, characterized by peace; it is an essential character trait, as the phrase "the God of peace" conveys. This phrase describing God's character appears four times in Paul's letters (Rom. 15:33; 16:20; Phil. 4:9; 1 Thess. 5:23), while the phrase "the God of love and peace" appears once (2 Cor. 13:11).[33] These phrases occur at the end of Paul's letters, situated within final benedictions or promises and serving as bookends to the letters' greetings of peace.[34] The brief theological claims and benedictions that open and close the letter also serve as liturgical reminders to the letter's readers and hearers that the God worshiped by those in Christ is first and foremost the God of grace and peace.[35]

Second, Paul is saying that the peace promised in those Scriptures has now come to expression and fulfillment in a fresh way; in fact, the promise

---

31. In fact, the grammar itself expresses this reality, as the word "from" (Greek *apo*) appears only once in each verse: that is, "from God and Christ," not "from God and from Christ."

32. Although the phrase "the God of peace" does not appear in the Old Testament, God is essentially named "peace" in Judges 6:24 ("Then Gideon built an altar there to the Lord, and called it, The LORD is peace."). God is described as the one who gives peace (Lev. 26:6; Num. 6:26; 2 Chron. 14:6; Ps. 4:8; 29:11; 147:14); makes peace (Isa. 27:5), even between Israel and its enemies (Prov. 16:7); speaks peace (Ps. 85:8); will establish a covenant of peace (Isa. 54:10; Ezek. 34:25; 37:26); will lead forth the people in peace (Isa. 55:12); will establish peace in the sense of healing (Isa. 57:19); and will send peace (Isa. 66:12). Moreover, God's royal representative on earth, or at least the ideal one, is a prince of peace (Isa. 9:6-7; cf. Zech. 9:10), and God's messenger will announce peace (Isa. 52:7). At times, peace is seen as the consequence of righteousness (e.g., Isa. 32:17-18; cf. Rom. 5:1-2), and the lack of peace is a sign of, or an aspect of, unrighteousness (e.g., Isa. 57:21; 59:8; Jer. 6:14; 8:11). The phrase "the God of peace" does appear in *Testament of Daniel* 5:2.

33. In addition, Paul says "God is a God not of disorder but of peace" (1 Cor. 14:33).

34. On "God of peace," see also Swartley, *Covenant of Peace*, pp. 208-11; Mauser, *Gospel of Peace*; William Klassen, "The God of Peace: New Testament Perspectives on God," in *Towards a Theology of Peace: A Symposium*, ed. Stephen Tunnicliffe (London: European Nuclear Disarmament, 1989), pp. 121-30.

35. So also de Villiers, "Peace in the Pauline Letters," pp. 7-8.

of peace as an eschatological gift has become a reality in and through God's activity in Jesus, the Jewish Messiah and universal Lord. In Romans, Paul asserts that the gift of peace is the consequence of God's justice/righteousness, God's right-wising activity:

> [1]Therefore, since we are <u>justified</u> by faith, <u>we have peace with God</u> through our Lord Jesus Christ, [2]through whom we have obtained access to this grace in which we stand. . . . (Rom. 5:1-2a)

It seems quite possible that Paul has Isaiah in mind here, who also promised that peace would flow from God's saving righteousness:

> [16]Then <u>justice</u> will dwell in the wilderness, and <u>righteousness</u> abide in the fruitful field. [17]The <u>effect of righteousness will be peace</u>, and the result of righteousness, <u>quietness and trust forever</u>. [18]My people will abide in a <u>peaceful</u> habitation, in <u>secure</u> dwellings, and in <u>quiet resting places</u>. (Isa. 32:16-18)

As we will see again in the chapter on justice, Paul almost certainly saw in Christ the fulfillment of the psalmist's hope, noted above, that righteousness/justice and peace would kiss:

> For the kingdom of God is not food and drink but <u>righteousness</u> [or "<u>justice</u>"; *dikaiosynē*] <u>and peace</u> and joy in the Holy Spirit. (Rom. 14:17)[36]

Of course for Paul life in the Spirit is life in Christ (e.g. Rom. 8:1-17), which is also life in God (1 Thess. 1:1). It should not surprise us, then, that Paul (or perhaps his disciple) calls the Lord Jesus "the Lord of peace" (2 Thess. 3:16), echoing the descriptor of God as "the God of peace."[37] Similarly, the phrase "the peace of God" becomes "the peace of Christ" in Colossians 3:15.

---

36. Unfortunately, Mauser mischaracterizes Paul's understanding of peace as "hav[ing] lost touch with concrete and individual problems and needs" and as "determined by the internal struggle between Spirit and flesh" such that "the peace of God [in the concrete ways Jesus embodied it] is still relegated to its disclosure in the future" and Paul's "admonitions for peace . . . , in comparison to the Gospels, appear pale and abstract" (*The Gospel of Peace*, p. 130). His own actual discussions of specific texts do not give support to this interpretation.

37. The word "Lord" appears twenty-one times in 2 Thessalonians, often (twelve times) explicitly identified with Jesus, and otherwise often implicitly identified with him. Although there is some ambiguity in the use of the word "Lord" in 2 Thess. 3:1-5, in the passage imme-

For Paul this gift of peace and reconciliation is not an addendum to something else, such as salvation; it *is* salvation, it *is* the mission of God, the *missio Dei*. And it has two inseparable dimensions, the reconciliation of people to God and the reconciliation of people to one another; we find both dimensions whenever Paul discusses peace, with special emphasis on both in Romans, 2 Corinthians, and Ephesians.

We see the "vertical" (God-humanity) dimension of peace powerfully on display in this well-known text:

> [I]n Christ <u>God was reconciling the world to himself</u>, not counting their trespasses against them. (2 Cor. 5:19)

This sentence appears in the context of a letter in which Paul is trying to effect reconciliation within the Corinthian congregation as well as between himself and the Corinthians. The entire letter is a striking example of the inseparability, in Paul's mind, between the vertical and the horizontal dimensions of reconciliation. This theological connection is not limited to 2 Corinthians; it is succinctly summarized in the following exhortation to the disharmonious Roman congregations:

> <u>Welcome one another, therefore, just as Christ has welcomed you</u>, for the glory of God. (Rom. 15:7)[38]

The letter to the Ephesians famously extols God's grace in saving us while we were dead in our trespasses and sins (Eph. 2:1-10), yet because this mercy extends to Gentiles as well as Jews (Eph. 2:11-13; cf. Romans, e.g., 3:27-31), the vertical reconciliation between God and people necessarily means horizontal reconciliation between people:

> [14]For he [Christ] is our <u>peace</u>; in his flesh he has made both groups [Jews and Gentiles] into one and has <u>broken down the dividing wall</u>, that is, the

---

diately preceding the peace greeting (2 Thess. 3:6-15; see vv. 6, 12) and in the final benediction following the peace greeting (3:18), the Lord is named three times, always as the, or our, "Lord Jesus Christ." Thus the larger context of 2 Thess. 3:16 makes it likely, and the immediate context makes it virtually certain, that "the Lord of peace" refers specifically to Jesus, without thereby excluding God the Father as associated with peace.

38. There is significant scholarly disagreement over the ethnic makeup and social location of the communities Paul addresses in Romans, particularly Romans 14-15, but that contentions among them exist is widely acknowledged.

hostility between us. [15]He has abolished the law with its commandments and ordinances, that he might create in himself one new humanity in place of the two, thus <u>making peace</u>, [16]and might <u>reconcile both groups to God in one body through the cross</u>, thus putting to death that hostility through it. (Eph. 2:14-16)

Even this apparently comprehensive understanding of reconciliation as encompassing human relations with both God and one another is set within a larger, cosmic context, according to Colossians:

[19]For in him [Christ] all the fullness of God was pleased to dwell, [20]and through him God was pleased <u>to reconcile to himself all things</u>, whether on earth or in heaven, <u>by making peace through the blood of his cross</u>. [21]And you who were once estranged and hostile in mind, doing evil deeds, [22]<u>he has now reconciled in his fleshly body through death</u>, so as to present you holy and blameless and irreproachable before him. . . . (Col. 1:19-22)

Similar in tone is Romans 8:18-39, where we find images of God's new creation and loving victory over suffering and evil that rightly prompt Willard Swartley to ask, "Where else in all God's creation is there a grander vision of shalom for God's people?"[39] Likewise, Gordon Zerbe contends that everything Paul says about peace (personal, corporate, missional) is rooted in his core vision of cosmic restoration and peace, "the final triumph of God over the hostile and destructive powers of this age."[40] In other words, the Old Testament's overall vision of *shalom* shapes the Pauline vision of peace as having three dimensions — vertical, horizontal, and cosmic.[41]

We must stress that this divine peacemaking project is not some vague form of reconciliation but is robustly theocentric and Christocentric: God in and through Christ, and then humanity — and even the cosmos — in and through Christ. Furthermore, God's peacemaking will inevitably involve the

---

39. Swartley, *Covenant of Peace*, p. 217.

40. Gordon Mark Zerbe, *Citizenship: Paul on Peace and Politics* (Winnipeg, MB: CMU Press, 2012), p. 145. See also N. T. Wright, *Paul and the Faithfulness of God*, vol. 4 of Christian Origins and the Question of God (Minneapolis: Fortress, 2013), p. 1491, who says that "the renewal of humans is the prelude to, and the means of, the renewal of all creation. Paul's work both as an evangelist and as a pastor and teacher was therefore in the service of the unity and holiness of the church. . . . But the unity and holiness of the church was itself in the service of this larger aim."

41. Similarly, Talmon, "Signification," p. 107.

judging and removing of evil, as Romans 16:20 makes clear: "The God of peace will shortly crush Satan under your feet."[42]

Third, however, this eschatological peace is the gift that keeps on giving, or (rather) this God of peace is the God who keeps on giving the peace of God to the people of God. It is an ongoing gift, needed again and again by Paul's letter recipients and, we should add, by all who continue to read his letters as Scripture.

This dual reality of God's peaceable character and God's gift of peace sometimes comes to succinct expression near the closings of Paul's letters, in addition to the openings. For instance, we find this in the form of a promise in the last chapter of Philippians, which we noted at the beginning of the chapter:

> [7]And the peace of God, which surpasses all understanding, will guard your hearts and your minds in Christ Jesus. . . . [9]Keep on doing the things that you have learned and received and heard and seen in me, and the God of peace will be with you. (Phil. 4:7, 9)

And in 2 Thessalonians it appears in the form of a benediction, or prayer-wish, as well as a promise:

> Now may the Lord of peace himself give you peace at all times in all ways. The Lord be with all of you. (2 Thess. 3:16)

These two texts are significant also because they witness to the inner peace and calm that are given to those in Christ. This is a precious gift for all believers, and it has its roots in the promises of peace found in the Psalms. But in the history of interpretation, especially at the popular level, the peace of God is often restricted, explicitly or implicitly, to this sense of inner tranquility. Paul would say — Paul does say — that inner peace is a necessary and real aspect of God's peace, but it is not the entire, or even the principal, meaning of peace.[43]

The text from 2 Thessalonians is particularly interesting for another reason: because (as noted above) "the Lord" to whom it refers is almost certainly, in the context of the end of 2 Thessalonians, Jesus. Moreover, peace is arguably the primary theme of 2 Thessalonians.[44] Whether or not Paul

---

42. See Swartley, *Covenant of Peace*, pp. 210-11: "the 'God of peace' blessing and delivering from evil/crushing Satan cohere" in Paul's theology.

43. Even the interiority of a text like "let the peace of Christ rule in your hearts" (Col. 3:15), in context, includes communal practices of love and forgiveness (Col. 3:12-14).

44. "[T]he main sections of the letter . . . are, in fact, concerned with peace and . . .

wrote 2 Thessalonians,[45] the identification of Jesus as peacemaker suggests that either Paul or the Pauline tradition associated Jesus with God the Father in his character and role as peacemaker.

A benediction for peace also appears at the end of two other Pauline letters:

> As for those who will follow this rule — peace be upon them, and mercy, and upon the Israel of God. (Gal. 6:16)

> Peace be to the whole community, and love with faith, from God the Father and the Lord Jesus Christ. (Eph. 6:23)

If we add the three other uses (in addition to Phil. 4:9) of Paul's phrase "God of peace," which always appears near the end of a letter, to these, we have a pattern of Paul starting and concluding his letters with a word of peace, the closing word taking the form of a benediction or a promise or both:

> The God of peace be with all of you. Amen. . . . The God of peace will shortly crush Satan under your feet. The grace of our Lord Jesus Christ be with you. (Rom. 15:33; 16:20)

> May the God of peace himself sanctify you entirely; and may your spirit and soul and body be kept sound and blameless at the coming of our Lord Jesus Christ. (1 Thess. 5:23)

That is to say, Paul literally wraps his correspondence in a peace-blessing, wishing and praying for his communities that they will know the *shalom* of God in their life together, both in church and in daily life.[46] He both begins and ends his communiqués, which function in his place when he is absent,

---

peace in its eschatological, ecclesiological, and social dimensions is the theological goal of this letter" (Jouette M. Bassler, "Peace in All Ways: Theology in the Thessalonian Letters. A Response to R. Jewett, E. Krentz, and E. Richard," in *Pauline Theology*, Vol. 1, *Thessalonians, Philippians, Galatians, Philemon*, ed. Jouette Bassler [Minneapolis: Fortress, 1991], pp. 71-85 [here p. 75]).

45. For a recent argument in favor of Paul's authorship of 2 Thessalonians, see Paul Foster, "Who Wrote 2 Thessalonians? A Fresh Look at an Old Problem," *Journal for the Study of the New Testament* 35 (2012): 150-75.

46. "The worship meetings of early Christianity are portrayed [in Paul's letters] in terms of God's peaceable presence" (de Villiers, "Peace in the Pauline Letters," p. 8).

with a heartfelt wish for them to experience God's peace through Jesus the Messiah and in the Spirit.

Fourth, then, in considering the peace of God and the God of peace, we are driven inevitably to the Trinitarian character of each. Romans 5 (vv. 1-11) makes it clear that the divine reconciliation of rebellious humanity involves God the Father; Christ, whose death is the divine means of reconciliation; and the Spirit, who makes the divine reconciling love an experiential reality (Rom. 5:5). Indeed, this Trinitarian act of reconciliation is ultimately precisely that — an act of love.[47] Alluding perhaps to Romans 5, Ephesians rightly says, with a Christological focus, that "he [Jesus] is our peace" (Eph. 2:14). But the same letter also acknowledges the Father as well as the Son as the source of peace (Eph. 1:2; 6:23), and the Spirit as the practical agent of peace in the community (Eph. 4:3).[48]

Finally, we must highlight the transformative character of God's peacemaking initiative. One of the overlooked dimensions of Paul's assessment of the human condition apart from Christ is the normalcy of violence and the absence of peace. Quoting Scripture, Paul makes this point most emphatically in Romans 3, in the powerful conclusion to his indictment of humanity:

> [9] . . . [W]e have already charged that all, both Jews and Greeks, are under the power of sin, [10]as it is written: "There is no one who is righteous, not even one; [11]there is no one who has understanding, there is no one who seeks God. [12]All have turned aside, together they have become worthless; there is no one who shows kindness, there is not even one." [13]"Their throats are opened graves; they use their tongues to deceive." "The venom of vipers is under their lips." [14]"Their mouths are full of cursing and bitterness." [15]"Their feet are swift to shed blood; [16]ruin and misery are in their paths, [17]and the way of peace they have not known." [18]"There is no fear of God before their eyes." (Rom. 3:9b-18)

Violent speech and action, Paul says, is the way of lost humanity, summarized in verse 17 and the words of Isaiah 59:8 — "The way of peace they do not know."[49]

---

47. The role of the Spirit in the divine peace is stressed also in Rom. 8:6; 14:17; 15:13.

48. We will return to Ephesians, for a fuller exploration of peace in that letter, in the next chapter.

49. In addition to Isaiah, this "catena," or chain, of Scripture texts includes quotations of or allusions to various psalms and wisdom texts. We will return to this text in the chapter on justice.

What God has done and is doing in Christ, therefore, is an act of radical pacification, of radical transformation. God has made friends out of enemies (Rom. 5:1-11, esp. v. 10: "while we were enemies, we were reconciled to God through the death of his Son").[50] Reconciliation is not merely a pronouncement of forgiveness, but an event of conversion, an act of new creation. Paul knew this to be true from his own experience of conversion away from hatred and violence — he had zealously wanted to destroy the church[51] — and as he makes clear in 2 Corinthians: "So if anyone is in Christ, there is a new creation: everything old has passed away; see, everything has become new! All this is from God, who reconciled us to himself through Christ" (2 Cor. 5:17-18a). Because they are *in* him, clothed by him, reshaped by him, those who are reconciled to God through Christ are already now being transformed into the righteousness/justice of God (2 Cor. 5:21). That is, they are not only *benefiting* from God's reconciling love but *participating* in it. They are becoming a peaceable people, a people that practices peace — and passes that peace on to others, in fact to the entire world:

> [18]All this is from God, who reconciled us to himself through Christ, and has given us the ministry of reconciliation; [19]that is, in Christ God was reconciling the world to himself, not counting their trespasses against them, and entrusting the message of reconciliation to us. [20]So we are ambassadors for Christ, since God is making his appeal through us; we entreat you on behalf of Christ, be reconciled to God. [21]For our sake he

50. It should be noted that both in Rom. 5:1-11 and in 2 Cor. 5:14-21 justification/righteousness language and reconciliation/peace language appear, the former more so in Romans and the latter more so in 2 Corinthians. Justification and reconciliation, I would argue, are two ways of referring to the same reality. See further James D. G. Dunn, *The Theology of Paul the Apostle* (Grand Rapids: Eerdmans, 1998), pp. 386-89; Michael J. Gorman, *Apostle of the Crucified Lord: A Theological Introduction to Paul and His Letters* (Grand Rapids: Eerdmans, 2004), pp. 364-66; Michael J. Gorman, *Inhabiting the Cruciform God: Kenosis, Justification, and Theosis in Paul's Narrative Soteriology* (Grand Rapids: Eerdmans, 2009), pp. 52-57; de Villiers, "Peace in the Pauline Letters," pp. 11-14.

51. Acts 7:58–8:1; 9:1-2; 22:3-5; 26:9-12; Gal. 1:13-14; 1 Cor. 15:9; 1 Tim. 1:13. See Gorman, *Inhabiting the Cruciform God*, pp. 129-60. A number of scholars have proposed that Paul himself was violent, in his use of language, his imposition of control, and so on. See my response to this perspective in *Inhabiting the Cruciform God* (pp. 129-60) and, for a more thorough analysis, with a theologically nuanced way forward, Zerbe, *Citizenship*, pp. 169-80. See also Jeremy Gabrielson, *Paul's Non-Violent Gospel: The Theological Politics of Peace in Paul's Life and Letters* (Eugene, OR : Pickwick, 2013), esp. pp. 91-101.

made him to be sin who knew no sin, so that in him we might become the righteousness of God. (2 Cor. 5:18-21)[52]

## *Pursuing the Things That Make for Peace: Peace as Ecclesial Practice*

Paul's language about peace is not limited, then, to its association with God's character and generosity. The peace of God carries with it a moral and missional imperative to be at peace, indeed to make peace, as Paul had no doubt learned from the Psalms: "seek peace, and pursue it" (Ps. 34:14; LXX 33:15 = *zēteson eirēnēn kai diōxon autēn*), to which he clearly alludes in Romans 14:19 (*ara oun ta tēs eirēnēs diōkōmen;* "Let us then pursue what makes for peace"). If the church formed by God's reconciling love (Rom. 5:1-11) is to embody the gospel in daily life, in its "spirituality," it too will practice love and thus reconciliation.[53] This is an inherent and inevitable dimension of participation in the life of the God who makes peace in Christ by the Spirit, but it is not natural to human beings. It requires conversion from the "normalcy" of conflict, violence, and the absence of peace.[54]

N. T. Wright is but the latest in a line of interpreters who have found reconciliation to be at the heart of Paul's soteriology. But Wright now wants us to be sure to see that the theology of reconciliation is also at the heart of Paul's ecclesiology, his vision of the church:

> I want . . . to argue that Paul's practical aim was the creation and mainte-
> nance of particular kinds of communities; that the means to their creation
> and maintenance was the key notion of reconciliation; and that these
> communities, which he regarded as the spirit-inhabited Messiah-people,
> constituted at least in his mind and perhaps also in historical truth a

52. There is scholarly debate about the implicit referents in Paul's use of first-person-plural (we/us) language in this text and throughout 2 Corinthians. It is possible and perhaps necessary to restrict this language to Paul and his apostolic colleagues in some instances, but since the scope of God's reconciliation and transformation is not just apostles but the entire church, it seems best to conclude that in some form, reconciliation is the work of the entire church. The beneficiaries of God's reconciliation are also its agents. See also Morna D. Hooker, "On Becoming the Righteousness of God: Another Look at 2 Cor. 5:21," *Novum Testamentum* 50 (2008): 358-75, esp. pp. 365, 373.

53. See also Swartley, *Covenant of Peace,* pp. 211-21; Klassen, "Pursue Peace."

54. Recent work on spirituality focuses on the centrality of transformation to the very definition of the word. For the connection of that emphasis with the spirituality of peace in Paul, see de Villiers, "Peace in the Pauline Letters."

new kind of reality, embodying a new kind of philosophy, of religion, and of politics, and a new kind of combination of those . . . a new kind of Jewishness, a community of new covenant, a community rooted in a new kind of prayer.[55]

What does all this mean for Paul, and for us, practically?

### A Community of Centripetal Peace, a "Sphere of Interrupted Violence"

First of all, Paul sees the church itself as a community of peace in its internal life, its centripetal activity. It is a "sphere of interrupted violence" in the midst of a violent world, the Roman Empire.[56] Ironically, Rome — via its emperors, citizens, poets, and propagandists — proclaimed itself the source of worldwide peace, even the bringer of the eschatological or golden age.[57] Of the many symbols and propaganda tools of the *Pax Romana*, we may point to the famous *Ara Pacis (Augustae)*, or altar of (the Augustan) peace, erected in 9 BCE in Rome. N. T. Wright describes it in the following way:

> To this day the huge altar, with its carved panels on every side, creates the strong impression of a solemn, devout, peaceful and (not least) prosperous society, in which the literal fruits of peace are displayed in a cornucopia, and a kind of rural idyll is invoked, as in Virgil's *Georgics,* of a countryside enjoying the chance to get on with its quiet round of harvests and animal husbandry. The larger scheme, however, of which this celebration of peace forms a part, is unambiguously and unashamedly a celebration of the military victory which brings peace about. The goddess Roma sits triumphantly on top of a pile of arms; it is because the whole world now lives in fear of Rome that Rome herself can be at peace. "Peace and security," indeed, are regularly combined: military might guarantees imperial stability. But such thoughts, though present and relevant, seem miles away from the overall impression of the altar, which offers a serene combination of devout formality and familial informality, with (unusu-

---

55. Wright, *Paul and the Faithfulness of God,* p. 1476.

56. Wengst, *Pax Romana,* p. 88.

57. See texts in, e.g., Mark Reasoner, *Roman Imperial Texts: A Sourcebook* (Minneapolis: Fortress, 2013). The sentiment was not confined to literary texts but was expressed also in inscriptions and on coins.

ally) women and children portrayed attractively as part of the family party in sacrificial procession.[58]

The *Pax Romana,* then, meant prosperity, peace, and security by intimidation and subjugation, for the Romans believed that it was the will of the gods that Rome rule the world — politically, militarily, economically — and that only as such a divinely sanctioned power did Rome gain its peace and security, by whatever means necessary. The peace of Rome was the peace of its gods *(pax deorum);* indeed, Rome even made *Pax* a Deity (as it did *Iustitia,* justice, and *Fides,* fidelity).[59] While Rome may have believed it had a divine mission of pacification through subjugation, Paul, as we have just seen, knew and proclaimed the peace of Israel's God, peacemaking and human flourishing through enemy-love.

Let me state what Paul is up to as bluntly as possible. To paraphrase the apostle in Galatians 2:15-21,

> *If violence and war is the way to peace, then Rome was right, and Christ died for nothing.*[60]

But Christ did not die in vain; rather, God in Christ was bringing the peace of God to the world. Jesus is the Messiah, the Prince of Peace.

In his earliest extant letter, Paul admonishes the Thessalonians to embody this peace of God within their community. This means, on the one hand, refusing to return evil for evil and, on the other, proactively seeking others' welfare:

> [13] . . . Be at <u>peace</u> among yourselves. [14]And we urge you, beloved, to admonish the idlers, encourage the faint-hearted, help the weak, be patient with all of them. [15]See that <u>none of you repays evil for evil</u>, but <u>always seek to do good to one another and to all</u>. (1 Thess. 5:13b-15)

The full implications of this admonition can be grasped only by noting the reference to the *absence* of peace mentioned in the immediately preceding passage:

58. Wright, *Paul and the Faithfulness of God,* p. 296.

59. For an excellent overview of these developments, see Wright, *Paul and the Faithfulness of God,* ch. 5 (pp. 279-347).

60. This sentence alludes to Gal. 2:21, which says, "I do not nullify the grace of God; for if justification comes through the law, then Christ died for nothing."

²For you yourselves know very well that the day of the Lord will come like a thief in the night. ³<u>When they say, "There is peace and security,"</u> then <u>sudden destruction</u> will come upon them, as labor pains come upon a pregnant woman, and there will be <u>no escape</u>! ⁴But you, beloved, are not in darkness, for that day to surprise you like a thief; ⁵for you are all children of light and children of the day; we are not of the night or of darkness. (1 Thess. 5:2-5)

It is now widely recognized that in this text Paul is referring to the Roman claim to offer *pax et securitas,* a claim that Paul finds empty.[61] It is not the Empire that offers peace and security, but God, in fulfillment of the promise recorded in Isaiah 32:18 noted earlier: "My people will abide in a peaceful habitation, in secure dwellings, and in quiet resting places." Specifically, the space of peace is the apocalyptically shaped community in Christ, where the children of light practice peace as an inherent part of their common life of faith, hope, and love (1 Thess. 5:8). In Galatians, Paul will say that this divinely given peace is the fruit of the Spirit, inseparable from love, patience, joy, and so on (Gal. 5:22-23).[62] Even in 1 Thessalonians, the practices of love, joy, and peace are implicitly identified as the work of the Spirit in the community (cf. 1 Thess. 5:19).[63] It is the God of peace (1 Thess. 5:23a) who is creating a peaceful people as part of their thorough sanctification (1 Thess. 5:23b).

First Thessalonians also makes it clear that the community's peaceable nature and peacemaking mission are due to its existence as an apocalyptic, or eschatological, community — a community that anticipates the coming reign of God by participating in it already. In earlier chapters, we have referred to this apocalyptic existence as "anticipatory participation." A foretaste of the promised messianic era of peace is possible, by the work of the Spirit who is the "first installment" of future salvation (2 Cor. 1:22; Eph. 1:14), in and

61. See, e.g., Jeffrey A. D. Weima, "'Peace and security' (1 Thess. 5.3): Prophetic Warning or Political Propaganda?" *New Testament Studies* 58 (2012): 331-59.

62. See also Col. 3:12-17, where peace is prominent along with love and gratitude, all of which seem to relate to compassion, kindness, humility, meekness, patience, and forgiveness.

63. The exhortations regarding community life in 1 Thess. 5:11-22 include only one explicit mention of the Spirit, namely, "Do not quench the Spirit" (5:19), which refers most directly to permitting and discerning prophetic utterances in the assembly (5:20-22). Nevertheless, given Paul's understanding of the Spirit's activity from other letters, we should see all of the practices and attitudes promoted in this section of 1 Thessalonians as ways in which the Spirit works in the community. (See, for instance, the association of the Spirit and joy in 1 Thess. 1:6 — "you received the word with joy inspired by the Holy Spirit" — foreshadowing the same association in Gal. 5:22 and suggesting a link between the Spirit and joy in 1 Thess. 5:16-19.)

through those who live in the Messiah Jesus, the prince of peace. Therefore, this peace

> is not only about incidental or individual aspects like greeting each other, experiencing an inner peace or displaying a peace-loving lifestyle. *It is an abiding, sustainable new way of existence and lifestyle that characterize God's new community and creation.* The transformation of humanity to become peaceful and peace-loving has a cosmic nature and implies a new way of thinking and a new lifestyle.[64]

Another exhortation to peacemaking as the responsibility of all in the community, and also as the work of the Spirit, is found in Romans, in the context of dissension among those with differing cultural expressions (in the matter of diet) of their faith in the gospel:

> [17]For the kingdom of God is not food and drink but righteousness and peace and joy in the Holy Spirit. [18]The one who thus serves Christ is acceptable to God and has human approval. [19]Let us then pursue what makes for peace and for mutual upbuilding. (Rom. 14:17-19)

As in 1 Thessalonians, here in Romans peacemaking is an active task, a practice focused on community edification, which is what Paul means, practically speaking, by love (cf. 1 Cor. 8:1 — "love builds up"). Paul takes this communal responsibility so seriously that he finds an inseparable connection between practicing peace toward others and experiencing the promised peace of God, as we see in the conclusion of 2 Corinthians:

> Finally, brothers and sisters, farewell. Put things in order, listen to my appeal, agree with one another, live in peace; and the God of love and peace will be with you. (2 Cor. 13:11)[65]

---

64. De Villiers, "Peace in the Pauline Letters," pp. 15-16 (emphasis added).

65. This connection is reminiscent of the teaching of Jesus summarized in the Lord's prayer and the brief interpretation of it in Matthew's Gospel: "And forgive us our debts, as we also have forgiven our debtors. . . . For if you forgive others their trespasses, your heavenly Father will also forgive you; but if you do not forgive others, neither will your Father forgive your trespasses" (Matt. 6:12, 14-15). As Swartley puts it, in 2 Cor. 13:11 we see a "synergistic relation between God's empowerment and human responsibility" (*Covenant of Peace*, p. 211). He notes that a similar synergy is implied in 1 Cor. 14:33.

While in some instances it may be true, as Swartley maintains,[66] that Paul subordinates peace to the primary Pauline virtue of love, what seems more significant is the symbiosis of, or close connection between, the two practices of loving and peacemaking.[67]

Also closely connected in Paul's theology are practices of peace and justice, especially in relations between Gentiles and Jews and between the haves and the have-nots. These two interests coalesce in Paul's ongoing interest in the collection for the poor, especially the poor of Jerusalem (Rom. 15:22-32; 1 Cor. 16:1-4; 2 Corinthians 8–9), as we will see in chapter seven. If God has brought *shalom* to the world in Christ, one of the concrete fruits of that *shalom* is the sharing of material goods with those in need so that those who are one in Christ may experience, in some sense, "equality" (Paul's word, *isotēs*, in 2 Cor. 8:13-14; NRSV "fair balance").

*A Community of Centrifugal Peace:*
*Pursuing Peace, Rejecting Retaliation*

Secondly, however, the peace of the church is not merely for insiders, for life within the body of Christ; its inner life spirals out into the world. Paul already makes this centrifugal dimension of the church peace clear early in his writing career when he urges the Thessalonian believers to practice peacemaking (1 Thess. 5:13b) by "not repay[ing] evil for evil" and by "do[ing] good to one another and to all" (1 Thess. 5:15), which reemphasizes the prayer of 3:12: "And may the Lord make you increase and abound in love for one another and for all." This exhortation to peacemaking in the world appears in a list of final admonitions at the end of the letter, none of which, unfortunately, gets developed at any length.

A comparable exhortation appears in a similar passage in Romans. After admonishing the believers in Rome to excel in mutual love, honor, and practical care toward one another, as well as hospitality to strangers (Rom. 12:9-13), Paul shifts briefly to outsiders, specifically persecutors: "Bless those who persecute you; bless and do not curse them" (Rom. 12:14). After turning once again to internal affairs, urging empathy, harmony, and humility (Rom. 12:15-16), Paul turns his attention once more toward (at least primarily) outsiders:

---

66. Swartley, *Covenant of Peace*, p. 212.

67. See also 2 Tim. 2:22-24, which begins, "Shun youthful passions and pursue righteousness, faith, love, and peace, along with those who call on the Lord from a pure heart. Have nothing to do with stupid and senseless controversies; you know that they breed quarrels."

Do not repay anyone evil for evil, but take thought for what is noble in the sight of all. If it is possible, so far as it depends on you, live peaceably [Greek *eirēneuontes*] with all. Beloved, never avenge yourselves, but leave room for the wrath of God; for it is written, "Vengeance is mine, I will repay, says the Lord." No, "if your enemies are hungry, feed them; if they are thirsty, give them something to drink; for by doing this you will heap burning coals on their heads." Do not be overcome by evil, but overcome evil with good. (Rom. 12:17-21)

The echoes of 1 Thessalonians in Romans 12 reveal a pattern in Paul's thinking and speaking about peace vis-à-vis outsiders ("all"). The pattern includes prohibitions against evil — cursing, retaliation, and the like — on the one hand, and positive admonitions about doing good — blessing, feeding, and so on — on the other.

It would be fair to conclude, therefore, that peacemaking toward outsiders for Paul has a special focus because of the frequent hostility generated toward believers by those outsiders.[68] In other words, the practice of peace is a sort of apologetic, a form of bearing witness to the gospel in the most difficult of circumstances. It is the active expression of the command of both Jesus and Paul to love one's enemies.[69] As the communities and individual believers bear faithful witness to the Messiah who taught and practiced peacemaking toward enemies, they become a living exegesis of the gospel; indeed, once again they become the gospel.[70] Such peaceful relations with outsiders will rather obviously include the rejection of violence; as Richard Hays has put it, "There is not a syllable in the Pauline letters that can be cited in support of Christians employing violence."[71] This commitment to nonvi-

---

68. See also Heb. 12:14, an imperative issued in a similar, indeed more grave, instance of believers encountering hostility from outsiders.

69. On Romans 12 and love, see Zerbe, *Citizenship*, pp. 148-50.

70. On enemy-love in Paul, see Swartley, *Covenant of Peace*, pp. 213-15 and, for more detail, Gordon Zerbe, "Paul's Ethic of Nonretaliation and Peace," in *The Love of Enemy and Nonretaliation in the New Testament*, ed. Willard M. Swartley (Louisville: Westminster John Knox, 1992), pp. 177-222, now reprinted in his *Citizenship*, pp. 141-68. Zerbe calls what I have termed prohibitions against evil and positive admonitions about doing good "passive" and "active" responses, respectively, to enemies. Zerbe (*Citizenship*, pp. 143-44) lists passive responses as not repaying evil for evil, not taking vengeance for oneself, not cursing, clemency/long-temper, endurance, not litigating, and not reckoning evil; active responses include responding with good deeds, blessing, conciliating, being at peace, showing grace, and loving.

71. Richard B. Hays, *The Moral Vision of the New Testament: Community, Cross, New*

olence is grounded in the very heart of the Pauline gospel, the discussion of Christ's death for God's enemies as the manifestation of God's reconciling and justifying love (Rom. 5:1-11; Ephesians 2–3). Thus John Howard Yoder rightly observed that justification is "the Good News that I and my enemy are united, through no merit or work of my own, in a new humanity that forbids henceforth my ever taking his life in my hands."[72]

At the same time, however, it seems just as likely that Paul does not want to limit peacemaking to a sort of *apologia* in the form of reactionary measures of beneficence rather than retaliation. On the contrary, Paul would want his communities to practice peacemaking as a proactive way of life. Gordon Zerbe has shown that Paul's "ethic of non-retaliation and peace" appears in general exhortations on the topic (e.g., Rom. 12:9-21), in catalogs of Paul's hardships (e.g., 1 Cor. 4:12-13a), in lists of virtues and vices (e.g., Gal. 5:16-24), in reference to a concrete situation (1 Cor. 6:1-8), and in his poem on love (1 Corinthians 13).[73] This pervasive presence of peace-language suggests a proactive, rather than simply reactive, posture as a fundamental dimension of Pauline ethics.

Practical concern for harmony in the church and for care for the weak can and should translate into similar practices outside the community. The admonition to "live peaceably with all" may have its origins in the context of harassment and other forms of persecution, but unless we assume that Paul thought *every* nonbeliever was a persecutor, we need to interpret the universality of the admonition to mean a commitment to practicing Christ-shaped, or cruciform, *shalom* always and everywhere.[74]

This, indeed, is what Paul, in 2 Corinthians 5:20, claims that he and his coworkers do as "ambassadors for Christ" — though even here the lines between the church and the world are blurred, since Paul is writing to members of the church to be "reconciled with God." Throughout much of 2 Corinthians (especially chapters 1–7), Paul engages in a ministry of reconciliation, and in the letter he repeatedly describes apostolic existence as inherently Christlike, indeed cruciform. Since, however, in his earlier letter to the Corinthians (1 Cor. 4:16; 11:1) Paul had urged them to imitate his imitation of Christ, it would be inappropriate to conclude that reconciliation is *solely*

---

*Creation; A Contemporary Introduction to New Testament Ethics* (San Francisco: HarperCollins, 1996), p. 331. See also my *Inhabiting the Cruciform God*, pp. 129-60.

72. Yoder, *Politics of Jesus*, p. 224.

73. Zerbe, *Citizenship*, pp. 141-43.

74. See also Paul's words about the divine calling to peace in general, including relations with outsiders, finding expression in the marriage of a believer to an unbeliever (1 Cor. 7:15).

an apostolic activity. In fact, in the beginning of 2 Corinthians Paul specifically urges the Corinthians to practice reconciliation within their community (1:23–2:11). Even though he does not use the word "reconciliation" in that passage, he does call on the Corinthians to imitate his forgiveness of a member of their community (2:7, 10) and thus, ultimately, to imitate God's act of reconciliation, for God did not count the world's trespasses against them (2 Cor. 5:19). For Paul, forgiveness is clearly at the heart of reconciliation, whether by God or by humans. Moreover, the occurrence of the word "world" in 2 Corinthians 5:19 ("reconciling the world") is reminiscent of John 3:16-18 ("God so loved the world . . .") and reinforces the claim made above that the kind of forgiveness and reconciliation about which Paul writes cannot be limited to insiders if it is to imitate — or, better, participate in — God's reconciliation.

In other words, (1) the ministry of reconciliation is ultimately a ministry for all believers and for all communities in Christ, and (2) its divinely derived focus is the entire world — one conflict at a time, whether in the church or not. To ground this more broadly in Paul's theology of divine reconciliation, we can put it this way: just as God was in Christ to effect reconciliation, all who are now in Christ participate in the Christocentric divine mission of reconciliation. To be sure, "we" — meaning all believers — are not in Christ in the same way that God was in Christ. But Paul's use of locative language in both cases, which creates an implicit connection between us and God in Christ, is not to be dismissed as an unimportant coincidence. Furthermore, whatever rhetorical and relational situation moved Paul to stress his own ministry throughout 2 Corinthians should not stop us from following the trajectory of his own theo-logic. In some significant sense, all those who are in Christ are Christ's ambassadors, God's means of proclaiming and continuing the work of reconciliation offered in Christ.[75] *The church that does not practice peace, both internally and externally, will not be a credible witness to others that God was, and is, reconciling the world in Christ and through the body of Christ, the church.*

Thus, although Paul does not elaborate on what peace means concretely for believers with respect to outsiders, the contexts in which the admonitions appear allow us to draw a few general conclusions about what the practice of peace, the ministry of reconciliation, "in the world" means for Paul:

---

75. As we will argue in chapter seven, Paul does not limit becoming the justice of God (2 Cor. 5:21) to apostles, and since throughout his letters he exhorts all believers to practice peace and reconciliation, the ministry of reconciliation is a ministry of the entire church, even if apostles (and others) have special roles in that ecclesial mission.

1. Peacemaking means embodying the same virtues in the world as in the church; there can be no ethical dualism of "churchly" and "worldly" activity; centripetal and centrifugal activity cohere.

2. Peacemaking means renouncing retaliation for evil, even the kind of extreme evil (persecution) experienced by contemporary believers as their faithfulness connects them to the experiences of the prophets, Jesus, Paul, and the Thessalonians (see 1 Thess. 1:6-7; 2:14-16; 3:1-10).

3. Peacemaking means seeking the common good, especially by attending to the needs of the weak, promoting a spirit of forgiveness, striving for harmony, and encouraging all to take responsibility for their role in furthering the common good.

4. Peacemaking in the present is grounded in the past world-reconciling love of God in Christ and the future world-redeeming salvation of God promised in such texts as Romans 8 and Colossians 1. Thus it both reflects and integrates the two Pauline theological emphases of cross and parousia, a truly Christologically grounded, apocalyptically oriented practice that includes both humans and the rest of the created order, as does the larger biblical vision of *shalom*.[76]

We have emphasized the specifically Christological understanding of peace that we find in Paul, but we should remember, as Swartley, Klassen, and others have rightly stressed, and as we have already discussed, that Paul's devotion to peace has its origins in the Scriptures of Israel and in Jewish ethics.

## Summary: Overview of Paul and Peace

We may summarize our argument concerning Paul and peace so far in this chapter with the words of Pieter de Villiers of South Africa:

> In this reconciliation [described in Rom. 5:1-11] salvation was established through the death and resurrection of Christ which removed the hostile relationship with God and brings about a new condition in Christ (Rom. 5:11). . . . For Paul the human condition is in need of radical transformation by a peaceable God so that humanity can reflect God's peaceable

---

76. For a contemporary theology of creation that develops these connections among creation, peace, and apocalyptic hope, see Jonathan R. Wilson, *God's Good World: Reclaiming the Doctrine of Creation* (Grand Rapids: Baker Academic, 2013), esp. pp. 120-26.

image. The faith of Pauline communities is delineated in these terms. Peace thus is much more than an option. Faith is all about peace as the prerequisite for a meaningful lifestyle. For Paul the divine touch results in humanity being transformed to become peaceful and to work for peace.[77]

We turn now, briefly, to the working out of Paul's peace theology and vocabulary in one specific letter (Romans) before turning, in the next chapter, to a longer treatment of Ephesians.[78] Like all Pauline letters, Romans and Ephesians both begin with a greeting that includes a prayer-wish for peace (Rom. 1:7; Eph. 1:2). As noted above, this is no mere formality in any of Paul's letters, but that is particularly the case with Romans and Ephesians, in which peace is a central theme. The "peace" word-family appears eleven times in Romans and seven times in Ephesians, with related terms also figuring critically in the argument of each letter. Both letters focus on what God has done in Christ to make peace both *with* humanity and *within* humanity — the so-called vertical and horizontal dimensions of peace discussed earlier — as well as the cosmic dimensions of God's peace initiative and our anticipatory participation in it.

## Peace in Romans

Why should a discussion of peace in Paul focus on Romans? The most obvious answer is that Romans is Paul's most comprehensive, systematic, and influential letter. It contains the fullest exposition of his gospel. If peace is a significant aspect of Romans, that fact in and of itself is significant for both our understanding and our appropriation of the letter.[79]

The argument of Paul's letter to the Romans has often been traced in terms of a narrative flow — from (1) the human condition, to (2) the divine solution and human response, to (3) the consequences for those who believe, to (4) the plight and fate of Israel, to (5) life in the community of Gentile and Jewish believers. This narrative is bracketed by bookend-like opening and closing remarks, including greetings. This narrative argument, surrounded by the bookends, can be displayed in the following table:

---

77. De Villiers, "Peace in the Pauline Letters," pp. 13, 15.

78. I am of course aware that the authorship of Ephesians is disputed, a matter we will consider in the next chapter.

79. This brief paragraph should not be misunderstood either as a denial that Romans is a real letter or a suggestion that peace is the *only* theme in the letter. Indeed, we will consider a different, though related, theme in chapter eight of this book.

## THE NARRATIVE ARGUMENT OF ROMANS

| Section | Passage |
| --- | --- |
| Opening | 1:1-17 |
| (1) The human condition | 1:18–3:20 |
| (2) The divine solution and human response | 3:21–5:11[80] |
| (3) The consequences for those who have faith | 5:12–8:39 |
| (4) The plight and fate of Israel | 9:1–11:32 |
| (5) Life in the community of Gentile and Jewish believers | 12:1–15:13 |
| Closing | 15:14–16:27 |

What few interpreters of Romans have noted, however, is the prominent role of peace in this narrative. However, Klaus Haacker has in fact noticed its importance, identifying the letter as a "Friedensmemorandum," or "peace memorandum."[81] He calls the letter also a "proclamation of peace with God and on earth."[82] Indeed, peace plays a prominent role in Paul's narration of the gospel story from human need to life in the Christian community, with both bookends containing prayer-wishes for peace. It may well be that this emphasis appears in Romans because the letter was addressed to the capital of the Empire, the home of the emperors who were thought, from Augustus onwards, to be the architects of peace, the *Pax Romana*.[83] As noted above, Rome was (and is) also home to the famous altar to peace, the *Ara Pacis*.

We can see in a general way how this theme works itself out in Romans by simply noting the verses in which the vocabulary of peace (including reconciliation), and its opposites, appears:

### Opening

To all God's beloved in Rome, who are called to be saints: Grace to you and <u>peace</u> from God our Father and the Lord Jesus Christ. (1:7)

---

80. Rom. 5:1-11 is sometimes referred to as a bridge passage linking the discussion that ends at 4:25 with that which begins at 5:12 and continues through 8:39. I have placed it here with the earlier section of the letter because on the theme of peace and reconciliation it sums up the content of 3:21–4:25.

81. Klaus Haacker, "Der Römerbrief als Friedensmemorandum," *New Testament Studies* 36 (1990): 25-41. See also his discussion in Klaus Haacker, *The Theology of Paul's Letter to the Romans* (Cambridge: Cambridge University Press, 2003), pp. 45-53, 116-24.

82. Haacker, *Theology*, p. 45.

83. See, e.g., Haacker, *Theology*, pp. 45-53, 116-24 as well as the resources mentioned in previous notes in this chapter.

### *(1) The human condition*

They were filled with every kind of wickedness, evil, covetousness, <u>malice</u>. Full of envy, <u>murder</u>, <u>strife</u>, deceit, craftiness, they are gossips, <u>slanderers</u>, <u>God-haters</u>, <u>insolent</u>, haughty, boastful, inventors of evil, rebellious toward parents, foolish, faithless, <u>heartless</u>, <u>ruthless</u>. (Rom. 1:29-31)

For he [God] will repay according to each one's deeds: to those who by patiently doing good seek for glory and honor and immortality, he will give eternal life; while for those who are self-seeking and who obey not the truth but wickedness, there will be wrath and fury. There will be anguish and distress for everyone who does evil, the Jew first and also the Greek, but glory and honor and <u>peace</u> for everyone who does good, the Jew first and also the Greek. (2:6-10)

"Their feet are swift to shed blood; ruin and misery are in their paths, and the way of <u>peace</u> they have not known." "There is no fear of God before their eyes." (3:15-18)

### *(2) The divine solution and human response*

Therefore, since we are justified by faith, we have <u>peace</u> with God through our Lord Jesus Christ, through whom we have obtained access to this grace in which we stand; and we boast in our hope of sharing the glory of God. (5:1-2)

For if while we were enemies, we were <u>reconciled</u> to God through the death of his Son, much more surely, having been <u>reconciled</u>, will we be saved by his life. But more than that, we even boast in God through our Lord Jesus Christ, through whom we have now received <u>reconciliation</u>. (5:10-11)

### *(3) The consequences for those who have faith*

To set the mind on the flesh is death, but to set the mind on the Spirit is life and <u>peace</u>. (8:6)

### *(4) The plight and fate of Israel*

For if their rejection is the <u>reconciliation</u> of the world, what will their acceptance be but life from the dead! (11:15)

### (5) Life in the community of Gentile and Jewish believers

If it is possible, so far as it depends on you, live peaceably with all. (12:18)

For the kingdom of God is not food and drink but righteousness and peace and joy in the Holy Spirit. . . . Let us then pursue what makes for peace and for mutual upbuilding. (14:17, 19)

May the God of hope fill you with all joy and peace in believing, so that you may abound in hope by the power of the Holy Spirit. (15:13)

### Closing

The God of peace be with all of you. Amen. (15:33)

The God of peace will shortly crush Satan under your feet. The grace of our Lord Jesus Christ be with you. (16:20)

We may now therefore reconfigure the table displayed above to include peace and peacemaking as an essential component of the entire letter, from opening to closing:

#### PEACE IN THE NARRATIVE ARGUMENT OF ROMANS

| Section Topic | Passage | Key Concerns | Key Texts |
|---|---|---|---|
| Opening | 1:1-17 | Peace to you from God and Christ | 1:7 |
| (1) The human condition | 1:18–3:20 | (1) Peace is the divine intention, but not the human reality. | 1:29-31; 2:6-10; 3:15-18 |
| (2) The divine solution and human response | 3:21–5:11 | (2) Peace and reconciliation with God come through Christ, appropriated by faith. | 5:1-2, 10-11 |
| (3) The consequences for those who have faith | 5:12–8:39 | (3) Life in the Spirit is life marked by God's peace. | 8:6 |
| (4) The plight and fate of Israel | 9:1–11:32 | (4) The mystery of God's will includes reconciliation for all. | 11:15 |
| (5) Life in the community of Gentile and Jewish believers | 12:1–15:13 | (5) The kingdom of God means living peaceably with all; there should be peace both between Gentiles and Jews and between the church and outsiders. | 12:18; 14:17, 19; 15:13 |
| Closing | 15:14–16:27 | The God of peace blesses with peace now and later. | 15:33; 16:20 |

This table and the verses to which it refers do not exhaust the meaning of peace and peacemaking for Paul in Romans; they only highlight and summarize the theme. Much more can and should be said. The following discussion will flesh out a bit what has been presented so far in summary fashion and will recall points made earlier in the general discussion of peace in Paul, where Romans has figured significantly. It will also anticipate the fuller treatment of Romans, from a different perspective, in chapter eight.

*Opening (Rom. 1:1-17)*

As always, Paul begins his letter with a greeting of grace and peace from God and Christ (1:7), but he does so only after introducing himself by summarizing his gospel of God's Messiah, the Son of God, and his apostolic ministry to the Gentiles, or nations (1:1-6). It is hard to avoid the conclusion that Paul's theopolitical language, intentionally or not, would challenge the "gospel" of Rome and the *Pax Romana.* In what follows, Paul says, readers and auditors will be reminded of the true good news, the true peace that the world — including Rome and its so-called peacemaking son of God (the emperor) — cannot and does not give. But God in Christ does provide it.

*(1) The human condition (Rom. 1:18–3:20)*

In the first part of Romans, however, Paul first depicts the hopeless situation of humanity as one of *asebeia* and *adikia,* ungodliness and injustice/unrighteousness (1:18). Conflict is the order of the day, both between humans and God and within humanity itself (1:18-32). God has created humans for a life that will lead to eschatological "glory and honor and peace" (2:10), but humans have turned their back on God and the ways of God. Having forsaken God and replaced God with idols, they lack the glory of God that was theirs by creation (3:23), and they have replaced the doing of good and the practice of peace with violence of both mouth and hand (3:10-18). As we saw earlier in the chapter, Paul summarizes the nature and extent of this violent speech and action in the words of Scripture, culminating in this powerful indictment:

> [15]Their feet are <u>swift to shed blood</u>; [16]ruin and misery are in their paths, [17]and <u>the way of peace they have not known.</u> [18]There is no fear of God before their eyes. (3:15-18)

The way of peace they have not known, for they have no fear of God: this is a poignant summary of Paul's perspective on the human condition from his new perspective of being in Christ.

### (2) The divine solution and human response (Rom. 3:21–5:11)

In part 2 of Romans, Paul depicts Christ's death as God's dramatic, faithful, and loving means of restoring rebellious, even warring, human beings to a proper relationship with him, to new life (3:21-26). This divine action is depicted in the language of justification, resurrection, and reconciliation. Of greatest importance to our discussion here is the language of reconciliation (5:1-11).[84]

In antiquity, as today, reconciliation could refer to the cessation of hostilities in marriage, civic life, the international sphere (e.g., war), and so on. The dominant tone in Romans seems to be political — the termination of hostilities.[85] God's action in Christ's death is no ordinary conflict resolution mediated by a third party but the surprising, loving initiative of the grieved party, God, for the benefit of the self-made enemies of God — all human beings. It is divine enemy-love, and the result is peace with God (5:1).[86] God in Christ is the reconciler, the peacemaker. The Messiah's death is the demonstration of God's way of dealing with rebellious humanity — spiritual insurgents, so to speak. It is the definitive sign of God's love for enemies and God's nonviolent reconciliation of them.[87] It is "'peace after enmity.'"[88]

What is absent from Romans 5, however, is any explicit call to cruciform existence in the form of loving enemies or practicing reconciliation. This la-

---

84. As I have argued elsewhere and noted in a previous note, reconciliation is not something different from justification, as the parallel constructions in Rom. 5:1 and 5:9-11 manifest quite clearly.

85. So also, e.g., Robert Jewett, *Romans*, Hermeneia (Minneapolis: Fortress, 2007), pp. 365-68.

86. Some (in fact, some of the best) manuscripts of Rom. 5:1 read "let us have peace with God" rather than "we have peace with God." If this reading is correct, then it would likely refer to the lack of harmony within the church(es) in Rome and the need for "horizontal" peace to be practiced in order for the "vertical" peace with God to be fully realized (so Jewett [*Romans*, p. 348]). Although this sentiment is theologically correct, and Paul affirms it, he does so in the larger context and argument of the letter (as Jewett also says [*Romans*, p. 349]), not here. Paul's point here is the indicative situation, the reality of peace with God for those who believe the good news and are justified.

87. See further my *Inhabiting the Cruciform God*, pp. 129-60.

88. Haacker, *Theology*, p. 45.

cuna is more a function of context than conviction, however. At this point in Romans Paul has been establishing the need for, and the reality of, God's rescue of sin-enslaved humanity through the Messiah's death and resurrection. Romans 5:1-11 serves as a sort of bridge passage to the apostle's discussion of the existential significance of that reality. Later in the letter Paul will, in fact, draw parallels between the love of God and Christ for enemies and the praxis of those in Christ. But even here there is a hint in that direction, as Paul indicates that "God's love has been poured into our hearts through the Holy Spirit that has been given to us" (v. 5). In other words, those who have received the Spirit of God have also received the dynamic love of God and will, implicitly, love others — even enemies — as God in Christ has loved them.

### (3) *The consequences for those who have faith (Rom. 5:12–8:39)*

The third part of Romans depicts, in various ways, the contrast between life outside of Christ and life in Christ.[89] One overarching theme in this portrayal of transformation is death and the various aspects of its antithesis, life. Death came through one individual's sin and spread to all as they affirmed that "original" sin (as it was later labeled), resulting in a "reign" of death (5:12-21; cf. 7:5, 10, 13, 24). This reign of death is undone, paradoxically, by Christ's life-giving, peacemaking death and by his resurrection, giving life to all who believe and thus share in that death and resurrection (6:1-14). The result is newness of life now and eternal life to come (5:18, 21; 6:4, 13, 22-23).

If *shalom* is wholeness and fullness of life, then Paul has been talking about *shalom* without using the specific vocabulary of peace. In Romans 8, however, we find a celebration of God's gift of life in Christ by the Spirit, including the gift of peace previously mentioned in 5:1-11 and described in other language in the intervening chapters: "To set the mind on the flesh is death, but to set the mind on the Spirit is life and peace" (8:6). By the Spirit believers can do what God desires of human beings (8:3-4) and thereby receive the honor, glory, and peace that previously eluded them (2:10; 8:29-30).

Romans 8 speaks of the eschatological *shalom* of God as the final redemption, liberation, and glorification of those in Christ, and also of the whole creation (8:18-25).[90] While humans cannot, of course, cause this to

---

89. For a helpful overview, see the table in Craig S. Keener, *Romans*, New Covenant Commentary Series (Eugene, OR: Cascade, 2009), pp. 87-88.

90. On Romans 8 and peace/reconciliation, see Wilson, *God's Good World*, pp. 142-46:

happen, they can bear witness to it in the Spirit. But they moan and groan with the creation in its labor pains, which implies not only that they identify with creation's suffering — a common emphasis in the interpretation of this passage — but also that they act in ways that display the peace of God, the *shalom* that has already arrived in Christ and the Spirit, even if it is not yet fully present. That is, Christian existence is characterized by anticipatory participation in God's peaceful future.

### (4) The plight and fate of Israel (Romans 9-11)

The next part of Romans does contain only one occurrence of the word "peace" or "reconciliation" (11:15). Even in chapters 9–11, however, we see implicit references to Paul's concern for peace. In chapter 10, for instance, Paul discusses the means of salvation for Jew and Greek alike, claiming that those who confess Jesus as Lord and believe God raised him from the dead will be justified and saved (Rom. 10:9-10). This passage contains an intra-textual echo of Romans 5:1-11, which speaks of justification and salvation in relation to the gifts of peace and reconciliation with God. Furthermore, in chapter 11 Paul clearly wants Gentile believers to live in harmony with and appreciation for ethnic Jews, whether they are believers or not, even as he promises that God's mercy and forgiveness will extend to those who are currently part of unbelieving Israel. All of this suggests that the gift of peace from God in Christ — both its vertical and its horizontal dimensions — is front and center in chapters 9–11, even if the explicit vocabulary is absent.

### (5) Life in the community of Gentile and Jewish believers (Rom. 12:1–15:13)[91]

Commenting on Romans 5:10a ("For if while we were enemies, we were reconciled to God through the death of his Son"), John Howard Yoder claims,

---

"Since the present order of things is incapable of fulfilling its telos, we cannot expect to make the world right by our actions. . . . At the same time, however, God through Jesus Christ 'justifies' sinners. That is, those who believe in Christ are justified, aligned with the telos of creation, so that our lives bear witness to the final justification, which is the redemption of the world in the new creation" (p. 145). Wilson also sees the church's witness to this new creation as anticipatory participation.

91. Parts of this section are drawn from and abridge Michael J. Gorman, "Paul and the Cruciform Way of God in Christ," *Journal of Moral Theology* 2 (2013): 64-83.

"The Christian has no choice. If this was God's pattern, if his strategy for dealing with his enemies was to love them and give himself for them, it must be ours as well."[92] We see that Paul drew the same conclusion when, in chapters 12 through 15, he calls the Romans to peaceful living within their diverse community and to peacefulness toward outsiders, even including non-retaliation toward persecutors.

To repeat some of the texts cited above, we recall these well-known words of Paul that are rooted in the teaching of Jesus, and which he attempted to embody in his own life:[93]

> [14]Bless those who persecute you; bless and do not curse them. . . . [17]Do not repay anyone evil for evil, but take thought for what is noble in the sight of all. [18]If it is possible, so far as it depends on you, live peaceably [Greek *eirēneuontes*] with all. [19]Beloved, never avenge yourselves, but leave room for the wrath of God; for it is written, "Vengeance is mine, I will repay, says the Lord." [20]No, "if your enemies are hungry, feed them; if they are thirsty, give them something to drink; for by doing this you will heap burning coals on their heads." [21]Do not be overcome by evil, but overcome evil with good. (Rom. 12:14, 17-21)

Such robust peaceableness is constitutive of the Roman believers' identity and of their mission in the world; they are even to give food and drink to their enemies. Why? For one all-sufficient and all-compelling reason: *because it is constitutive of the identity and mission of God displayed in Christ.* Paul suggests that the ability to love enemies depends, not on ignoring evil, but on recognizing and naming it. Just as God in Christ named humans as sinners and enemies (Rom. 5:6-10), Paul's audience must name evil as such in order not to "repay" it or "be overcome" by it but to conquer it by doing good. This is precisely what God has done in the Messiah: overcome evil with good.

This is why Paul comes back to the story of Jesus when he pleads for the end of mutual judgmentalism about matters that don't matter (such as food and calendar preferences) in the house churches of Rome, and as he tells the Roman believers whom he labels "strong" to look out for the "weak":

---

92. Yoder, *He Came Preaching Peace*, p. 21.

93. See Matt. 5:43-48; Luke 6:27-33; 1 Cor. 4:10-13. We have in Romans a remarkable confluence of the *teaching* of Jesus and the *death* of Jesus on the subject of loving enemies/persecutors, for although Romans 5 is not explicitly recalled here, the astute hearer/reader of the letter will not have forgotten the repeated emphasis in that chapter on Jesus' death as God's reconciling of enemies.

¹³Let us therefore no longer pass judgment on one another, but resolve instead never to put a stumbling block or hindrance in the way of another. ¹⁴I know and am persuaded in the Lord Jesus that nothing is unclean in itself; but it is unclean for anyone who thinks it unclean. ¹⁵If your brother or sister is being injured by what you eat, you are no longer walking in love. Do not let what you eat cause the ruin of one for whom Christ died. ¹⁶So do not let your good be spoken of as evil. <u>¹⁷For the kingdom of God is not food and drink but righteousness and peace and joy in the Holy Spirit.</u> ¹⁸The one who thus serves Christ is acceptable to God and has human approval. <u>¹⁹Let us then pursue what makes for peace and for mutual upbuilding.</u> (Rom. 14:13-19)

¹We who are strong ought to put up with the failings of the weak, and not to please ourselves. <u>²Each of us must please our neighbor for the good purpose of building up the neighbor. ³For Christ did not please himself;</u> but, as it is written, "The insults of those who insult you have fallen on me." ⁴For whatever was written in former days was written for our instruction, so that by steadfastness and by the encouragement of the scriptures we might have hope. <u>⁵May the God of steadfastness and encouragement grant you to live in harmony with one another, in accordance with Christ Jesus,</u> ⁶so that together you may with one voice glorify the God and Father of our Lord Jesus Christ. ⁷Welcome one another, therefore, just as Christ has welcomed you, for the glory of God. (Rom. 15:1-7)

Here Paul is energetically calling the church(es) in Rome to *shalom*, grounding the ideal not in an idealistic hope but in the narrative of Jesus' others-oriented, sin-absorbing death on the cross (14:15; 15:1-7). It is the reality of cruciform love to which that story bears witness, and thus to the paradigm it offers, that gives Paul reason for hope — hope for harmony, for *shalom*, not only in Rome but throughout the church and the world. Pursuing peace, therefore, is one of the most concrete ways of expressing Christlike love and concern for others. In fact, love and peace overlap in meaning insofar as each requires a refocusing of the self away from the self and toward the other and the community.

In Romans as elsewhere in Paul's letters, *to be like Christ is to be like God,* for God was in Christ, loving enemies, reconciling the hostile world, welcoming all. To follow Paul's admonitions in Romans 14 and 15 is to participate not merely in the mission of Paul but in the mission of God (15:8-12).

We will return to this aspect of Romans more fully in the final chapter.

In the meantime, we note Paul's prayer-wish for those who live and love in this community of God's *shalom:* "May the God of hope fill you with all joy and peace in believing, so that you may abound in hope by the power of the Holy Spirit" (15:13).

### *Closing (Rom. 15:14–16:27)*

Finally, as noted earlier, in Romans 16:20, after Paul has offered a peace benediction (15:33) and urged his readers to avoid contentious members (or interlopers), he promises, "The God of peace will shortly crush Satan under your feet," and offers one final benediction: "The grace of our Lord Jesus Christ be with you." This eschatological promise that the God of peace will bring final peace through the crushing of Satan does not mean that the God of peace and the peace of God are not at work now. Indeed, just the opposite is the case: what God has done in Christ, what God is doing in and through congregations, and what God will do at the eschatological moment are all of a piece: the defeat of evil and its replacement with the triumphant *shalom* of God.

Thus in Romans, the "peace memorandum" (Haacker's term), we find Paul speaking of peace with God, peace with one another in the church, a peaceful and peacemaking presence in the world, and a final, eschatological peace.[94] The peacemaking missional God has created, and is creating, a peacemaking missional church.

### Conclusion

In a book not primarily on Paul but one that is deeply sympathetic with the direction of this chapter, Ross Hastings suggests that the mission of the church as participation in the life and mission of God is essentially twofold: discovering *shalom* and disseminating *shalom*.[95] This is what we have referred to in this chapter as peace being both a divine gift, or grace, and an ecclesial task, or practice.

The apostle Paul, not least in Romans — but not only in Romans —

94. Similarly Haacker, *Theology,* p. 53.

95. Ross Hastings, *Missional God, Missional Church: Hope for Re-evangelizing the West* (Downers Grove, IL: InterVarsity, 2012). After four introductory chapters, he structures the book into two parts, four chapters in part one, "Discovering Shalom," and four in part two, "Disseminating Shalom."

reminds his audiences, both ancient and contemporary, that in the gifts of Christ and the Spirit God has inaugurated the prophetically promised age of *shalom*. The church has the privilege and the mission of participating in that age of peace — which is also, as we will see in chapter seven, the age of justice. Those in Christ, empowered by the Spirit, become the gospel they believe; they embody the peace of God within the community, with outsiders, and wherever they are in the world. They become agents of reconciliation. They become, that is, the gospel of peace.

Lest those concerned that too much Christian attention to peacemaking might have a negative effect on what is traditionally called evangelism, I conclude with the following perspective from a Christian pacifist and an atheist.

Theologian Stanley Hauerwas has written a brilliant book titled *War and the American Difference: Theological Reflections on Violence and National Identity.*[96] In response to a critical review of that book, self-confessed atheist Noah Berlatsky lauds the intellectual and theological perceptiveness of Hauerwas, concluding his main remarks as follows:

> Hauerwas is definitively, defiantly Christian. His message, therefore, is specifically to Christians. It is Christians, first, he believes, who must determine not to kill each other. It is Christians, first, who must reject the morality of war for the morality of the Cross. On the one hand, this is something of a relief for atheists like myself. Since I'm not a believer, I can cheerfully keep paying taxes for cluster bombs and hating my neighbor just as I've always done. Still, there is a bit of discomfort there too. If, after all, Christians were actually to take up Hauerwas' challenge, if they were actually to bear witness to nonviolence and transform the world — well, I'd hate to say it, obviously, but it would be hard to escape the suspicion that that might actually be the work of God.[97]

Perhaps the world might actually sit up and take notice of the Christian faith if Christians really did embody the gospel of peace. For that reason, we will briefly consider a few contemporary practices of missional peace at the end of the next chapter, which will focus on peace in the letter to the Ephesians — another letter about "the gospel of peace" (Eph. 6:15).

---

96. Stanley Hauerwas, *War and the American Difference: Theological Reflections on Violence and National Identity* (Grand Rapids: Baker Academic, 2011).

97. Noah Berlatsky, "Bend Your Knee," n.p. Online at http://www.hoodedutilitarian .com/2012/04/bend-your-knee/, accessed December 11, 2013.

# CHAPTER 6

# Becoming the Gospel of Peace (II): Ephesians

"Among the Pauline writings," wrote Raymond Brown, "only Romans can match Ephesians as a candidate for exercising the most influence on Christian thought and spirituality."[1] Moreover, as we noted in the previous chapter, "peace" is central to Ephesians, so we might add to Brown's comment that Ephesians easily matches, and in fact probably exceeds, the influence that Romans has had on Christian understandings of peace and peacemaking. In this chapter we consider peace in Ephesians and then, briefly, some aspects of peacemaking in contemporary Christian life.

The noun "peace" appears eight times in the letter to the Ephesians, and the verb "reconcile" once.[2] The document is liturgically wrapped in peace (1:2; 6:23), its theological substance is peace (2:14-17, where the words "peace" and "reconciliation" are clustered in five occurrences), it calls for the inner life of the church to be a life of peace (4:3), and it characterizes the gospel the church is to share with the world as "the gospel of peace" (6:15). Thus the message of Ephesians can be summarized in that signature phrase: "the gospel of peace."[3] Indeed, it is significant that the letter's final prayer-wish seems to turn the Pauline triad of faith, hope, and love into faith, *peace,* and love:

---

1. Raymond E. Brown, *An Introduction to the New Testament,* Anchor Yale Bible Reference Library (New York: Doubleday, 1998), p. 620.

2. Although the "reconcile" word-family does not appear frequently in the letter, Andrew Lincoln is nonetheless right to say that reconciliation is an especially key aspect of its "distinctive treatment of salvation" (Andrew T. Lincoln, *Ephesians,* Word Biblical Commentary 42 [Dallas: Word, 1990], p. xcii).

3. Similar in tone and theological concern to Ephesians is Colossians, in which reconciliation is extended to all creation. Space does not permit a detailed examination of both letters in this chapter. For excellent theological commentaries on Colossians, see Andrew T. Lincoln, "The Letter to the Colossians: Introduction, Commentary, and Reflections," in *The New In-*

Peace be to the whole community, and love with faith, from God the Father and the Lord Jesus Christ. (Eph. 6:23)[4]

We will see in the letter that this "gospel of peace" is a message about what God has done in and through Christ's death, and what God is now wanting to do in and through the readers/hearers of this letter: effect the reconciliation of people to God and to one another. This is not to say that God has changed the means of peacemaking from Christ to the church, but rather that God now uses the church to make known, in deed and word, the reconciling death of Christ. As elsewhere in the Pauline corpus, we will see that the "vertical" (people's relationship with God) and the "horizontal" (people's relationships with one another) dimensions of salvation are inseparable.[5] Also inseparable, we will discover, are the twin realities of the church's centripetal activity and its centrifugal activity in the world — both of which are aspects of its participation in the *missio Dei*. And finally, as noted in the previous chapter, Ephesians also testifies to the peacemaking work of the one God as the inseparable activity of three persons: Father, Son, and Spirit.

Ephesians, then, which is sometimes appropriately described as a narration of the "drama" of salvation, needs also to be viewed as a narration of the drama of the triune God's peacemaking mission, and of our participation in it.[6] Ironically, this divine peacemaking mission will be expressed, in part, in the language of divine warfare and thus our warfare, too.[7] This irony is not

---

*terpreter's Bible* 11:551-669 (Nashville: Abingdon, 2000); Nijay K. Gupta, *Colossians,* Smyth & Helwys Bible Commentary (Macon, GA: Smyth & Helwys, 2013); and other commentaries cited in those works. For a penetrating theological discussion of creation and ecclesial practices of reconciliation, see Jonathan R. Wilson, *God's Good World: Reclaiming the Doctrine of Creation* (Grand Rapids: Baker Academic, 2013), pp. 138-42.

4. The context confirms that peace is a substitute for hope, indeed a close semantic cousin. Paul is telling his readers/hearers that he is sending Tychicus to inform them about his imprisonment, solicit their prayers for his evangelistic boldness, and, especially, "encourage [their] hearts" (Eph. 6:19-22).

5. See also, e.g., Lincoln, *Ephesians,* pp. xcii, 144-45, 148, 160-61, 346, and 449.

6. For "the drama of salvation," see, e.g., Stephen E. Fowl, *Ephesians: A Commentary,* The New Testament Library (Louisville: Westminster John Knox, 2012), pp. 3-4 et passim. Fowl uses the phrase (including three occurrences of "drama of redemption") some thirty times. On both the dramatic and the participatory nature of salvation in Ephesians, see, in addition to Fowl, Timothy G. Gombis, *The Drama of Ephesians: Participating in the Triumph of God* (Downers Grove, IL: InterVarsity, 2010).

7. See especially Gombis, *Drama of Ephesians.*

a mere literary device but expresses, as we will see, a profound theological truth about the nature of the *missio Dei* and of our part in it.

## Three Preliminary Issues

Before we consider the letter's peace theme in more detail, we need to pause briefly to consider three issues associated with the letter to the Ephesians: the question of authorship and audience, and then two interpretations of the letter (often amounting to theological criticisms of it) that have sometimes been put forth.

Ephesians is one of the six disputed or contested letters in the Pauline corpus, meaning that scholars debate its authorship by Paul. A slight majority of scholars today would argue that Ephesians is not by the apostle, but rather by a later interpreter or disciple, perhaps writing a generation after Paul's death. An even greater majority have concluded, based on manuscript evidence, that Ephesians was not originally addressed to the church(es) in Ephesus.[8]

For our purposes, the issue of authorship and audience is of little consequence. In my opinion, Paul's mind is in fact the main genius behind the letter, and I will refer to its author as Paul. Nevertheless, it is also likely in my view that the apostle, following the conventions of his day, gave a scribe (perhaps Tychicus; cf. 6:21-22) some leeway in composing the letter.[9] My interpretation of the text, however, is not greatly affected by this position.[10] With respect to the question of audience, if Ephesians was intended as more of a circular letter, as some have claimed, that would simply broaden the intended original audience, which would mean more churches than just those in Ephesus would have heard this version of Paul's gospel of peace.

The two interpretive issues do relate, however, to the otherwise relatively insignificant question of authorship. The first of these issues is whether Ephesians represents a time in which Gentile-Jewish relations are in harmony, which would most likely be after the time of Paul himself, since he was frequently dealing with Gentile-Jewish tensions in the communities he addressed. Such harmony may or may not have actually existed later in time, but the alleged claim of the letter that all is well is sometimes seen as pre-

---

8. The earliest and best manuscripts lack the phrase "in Ephesus" from 1:1.

9. See the discussion in my *Apostle of the Crucified Lord: A Theological Introduction to Paul and His Letters* (Grand Rapids: Eerdmans, 2004), pp. 501-2.

10. Similar is the position of Fowl, *Ephesians*, pp. 16-28.

tentious or even triumphalistic — peace and harmony appear to be a done deal, a *fait accompli*. The second interpretation/criticism is that Ephesians depicts and underwrites a patriarchal structure that is theoretically distinct from, and even withdrawn from, "the world" (see 5:7), but that is ironically imbued with the very spirit of its age, as seen especially in its (again, alleged) support of the patriarchal status quo and the institution of slavery.

Regarding the first issue, we should note that the message of Ephesians is similar to that of Galatians: Galatians 3:28 reads, "There is no longer Jew or Greek, there is no longer slave or free, there is no longer male and female; for all of you are one in Christ Jesus," while Ephesians 2:14 says, "For he is our peace; in his flesh he has made both groups into one and has broken down the dividing wall, that is, the hostility between us." In each case, Paul makes a claim about the result of what God has done in Christ and in creating a new people in him, a people that can be described only in relation to Israel. This is the "indicative" of the gospel — that which God has done, that which is. The indicative carries within it an "imperative" — that which now needs to be. The divine gift, once again, implies ecclesial practice.

Thus Paul warns the Galatians not to destroy the work of God either by refusing table fellowship with others (as Peter and others wrongly did; Gal. 2:11-21) or by creating enmity and strife rather than allowing the peace of the Spirit to pervade the community (Gal. 5:13-26). Similarly, in Ephesians Paul urges the community to maintain that which God has brought into being, "the unity of the Spirit in the bond of peace" (Eph. 4:3) by practices of mutual edification, rather than mutual destruction, that honor and please God's Spirit (e.g., Eph. 4:29-32). In both letters the divine indicative and the human imperative together create neither an idealistic nor a triumphalistic vision of the church but, instead, a real place of peace in need of ongoing maintenance. That is, in neither letter does the strong indicative — "there is no longer Jew and Greek . . ." (Galatians) and "made both groups into one" (Ephesians) — suggest that God's reconciling work is done. Despite the very different circumstances of the letters (prominent *ethnic* tension being clearly reflected only in Galatians), Paul reflects theologically about the church and its practices in these letters in very similar ways.[11]

As for the second issue, the charge of both worldly patriarchy and si-

---

11. Noting the differences between Ephesians and other letters in this regard, Fowl (*Ephesians*, p. 101) wisely notes, "It appears that whether or not Christians in Ephesus or elsewhere are subject to Judaizing pressures, they must understand themselves as Christians in relation to Israel and Israel's God."

multaneous withdrawal from the world, it should be clear from Ephesians 6:10-22 that the church in Ephesians is hardly an entity unto itself, but is in fact a missional body that needs to be clothed with the essentials needed for a real-life struggle in the world. We shall return to this below. But is this mission betrayed by the church's apparently demeaning, patriarchal view of women, slaves, and children? In other words, can the church we see in Ephesians bring men and women, slaves and free, parents and children together in the same way it (claims to) bring Gentiles and Jews together? Is the apostle of unity and equality in Christ actually betrayed by this letter?

A superficial reading of Ephesians, especially of 5:22–6:9, could lead to the conclusion that the letter perpetuates disdain for women, slaves, and children, and that this message can hardly be called good news of peace, of *shalom*, for these groups of people. A full response to this concern could occupy an entire chapter, indeed a book, so we will need to limit ourselves to a few key points. The most significant aspect of a response to these concerns is the larger context of the letter.

First of all, the nature of life in the church that the letter holds forth in the section immediately preceding 5:22–6:9 needs to be seen as the interpretive lens through which to read the controverted passages.[12] The letter prescribes practices of peacemaking, harmony, self-giving love, and forgiveness that are intended to be evidenced in *all* relationships in which believers participate, including those of the household portrayed in chapters 5 and 6. Of particular importance is the language of 4:31–5:2, which foreshadows some of the most controversial admonitions in 5:22–6:9:

> [31]Put away from you all bitterness and wrath and anger and wrangling and slander, together with all malice, [32]and be kind to one another, tenderhearted, forgiving one another, as God in Christ has forgiven you. 5[1]Therefore be imitators of God, as beloved children, [2]and live in love, as Christ loved us and gave himself up for us, a fragrant offering and sacrifice to God.

Since the exhortations to engage in these practices (and the others in the context) are generic and universal for ecclesial relationships, then *nothing that is said in the specifics of 5:22–6:9 should be interpreted in a way that would contradict the earlier admonitions.* In other words, the male Christian

---

12. This section of the letter is generally referred to as the "household code" or *Haustafel*, a rather common literary form in antiquity.

head of household cannot mistreat his wife, children, and slaves but must act lovingly and peaceably toward them. They are no longer, despite Roman law and practice, his possessions.

Second, this principle of interpreting the specific relationships in light of the general call to practices of peace and love is demonstrated explicitly in 5:21-22, where mutual submission and sacrificial love among believers as a sign of being filled with the Spirit leads to mutual submission and sacrificial love in the husband-wife relationship.[13] A careful translation of these verses and those on either side of them, displayed graphically, reveals these connections:

[B]e filled with the Spirit, by
- singing psalms and hymns and spiritual songs among yourselves,
- singing and making melody to the Lord in your hearts,
- giving thanks to God the Father at all times and for everything in the name of our Lord Jesus Christ, and
- being subject to one another out of reverence for Christ,
  - wives to your husbands as you are to the Lord. . . .
  - Husbands, love your wives, just as Christ loved the church and gave himself up for her [*as I have just said in 4:31–5:2*]. . . . (Eph. 5:18b-22, 25)

To summarize: properly read in its literary and canonical contexts, Ephesians presents a vision of the church as a place of peace that is already realized, though not fully realized, and is inclusive of all groups that may naturally be at odds in their secular "natural habitat." It is the task of the church to work out the details of this countercultural peaceful gift and calling in its concrete cultural existence.[14]

## Ephesians: The Triune God's Peacemaking Mission and the Church's Participation in It

We turn now to a brief walk through Ephesians to see how it narrates the peacemaking *missio Dei*. Imitating the second table from our discussion of Romans, we may display this narrative of Ephesians graphically as follows:

13. See further the excursus on 5:21-33 in my *Cruciformity: Paul's Narrative Spirituality of the Cross* (Grand Rapids: Eerdmans, 2001), pp. 261-66.

14. In personal correspondence to the author (February 12, 2014), Dean Flemming has said that this section of Ephesians "seems to be an example of embodying the gospel in the existing structures and relationships of society in a transforming way — the way of Christ."

## PEACE IN THE NARRATIVE ARGUMENT OF EPHESIANS

| Section Topic | Passage | Key Concerns | Key Texts |
|---|---|---|---|
| Opening | 1:1-23 | "Grace to you and peace from God our Father and the Lord Jesus Christ." | 1:2 |
| Theme | | God has a plan for the fullness of time: to gather up all things in Christ. | 1:10 |
| The human condition of death and estrangement/ hostility, and the divine solution of life and peace | 2:1-22 | Humanity without Christ is dead in trespasses and sins. | 2:1-3 |
| | | God makes people alive in Christ. | 2:4-10 |
| | | Humanity apart from Christ is divided and in a state of hostility, with Gentiles separated from the people of God. | 2:11-12 |
| | | God in Christ makes peace, creating one new humanity. | 2:13-22 |
| Paul's role in, and prayer for the Ephesians in, God's peace mission | 3:1-21 | The mystery of God's eternal plan for the inclusion of the Gentiles in one body has been revealed in Christ. | 3:1-13 |
| | | Paul and his readers need prayer to experience God's love and power in Christ. | 3:14-21 |
| The church as a place of unity and peace | 4:1–6:9 | This new humanity, the church, must make "every effort to maintain the unity of the Spirit in the bond of peace" (4:3) through practices of humility, gentleness, patience, edifying speech, forgiveness, mutual submission, non-threatening behavior, etc. | 4:2-3, 25-32; 5:1-2, 21; 6:9 |
| The church and Paul as proclaimers of the gospel of peace | 6:10-22 | The church is engaged in a spiritual apocalyptic struggle, and must clothe itself for the struggle in order to proclaim the gospel of peace. | 6:15 |
| | | Paul, ambassador for the gospel in chains, requests prayer for boldness in his proclamation. | 6:19-20 |
| Closing | 6:23-24 | Peace to all, with love and faith. | 6:23 |
| | | Grace to all. | 6:24 |

With this overview of peace in Ephesians in mind, we may now look at the letter section by section.

## Opening and Theme: The Liturgical and Cosmic Contexts of Peace (1:1-23)

After introducing Paul and the recipients, the letter begins with the standard — though not insignificant — Pauline greeting of grace and peace from God the Father and Christ Jesus the Lord (1:2). This greeting, which is really a prayer-wish or opening benediction, sets the letter in its proper context. Together with the peace-and-grace benediction of 6:23-24, it forms a pair of bookends, reminding the letter's recipients that the production and reception of this document constitute a liturgical and theological event, not the mere sending and receiving of a letter or treatise.

This liturgical mode continues as the first main part of the letter is a *berakah,* or blessing — one long sentence (in Greek) lauding God the Father for what he has done for us in Christ (1:3-14): "Blessed be the God and Father of our Lord Jesus Christ, who has blessed us in Christ with every spiritual blessing in the heavenly places" (1:3). Although the word "peace" does not appear explicitly in this passage, the text describes the eternal plan of God to create a family of adopted children (1:5), God's very own people, who have been redeemed and forgiven in Christ (1:6-7), and who are marked with the Spirit (1:13-14) as heirs of a salvation that will encompass not merely all humanity, but the entire cosmos:

> [9][God] has made known to us the mystery of his will, according to his good pleasure that he set forth in Christ, [10]as a plan for the fullness of time, to gather up all things in him, things in heaven and things on earth. (Eph. 1:9-10)

We will learn in chapter 2 that this "mystery" (1:9; cf. 3:1-10, where the word appears four more times, and 6:19) made known in the gospel, is indeed best characterized with respect to humanity as a divine peace mission, and in chapter 6 that this "gospel of your salvation" (1:13; cf. 3:6-7) is in fact "the gospel of peace" (6:15). Here, however, Paul has the cosmic view in mind. The divine plan of "gather[ing] up all things" in Christ (1:10; *anakephalaiōsasthai,* "to recapitulate," "to sum up again") suggests a metanarrative of creation and recreation, and specifically of bringing unity to that which is now scattered in order to restore harmony in the creation: "when God brings all things in heaven and earth to their proper end through and in relation to Christ."[15] This is a new way of stating an old vision, the prophetic vision of new creation and of the *shalom* it will bring into being for all creation. Human beings will be part of this; they will share in the inheritance of glory (1:18). Thus the church, as described briefly here and in more detail in the rest of the letter, is intended by God to be a foretaste of the future cosmic peace and harmony that has been the eternal divine plan. It is Christ's body, "the fullness of him who fills all in all" (1:23).

## Human Death and Hostility, Divine Life and Peace (2:1-22)

The second chapter of Ephesians functions as a summary of the Pauline gospel. It depicts the human condition as one of death vis-à-vis God (2:1-3), and of estrangement and hostility among humans (2:11-22). In grace and kindness, God has brought the dead to life and put them into the "heavenly places" in Christ (2:6) — the ultimate act of restoration. Because that grace and kindness are extended to Gentiles as well as Jews, specifically in Christ's death, the salvation that the gospel proclaims reconciles people not only to God, but also to one another. In fact, the latter — the horizontal dimension of salvation — receives more attention in this letter than the vertical.[16]

The description of the Gentiles in their pre-salvation state is quite emphatically one of exclusion, and the resulting relationship between Gentiles and the people of God one of hostility. A variety of phrases emphasize this situation:

- without Christ . . . aliens from the commonwealth of Israel . . . strangers to the covenants of promise (v. 12)
- having no hope and without God in the world (v. 12)
- far off (v. 13)
- the dividing wall, that is, the hostility between us (v. 14)
- two [humanities] (v. 15), both groups (v. 16)
- hostility (v. 16)
- far off (v. 17)
- strangers and aliens (v. 19)

15. Fowl, *Ephesians*, p. 47.
16. So also, e.g., Lincoln, *Ephesians*, p. xcii.

The divine solution to this crisis is Christ, and specifically his death, as the means of peacemaking:[17]

> [14]For he is our peace; in his flesh he has made both groups into one and has broken down the dividing wall, that is, the hostility between us. [15]He has abolished the law with its commandments and ordinances, that he might create in himself one new humanity in place of the two, thus making peace, [16]and might reconcile both groups to God in one body through the cross, thus putting to death that hostility through it. [17]So he came and proclaimed peace to you who were far off and peace to those who were near; [18]for through him both of us have access in one Spirit to the Father. (Eph 2:14-18)

Christ, who "is our peace" (2:14), Paul says, "came and proclaimed peace [euēngelisato eirēnēn] to you who were far off and peace to those who were near" (2:17). Paul is drawing on two texts from Isaiah, paraphrasing Isaiah 52:7 and quoting part of Isaiah 57:19:

> How beautiful upon the mountains are the feet of the messenger who announces peace, who brings good news [LXX podes euangelizomenou akoēn eirēnēs hos euangelizomenos agatha], who announces salvation, who says to Zion, "Your God reigns." (Isa. 52:7)

> Peace, peace, to the far and the near, says the Lord; and I will heal them. (Isa. 57:19)

Paul assigns to Jesus both the human activity of announcing God's peace (Isa. 52:7) — the work of the herald — and the actual saving, peacemaking activity — the work of God (Isa. 57:19).[18] This claim needs to be partly qual-

---

17. A full exploration of the theology of atonement in this passage would make for a very long chapter. Paul is much more interested in the result of that death (peace in all its dimensions) than in the specifics of how it occurs (the "mechanics"). The phrases that come closest to a theology of the atonement, such as "[he] has broken down the dividing wall" (v. 14) and "He has abolished the law with its commandments and ordinances" (v. 15), are metaphors, and cannot be pressed too literally as statements of Paul's theology of atonement. It is possible that Paul has texts or traditions about God as a "divine warrior" in mind here, though that is disputed. If he does, God's warfare is clearly paradoxical, for God in Christ makes and wins a peaceful war by apparently suffering defeat (crucifixion) in order to make peace and create unity.

18. As Lincoln suggests (Ephesians, p. 140), other key scriptural texts about eschatological

ified, however, for although "Christ" is the implicit grammatical subject of "he came and proclaimed peace" in verse 17, verse 18 makes it clear that the resulting salvation is participation in the life of the triune God ("for through him both of us have access in one Spirit to the Father"); it therefore implies that Christ the mediator is not acting alone, but in partnership with the Father and the Spirit.

The proclamation of peace to which Paul refers is less a reference to the ministry of Jesus narrated in the Gospels than it is a description of the eternal plan of God manifested in the death and resurrection of Jesus, and carried forward in the proclamation of the gospel through the church after the resurrection. Once again, a variety of phrases stress this radically new situation:

- brought near (v. 13)
- has made both groups into one and has broken down the dividing wall, that is, the hostility between us (v. 14)
- one new humanity in place of the two, thus making peace (v. 15)
- reconcile both groups to God . . . thus putting to death that hostility (v. 16)
- through him [Christ] both of us have access in one Spirit to the Father (v. 18)
- no longer strangers and aliens (v. 19)
- citizens with the saints and also members of the household of God (v. 19)
- a holy temple in the Lord . . . [being] built together spiritually into a dwelling place for God (vv. 21b-22)

In addition to these explicit phrases, all of the other phrases in the text reflecting the existence of hostility (listed above) are implicitly undone by this one act of peacemaking.

Three additional elements of Ephesians 2 are especially noteworthy. First, in his death Christ has "pacified" both the people of God and the Gentiles, the nations, not by the shedding of *their* blood — as the Romans often did — but by the shedding of his own blood. Moreover, by simultaneously delivering us from "the power of the air" (2:2, referring to Satan's sphere of influence on humanity), Christ's death "allows the church to be established as a political space or realm that recognizes Christ's dominion."[19]

---

peace, such as Isa. 2:2-4 and Mic. 4:1-4, may also be present in the mind of the author or heard by the audience, at least its Jewish members.

19. Fowl, *Ephesians*, p. 74.

*Thus the mission of God, and of Paul, the Ephesians, and all Christians, is to bring people from the realm of sin, death, and alienation governed by anti-God powers into the realm of forgiveness, resurrection life, and peace ruled by Jesus the Messiah and Lord.*

Second, a single act, Christ's death, both reconciles people to God and reconciles people to one another (see esp. 2:16-17). This reinforces the inseparability of the two dimensions of reconciliation (vertical and horizontal), as we have seen earlier. There is no reconciliation with God without reconciliation with others, for this is what God in the cross was up to, and what God in the church is still up to. "The major division within humanity in the first-century world is reckoned to have been overcome, as Jews and Gentiles with their ethnic and religious differences are seen to have been reconciled in the one body of the Church."[20] It is therefore the case that the gospel can continue today to unite people with great ethnic, cultural, and religious differences.

Third and finally, then, the emphasis on the creation of one humanity out of two groups suggests that Paul would contend that *all* binaries (categories built on the splitting of humanity into two groups) constructed by humans about humans are subverted by the gospel of Christ the peacemaker.[21] That is, although the primary emphasis in Ephesians is clearly on the joining of Jews and Gentiles into one, the reality of one and only one humanity means that God's plan is to join all divided groups into one new humanity: men and women, slaves and free, parents and children, but also — moving forward in history — all other divisions in the human race that have emerged since the first century and will emerge in the years to come. These would, of course, include blacks and whites, Hutus and Tutsis, and so on. Missiologists and other theologians have rightly looked to Ephesians 2 in order to proclaim the truth that "the reconciliation of previously hostile groups into the body of Christ . . . transform[s] but do[es] not require the erasure of national,

---

20. Lincoln, *Ephesians*, p. xcii.

21. This should not be taken to mean either that the differences among human beings are nonexistent ("Peacemaking here is not homogenizing" — Fowl, *Ephesians*, p. 90) or that toleration of sin or evil is an appropriate Christian stance. Rather, in Christ binaries — the natural, created ones (such as male and female) or the more arbitrary ones we create and impose on the human community (such as native and immigrant) — that divide the world into "us" and "them" are transcended in the creation of one humanity/person. At the same time, in Christ sin and evil, the marks of those dead through their trespasses and sins (2:1), no matter their "membership" in any of the binaries, are meant to be ended as new creation issues in the good works intended by God for all humans to practice (2:9).

ethnic, or cultural identity."[22] This does not mean, however, that there is no human effort or cost involved in reconciliation. Reconciliation may require repentance, forgiveness, restitution, and transformation on the part of one or more of the parties involved.[23]

For Paul, then, Jesus on the cross embodied and performed the divine act of peacemaking that constitutes the human dimension, so to speak, of the eternal, cosmic mystery and plan of God. The cross is the divine per-formative utterance of reconciliation. Or, more simply, Christ is our peace, our *shalom. He is God's peace in person — in the flesh.*[24] He — that is, God the Father acting in him, and the Spirit continuing his work now — is the one who restores right relations between people and God, as well as among people(s); transfers them into the sphere of Christ's lordship, where love and forgiveness replace hate, retaliation, and violence (e.g., war); and fulfills the prophetic promise that a Prince of Peace (Isa. 9:6) would do precisely that (e.g., Isa. 2:1-4).[25] He has established a new covenant, a covenant of peace (see Ezek. 34:25; 37:26).

## The Apostle, the Church, and God's Peace Mission (3:1-21)

Of this gospel of peace Paul is a glad proclaimer (3:1-13), and he is also a fervent pray-er (3:14-21) for those he addresses in this letter, those who have come to share in the "boundless riches of Christ" (3:8). Although the word "peace" does not occur in Ephesians 3, Paul does use a number of phrases echoing the first two chapters that indicate that his apostolic mission is to make known the peacemaking initiative of God to the Gentiles (3:1, 6), "the mystery of Christ" (3:4; cf. 3:5, 9) that means the inclusion of the Gentiles, which is in fact the gospel (3:6-7).[26]

Four interrelated things are absolutely critical in what Paul says here. The first three all appear in 3:8-10:

---

22. Fowl, *Ephesians,* p. 102.

23. The unifying of Jews and Gentiles in the early church was challenging work, as Acts and the letters testify.

24. In his translation of Eph. 2:14-18, Markus Barth renders three words or phrases as "in person." See Markus Barth, *Ephesians: Introduction, Translation, and Commentary on Chapters 1-3,* AB 34 (Garden City, NY: Doubleday, 1974), pp. 253, 260-62. Cf. Lincoln, *Ephesians,* p. 140.

25. Similarly, Fowl, *Ephesians,* p. 90.

26. So also Fowl, *Ephesians,* pp. 109-10.

> [8]Although I am the very least of all the saints, this grace was given to me to bring to the Gentiles the news of the boundless riches of Christ, [9]and to make everyone see what is the plan of the mystery hidden for ages in God who created all things; [10]so that through the church the wisdom of God in its rich variety might now be made known to the rulers and authorities in the heavenly places.

First, Paul stresses that God's mystery, and therefore his (Paul's) gospel, centers on the church, not merely on individuals. Second, Paul avers that the church has a mission, which is to make known the wisdom of God — God's mystery, plan, and salvation — to rulers and authorities. And third, implicitly but clearly, the church can fulfill its witness-bearing mission only as it embodies the gospel, only as the "rich variety" of divine wisdom is represented in a diverse but reconciled new humanity. This is precisely what many rulers and authorities do not want or seek — reconciliation with the other, the enemy, the perceived threat to social, political, or economic stability. For Paul, therefore, the church as a reconciled body of Jews and Gentiles (and other "binaries" as well) is both the witness to God's redemptive plan for the world and the primary means God has established for drawing a fractured, hostile, and violent world together. That is, to say the least, a weighty responsibility for the church, and it can become reality, as Paul readily acknowledges, only because of God's power at work in and through the church (3:20).

There is a fourth noteworthy aspect of the first part of chapter 3. Like bookends on a shelf — the shelf being Paul's self-description of his role in God's gospel and of that gospel's ecclesial, missional focus — are two similar sentences in which Paul says that this gospel is something worth suffering for (vv. 1, 13). Paul's imprisonment and other sufferings are, paradoxically, the source of the Gentiles' glory, both present (i.e., honor/pride rather than shame) and future (eschatological bliss). In this respect, Paul has himself become the gospel by offering glory to others through his suffering, like Jesus himself (cf. 2 Corinthians 3–4, esp. 4:8-12).[27]

Intercessory prayer, then, is for Paul an instrument of his mission and that of the church, as he prays that the church will be strong, grounded in

---

27. For Paul as an embodiment of the gospel in his loving, cruciform apostolic existence (which is intended to be a model for all believers — 1 Cor. 11:1), see my *Cruciformity*, ch. 9 (pp. 178-213). Of course this does not mean that either Paul or others who imitate Paul do for others precisely what Jesus did on the cross, for only Jesus died for the sins of the world. But, by analogy, the self-giving love of Paul and others allows for others to benefit from the death of Jesus on their behalf and participate in the life that his death and resurrection effect.

love, and full of the fullness of God (3:14-21). Why this prayer? He offers it not merely so that individuals in the church will be comforted by such strength and the assurance of God's love. He prays in this way so that the church's imagination will be stretched and its corporate jaw be found wide open in amazement at what God — the true Father of all the families of the earth (3:14-15) — can accomplish in and through the church:

> [20]Now to him who by the power at work within us is able to accomplish abundantly far more than all we can ask or imagine, [21]to him be glory in the church and in Christ Jesus to all generations, forever and ever. Amen. (Eph. 3:20-21)

This means that the church occupies a public space, not a corner hidden from view. And that public space is decidedly also political space, because the gospel the church proclaims in word and deed, a gospel of unity and reconciliation — the creation of a new family under one Father — is a challenge to claims like those of the empire, and like many subsequent powers, to be the great unifier of human beings. The emperor was even perceived as the great father of a unified (and pacified) family. But the real family, says Paul, the true place of unity for all the families of the earth, is not the empire with its so-called father, but the church with its heavenly Father. The church needs prayer to sustain that vision and to actualize it in daily life.

This challenge to the powers, as benignly proclaimed as it may be by apostles ancient and modern, and as peacefully (though imperfectly) embodied as it may be by churches then and now, will often be met with suspicion, especially by the very powers it challenges. Sometimes it will even be met with aggressive action, as Paul well knew. Yet, in spite of all this, people of all ethnicities have been attracted to the gospel of this Father and his family, and continue to be attracted when it is embodied in biblically faithful, culturally appropriate, and missionally imaginative ways. All of this is why the church needs to be unified by the Spirit in the bond of peace — the subject of the final three chapters of Ephesians.

## The Church as a Place of Unity and Peace (4:1–6:9)

Having narrated in chapters 1–3 God's salvific peace mission in Christ, as well as his own role in it, Paul moves on in the second half of the letter to describe the church's role in that divine drama: to live worthily of its calling

(4:1; cf. Phil. 1:27; Col. 1:10; 1 Thess. 2:12). The Greek has the verb "walk" *(peripatēsai),* though many translations now render it like the NRSV: "lead a life ['walk'] worthy of the calling. . . ." Walking implies involvement in the world — mission — not existence in an isolated holy huddle. The church, Paul says, is to be a place of peace and unity sustained by inner, centripetal practices that embody the gospel (4:1–6:9) and external, centrifugal practices that proclaim the gospel (6:10-22). These two sets of missional practices, of course, are not unrelated but overlapping.

Paul begins by showing the fundamental connection between the gospel and the church's life together. The corporate life of the church means walking

> with all humility and gentleness, with patience, bearing with one another in love, making every effort to maintain the unity of the Spirit in the bond of peace. (Eph. 4:2-3)

The task of the Christian community is not first of all to *make* peace but to *keep* the peace it has been given in the gospel, the peace that has made it one body in the one God: Father, Son, and Spirit (4:4-6). The "seven unities" of the church (4:4-6) are aspects of the one reality of unity and *shalom* given in the gospel.[28] *Shalom,* then, fundamentally means harmony, not as a human achievement but as a divine gift, but a divine gift needing the church's devoted care and nurture: the verb translated "making every effort" *(spoudazontes)* suggests "the utmost importance and urgency" and thus sparing no effort.[29] This is not to excuse the church from responsibility; as Christopher Marshall puts it, focusing first on peace in the church, "Without a commitment to peace, we deny the very 'gospel of peace' (6:15) we proclaim. Without peacemaking, our Christian lives are, simply, *unworthy* of the calling to which we have been called."[30] Sustaining *shalom* — the church's first task — requires the same kind of cruciform love (4:2; cf. 4:31–5:2) that created the church. Without forbearing, forgiving love, there is no hope for peace.[31]

---

28. They are: "one body and one Spirit . . . the one hope of your calling, one Lord, one faith, one baptism, one God and Father of all."

29. Lincoln, *Ephesians,* p. 237. On this entire passage, see Christopher Marshall, "'Making Every Effort': Peacemaking and Ecclesiology in Ephesians 4:1-6," in *Struggles for Shalom: Peace and Violence Across the Testaments,* ed. Laura L. Brenneman and Brad D. Schantz (Eugene, OR: Pickwick, 2013), pp. 256-66.

30. Marshall, "'Making Every Effort,'" p. 261.

31. Yet this is not a "cheap peace," as Paul will make clear especially beginning in 4:17. It is a peace rooted in a calling, specifically God's call to holiness, and the church must learn in

Christ our peace, who in his death is the ultimate gift-giver, offering himself in love, continues to give to the church, now in the form of gifts (4:7-16). The role of gifts is, in part, to edify the church as the peaceable community to ensure that its life — and therefore its ministry and public witness — embodies the gospel of peace and unity (4:12, 16). These gifts need to be exercised, as Paul says also in 1 Corinthians 12–14, in love, which is the church's *modus operandi* for the use of its various gifts (4:15-16). It is love, moreover, that must govern the exercise of the tongue as well, such that the virtuous and appropriate practice of truth-telling within the church does not become an exercise in disunity and disharmony (4:15).

As already noted, the church needs appropriate ecclesial practices to sustain its holiness and harmony. Paul has already named some (4:2-3, cited above) and will enumerate several others in 4:18-32, noting that, inasmuch as such ecclesial practices reflect God's righteousness, they are in fact radically countercultural practices (4:17-24). Among these are truth-telling, ongoing reconciliation, honesty in work, generosity to the needy, kindness and grace in speech, and forgiveness (4:25-32), all done in Christlike, Godlike love (5:1-2). Not coincidentally, some of these practices will also be specifically mentioned as necessary for mission, particularly truth and righteousness (5:8-11; 6:14). It is this form of life that is both true human living (4:24) and, simultaneously, participating in the "life of God" (4:18). In fact, we could describe the mission of the church in this very language: to participate in, and to be agents of enabling others to participate in, the life of God.[32] Paul can also call it "learning Christ" (4:20).

As Paul continues his plea for this holy, righteous, Spirit-filled, counter-cultural living in God/Christ (5:3-21), we find a text that might be taken as a call for withdrawal from the world, for disengagement:

> [6]Let no one deceive you with empty words, for because of these things the wrath of God comes on those who are disobedient. [7]Therefore do not be associated with them. (Eph. 5:6-7)

---

every age how to balance the divine gift of, and call to, peace and unity with the divine gift of, and call to, holiness. For God, these are synonymous realities; for us, they are overlapping at best, fraught with ambiguity and struggle, and are sometimes even (apparently) antithetical. At the very least, the church must recognize that when Paul advocates certain practices, he also forbids others.

32. The traditional Christian language for participation in the life of the triune God is theosis, or deification. For much more on this, see chapter eight on Romans.

It is hard to imagine a missional church that does not associate with outsiders; it is even harder to imagine a group of disciples of Jesus refusing to associate with "sinners," since that is what Jesus was known to have done.

Paul's words can actually be read in a quite different way with very different consequences. To the Corinthians, Paul had written the following:

> [9]I wrote to you in my letter not to associate with sexually immoral persons — [10]not at all meaning the immoral of this world, or the greedy and robbers, or idolaters, since you would then need to go out of the world. [11]But now I am writing to you not to associate with anyone who bears the name of brother or sister who is sexually immoral or greedy, or is an idolater, reviler, drunkard, or robber. Do not even eat with such a one. (1 Cor. 5:9-11)

As in the lost letter that Paul wrote to the Corinthians, also advocating disassociation with the immoral and idolatrous, Paul may not be referring in Ephesians 5 to nonbelievers but to (so-called) believers who continue in their old ways.[33]

If, however, this reading is incorrect and Paul is in fact referring to non-association with outsiders, this still does not mean complete withdrawal and disengagement. Rather, in 5:7 Paul prohibits full participation (*symmetochos*, as in 3:6, of Gentile participation in Christ), for Christ represents one of "two incommensurable realms in which one might participate"[34] — i.e., in which one might "walk" and by which one might be formed. The church is a counterculture or, better, an alter-culture, and it needs to preserve its distinctive form of life in order to bear witness to its neighbors.

In either reading, Paul is not urging withdrawal from the world. Rather, Paul says, now that those in the Lord are "light," they should walk "as children of light" (5:8).[35] As they embody the light of the gospel in their "walk" among

---

33. Although a casual glance only at 5:6-7 may make this reading seem implausible, the context actually suggests that Paul is concerned about inappropriate behavior among "the saints" (5:3), for such behavior puts at risk one's inheritance in the kingdom of Christ and God (5:5). In other words, the danger is that old, pagan behaviors may persist in the church.

34. Fowl, *Ephesians*, p. 168 n. 6. Fowl rightly sees this passage as "a strategy of engagement and not withdrawal" (p. 169 n. 7). So also Lincoln, *Ephesians*, p. 326 — the withdrawal is moral, not isolationist.

35. Once again, the more "literal" translation "walk," rather than "live," conveys the sense of the church going somewhere, of being in mission. The NRSV ("live"; 5:8b) and other translations miss this missional sense.

the disobedient in the darkness, they will "expose" the "unfruitful works of [the] darkness" (5:11). This should not be understood as self-righteous finger-pointing, but as the preparatory work of mission, similar to that of the Spirit (Paraclete/Advocate), according to John's Gospel: "And when he comes, he will prove the world wrong about sin and righteousness and judgment; about sin, because they do not believe in me . . ." (John 16:8-9).[36]

Paul does indeed counsel nonparticipation (5:11), but that is not the same as nonpresence or even nonengagement. Paul's hope, in fact, is that just as his hearers/readers have been transformed from darkness to light, so also will Christ the light shine on others, through his hearers/readers, so that all will be raised from their spiritual death into new life in the new humanity (5:13-14). "[T]he challenge to the church is to stand as an appealing alternative to the world," not so much by virtue of its "moral superiority" but by virtue of the way "believers confront their sins, seek and offer forgiveness, and live reconciled and reconciling lives"[37] — that is, by becoming the gospel of peace. The final admonition in this context — "Be careful then how you live, not as unwise people but as wise, making the most of the time, because the days are evil" (5:15-16) — is therefore a missional admonition for the church to be the light of the world (cf. Matt. 5:14) in the midst of days of darkness.

A detailed examination of the household code in 5:22–6:9 is beyond the scope of this chapter. We have already addressed certain major issues at the beginning of this chapter. Given the overall context that we have been exploring, we may suggest that, despite their difficulties, the agenda of these texts is generally consonant with the overall goal of the letter: to enunciate and further the peace of God that reconciles humanity's binaries. Men and women in Christ are to be mutually loving, in Christlike fashion, and submissive (5:21-33); children and parents in Christ are to be mutually respectful (6:1-4); and slaves and masters in Christ are to recognize their common Master in Christ, and to treat one another within that framework (6:5-9). Rather than being a justification of the status quo, then, these verses challenge the status quo of patriarchal control and even violence with the peace of Christ.

Paul's references to darkness and light in this quite lengthy discussion of the church's life in 4:1–6:9 remind us that he and his hearers/readers are walking in a dangerous, apocalyptic world, where the battle between the realities of light and darkness is very real and experienced existentially, both

---

36. On the countercultural and subversive yet edifying and missional nature of Christian existence, see Gombis, *The Drama of Ephesians,* esp. ch. 6 (pp. 133-54).

37. Fowl, *Ephesians,* p. 171.

within the household and outside of it. Paul takes up that dimension of his and our mission in 6:10-22.

## Waging War with Peace: The Church and Paul as Proclaimers of the Gospel (6:10-22)

This section of Ephesians has been interpreted from a variety of angles, most often focusing on the church's (or the believer's) battle with, and/or witness to, "the powers," those forces of evil named in 6:12 (more popularly called "spiritual warfare"). Here we will take a slightly different approach, focusing primarily on the gospel of peace and the church's embodied proclamation of it. (These two approaches, however, are not mutually exclusive but complementary.)

In Ephesians 6:10-22 Paul depicts life in Christ as an apocalyptic battle. It is a "rousing call" — even a call to arms — that summons the church to embody the kind of life in the world that the entire letter depicts.[38] The church, and not merely the individual believer, is engaged in a war with cosmic powers that requires divine strength and provision — armor. This metaphor has often led interpreters down a path of arguing about whether Paul is depicting an offensive or a defensive battle, which may be an exercise in missing the point. What Paul is focusing on here, using the paradoxical metaphor of military gear, is the set of godly virtues and practices the church needs in order to move out into a hostile world with the gospel, the gospel of peace. Theologically, Paul portrays this as participation in a divine war by taking on divine attributes — by "wearing" what God wears: righteousness, truth, and so on.[39] Furthermore, and again rather paradoxically, this moving out while dressed in God-clothes both requires the church to be able to stand firm ("stand against the wiles of the devil," 6:11;

---

38. Lincoln, *Ephesians*, pp. 432-33. Elsewhere in Paul, we find warfare imagery in 1 Thess. 5:8 (which similarly draws on Isa. 59:17); Rom. 6:13; 13:12-14; 1 Cor. 16:13; 2 Cor. 6:7; 10:3-5; Phil. 2:25; Philem. 2; cf. 1 Tim. 1:18; 2 Tim. 2:3-4.

39. So also Lincoln, who says that "it is hard to avoid the impression that more is intended [than simply that God supplies the armor] and that the armor given by God to believers is in some sense his own" (*Ephesians*, p. 442). Gombis calls the church the *"embodiment of the divine warrior,"* though he does not stress the peacemaking dimension of the church's life per se ("The Triumph of God in Christ: Divine Warfare in the Argument of Ephesians" [Ph.D. diss., University of St. Andrews, 2005], p. 3; http://research-repository.st-andrews.ac .uk/bitstream/10023/2321/6/TimothyGombisPhDthesis.pdf).

"withstand on that evil day . . . stand firm," 6:13; "Stand therefore," 6:14), and empowers it do so.[40]

As all interpreters recognize, Paul draws on scriptural texts from the prophet Isaiah that associate God with a kind of warfare.[41] Ironically, however, this divine warfare establishes justice and peace. Paul's contribution is to assert that the church participates in this paradoxical, divine, *shalom*-making warfare by putting on the gospel of peace. He writes, in part, as follows:

> [11]Put on the whole armor of God, so that you may be able to stand against the wiles of the devil. . . . [13]Therefore take up the whole armor of God, so that you may be able to withstand on that evil day, and having done everything, to stand firm. [14]Stand therefore, and fasten the belt of truth around your waist, and put on the breastplate of righteousness. [15]As shoes for your feet put on whatever will make you ready to proclaim the gospel of peace. [16]With all of these, take the shield of faith, with which you will be able to quench all the flaming arrows of the evil one. [17]Take the helmet of salvation, and the sword of the Spirit, which is the word of God. (Eph. 6:11, 13-17)

The main texts on which Paul draws (from the Greek Bible, or LXX) are from Isaiah 11, 59, and 52. First, Isaiah 11, from which Paul draws parts of verses 4-5:

> [1]A shoot shall come out from the stump of Jesse, and a branch shall grow out of his roots. [2]The spirit of the Lord shall rest on him, the spirit of wisdom and understanding, the spirit of counsel and might, the spirit of knowledge and the fear of the Lord. [3]His delight shall be in the fear of the Lord. He shall not judge by what his eyes see, or decide by what his ears hear; [4]but with righteousness he shall judge the poor, and decide with equity for the meek of the earth; he shall strike the earth with the rod [LXX *tō logō*] of his mouth, and with the breath [LXX *en pneumati*] of his lips he shall kill the wicked. [5]Righteousness shall be the belt around his

---

40. As Fowl notes, the images of "walking" (and we might add walking in the shoes of the gospel of peace) and "standing firm" are "not incompatible" (*Ephesians*, p. 200). The church is being called "both to be ready for battle and to stand firm in the battle that is already in progress" (Lincoln, *Ephesians*, p. 433).

41. For more detailed discussion, see the commentaries (e.g., Lincoln, *Ephesians*, pp. 436-37).

waist, and faithfulness [LXX *alētheia,* truth/fidelity] the belt around his loins. ⁶The wolf shall live with the lamb, the leopard shall lie down with the kid, the calf and the lion and the fatling together, and a little child shall lead them. ⁷The cow and the bear shall graze, their young shall lie down together; and the lion shall eat straw like the ox. ⁸The nursing child shall play over the hole of the asp, and the weaned child shall put its hand on the adder's den. ⁹They will not hurt or destroy on all my holy mountain; for the earth will be full of the knowledge of the Lord as the waters cover the sea. (Isa. 11:1-9)

This passage is a description of the person and mission of the Spirit-empowered "stump of Jesse," or coming Davidic ruler, the "messiah" to many later readers (Isa. 11:1-2). He does what God does, and what the king in Israel was supposed to do: he effects justice and peace. By the Spirit of YHWH, he is given the ability to "do what the world believes is impossible."[42] As he judges the poor with righteousness and slays the wicked with his breath, his righteousness and faithfulness will usher in an era of *shalom,* when "[t]he wolf shall live with the lamb" (Isa. 11:6) and "[t]hey will not hurt or destroy on all my [the Lord's] holy mountain; for the earth will be full of the knowledge of the Lord as the waters cover the sea" (Isa. 11:9). Thus when Paul calls the church to "fasten the belt of truth [*alētheia*] around your waist, and put on the breastplate of righteousness" (Eph. 6:14), he is doing more than reinforcing two of the basic virtues he has already mentioned (1:13; 4:15, 21, 24, 25; 5:9). He is also associating the "wearing" of truth and righteousness with the messianic reign of peace.

The church is the place where believers embody the virtues of the messianic era of peace as a foretaste of the full and future reign of the messiah's peace, for Christ *is* our peace — present tense. The vision of animals that are normally related to one another as enemies, perpetrators and victims of violence, being reconciled and living in harmony, is, or should be, an icon of the church. For the church, knowing that the messianic age has begun in Jesus, anticipates the future by rejecting violence in the present, becoming a foretaste of the "new world [that] will indeed be safe for the vulnerable."[43] Its "offensive warfare," therefore, is conducted with one and only one weapon, the sword of the Spirit [*pneumatos*] — the word [*rhēma*] of God. The church

---

42. Walter Brueggemann, *Isaiah 1–39,* Westminster Bible Companion (Louisville: Westminster John Knox, 1998), p. 99.

43. Brueggemann, *Isaiah 1–39,* p. 103.

takes on the role of God's servant in Isaiah, not by slaying the wicked (for that kind of role is reserved for God alone, according to Paul: Rom. 12:19) but by bearing witness to the nations (Isa. 49:1-6).[44]

We turn next to Isaiah 59; Paul draws from verse 17 of that chapter:

> He [YHWH] put on righteousness like a breastplate, and a helmet of salvation on his head; he put on garments of vengeance for clothing, and wrapped himself in fury as in a mantle. (Isa. 59:17)[45]

This verse appears in the context of the prophet's lament about the people's sins, which the prophet enumerates to include "deeds of violence" (59:6) as people's "feet run to evil, and they rush to shed innocent blood" (59:7), for "[t]he way of peace they do not know, and there is no justice in their paths. Their roads they have made crooked; no one who walks in them knows peace" (59:8).[46] The prophet says that the absence of justice and righteousness means that the people are walking in darkness rather than light (59:9-10). Into this dire situation, where justice and salvation are "far from us" (59:11), God — "displeased . . . that there was no justice" (59:15) — enters, bringing righteousness and salvation, vengeance and fury (59:17). That is, God brings the *shalom* that humans need but cannot attain on their own. Therefore, once again, when Paul says, "put on the breastplate of righteousness" (6:14) and "[t]ake the helmet of salvation" (6:17), he is encouraging believers to participate actively in the divine mission of bringing humanity from darkness to light (Isa. 59:9-10; cf. Eph. 5:8-14), from sin to salvation and *shalom*.[47] That is, when Paul says to put on the armor "of God," he is not simply identifying God as the source of the armor but as the first bearer of the armor, who now shares it with the people of God.

---

44. "He [YHWH] made my [YHWH's servant's] mouth like a sharp sword." . . . "I [YHWH] will give you [YHWH's servant] as a light to the nations, that my salvation may reach to the end of the earth" (Isa. 49:2, 6). It should be especially emphasized that Paul does not encourage his audience to assist God in slaying the wicked. As Paul says in Rom. 12:19, where he also quotes Scripture (Deut. 32:35), "Beloved, never avenge yourselves, but leave room for the wrath of God; for it is written, 'Vengeance is mine, I will repay, says the Lord.'" Rather, the church in Rome, as in Ephesus, is to be a community that practices peace in the world (Rom. 12:18, discussed in the previous chapter).

45. Similar language appears in Wisd. 5:18, which is likely indebted to Isaiah here.

46. Paul quotes Isa. 59:7-8 in Rom. 3:15-17, his final description of humanity's sinfulness, revealing the need for the gospel.

47. Once again, Paul does not promote the church's participation in executing the divine wrath.

This divine rescue mission centers, of course, in Jesus, who brings righteousness and salvation to humanity. Given that elsewhere in his correspondence Paul speaks of putting on, or clothing ourselves with, Christ (Rom. 13:14; Gal. 3:27), it is quite possible that Paul wants us to understand the divine peacemaking warrior to be — or perhaps to include (i.e., within the identity of God) — Christ.[48] That is, those who wrap themselves in the clothes of Christ are thereby donning the armor of God, and vice versa. Paul says something very close to this in Romans 13, where he seems to equate putting on the "armor of light" with putting on Christ (Rom. 13:11-14). Moreover, already in Ephesians Paul has spoken of his readers "know[ing] the love of Christ that surpasses knowledge, so that you may be filled with all the fullness of God" (3:19) and having learned Christ (4:20), which means in part "to clothe yourselves with the new self, created according to the likeness of God in true righteousness and holiness" (4:24).[49] To learn Christ means to be re-clothed in Godlikeness.[50]

This way of understanding Paul's armor-donning language in Ephesians 6 would reinforce the significance for him of interpreting God, and God's attributes, in light of Christ (cf. 1 Cor. 1:18-31). This interpretive move means for Paul, and for us, that to be Godlike means to be Christlike, and vice versa. And this, in turn, means that Godlikeness means conformity to the self-giving, peacemaking love revealed on the cross. The cross, then, reconfigures our understanding of Isaiah 59:17 and of its use in Ephesians 6 as a call to nonviolent, cruciform arms.[51]

Finally, we consider Paul's use of Isaiah 52, which we have already noted:

> How beautiful upon the mountains are the feet of the messenger who announces peace, who brings good news, who announces salvation, who says to Zion, "Your God reigns." (Isa. 52:7)

48. This suggestion is made also by Peter S. Williamson (*Ephesians,* Catholic Commentary on Sacred Scripture [Grand Rapids: Baker, 2009], p. 194), based on his interpretation of Rom. 11:26 as Paul's identification of the Lord named in Isa. 59:20 with Jesus.

49. The Greek text says simply "according to God" *(kata theon),* not "according to the likeness of God."

50. Similarly, Col. 3:12-15 suggests a close correspondence between being God's chosen holy ones and being imitators of Christ. The Colossians are instructed to "clothe themselves" (3:12, 14) with the virtues and practices of love and reconciliation. And Christ in Colossians is the fullness of God (1:19; 2:9).

51. For an extended discussion of this argument, see my *Inhabiting the Cruciform God: Kenosis, Justification, and Theosis in Paul's Narrative Soteriology* (Grand Rapids: Eerdmans, 2009).

The people of God addressed by this text were in exile waiting for deliverance, for restoration, for their return, and for the return of YHWH, their king, to Zion (Jerusalem). In four phrases of overlapping significance, the prophet here describes the messenger who proclaims that this hope is about to be realized: announcing peace, bringing good news (LXX *euangelizomenou akoēn eirēnēs hos euangelizomenos agatha*), announcing salvation, and proclaiming the arrival of God as king. Although this text is not as explicitly cited in Ephesians 6 as the previously discussed verses from Isaiah, three of its key words, "feet," "peace," and "good news"/gospel *(euangeliou)* are echoed in Ephesians 6:15. Moreover, in Romans 10:15 Paul quotes this text from Isaiah in reference to those who spread the gospel. Thus it is likely that Paul has the task of evangelization (broadly understood) in mind here. The lack of a military image in Isaiah 52:7 simply underscores the main point we have been making in this section: the warfare imagery in Ephesians serves, and is therefore secondary to, Paul's principal concern: the calling of the church to embody the gospel of peace in the world.

Peace, as we have seen, is a key theme in this letter. We learn now that the Christ-shaped community of peace, of people reconciled to God and to one another, has a task in the world, the same sort of task given to heralds long ago: to announce the good news of peace — not just any peace, but God's peace, the *shalom* of God's victorious salvation. As in the time of announcements about a return from exile, the subject of Isaiah 52, so also now those who *wear* the good news must *share* the good news; Paul states this imaginatively by speaking of the church's preparation to proclaim the gospel of peace as putting on its "shoes" — its (peaceful) combat boots, so to speak. That is, by ongoing attention to its life of peace, love, and righteousness, the church's internal life becomes both the shape of and the impetus for its embodied witness in the world. For this reason, it is critical to the church's witness that it "mak[e] every effort to maintain the unity of the Spirit in the bond of peace" (4:3).[52] It is this one, unifying, peace-creating Spirit who empowers the church to proclaim the gospel by means of the word of God (Eph. 6:17).

At the same time, we see the participatory nature of the church's peace witness. In chapter 2 Paul had interpreted the preacher of peace in Isaiah 52:7 as Christ, but now he applies that image to the church. What does this

---

52. One is reminded of John 17 (esp. vv. 20-23), where Jesus prays that his disciples will be unified in order to bear appropriate and convincing witness to the world. A sense of spiritual warfare appears in John 17 as well (esp. vv. 14-16).

mean? Fundamentally, that the church now shares in the work of God begun in Christ; it continues to proclaim the good news of peace by bearing faithful witness, word and deed, to the one who "is our peace." Paul's *Christological* reading of Isaiah has become a *missiological* reading without ever losing its focus on Christ. In other words, the church has the privilege and responsibility of participating in God's work of peace, but it is called to do so in a fully Christological way, that is, being both Christ-shaped and Christ-focused.

To conclude our consideration of Ephesians 6: when we put this passage in conversation with its chief sources, or intertexts, namely Isaiah 11:5, 59:17, and 52:7, we are pressed to conclude that peacemaking is more than obeying or even imitating God. It is, in a profound sense, wearing God, putting God on, dressing in God's attributes, all understood Christologically. This is not make-believe dressing, like that of a small child putting on his or her parents' shoes, or a costume. Rather, it is *participating* in the very life of the God who makes peace in and through Christ. We are transformed into the likeness of God when and as we embody — and thus become — the gospel of peace. Such embodiment will be proactive and will involve movement, for that is, after all, the purpose of shoes. The gospel must not be *taken to* the world but *walked into* the world, incarnationally, we might say.

It is worth noting that the understanding of missional identity and strength in this passage has a rather Trinitarian texture: the church is called to be "strong in the Lord [Jesus]" (6:10), clothed with the "whole armor of God [the Father]" (6:11, 13), and equipped and empowered "in the Spirit" (6:17-18). The two locative phrases ("in" — referring both to Jesus and the Spirit), meshed with the image of wearing armor, also suggest a highly participatory form of missional spirituality. It is participation in the missional life of the triune God.

Such a missional vocation requires prayer, Paul says, for it to be faithful and effective. He calls on his readers to pray for themselves (6:18a), for "all the saints" (6:18b), and for himself (6:19-20). He specifically asks (twice) for boldness in his preaching as the ambassador of the gospel (cf. 2 Cor. 5:20), even as he has been imprisoned for doing exactly that. An ambassador in chains is of course precisely what most diplomats wish never to become (and normally *could not* become, having diplomatic immunity[53]), but in this case the punishment is, in an important sense, both a reward and an opportunity for Paul. It is an occasion to proclaim the gospel in a way that powerfully embodies its message, to connect with his readers and receive their spiritual

---

53. Lincoln, *Ephesians*, p. 454.

support, and to encourage his readers then and now, in their own situations, also to be faithful ambassadors of the gospel, even when faced with hostility.

## Conclusion: Peace in Paul and Contemporary Practices of Peace

For Paul, to practice Christ-shaped peacemaking is to participate in the life and mission of the God whose very nature, revealed most fully in Christ the peacemaker, is peaceable and peacemaking. To practice and to make peace is to partake of the very character of God, of the divine nature. Paul would agree with Jesus as recorded in Matthew's Gospel: "Blessed are the peacemakers, for they shall be called children of God" (Matt. 5:9). That is, *peacemakers have the DNA of God, and those who claim to have that DNA will be peacemakers.*

The term "peace churches" should be redundant, but sadly it is probably more often at least somewhat oxymoronic. "Peace churches" is theologically repetitive because the gospel that the church has been given is God's peace initiative. The implications of this reality may be stated rather forcefully: there is no gospel other than the gospel of peace. *Peace — both as peaceableness and as peacemaking — is not a supplement to the gospel but a non-negotiable and constitutive element of it.* In fact, peacemaking, between humanity and God and between people and other people, is arguably for Paul the central reality that Christ's death effects and that the gospel makes known and makes real in concrete, everyday situations.

Such forms of concrete peacemaking will reflect the character of God's work in Christ in imaginative, creative ways. They may be referred to as "improvisations" on the gospel. Timothy Gombis, for instance, says that Paul and the church participate in God's drama of salvation through "gospel performances that are both cruciform and subversive."[54] This does not mean that the church is "rebellious or a band of troublemakers," but rather that

> God calls the church to become communities that subvert corrupted and destructive patterns of life. . . . The church cultivates communal practices that embody the grace and love of Jesus for a broken, fractured and tired world. . . . [W]e wage our warfare . . . when we resist idolatrous and destructive patterns of life.[55]

54. Gombis, *Drama of Ephesians*, pp. 124-25, 133-53 (quote from p. 124).
55. Gombis, *Drama of Ephesians*, pp. 182-83.

Ironically, therefore, the church's peacemaking life will sometimes be perceived as troublemaking. Subversion of the status quo, even when done unintentionally and in love, can provoke opposition, as the Prince of Peace, who called his followers to be peacemakers, told them: "Do not think that I have come to bring peace to the earth; I have not come to bring peace, but a sword" (Matt. 10:34). The divine peace mission may, in fact, lead to the cross, but eventually the cross leads to resurrection and renewal. That is the ultimate hope and ground of all Christian mission (1 Cor. 15:58).

The church, then, is — or should be — a sign of hope in a fractured world. It can be the bridge between enemies, between the realities of this broken age and those of the coming age of *shalom,* and between the hatred and violence in our own hearts and in the hearts of others. As Andrew Lincoln puts it, the church's part in God's plan to bring "peace and reconciliation on a universal and cosmic scale," which happens "through a life of holiness and love," can "still be immensely attractive and provides a powerful incentive for hope."[56]

The church's peacemaking takes place in concentric circles, beginning within the church itself, and extending to the home, the community, the nation, and the world. It has, in other words, five spheres: ecclesial, domestic, communal, national, and international. Since many Christians and churches may know of ministries in some of these spheres closer to home, it might be useful to consider for a moment the international sphere. How can a church, or individual believers, make a difference at the global level?

Christian Peacemaker Teams (CPT) is one answer.[57] CPT's mission and motto is "Building partnerships to transform violence and oppression." Its vision, according to its website, is a "world of communities that together embrace the diversity of the human family and live justly and peaceably with all creation." It is "committed to work and relationships that honor and reflect the presence of faith and spirituality; strengthen grassroots initiatives; transform structures of domination and oppression; and embody creative non-violence and liberating love."

CPT began as a response to the 1984 challenge of theologian Ron Sider, issued to an international meeting of Mennonites, to take the call to cross-shaped discipleship, specifically the cross as an alternative to the sword, seriously — perhaps to the point of martyrdom. By 1986 a vision was formed, and the first ministry activities began a few years later.

56. Lincoln, *Ephesians,* p. xcvi.
57. See http://www.cpt.org/.

What does this mean on the ground? Now an ecumenical ministry, CPT hopes to inspire all Christians to seek nonviolent alternatives to conflict and to bear witness to the peace Jesus offers by practicing nonviolence and reconciliation in the world's hot spots. They call this work "violence-reduction ministry." CPT focuses on placing small groups of trained individuals in areas of conflict to observe, document, be present, and nonviolently intervene. It maintains an ongoing presence in Palestine, Iraq, Colombia, and certain aboriginal/First Nation areas. It has also had periods of presence in the Congo, on the Mexico/U.S. border, and elsewhere. CPT sponsors delegations to such areas for first-time participants, who work with long- or short-term staffers in their areas. The peacemaker "corps" consists of members who serve for three years and "reservists" who commit to a period of two to twelve weeks annually. CPT solicits the support of individuals and churches and, in turn, provides not only ministry opportunities but also resources for training, worship, and the church's public witness to peace.

In some situations, being a Christian peacemaker seems an impossible task, especially in the places CPT is active. On a more local but no less challenging level, I know of one pastor who, during the apartheid era in South Africa, was willing to take serious risks in order to try to bring justice and peace to his fellow blacks. His denomination, however, forbade any "political activity" on the part of its clergy in order not to put the message of the gospel at risk. (The denomination later apologized for its own failure to address the oppression of apartheid.) This pastor, committed to nonviolence and reconciliation, decided that if he could not participate in peacemaking between the races, he would do so within his own race. He lived in Soweto, where there was much black-on-black violence in those horrible years. He therefore dedicated himself to peacemaking within the black community. It was not the wider ministry of reconciliation he wanted, and he knew his work would not end apartheid, but it was nonetheless an amazing ministry, one that contributed positively to the reality of peace within the community in the post-apartheid era.

Similarly, my friend Dr. Bungishabaku Katho, an Old Testament scholar, is the principal, or president, of Shalom University of Bunia in the Democratic Republic of Congo. The Christian university's name is not only biblical and beautiful, it is appropriate. Its principal, staff, students, and graduates have worked tirelessly to promote peace and reconciliation in that strife-torn nation. First a Bible school and then a seminary, Shalom became a university after eight years of war in the country. During the war, the warring sides approached the seminary, and everyone feared a major battle would occur on the campus in the spring of 2003. But the seminary officials proclaimed their space a place of peace, not war. Eventually each side recognized the sanctity of the seminary and did not damage it. In fact, once students and staff evacuated the campus, more than one thousand people were able to find sanctuary in the seminary. When the war ended, the first peace talks were held at the seminary. Hence in the midst and aftermath of war was born the need for, and the name of, Shalom University.

The fundamental postwar question the school perceived the need to address was how pastors and other Christian leaders could be agents of transformation. Facing many issues, from ethnic reconciliation to community development to deforestation and other environmental concerns, the school's leaders made the decision to link every aspect of the program to theology. They understood, and continue to understand, the biblical vision of *shalom,* the *missio Dei,* as an integrated, comprehensive reality.

As I was completing this chapter, an image of the church as agent of reconciliation came across the Internet. It was a photo of four Orthodox priests standing in the middle of a public square between Ukrainian protesters and Ukrainian police forces, armed with riot gear. The priests were praying for peace, putting themselves in harm's way as an icon of the peace of Christ that passes all understanding and that can unite even enemies. These priests were not the first, and will not be the last, to become the gospel of peace in such a powerful way. (In fact, I also recently saw similar images of priests in Egypt.)

Another incident occurred while I was finishing this chapter. A Dutch Jesuit priest in war-torn Syria, a man who had spent his life caring for his flock and working for peace, especially on improving Christian-Muslim relations, had refused to leave his greatly diminished parish. Fr. Frans van der Lugt had repeatedly said he would stay with his people and share their fate. Sadly, one April morning he was murdered, shot in the back of his head, at age seventy-six.

Not every Christian peacemaker is called to martyrdom, of course, or even to national or international work for peace. The church need only open its eyes, and enlarge its imagination, to find ways to imitate the example of these more dramatic cases of peacemaking in the community, the home, and the church in more modest ways. As events that continue to transpire in the United States (and elsewhere) make painfully clear, injustice to ethnic and racial minorities persists, and reconciliation is needed at the national and local levels. Like judgment (1 Pet. 4:17), such reconciliation begins, or should begin, with the household of God — both centripetally and centrifugally. If, for instance, "11 a.m." (metaphorically speaking) is still the most segregated hour in the U.S., then the church has failed to become the gospel in a radical and highly significant way. Yet there are signs of hope: Christian communities as diverse ethnically and racially as Paul's vision in Ephesians requires. In my immediate experience alone, there are such instantiations of the gospel in churches that are otherwise very different from one another: for example, a stately, urban Episcopal cathedral with a multiracial and international flavor; a young "emergent" church that especially brings Asians and those of European descent together; and a suburban Lutheran congregation of blacks and whites, Africans and African-Americans, Hispanics and more. Such unity in diversity is both a gift and a demand for those who participate in God's peacemaking mission.

One last example. A few years ago a Christian man I know decided to address the problem of bullying on the local school bus by volunteering to ride it each morning for a while. The driver had not been able to curb the problem. But the addition of a friendly and fun personality (and that describes this man perfectly) not only stemmed the rising tide of bullying, it also made for a more interesting bus ride for all and a not insignificant witness to the man's faith and church.

Even the most mundane actions for peace — such as a Christian in suburban America riding a school bus that was plagued with bullying and other tensions — can be witnesses to the good news promised by the prophets, inaugurated by Jesus, and celebrated by Paul. The challenge to the church, and to each Christian, is to hear and see what the Spirit might be saying through Ephesians, Romans, Isaiah, and the rest of Scripture's witness to Jesus. It is a message of nonviolent peacemaking in his Spirit, and thus also in the spirit of Paul.[58]

---

58. On nonviolence as an effective means of seeking justice and peace, see especially Ronald J. Sider, *Nonviolent Action: What Christian Ethics Demands but Most Christians Have Never Really Tried* (Grand Rapids: Baker Academic, 2015).

# CHAPTER 7

# Becoming the Justice of God: 1 & 2 Corinthians

In the last two chapters we have considered the gospel of peace in the letters of Paul. In the early part of that discussion, we noted that there is an inseparable link in the Bible between peace *(shalom)* and justice. Indeed, justice is a constitutive dimension of *shalom*. Nevertheless, the phrase "Paul and justice" rolls off the tongue no more rapidly than does the phrase "Paul and peace." In fact, it probably rolls off more slowly — if at all. In this chapter, then, we look at Paul, the church, and the justice of God by way of Paul's Corinthian correspondence. We will perhaps be surprised at the crucial role that justice plays in Paul's missional theology and practice, and how it is a critical aspect of his understanding of transformative participation in the life of God, the God of justice.

## Introduction: God of Justice, People of Justice

One definition of a good Jew is someone who cares about what God cares about. That is not a bad description of a Christian, either. The great Jewish writer Abraham Joshua Heschel claimed that "the fundamental experience of the prophet is a fellowship with the feelings of God" and that "[t]o be a prophet means to identify one's concern with the concern of God."[1] It is difficult to resist the conclusion that to be a Jew or a Christian means, in some sense, to be "prophetic" — not first of all in the sense of being socially "progressive" or vocally critical of perceived injustices, but simply in Heschel's sense of having a passionate concern about God's concerns.

---

1. Abraham J. Heschel, *The Prophets,* Perennial Classics (New York: HarperCollins, 2001 [1962]), p. 31; and *Between God and Man: An Interpretation of Judaism* (New York: Free Press, 1997 [1959]), p. 126.

The Scriptures of Israel, the Christian Old Testament, testify that one of the things God cares most about is justice (*mishpat;* LXX *krima* and related words) and its cousin, righteousness *(tsedheq, tsedhaqah;* LXX *dikaiosynē).*[2] Discussing the biblical injunction to "listen to" YHWH, Walter Brueggemann rightly claims that even though this call to listen has many dimensions, "we may say in sum that *Israel's obligation is to do justice.*"[3] The two terms *mishpat* and *tsedhaqah* often appear together,[4] constituting an idiom of sorts that might be translated as "social justice."[5] "The prophetic passion for justice is the *social face of righteousness.*"[6]

Yet, biblically speaking, justice is not an autonomous ethical principle. It is a comprehensive, covenantal, relational mandate.[7] It is part of being in relationship with God, part of "walking" with God:

> [6]"With what shall I come before the Lord, and bow myself before God on high? Shall I come before him with burnt offerings, with calves a year old? [7]Will the Lord be pleased with thousands of rams, with ten thousands of rivers of oil? Shall I give my firstborn for my transgression, the fruit of my body for the sin of my soul?" [8]He [the Lord] has told you, O mortal, what is good; and what does the Lord require of you but to do justice

2. I have generally indicated in transliteration the Hebrew and Greek words for justice from the Hebrew Bible, the Septuagint (LXX), and the New Testament. In addition to works mentioned in some of the following notes, for a brief summary, arguing for biblical justice as primarily distributive rather than retributive, see Walter Brueggemann, *Theology of the Old Testament: Testimony, Dispute, Advocacy* (Minneapolis: Fortress, 1997), pp. 735-42. See also Bruce V. Malchow, *Social Justice in the Hebrew Bible* (Collegeville, MN: Liturgical, 1996) for a historical-developmental approach, and Christopher J. H. Wright, *Old Testament Ethics for the People of God* (Downers Grove, IL: InterVarsity, 2004), pp. 253-80, for a more synthetic, thematic treatment. Wright says that God (1) displays, (2) demands, and (3) will deliver justice.

3. Brueggemann, *Theology of the Old Testament,* p. 421.

4. E.g., Ps. 33:5; 89:14, all connected with God's "steadfast love" *(hesed);* also Gen. 18:19; Ps. 72:1-2; 99:4; Prov. 2:9; 8:20; Isa. 5:7; 32:16; 33:5; Jer. 22:3.

5. So, e.g., Wright, *Old Testament Ethics,* p. 257. For some, the term "social justice" connotes a humanly conceived project with certain fundamental dimensions arising from the Enlightenment project. It should be clear from this chapter, however, that the social justice of the prophets and (I will argue) of Paul is decidedly theological and theocentric. Indeed, for Paul it is also decidedly Christological and Christocentric.

6. Willard Swartley, "The Relation of Justice/Righteousness to *Shalom/Eirēnē,*" *Ex Auditu* 22 (2006): 29-53 (p. 33).

7. See, e.g., Bruce C. Birch, "Reclaiming Prophetic Leadership," *Ex Auditu* 22 (2006): 10-25, esp. pp. 11-13.

[*mishpat;* LXX *krima*], and to love kindness, and to walk humbly with your God? (Mic. 6:6-8)

Thus justice, biblically speaking, is a dimension of spirituality. And if spirituality is ultimately about having such deep communion with God that one takes on God's character, then doing justice is one of the richest spiritual experiences and practices. Why? Because the God of the Bible is just and practices justice. This divine justice is rooted in God's character (YHWH is "a lover of justice"; Ps. 99:4) and God's *hesed,* or steadfast covenant love. Accordingly, the corollary covenantal command for God's people to love their neighbor finds expression in practices of justice. To be like God means to do justice.

At the same time, justice is obviously about mission, about participating in the activity of this justice-loving, justice-doing God. It is an unfortunate reality of contemporary church life and language, however, that "spirituality" and "mission" (including "justice") are still frequently seen as separate from each other, and at times even at odds with each other. This is hardly characteristic of the emphasis on justice found in the Christian Old Testament.

We see this concern for justice, articulated in various ways, throughout the Torah, the Writings, and the Prophets. It comes to richest expression in parts of the prophetic tradition, with texts such as Micah 6:8, quoted above, and the following:

- [L]earn to do good; seek justice [*mishpat;* LXX *krisin*], rescue the oppressed [LXX *adikoumenon*], defend the orphan, plead for the widow. (Isa. 1:17)
- [L]et justice [*mishpat;* LXX *krima*] roll down like waters, and righteousness [*tsedhaqah;* LXX *dikaiosynē*] like an everflowing stream. (Amos 5:24)

To repeat, this missional imperative to practice justice, including special regard for the poor, is not an arbitrary command but an extension of God's own identity onto and into the people of God. It is "rooted in Yahweh's own practice and inclination, so that in the practice of justice Israel is indeed to imitate Yahweh," writes Brueggemann,[8] citing Deuteronomy 10:

---

8. Brueggemann, *Theology of the Old Testament,* p. 422. Brueggemann cites additional texts, including Prov. 14:31, which reads, "Those who oppress the poor insult their Maker, but those who are kind to the needy honor him."

[17]For the Lord your God is God of gods and Lord of lords, the great God, mighty and awesome, who is not partial and takes no bribe, [18]who executes justice for the orphan and the widow, and who loves the strangers, providing them food and clothing. [19]You shall also love the stranger, for you were strangers in the land of Egypt. (Deut. 10:17-19)

Lest we import a foreign, twenty-first-century definition of justice into this prophetic concern, we need to hear the prophetic words "justice" and "righteousness" as relational terms.[9] They have to do not with retribution, for instance, but with human community and wholeness, the setting right of wrongly configured relationships, the liberation of the oppressed, and attention to the poor and otherwise needy. Justice is, in other words, closely related to the biblical vision of *shalom*.[10] Being grounded in God's character, justice is not a *footnote* to biblical religion but rather at the very *heart* of biblical faith.

The prophets knew, however, that God's people often did not practice justice:

"How the faithful city has become a whore! She that was full of justice, righteousness lodged in her — but now murderers!" . . . They do not defend the orphan, and the widow's cause does not come before them. (Isa. 1:21, 23c)[11]

But they had visions of a new day when there would be peace and justice, as Isaiah famously foresaw:

[2]In days to come the mountain of the Lord's house shall be established as the highest of the mountains, and shall be raised above the hills; all the nations shall stream to it. [3]Many peoples shall come and say, "Come, let us go up to the mountain of the Lord, to the house of the God of Jacob; that he may teach us his ways and that we may walk in his paths." For out of Zion shall go forth instruction, and the word of the Lord from Jerusalem.

9. On the relational character even of *mishpat,* the more legal of the two Hebrew terms, see Harold V. Bennett, "Justice, OT," in *The New Interpreter's Dictionary of the Bible* 3:476-77 (Nashville: Abingdon, 2008).

10. See, e.g., Swartley, "Relation," and cf., e.g., Isa. 60:17b. We note this relationship in the chapters on peace, as well.

11. Isaiah and other prophets associate such injustice with forsaking YHWH and practicing idolatry (e.g., Isa. 2:2-4), as does Paul (Rom. 1:18-32).

⁴He shall judge between the nations, and shall arbitrate for many peoples; they shall beat their swords into plowshares, and their spears into pruning hooks; nation shall not lift up sword against nation, neither shall they learn war any more. (Isa. 2:2-4; cf. Mic. 4:1-4)

At least some of the prophets predicted that God's people would have a new heart, animated by God himself, that would empower them to embody God's will in the world: "I will put my spirit within you, and make you follow my statutes and be careful to observe my ordinances" (Ezek. 36:27). One of those chief ordinances is the call to practice justice, especially for the poor. Justice, integral to *shalom,* is part and parcel of the new covenant, the covenant of peace.[12]

It is widely recognized today that Jesus, the bringer of the new covenant, shared this biblical vision of justice, attested in such texts as his "inaugural sermon" at Nazareth (Luke 4:14-30):

¹⁶When he came to Nazareth, where he had been brought up, he went to the synagogue on the sabbath day, as was his custom. He stood up to read, ¹⁷and the scroll of the prophet Isaiah was given to him. He unrolled the scroll and found the place where it was written [Isa. 61:1-2a]: ¹⁸"The Spirit of the Lord is upon me, because he has anointed me to bring good news to the poor. He has sent me to proclaim release to the captives and recovery of sight to the blind, to let the oppressed go free, ¹⁹to proclaim the year of the Lord's favor." ²⁰And he rolled up the scroll, gave it back to the attendant, and sat down. The eyes of all in the synagogue were fixed on him. ²¹Then he began to say to them, "Today this scripture has been fulfilled in your hearing." (Luke 4:16-21)

These words became the substance and shape of Jesus' ministry. More precisely, then, Jesus, filled with God's Spirit, *embodied* biblical justice, especially in his concern for the weak and marginalized; the evangelists bear witness to this, most especially Luke. It was integral to his identity and his mission. We might even say that Jesus not only *proclaimed* the good news to the poor that was promised by Isaiah, but he also *became* that gospel. And, like the God of Israel's Scriptures, Jesus expected those who walked with him to do

---

12. On the new covenant, see my *The Death of the Messiah and the Birth of the New Covenant: A (Not So) New Model of the Atonement* (Eugene, OR: Cascade, 2014). Chapters six and seven focus on *shalom,* the new covenant as the covenant of peace.

likewise, as texts such as the parables of the Good Samaritan (Luke 10:25-37) and the sheep and the goats (Matt. 25:31-46) make clear.

Furthermore, of course, in the New Testament (new covenant) the letter of James recognizes the centrality of justice, summarized in texts like "Religion that is pure and undefiled before God, the Father, is this: to care for orphans and widows in their distress, and to keep oneself unstained by the world" (James 1:27). It is difficult to read the gospels or James without seeing the ongoing importance of justice for those who belong to the new covenant that was promised by the prophets and inaugurated by Jesus.

But what about Paul?

## Paul the Anomaly or a Voice for Justice?

Did Paul care about *dikaiosynē* in the sense of prophetic justice? Or was he only concerned about *dikaiosynē* in the sense of justification, whether understood in the traditional, individualist manner — "How can a sinful human being be put into right relationship with God?" — or from some version of the "new perspective on Paul" — "Who is to be identified as part of the people of God, and by what criterion?"[13] To put it more bluntly, was Paul simply a bad Jew and a failed prophet, claiming to be called like a prophet to speak for God (Gal. 1:15-16) but apathetic about justice? Was Paul out of sync with the prophets and with Jesus? Indeed, to put the question theologically and more bluntly still, was Paul out of sync with God?

That I am not alone in raising this question became clear to me some years ago when a senior New Testament scholar, writing a chapter on social justice in the Bible, asked me if I could provide any help in discussing Paul as a potential resource, for he himself had found very little. More recently, a graduate student from Latin America but educated in the U.S. expressed to me his impression, gained from his recent academic study of Paul, that the apostle did not care about justice but only about justification (i.e., of the individual).

Did Paul care about biblical justice? And, perhaps more importantly, what should those who read Paul's letters as inspired and inspiring texts

---

13. Proponents of the "new perspective" on Paul (such as James Dunn and N. T. Wright) contend, among other things, that justification in Paul's theology is about the inclusion of the Gentiles as Gentiles in God's people in Christ, and not (or not merely, or not primarily) about how individuals are put right with God.

conclude about *our* missional responsibility to practice justice? Does Paul change the rules of the biblical game? Does he refocus concern away from justice and onto something else?

*Mē genoito!*, as Paul himself frequently said in Greek: "By no means!"[14] Paul has often been misread, and that misreading has created the situation we face today, wondering whether he cares one whit about what the prophets, Jesus, James, and the God to whom they testify care about. Rather, we should conclude, with Clement of Rome, writing at the end of the first century, that Paul "taught justice [*dikaiosynē*]" — in the fullest sense of that word — "to the whole world" (*1 Clement* 5:7).

## The Problem and a Proposal

More than two decades ago, James D. G. Dunn published a compelling article titled "The Justice of God: A Renewed Perspective on Justification by Faith."[15] Dunn not only summarized his "new perspective" on justification with respect to Jews and Gentiles, but also argued for the importance of justice — biblical, saving, restorative, relational justice — in Paul's theology of justification. This "horizontal dimension of righteousness," Dunn contended, was inseparable in Jewish thought from the "vertical relationship": right relations with God cannot exist without right relations with others, especially the disadvantaged.[16] He even suggested that a good starting place

14. This is Paul's response, meaning literally "may it not be," to preposterous conclusions that might be wrongly drawn from his gospel or his theologizing, especially in Romans. See Rom. 3:4, 6, 31; 6:2, 15; 7:7, 13; 9:14; 11:1, 11; 1 Cor. 6:15; Gal. 2:17; 3:21. Other possible translations or paraphrases include "No way!" and "Are you out of your mind?"

15. James D. G. Dunn, "The Justice of God: A Renewed Perspective on Justification by Faith," *Journal of Theological Studies* n.s. 43 (1992): 1-21. Perhaps the article would have been more influential had it been published in a journal of strictly biblical studies. The argument was popularized and brought into conversation with twentieth-century concerns in James D. G. Dunn and Alan M. Suggate, *The Justice of God: A Fresh Look at the Old Doctrine of Justification by Faith* (Carlisle, UK: Paternoster, 1993; Grand Rapids: Eerdmans, 1994). Curiously, Dunn's *The Theology of the Apostle Paul* (Grand Rapids: Eerdmans, 1998) echoes his earlier focus on relationality but does not develop the justice theme per se. Dunn's concerns in the journal article were anticipated already by Markus Barth, "Jews and Gentiles: The Social Character of Justification in Paul," *Ecumenical Studies* 5 (1968): 241-67: "Pauline writings indicated that justification involves all that is good for the human community and for the life of its individual members. . . . Justification is a social event" (p. 241).

16. Dunn, "The Justice of God," pp. 18-19.

for acknowledging the significance of justice for Paul would be to render the important Pauline phrase *hē dikaiosynē theou,* normally translated as "the righteousness of God," as "the justice of God." Dunn argued that this change in translation, despite some possible problems, would "at least . . . [avoid] the fatal disjunction of terminology which has been the consequence of English having to translate what in Hebrew and Greek are integrated concepts — justify, righteous, righteousness, justice."[17]

The "terminology" problem to which Dunn refers is complicated but important. First, it refers to the fact that English has two different word-families that seem unrelated to each other: the "just-" family (just, justice, etc.) and the "right-" family (righteous, righteousness, etc.), whereas both Hebrew and Greek each have one word-family to express such concepts. English makes these various concepts seem unrelated, while the Hebrew and Greek words suggest their interconnections. Second, furthermore, much theological discourse in English tends to make distinctions within the "just-" family between words and concepts like "justice" and "just," on the one hand, and "justification" and "justified," on the other. Such discourse obscures the close linguistic and theological ties within the "just-" family of words.[18]

Dunn's translational suggestion seeks to overcome these linguistic and theological problems. Unfortunately, however, neither Dunn's stress on the connection between justification and justice nor the phrase "the justice of God" has become a staple of the justification diet in Pauline studies. To be sure, there have been a few voices echoing this aspect of Dunn's new perspective in one way or another, including N. T. Wright, who has claimed that "[j]ustification is ultimately about justice, about God putting the world to rights."[19] In fact, Wright asserts that "we should in fact follow Paul's own

17. Dunn, "The Justice of God," p. 21. Dunn does not argue that justice should replace justification as the "leading motif" in Paul, so he does not wish to use "justice of God" all the time. He is also concerned that, in English, the phrase hides the "relational character" of justice in Paul (p. 21).

18. N. T. Wright (*Paul and the Faithfulness of God,* vol. 4 of Christian Origins and the Question of God [Minneapolis: Fortress, 2013], p. 801) laments regarding the translation of *dikaiosynē,* "We simply do not have, in contemporary English (or, I think, German or French), a word or even a single phrase that can sum up the broad ethical and 'relational' sense [of *dikaiosynē*], add to it the overtones of the law court, give it the extra dimensions of the divine covenant with Israel and set it within a worldview-narrative that looked ahead to a final judgment in which the creator would set all things right at last."

19. N. T. Wright, "New Perspectives on Paul," in *Justification in Perspective: Historical Developments and Contemporary Challenges,* ed. Bruce L. McCormack (Grand Rapids: Baker

train of thought on 'justification' itself into the wider notion of 'justice,' that is, of a community that embodies in its own life the wise ordering which is the creator's will."[20] But the concern of Dunn, Wright, and others has been far too neglected as scholars have debated other aspects of the new perspective and the issue of justification. For instance, in a 2005 review article of four then-recent books on justification, Douglas Harink found a few theologically interesting insights but ultimately lamented that each one remained bound by a narrow, individualistic notion of justification without concern for justification's social and political consequences.[21]

Furthermore, despite Dunn's important contribution, he inadvertently weakens his own thesis by speaking of "the relative absence of these fuller social dimensions in Paul's teaching," mentioning in passing as examples only Romans 12:9-21 and 14:1–15:9.[22] As we will see below, Paul's concern for justice is both more widespread and more central to his theology than even Dunn claimed.

In the remainder of this chapter, I briefly propose seven connections between justification and justice in Paul, with the sixth connection consisting of examples drawn from 1 and 2 Corinthians. First, however, I wish to offer an overarching working hypothesis. In the Greek Bible (Septuagint [LXX] plus New Testament) the phrase *dikaiosynē kai eirēnē*, "righteousness/justice and peace," appears twice, and only twice — in Psalm 85:10 (LXX translating the Hebrew *tsedheq weshalom*) and Romans 14:17.[23]

In the NRSV, Psalm 85:10 is translated "Steadfast love and faithfulness will meet; righteousness and peace will kiss each other." Most translations

---

Academic, 2006), pp. 243-64 (here p. 264). See also, e.g., Barth, "Jews and Gentiles"; Elsa Tamez, *The Amnesty of Grace: Justification by Faith from a Latin American Perspective,* trans. Sharon H. Ringe (Nashville: Abingdon, 1993); John Reumann, "Justification and Justice in the New Testament," *Horizons in Biblical Theology* 21 (1999): 26-45; Miroslav Volf, "The Social Meaning of Reconciliation," *Interpretation* 54 (2002): 158-72; A. Katherine Grieb, "'So That in Him We Might Become the Righteousness of God' (2 Cor. 5:21): Some Theological Reflections on the Church Becoming Justice," *Ex Auditu* 22 (2006): 58-80; Willard M. Swartley, *Covenant of Peace: The Missing Peace in New Testament Theology and Ethics* (Grand Rapids: Eerdmans, 2006), pp. 189-221; and Gorman, *Inhabiting the Cruciform God: Kenosis, Justification, and Theosis in Paul's Narrative Soteriology* (Grand Rapids: Eerdmans, 2009), pp. 40-104, esp. pp. 84-99.

20. Wright, *Paul and the Faithfulness of God,* p. 1097.

21. Douglas Harink, "Setting It Right: Doing Justice to Justification," *Christian Century* (June 14, 2005): 20-25.

22. Dunn, "The Justice of God," p. 20.

23. The terms are also linked, though not in this precise, short phrase, in, e.g., Ps. 34:14-15; Isa. 32:17; James 3:18.

follow suit, though the NAB (New American Bible) and the NJB (New Jerusalem Bible) have "justice" and "saving justice," respectively, for "righteousness." The NRSV renders Romans 14:17 as "For the kingdom of God is not food and drink but righteousness and peace and joy in the Holy Spirit." Once again, most translations are very similar, but the NJB replaces "righteousness" with "saving justice,"[24] which suggests the connection to Psalm 85 that I am proposing: *I suggest that Paul sees in Christ, in life in the Spirit, the fulfillment of the Psalmist's vision that the divine attributes and gifts of justice and peace would be present on earth, embodied in a joyful people.*[25] The connections we will explore support this claim.

A (re)turn to the link between justification and justice is one natural outgrowth of an understanding of justification as more than a mere verdict of acquittal for an individual sinner (the traditional understanding in Protestantism, the "old" perspective), and even more than a pronouncement of inclusion in the people of God (the emphasis of the new perspective). A more robust and faithfully Pauline understanding of justification, as I have argued at length elsewhere, is both participatory and transformative.[26] Space does not permit a detailed account of this interpretation of justification. Rather, it will have to be summarized as part of the foundation upon which the argument of this chapter is built. (The chapter will also, in turn, reinforce the foundation.) We will also see that a participatory and transformative account of justification is also inherently missional. Furthermore, such a participatory, transformative, and missional view of justification will be inherently countercultural, or alter-cultural. Paul's scripturally and Christologically shaped justice stands in stark opposition to Roman justice (and American justice, etc., too), and we will make some comments about this along the way. But the primary focus of the chapter will be Paul's continuity with the biblical tradition about justice.

---

24. The NAB, NIV, CEB, and NET all have "righteousness," not "justice."

25. Cf. the prophetic vision, summarized well in Isa. 32:16-17.

26. See especially my *Inhabiting the Cruciform God*, pp. 40-104. The argument of Douglas A. Campbell's *The Deliverance of God: An Apocalyptic Rereading of Justification in Paul* (Grand Rapids: Eerdmans, 2009) implies the same connection but does not make it, perhaps because Campbell is fighting against "retributive justice" and so identifies its antithesis as "benevolence" rather than, say, "restorative justice," though Campbell himself is committed theologically and personally to restorative justice. Nearly a half-century ago Markus Barth understood the link between participation in Christ and justice ("Jews and Gentiles," p. 243); see also Yung Suk Kim, *Christ's Body in Corinth: The Politics of a Metaphor* (Minneapolis: Fortress, 2008).

We turn, then, to seven connections between justification and justice in Paul. After briefly examining the first five of these, we will look closely at portions of 1 and 2 Corinthians to see how these connections play out in concrete ways in two of Paul's very practical letters. I have chosen these letters in part because they are not the letters people most often associate with Paul's teaching on justification (i.e., Romans and Galatians), and it may be especially edifying to discover unexpected perspectives in unexpected places.

## Seven Connections between Justification and Justice in Paul

### The Linguistic Link

The most fundamental and obvious connection between justification and justice in Paul is linguistic: the *dikaio-* family of words (*dikaioō, dikaiosynē, dikaios,* etc.). As noted above, in English, this one family gets translated into two families, the "right-" family (right, righteous, righteousness, rightwise, etc.) and the "just-" family (just, justification, justice, justify, etc.). English translations can either hide or reveal the Greek linguistic connections, but generally — unfortunately — they hide them.

For example, in the NRSV, forms of the *dikaio-* family in Paul's letters are translated as "justice," "injustice," "just," "unjust," etc. a mere six times, all in Romans (Rom. 3:5 [three times]; 7:12; 8:4; 9:14). Like most translations, the NRSV prefers the translation of the adjectives and nouns as "righteous" and "righteousness" even where various words in the *dikaio-* family appear together and the verbs are rendered as forms of "justify."[27] The Roman Catholic NAB translation is only slightly better. Readers/hearers of most English translations are therefore left with little or no clue that justification and justice may be related in Paul's theology. In Christian theological parlance, "righteousness" and "justice" are sometimes separated, the former referring to personal morality and holiness, the latter to social ethics. By omitting "justice," translations both reflect and further underwrite a bias, emerging especially from many forms of Protestantism, toward a privatistic interpretation of Paul.

Methodologically, translators and other interpreters of Paul should as-

---

27. E.g., Rom. 3:21-26; 4:5-6; 5:18-21; Gal. 3:11; and 1 Cor. 6:1-11, which we will consider at some length below.

sume that members of the *dikaio-* family are related to one another, especially when they occur in proximity to one another, unless there is strong
evidence to the contrary. Some interpreters, however, as we will see in our
discussion of 1 Corinthians 6:1-11, steadfastly contend that the *dikaio-* family
of words actually reflects two different concepts, one "forensic" (meaning
legal or juridical) and one ethical (or moral). The former would refer to God
pronouncing people righteous, and the latter to the righteous God actually
making people righteous, and thus to a righteous or just community. Although this distinction is certainly a theoretical possibility, more often than
not those who make the distinction do so because they perceive a difference
(or, in some cases, want to perceive a difference, for theological reasons) that,
in my view, is not supported by the evidence. Starting with the assumption
that members, and specific occurrences, of the *dikaio-* family of words are
interconnected — until and unless proven otherwise — is the most linguis-
tically and biblically appropriate way to proceed.

Translations that mask the contextual and/or linguistic connections
make it highly difficult to read Paul as one who stands in line with the prophets and Jesus and who subverts, at least implicitly, the Roman claim that
Roman justice — the justice of power and punishment — is divine justice.
It is therefore incumbent upon translators to begin showing these connections in English. One way would be to continue rendering *hē dikaiosynē
theou* (e.g., Rom. 1:17; 3:21) as "the righteousness of God" and use a verb
like "rightwise," "rectify," "set right," or even "make righteous" for *dikaioō*.
However, these renderings are all awkward, disputed, and/or subject to individualistic interpretation. It would therefore be preferable to keep the verb
"justify" and follow Dunn's suggestion of using the noun phrase "the justice
of God" — God's saving, liberating, and restorative justice — to show the
close connection between justification and justice.[28] Moreover, "the saving
justice of God," emphasizing the phrase "of God," reminds us also that Paul's
gospel is about a special kind of divine character trait and activity — *God's
justice* — that is radically different from other kinds of justice.

## The Human Condition and Injustice

A second connection between justification and justice in Paul can be seen
in the apostle's description of the human condition that justification is in-

---

28. Or perhaps "the saving justice of God," like the NJB, or "the restorative justice of God."

tended to affect — that God's action in Christ is intended to rectify. This situation may be described as one of covenantal dysfunctionality — people's disordered relations toward God (the "vertical" relation) and toward one another ("horizontal" relations). The former can be summarized in the term *asebeia*, "ungodliness" (NRSV), while the latter can be characterized as *adikia*, "wickedness" (NRSV), as Romans 1:18 puts it plainly: "For the wrath of God is revealed from heaven against all ungodliness [*asebeian*] and wickedness [*adikian*] of those who by their wickedness [*adikia*] suppress the truth." Other English translations largely echo the NRSV, rendering *adikia* as "wickedness" or "unrighteousness."

But a better contextual translation would be "injustice," understood in the broadest sense of the word as the mistreatment of other human beings. The CEB and the NJB break with the pack here and wisely translate *adikia* as injustice in Romans 1:18. The human condition of covenantal dysfunctionality summarized in Romans 1:18 and described in the rest of Romans 1:18–3:20 involves the breakdown of human relationships as well as direct rebellion against God per se.[29] Paul has a notion of sin that means breaking covenant with others, as well as with God. The word *adikia* — in 1:18 (twice), 29; 2:8; and 3:5 — sums up the situation for Paul.[30] Injustice reigns, and it will take the justice of God and the divine act of justification to undo the injustice and effect justice. *Consistent use of the "just-" family in English translation would remind us that the human condition and the divine solution are actually, and inseparably, related — and that the resulting new condition is the antithesis of the former situation.*

But we are getting a bit ahead of ourselves. For now, the point about the injustice-justification question is that any "solution" to such a human condition must address it directly and specifically, and not merely provide for the forgiveness of its various manifestations. *If justification does not renew and restore human relationships, it does not address the human condition as Paul perceives it.*

The various lists and brief discussions of symptoms of the disease "injustice" in Romans 1:18–3:20 are rather comprehensive, and God's project of restoration and renewal includes, for Paul, the undoing of it all — anything and everything evil the human race, or any individual, can concoct.[31] One of the

---

29. I obviously do not subscribe to Douglas Campbell's contention in *The Deliverance of God* that 1:18-32 and parts of 2:1–3:20 reflect the views of someone other than Paul.

30. The NJB consistently renders *adikia* as "injustice" in these verses, but the CEB changes to "wickedness" in 2:8 and 3:5.

31. For specific symptoms, see 1:24-32.

least noticed of these evil manifestations of *adikia* is violence — a phenomenon no less common in Paul's day than in ours, as we saw in chapter five:

> [15]"Their feet are swift to shed blood; [16]ruin and misery are in their paths, [17]and the way of peace they have not known." [18]"There is no fear of God before their eyes." (Rom. 3:15-18, quoting from Isa. 59:7-8; Prov. 1:16; and Ps. 36:1 [LXX 35:2])

Paul knows from the text of Isaiah to which he points that such practices are the antithesis of justice: "there is no justice [MT *mishpat;* LXX *krisis*] in their paths" (Isa. 59:8). Few interpreters of Paul, however, have drawn sufficient attention to this aspect of Paul's understanding of the human condition, as we note as well in the overview chapter on peace. Ironically, in fact, for some ancient versions of justice (Latin *iustitia*), as well as certain contemporary interpretations of justice, the use of violence — often in the name of making peace — is a central feature. The presence of violence in our homes, on our streets, within nations, and between peoples separated by thousands of miles — all are signs of the need for justification and reconciliation, both among people and between people and God, for all of this, Paul and his scriptural sources say, is rooted in humanity's rejection of God: "There is no fear of God before their eyes" (cf. Rom. 1:18-23).

If justification is supposed to repair the human condition, then justification must address injustice, including violence. That is, justification must do something about injustice by making liberation from practices of injustice possible and practices of justice attainable. That is, given the human condition, the justification of the unjust will mean both liberation and transformation.

## Justification as Transformative Participation

For many people, especially in the Protestant traditions, justification means simply acquittal, a divine pronouncement on the unrighteous that they are counted as righteous by God because of Christ's death for them and because of his righteousness. This is often taught as Paul's understanding of justification. But there are reasons to suggest that Paul has a fuller, more robust theology of justification. The letter to the Romans confronts us right away with the depth and complexity of Paul's theology of justice and justification in the thematic statement of the letter that precedes and links with the pronouncement of human injustice *(adikia)* noted above:

¹⁶For I am not ashamed of the gospel; it is the power *(dynamis)* of God for salvation to everyone who has faith, to the Jew first and also to the Greek. ¹⁷For in it the <u>righteousness</u> *(dikaiosynē)* of God is revealed through faith for faith; as it is written, "The one who is <u>righteous</u> *(dikaios)* will live by faith." ¹⁸For the wrath of God is revealed from heaven against all ungodliness and <u>wickedness</u> *(adikian)* of those who by their <u>wickedness</u> *(adikia)* suppress the truth. (Rom. 1:16-18; NRSV)

We could translate this as follows:

¹⁶For I am not ashamed of the gospel; it is the power of God for salvation to everyone who has faith, to the Jew first and also to the Greek. ¹⁷For in it the <u>saving justice</u> *(dikaiosynē)* of God is revealed through faith for faith; as it is written, "The one who <u>is just</u> *(dikaios),* that is, <u>part of the community of the just</u>, will live by faith." ¹⁸For the wrath of God is revealed from heaven against all ungodliness and <u>injustice</u> *(adikian)* of those who by their <u>injustice</u> *(adikia)* suppress the truth.

This is not the place to consider all the translational and interpretive issues related to this text.[32] Nonetheless, one thing should be quite clear. In contrast to a thin understanding of justification as merely acquittal, the juxtaposition of language about justice and the just *(dikaiosynē; dikaios)* in 1:16-17 and language about injustice *(adikian)* in 1:18, especially combined with references to power *(dynamis;* 1:16) and life *(zēsetai,* 1:17, related to the noun *zōē,* life), suggests that Paul sees justification as inherently transformative and life-giving.[33]

A third connection between justification and justice in Paul is therefore to be found in the meaning of justification itself. Interpreting baptism and the life it inaugurates as participation in Christ's death, burial, and resurrection, Paul refuses to separate this reality from justification. In fact, he uses a form of the verb *dikaioō (dedikaiōtai;* Rom. 6:7) to express his conviction that the inseparable realities of baptism and justification constitute a divine

32. The phrase "part of the community of the just" in 1:17 is offered to suggest that "justification" is about incorporation into a people. See further below, on Romans 6 and esp. 1 Cor. 6:1-11.

33. The theme of transformation as the mark of the justified community appears also in Rom. 12:1-2, which signals the undoing of the situation described in Rom. 1:18–3:20. The result is that the in-Christ community becomes the gospel, becomes the (embodiment of the) saving justice of God. This is the subject of Romans 12–15, anticipated in summary form in 2 Cor. 5:21 (see discussion below).

deliverance, a kind of release from slavery and new exodus. Specifically, it is deliverance from the reign of sin and injustice into justice and life:[34]

> [6]We know that our old self was crucified with him so that the body of sin might be destroyed, and we might no longer be enslaved to sin. [7]For whoever has died is freed *(dedikaiōtai)* from sin. . . . [13]No longer present your members to sin as instruments [weapons[35]] of <u>injustice</u> *(adikias)*, but present yourselves to God as those who have been brought from death to life, and present your members to God as instruments [or weapons] of <u>justice</u> *(dikaiosynēs)*. . . . [17]But thanks be to God that you, having once been slaves of sin, have become obedient from the heart to the form of teaching to which you were entrusted, [18]and that you, having been set free *(eleutherōthentes,* a form of the more common verb for "liberate") from sin, have become slaves of <u>justice</u> *(dikaiosynē;* lit. "slaves to justice"). (Rom. 6:6-7, 13, 17-18)

Thus, those who are justified/baptized are delivered or liberated *(dedikaiōtai* in 6:7; *eleutherōthentes* in 6:18) so that they/their "members" will no longer be weapons of injustice but of justice *(adikias . . . dikaiosynē;* Rom. 6:13, 18).[36]

What is going on here? *The human condition portrayed in Romans 1:18–3:20 is being addressed and undone. Justification means that the unjust are being liberated from injustice to live justly.* It means resurrection from death to life, from participation in sin and death to participation in justice and life. In fact, as Robert Jewett eloquently puts it in commenting on Romans 6, the justified are being given a new mission, even a new warfare, one that is more "risky" and "vulnerable" than any previous form of existence. "Such risks are counterbalanced by the idea of being a weapon in the hand of another, in this case the hand of God, which provides the impetus and courage for unprecedented forms of hospitality and other actions of love . . ."; the redeemed community serves "in the new, nonviolent campaign to restore righteousness in a corrupted world."[37]

---

34. The text that follows is adapted from the NRSV. I have substituted "injustice" for NRSV's "wickedness" and "justice" for NRSV's "righteousness." On justification as deliverance, see esp. Campbell, *The Deliverance of God.*

35. See Robert Jewett, *Romans,* Hermeneia (Minneapolis: Fortress, 2007), pp. 410-11.

36. On the overlapping meanings of (1) baptism as death and resurrection and (2) justification by faith — i.e., baptism and justification as new life by co-crucifixion, see my *Inhabiting the Cruciform God,* pp. 63-79.

37. Jewett, *Romans,* p. 411.

As noted earlier, space does not permit additional defense of the participatory and transformative model of justification for which I have argued elsewhere.[38] Here I offer the following definition of justification as one that captures elements of traditional interpretations but also places a more appropriately Pauline accent on its covenantal, corporate, participatory, liberative, transformative, and horizontal (as well as vertical) character:

> Justification is the establishment of right covenant relations — fidelity to God and love for neighbor — by means of God's liberating grace in Christ's faithful and loving death and our co-crucifixion with him. Justification therefore means co-resurrection with Christ to a new life of faithfulness toward God and love toward others, expressed concretely as biblical justice, within the Spirit-empowered people of God, with the certain hope of God's welcome, on the day of judgment, into the fullness of resurrection life.

Justification, then, is about reconciliation, covenant participation and faithfulness, community, resurrection, and life. And this reality is brought about by death — Christ's death *for us* in the past and our death *with him* in the present, all due to God's initiative and grace. Those who are justified — who are in Christ — will be conformed to his covenantal faithfulness and love.[39] This symbiosis of faith and love is not an addendum to justification but is constitutive of justification itself — the restoration of right covenant relations. Put differently, Paul understands justification as participatory transformation in the justice of God in Christ that creates a just people. *Justice is inherent in justification.*

This understanding of justification will have enormous effects on the church's understanding of mission. Like Paul, the church that lives by this

---

38. See especially *Inhabiting the Cruciform God*, pp. 41-104, and (more popularly) *Reading Paul* (Eugene, OR: Cascade, 2008), pp. 111-31. For a similar understanding of justification, see Campbell, *The Deliverance of God*.

39. Paul clearly sees Christ's death as his act of obedience to God (Rom. 5:19; Phil. 2:8) as well as his act of love for us. As noted earlier in this book, in the scholarly debate about how to translate the so-called *pistis Christou* ("faith of Christ" or "faith in Christ") texts in Paul, I have argued, along with Richard Hays, N. T. Wright, and others, for the "faith of Christ" translation. (See my *Cruciformity: Paul's Narrative Spirituality of the Cross* [Grand Rapids: Eerdmans, 2001], pp. 110-21.) If that translation is correct, then it reinforces my claim that Paul understands Christ's death as the quintessential covenantal act, the symbiosis of obedience, or fidelity, and love. It seems to me that this understanding is implied by Paul's missional goal — to bring people into Christ, which means into the sphere of "the obedience of faith" (Rom. 1:5; 16:26).

account of justification will not merely be trying to "save souls" but will want to be God's agent in the creation of a justified and just people — transformed and participating in Christ and his current work in and through the church. Evangelism — sharing the good news — will be a message about liberation from all sorts of sin, including hatred and violence and injustice, and into a new life. Centrifugal activity, or outreach — embodying the good news in the public square — will mean siding with those who are neglected and mistreated, whether in the neighborhood or in another part of the world. In fact, the differences between terms like "evangelism" and "outreach" will in part collapse, not because Jesus is being replaced with justice, understood in some generic, secular way, but because Jesus *is* justice, the justice of God incarnate. The result will be a *deeper* spirituality, not a lesser one, a closer walk with God (the God of justice), not a more distant one. In fact, the result will be a passion for Jesus *and* for justice.[40]

It is important to be crystal clear about this, as with peacemaking (remembering that, biblically speaking, justice and peace are actually both part of one reality, *shalom*). Christian commitment to justice must never be separated from Christian commitment to Jesus. When the two are severed, even partially, the Christian understanding of justice inevitably morphs into a sub-Christian one.[41] This does not mean that Christians can only work for justice with fellow Christians, or that Christians can only work for justice when they are allowed to speak the name of Jesus. But the shape of justice for which they work must conform to Christ.

## The Justice of God in the Cross of Christ

Fourthly, as we have just hinted in several ways, the correlation between justification and justice for Paul has its ultimate origin in Christ crucified as the supreme manifestation of divine justice. In 1 Corinthians 1:30, Paul proclaims that "Christ Jesus . . . became for us wisdom from God, and righteousness [*dikaiosynē*] and sanctification [*hagiasmos*] and redemption [*apolytrōsis*]." (Once again, only the NJB renders *dikaiosynē* as "saving justice.") Given the presence of the verbal phrase "became for us" (rather than, say, "gave to us")

40. See Esther Byle Bruland and Stephen C. Mott, *A Passion for Jesus, a Passion for Justice* (Valley Forge, PA: Judson, 1983).

41. On the unity of spirituality and social justice, see also Allan Aubrey Boesak and Curtiss Paul DeYoung, *Radical Reconciliation: Beyond Political Pietism and Christian Quietism* (Maryknoll, NY: Orbis, 2012).

and the fact that Paul has just contended that Christ (i.e., Christ crucified) is "the power of God and the wisdom of God" (1:24), we should read 1:30 not merely as a description of what Christ *provides* but primarily of what Christ *is,* that is, the divine attributes he embodies as the crucified one: not only (power and) wisdom, but also justice, holiness, and redemption/liberation.

What does it mean that Christ "became for us the justice of God"? The immediate answer is given in 1 Corinthians 1:18-31. Christ crucified reveals a God whose *modus operandi* is to work through, and to identify with, weakness and the weak.[42] That God identifies with the weak is of course a fundamental aspect of divine justice in the Scriptures of Israel. Here in 1 Corinthians 1:18-31 that justice is manifested first of all in the weakness (according to human standards) of the cross, and then also in the weakness (again, according to human standards) of the community:

> [22]For Jews demand signs and Greeks desire wisdom, [23]but we proclaim Christ crucified, a stumbling block to Jews and foolishness to Gentiles, [24]but to those who are the called, both Jews and Greeks, Christ the power of God and the wisdom of God. [25]For God's foolishness is wiser than human wisdom, and God's weakness is stronger than human strength. [26]Consider your own call, brothers and sisters: not many of you were wise by human standards, not many were powerful, not many were of noble birth. [27]But God chose what is foolish in the world to shame the wise; God chose what is weak in the world to shame the strong; [28]God chose what is low and despised in the world, things that are not, to reduce to nothing things that are, [29]so that no one might boast in the presence of God. (1 Cor. 1:22-29)

We should speak, therefore, of divine justice in Paul as *cruciform* justice. It is nonetheless in continuity with the liberating justice of God displayed throughout Israel's history, for, as Hannah prayed in a text to which Paul likely alludes in this passage,[43] the Lord "raises up the poor from the dust; he lifts the needy from the ash heap" (1 Sam. 2:8). This is the God who does "justice and righ-

---

42. See, for example, Kim, *Christ's Body in Corinth,* pp. 94-95. Also important, though unpublished, is Shannon Curran, "Become God's Justice (2 Cor. 5:21), Become Known by God (1 Cor. 8:3): How Paul Guides Corinth to Prefer Weakness and to Be Transformed through God's Justice" (M.A. thesis, St. Mary's Seminary & University, 2013).

43. So, cautiously but convincingly, Richard B. Hays, *First Corinthians,* Interpretation (Louisville: Westminster John Knox, 1997), pp. 32-35. The LXX of 1 Sam. [Kgdms.] 2:1-10 contains language very similar to Jer. 9:23-24 (LXX 9:22-23), often thought to be in Paul's mind here.

teousness" (*krima kai dikaiosynēn*; 1 Sam. [Kgdms.] 2:10 LXX). The Corinthian community will therefore be expected to embody the liberating, cruciform justice of God — a preferential option for the poor, to put it in contemporary terms — manifested both in Christ and in their communal constitution. However, as we will see below, the Corinthians generally fail to do so.

Understanding the character of divine justice revealed in Christ crucified according to 1 Corinthians sheds light on, and is confirmed by, Romans. If the gospel is the "power of God" that reveals the saving justice of God (Rom. 1:16-17) — phrases reminiscent of 1 Corinthians 1:18-31 — it is such only in this sense: the locus of God's powerful justice is Christ crucified. This is precisely what Romans 3:21-26 affirms:[44]

> [21]But now, apart from law, the saving justice (*dikaiosynē*) of God has been disclosed, and is attested by the law and the prophets, [22]the saving justice (*dikaiosynē*) of God through the faith of Jesus Christ for all who believe. For there is no distinction, [23]since all have sinned and fall short of the glory of God; [24]they are now justified [or "made just," "made part of the community of the just"; *dikaioumenoi*] by his grace as a gift, through the redemption that is in Christ Jesus, [25]whom God put forward as a sacrifice of atonement by his blood, effective through faith. He did this to show his saving justice (*dikaiosynēs*), because in his divine forbearance he had passed over the sins previously committed; [26]it was to prove at the present time that he himself is just (*dikaios*) and that [or "in that"] he justifies (*dikaiounta*) the one who has [or "shares"] the faith of Jesus.

That is, Paul is speaking of the justice (*dikaiosynē*; 3:21, 22, 25) of the just God (*dikaios*, 3:26) manifested in the faithful death of Jesus that effects justification (*dikaioumenoi*, 3:24; *dikaiounta*, 3:26) — forgiveness (3:25), liberation/ redemption (3:24; cf. 1 Cor. 1:30), and incorporation into the community of the just (see Romans 6, discussed above).

Paul also discusses Christ's death in relation to justice and injustice in Romans 5:

> [6]For while we were still weak, at the right time Christ died for the ungodly. [7]Indeed, rarely will anyone die for a righteous ("just"; *dikaiou*) person — though perhaps for a good person someone might actually dare to die.

---

44. Once again, I use the NRSV but substitute "saving justice" language for "righteousness" language, and I translate the *pistis Christou* phrases as "the faith of Christ."

> [8]But God proves his love for us in that while we still were sinners Christ died for us. [9]Much more surely then, now that we have been justified by his blood, will we be saved through him from the wrath of God. [10]For if while we were enemies, we were reconciled to God through the death of his Son, much more surely, having been reconciled, will we be saved by his life. (Rom. 5:6-10)

As in 1 Corinthians 1, also here Paul emphasizes that God's gracious, loving justice comes to the weak and helpless, even to the unjust (implied by *dikaiou*, 5:7) and to enemies (5:10). We could fairly paraphrase Romans 5:8 as follows: "But God demonstrates his kind of justice and his love for us in that while we still were unjust toward others and unloving toward God, Christ died for us to restore us to justice and love."

This is clearly not Roman justice, or the justice of anything that has resembled Rome over the last two millennia. Roman justice was the justice of the powerful that crushed the weak, not to mention anyone or any entity that dared to challenge the power of Rome; it was Roman justice, after all, that crucified Jesus. As N. T. Wright says, "It took genius to see that the symbol [the cross] which had spoken of Caesar's naked might now spoke of God's naked love. And I think that the genius in question belonged to Paul."[45] And Neil Elliott reminds us that Paul was not ashamed of the gospel (Rom. 1:16) for a very basic reason: "simply because in it, *real* justice was seen, 'the justice of God.' This was powerful, saving justice, experienced as genuine faithfulness between a faithful God and those who act in trusting obedience; it was the justice that Israel expected God to enact through the Messiah (Psalm 72)."[46]

The justification of the unjust as the justice of God means God's reconciliation of enemies and God's compassion for the weak.[47] It is restorative rather than retributive or retaliatory or Romanesque justice; it is the justice of the prophets. In the words of Pheme Perkins: "Prophetic hopes for the manifestation of God's salvation in a new order of justice have been fulfilled."[48] The Roman believers, like the Corinthians, will be expected to

---

45. N. T. Wright, *Paul: In Fresh Perspective* (Minneapolis: Fortress, 2005), p. 73.

46. Neil Elliott, *The Arrogance of Nations: Reading Romans in the Shadow of Empire,* Paul in Critical Contexts (Minneapolis: Fortress, 2008), p. 51.

47. Paul places justification and reconciliation in parallel in the inclusio (rhetorical bookends) of 5:1, 11, and in the two synonymous *qal we homer* ("from greater to lesser" forms of argumentation) texts in 5:9-10.

48. Pheme Perkins, "Justice, NT," in *The New Interpreter's Dictionary of the Bible* 3:475-76 (Nashville: Abingdon, 2008), p. 475.

practice the same kind of justice in their communities and toward their enemies as an essential component of that new order. *The missional justice of God creates a missional people of justice.*

## Paul's Own Transformation

Fifthly, Paul himself exemplifies the turn to justice that occurs when one is justified. Paul of course was a zealous public persecutor of the church.[49] He was most likely attempting to secure his justification before God through imitating, at least to some degree, the violent priestly hero Phinehas, who purified Israel and stayed God's wrath by killing an Israelite and his Midianite consort (Num. 25:6-13).[50] According to Psalm 106:31 (LXX 105:31), Phinehas was justified by his violent zeal: his act was "reckoned to him as righteousness" *(elogisthē autō eis dikaiosynēn);* the Greek phrase is exactly the same as the parallel text in Genesis 15:6 and in Romans 4:3, 5, 9, 22-24.[51]

When Paul was justified, reconciled to God, his oppressive, violent public behavior changed dramatically, and so did his spirituality, his relationship to God. In fact, the two changed simultaneously, and in tandem. Paul no longer sought justification in his misguided (as he later saw it) zeal for God that resulted in hatred for, exclusion of, and mistreatment of others. He would later describe his previous zealous, violent behavior as one of the manifestations of sin and *adikia* that generated the need for reconciliation/justification (Rom. 3:9-18). Paul's own life-story confirms that justification has a public, observable, social face: it includes the just practices of non-retaliation/nonviolence (1 Cor. 4:11-13) and reconciliation (cf. 2 Cor. 5:18-20),[52] as well as commitment to the poor (e.g., Gal. 2:10 and the Jerusalem collection). In other words, *to be justified is to be missionally rearranged and redirected.*

We have now considered the first five connections between justification and justice in Paul: the linguistic link, the human condition and injustice,

---

49. 1 Cor. 15:9; Gal. 1:13-14, 23; Phil. 3:6; 1 Tim. 1:13; cf. Acts 7:58–8:3; 9:1-2; 22:3-5; 26:9-12.

50. I do not mean to imply that Paul actually killed any Jesus-followers.

51. I explore the relationship between Phinehas and Paul, as well as the nonviolent character of justification in Paul, more fully in *Inhabiting the Cruciform God,* pp. 129-60. Others have also connected Paul to Phinehas (and sometimes to other Jews in Israel's history whose zeal led to violence); see, e.g., Wright, *Paul and the Faithfulness of God,* pp. 81-89, 167, 932, 1223; Dunn, *Theology of Paul,* pp. 350-53, 368-71, 375-76.

52. See, among others, Volf, "The Social Meaning of Reconciliation."

justification as transformative participation, the justice of God in the cross of Christ, and Paul's own transformation. We turn now to examine several passages from the Corinthian correspondence that demonstrate this link in action.

## Justification and Justice in the Christian Community

The sixth and most significant connection Paul draws between justification and justice is the link (or sometimes the lack of a link that should be present) between them in the concrete existence of the churches he founded. Paul believed that God's intention in justification was to create communities that are being transformed into the justice of God (2 Cor. 5:21; see discussion below). All of his letters serve this transformative goal, but for reasons of space and focus we will consider a limited number of texts. First and Second Corinthians supply several examples of how Paul deals with both human injustice and divine, cruciform justice. These are all related to what Yung Suk Kim calls "the Corinthians' failure to embody Christ crucified" and "Paul's exhortation . . . calling for participation in Christ crucified" in 1 Cor. 5:1–11:34.[53] Paul believes, as we have seen, that justification by participation in Christ crucified, the embodiment of God's saving justice, should produce a just community. What happens when it does not, and how can such situations be rectified?

### 1 Corinthians 6:1-11/The Tragic Irony of Injustice in the Community of the Just[54]

In 1 Corinthians 6:1-11, Paul provides a concrete and dramatic example of what the church becoming the justice of God means, first of all by showing what *not* being the justice of God entails. In doing so Paul reveals the inseparable connection between justification and justice.

Addressing the problem of Corinthian believers taking one another to court over "trivial," "ordinary" matters (1 Cor. 6:2-3, NRSV), Paul makes it clear that this practice is an injustice and needs to be replaced by practices of cruciform justice. He does this in large measure by means of a "deft word-

---

53. Kim, *Christ's Body in Corinth*, p. 76. Kim's focus is on 1 Corinthians, but the concern extends to 2 Corinthians as well.

54. The following discussion is expanded from my *Inhabiting the Cruciform God*, pp. 98-99.

play,"[55] deploying members of the *dikaio-* word-family five times. Unfortunately, the NRSV masks some of the most important links in the passage by using "unrighteous" and "wrong" to translate members of the *dikaio-* family while never using a form of "just" except for the word "justification." The NIV also has no "just" words except "justification." The NJB and especially the NAB do much better at revealing Paul's wordplay.

The key parts of the text of 1 Corinthians 6:1-11 are reproduced here (NRSV, with key Greek words; select NAB, NIV, and NJB renderings; and my own alternatives, marked MJG, in brackets):

> [1]When any of you has a grievance against another, do you dare to take it to court before the unrighteous [*adikōn;* NAB "**unjust**"; CEB "**people who aren't just**"; NIV "**ungodly**"[56]], instead of taking it before the saints? . . .

> [7]In fact, to have lawsuits at all with one another is already a defeat for you. Why not rather be wronged [*adikeisthe;* so also NIV; NAB "**put up with injustice**"; NJB "**suffer injustice**"; MJG "**be treated unjustly**" or "**endure injustice**"]?

> Why not rather be defrauded? [8]But you yourselves wrong [*adikeite;* NIV "**do wrong**";[57] NAB "**inflict injustice**"; NJB "(are) **doing the injustice**"] and defraud — and believers [*adelphous;* NAB, NIV "**brothers**"; MJG "**members of your own family**"] at that.

> [9]Do you not know that wrongdoers [*adikoi;* NAB "**the unjust**"; CEB "**people who are unjust**"; NJB "**people who do evil**"; NIV "**the wicked**"] will not inherit the kingdom of God? Do not be deceived! Fornicators, idolaters, adulterers, male prostitutes, sodomites, [10]thieves, the greedy, drunkards, revilers, robbers — none of these will inherit the kingdom of God.

> [11]And this is what some of you used to be. But you were washed, you were sanctified, you were justified [*edikaiōthēte;* MJG "**incorporated into the community of the just**"[58]] in the name of the Lord Jesus Christ and in the Spirit of our God.

55. Hays, *First Corinthians,* p. 98.

56. Oddly, the NJB has "sinners" here.

57. NIV "cheat and do wrong," apparently reversing the order of the Greek verbs.

58. Curiously, in verse 11 the CEB loses track of the "just-" family by rendering "you were justified" as "you were made right with God."

By consistently translating the *dikaio-* family with the English "just-" family (using existing translations as well as my alternatives), we arrive at the following translation for these verses:

> [1]When any of you has a grievance against another, do you dare to take it to court before the <u>unjust</u>, instead of taking it before the saints? . . . [7]In fact, to have lawsuits at all with one another is already a defeat for you. Why not rather be <u>treated unjustly</u>? Why not rather be defrauded? [8]But you yourselves <u>inflict injustice</u> and defraud — and members of your own family at that. [9]Do you not know that the <u>unjust</u> will not inherit the kingdom of God? Do not be deceived! Fornicators, idolaters, adulterers, male prostitutes, sodomites, [10]thieves, the greedy, drunkards, revilers, robbers — none of these will inherit the kingdom of God. [11]And this is what some of you used to be. But you were washed, you were sanctified, <u>you were justified — incorporated into the community of the just</u> — in the name of the Lord Jesus Christ and in the Spirit of our God.[59]

It is clear that Paul sees taking fellow believers to pagan courts, which are the courts of the unjust/unjustified (v. 1), as an act of injustice (v. 8) that betrays the divine action of rescue from such injustice that Paul calls justification (v. 11). To practice injustice is effectively to annul the justification wrought by God, to return to the realm of the unjust, and to jeopardize one's future inheritance of the kingdom of God (v. 9). It is evidence of an incomplete conversion.[60] The justified are expected to suffer injustice (v. 7), not to inflict it, because that is what Jesus the paschal lamb (1 Cor. 5:7) did on the cross.[61] Paul's words *may* be directed primarily to the elite, or strong,

---

59. We find something somewhat similar in N. T. Wright's translation (*Kingdom New Testament: A Contemporary Translation* [New York: HarperOne, 2011]. Here are the key lines: "to be tried before unjust people" (v. 1); "Don't you know that the unjust will not inherit God's kingdom?" (v. 9); "you were put back to rights" (v. 11). Unfortunately, Wright misses the verbal connections in verses 7-8, rendering the verbs "be wronged" and "are wronging." In addition to all that has been noted, the evangelical HCSB (Holman Christian Standard Bible) has the following: "[7]. . . Why not rather put up with injustice? Why not rather be cheated? [8]Instead, you act unjustly and cheat — and you do this to believers!" (1 Cor. 6:7b-8). A few translations, such as the CEV (Contemporary English Version), completely omit the "just-" family from the passage.

60. On this passage and conversion, see Stephen J. Chester, *Conversion at Corinth: Perspectives on Conversion in Paul's Theology and the Corinthian Church*, Studies of the New Testament and Its World (London: T. & T. Clark, 2003), pp. 125-48.

61. Paul does not say this explicitly in 1 Cor. 6:1-11, but the proximity of his reference to

who are oppressing certain non-elites, or weak, in the community, which would be a clear failure to heed the prophetic, and now Christian (implied by 1:18-31), call for justice for the weak. Yet Paul does not explicitly limit his concern to injustice directed at the weak; rather, he is simply concerned that there is injustice being practiced at all, especially toward family members ("brothers," *adelphous*, v. 8; cf. vv. 5, 6).

The clever but serious play on *dikaio-* words in this passage culminates in the occurrence of *edikaiōthēte*, traditionally translated "you were justified," in verse 11. It is clear from the context that Paul means something much more than a declaration of acquittal or of covenant membership. By God's gracious action the Corinthians have been washed, or baptized and forgiven ("washed" already implying transformation); sanctified, or set apart; and justified in the sense of incorporated into the community of the just (and thus made just) — or better yet, into the *family* of the just.[62] Thus the linguistic connections among the various *dikaio-* terms in these verses express a fundamental theological conviction that is basic to Paul's soteriology but is often overlooked by his interpreters: justification means a *transfer* from the realm of the unjust/unjustified into the realm of the just/justified, which simultaneously means a *transformation, a conversion* from being unjust people to being just people and thus a *transition* from practices of injustice to practices of Christologically shaped justice.[63]

Such cruciform justice means, first of all, the absorption rather than the infliction of injustice, especially (though not exclusively) within the family. Justification makes the unjust into the just; that is, as 2 Corinthians 5:21 puts it, justification is the divine act of transforming people into the justice of God. They become capable, by God's grace and power, of practicing the justice of God displayed on the cross. Here, too, we encounter the action of God, who is the implicit actor in the passive verbs in 1 Corinthians 6:11: "you were

---

the paschal lamb, his theology of the cross in places like Rom. 5:6-8, his allusions to Jesus' teaching on non-retaliation, and his own practice of non-retaliation combine to make it likely that he has Jesus' example in mind here.

62. The appropriateness of this interpretation/translation is clear from the way in which verses 1, 9, and 11, taken together, posit a clear contrast between the unjust, who are implicitly unholy, unwashed, unsanctified, and unjustified, and the washed, sanctified, justified, holy brothers (and sisters), who are implicitly now just.

63. Chester, *Conversion at Corinth*, rightly stresses (against Bultmann, Sanders, and Martyn) the importance of Paul's justification language in this passage as both forensic and participatory, expressive of Paul's understanding of conversion (and hence justification) as identity transformation with corresponding behavioral consequences. His argument would be strengthened by considering Paul's use of the *dikaio-* word-family.

washed, you were sanctified, you were justified/incorporated" means "God washed you, God sanctified you, and God justified/incorporated you. . . ."[64]

Accordingly, this passage demonstrates the error in the argument (or the assumption) that although Paul uses the *dikaio-* word family to refer to both the juridical reality of justification and the moral reality of justice, he is using that single word-family to express two different semantic domains, or fields of meaning. Douglas Moo, for example, says the following:

> Paul can certainly use the word *dikaiosynē,* in continuation with the Old Testament and other New Testament authors, to refer to appropriate ethical behavior. . . . But I am not convinced that these occurrences should be incorporated into the concept of Pauline "justification." . . . [W]hich occurrences of *dik-* language in Paul should be the building blocks in our construction of the *concept* of justification in Paul? I would argue, simply, that at least two distinguishable categories of *dik-* language — for the sake of brevity, the "moral" and the "forensic" — are identifiable, on the basis of sound syntagmatic considerations, in both the LXX and the New Testament, and that it is a mistake to merge these categories.[65]

To be fair to Moo, we should note that this passage is in an article on Galatians, not 1 Corinthians, yet here he is deliberately speaking more broadly about the "definitional issue" of justification in Paul generally,[66] and that is what is critical.

---

64. There is thus an implicit Trinitarian referent in 6:11, with God the Father as the primary actor in partnership with Christ and the Spirit.

65. Douglas J. Moo, "Justification in Galatians," in *Understanding the Times: New Testament Studies in the 21st Century; Essays in Honor of D. A. Carson on the Occasion of His 65th Birthday,* ed. Andreas J. Köstenberger and Robert W. Yarbrough (Wheaton, IL: Crossway, 2011), pp. 160-95.

66. Moo, "Justification in Galatians," p. 175, in continuity, he says (p. 176), with "the methodological issue" raised at the start of the essay (pp. 161-62). As for Moo's interpretation of justification in Galatians, he rightly argues (pp. 186-90) that "the hope of righteousness [*dikaiosynēs*]" mentioned in Gal. 5:5 is about hope for a future *dikaiosynē* (rather than a generic hope that comes from a *dikaiosynē* already experienced). But he interprets that *dikaiosynē* in a strictly forensic way. The context, however, could just as well suggest a moral understanding of *dikaiosynē,* or an understanding of *dikaiosynē* that is both forensic and moral — the hope of receiving a positive divine verdict by virtue of having been incorporated into the community of faith, hope, and love by means of the cross and of having exhibited the resultant cruciform faith, hope, love, etc. that is the fruit of the Spirit and the practical expression of *dikaiosynē* in daily life, the fullness of which awaits the future "harvest" (Gal. 6:7-8).

If the connections we saw in Romans were insufficient to convince some readers, the key linguistic-theological aspects of 1 Corinthians 6:1-11 we have examined expose the error of putting asunder that which Paul, in continuity with the biblical tradition, has brought together. In an almost nonchalant yet theologically powerful way, Paul has revealed that for him — and quite possibly for an early Christian (baptismal?) tradition to which he may refer in 1 Corinthians 6:11 — justification and justice are inseparable. This inseparability is not merely in a relationship of cause and consequence, whether a possible or even a necessary consequence (as Moo and others suggest[67]). Rather, each is part of the other. It is those who have been justified who practice justice, or at least ought naturally to do so. The clear language of justification in 1 Corinthians 6:11 — including the passive voice, as in Romans 5:1 and elsewhere[68] — flows smoothly from Paul's pen as the primary rationale for the cruciform justice advocated earlier in the passage and put forth as a constituent part of justification. Justification creates a just people, or at least it should do so, and when it does not, it is questionable whether the person or community in question has understood what justification is all about. It may even be appropriate to wonder if they are in fact justified.[69]

Justification as the creation of a just people raises in a sharp way the issue of Christian identity. Thus an implicit dimension of 1 Corinthians 6:1-11 and the social reality to which it attests is the issue of witness. When members of the community of the just take their matters to the courts of the unjust, they are obviously saying something to those courts and to all who are aware of their actions. Their actions, in fact, say several things. First, they constitute an implicit confession of the church's inability, or unwillingness, to settle its own internal "trivial matters." Second, they constitute an implicit proclamation of a counter-gospel to the gospel of the crucified Lord. This counter-gospel is focused on a form of justice that is opposed to the reconciling love of God in Christ. Furthermore, to the extent that the justified continue to practice injustice, they demonstrate their need for radical transformation into the justice of God to which they have been called in justification. They are proclaiming to all that they are still shaped more by their own culture than they are by the gospel of God. Should they continue to resist the trans-

67. For Moo, see "Justification in Galatians," pp. 176-77. Again, to be fair to Moo, he is an advocate of justice and of justification that leads to justice and righteousness, but he unnecessarily separates the two by insisting that justification is only forensic.

68. Romans 5:1 begins, "Therefore, since we are justified by faith. . . ." Cf. Rom. 2:13; 3:20, 24, 28; 4:2; 5:9; 8:30; 10:10; Gal. 2:16 (3x); 3:11, 24; Titus 3:7.

69. Cf. 2 Cor. 13:5.

formation that this gospel effects, their fate will be bound up with those who have never experienced the justifying justice of God (1 Cor. 6:10).

On the other hand, should they permit that transformation to occur, they will more fully embody the intentions — and the justice — of God in the world, both as individuals and as a community. Those who practice cruciform justice bear witness to the world — to their friends and maybe even to the public courts — concerning an alternative way of settling disputes. Jerome Murphy-O'Connor claimed, in fact, that Paul asks the Corinthians to "grasp the opportunity to demonstrate the power of grace to non-believers by resolving such disputes themselves."[70] The justified are, or should be, the justice-ized, and it should be a matter of public record, sometimes by virtue of what the justified don't do as well as what they do; the two go hand in hand.

In this regard it is impossible not to think of the incredible reaction of the Amish community in Nickel Mines, Pennsylvania, to the shooting of ten school-aged girls in 2006.[71] The immediate reaction, not just of affected individuals, but of an entire Christian community to horrible injustice was a witness to the world — and to the church universal — of a different way to respond to injustice. It was, and it continues to be, a cruciform response, profound Christ-shaped justice meeting profound injustice. No cries for vengeance, no lawsuits. Just forgiveness and hospitality and love. And to this day, the impact continues in a variety of ways, not least in and through the mother of shooter Charles Carl Roberts IV. Terri Roberts has begun a ministry of sharing her family's experiences: the power of forgiveness and the possibility of healing and joy after terrible events transpire.

In 1 Corinthians 6:1-11 and the remaining passages we will consider, Paul is exercising his prophetic (and apostolic) responsibility to name injustice among the people of God and to call them away from injustice and to justice. Perhaps Paul was, in some significant sense, Amish.

### 1 Corinthians 8:1–11:1/Injustice in the Assertion of Rights and the Withholding of Cruciform Love

The abundance of words from the *dikaio-* family in 1 Corinthians 6:1-11 is not matched in 8:1–11:1. In fact, there is no occurrence of any word from that

---

70. Jerome Murphy-O'Connor, *Paul: A Critical Life* (New York: Oxford University Press, 1996), p. 285.

71. See Donald B. Kraybill, Steven M. Nolt, and David L. Weaver-Zercher, *Amish Grace: How Forgiveness Transcended Tragedy* (San Francisco: Jossey-Bass, 2007).

family in these three chapters. This should not be taken, however, as a sign that justice is not on Paul's mind. It is clear from various factors that Paul sees the failure of love (8:1, implicitly on the part of the "strong") as another instance of *adikia*, injustice, within the community, this time explicitly injustice toward the weak. These factors include the use of the word "brother" (four times in 8:11-13; *adelphos*, lost in the NRSV's use of "believers," "family," and pronouns), as in 6:5-8, and the frequent use of the word "weak" (five times in 8:7-12). This is the language of inappropriate power relations among intimates — the language of domestic abuse.

The specific situation is the insistence by some at Corinth, since they know there is only one God, on eating meat in the precincts of pagan temples, no matter the possible effects on others who are less certain in their theological knowledge (1 Cor. 8:1-13). Paul refers to the latter group as "the weak" because their conscience is "weak" (8:7, 9, 10, 12). He calls this insensitive action toward the weak an instance of simultaneous sinning against the sibling and sinning against Christ (8:12), indicating once more that for Paul the vertical and horizontal obligations of the covenant are inseparable.

As we saw in the general discussion of biblical justice and the discussion of the cross as the revelation of God's justice, for the biblical writers, including Paul, justice is not the antithesis of love but its concrete expression. We might refer to this love as "just love" or, once again, cruciform justice. The Corinthians who insist on still visiting pagan temples have apparently unfurled the banner of "rights" (*exousia*; 8:9), translated "liberty" in the NRSV and NAB.[72] This is the language of justice in the sense of entitlement, or what one is due. Thus in Paul's exhortation about the treatment of the weak, he calls the Corinthians to practice a counterintuitive justice/love that is rooted in the cross and involves the renunciation of rights, for the benefit of the other, as the practical demonstration of just love.

Beginning with 8:13 and continuing through chapter 9, Paul offers himself as a paradigm of such rights-renouncing (9:4-6, 12, 15, 18), others-regarding love, as we saw in chapter three:

[12] . . . [W]e have not made use of this right [to financial support; Gk. *exousias*], but we endure anything rather than put an obstacle in the way of the gospel of Christ. . . . [15]But I have made no use of any of these rights

---

72. Here and throughout 1 Corinthians we do not know how many are actually participating in the various ills Paul addresses. Paul, however, seems to operate with the prophetic principle recognized by Heschel: "Few are guilty, all are responsible" (*The Prophets*, p. 17).

[financial support, accompaniment by a spouse], nor am I writing this so that they may be applied in my case. . . . [19]For though I am free with respect to all, I have made myself a slave to all, so that I might win more of them. (1 Cor. 9:12b, 15, 19)

It is clear that for Paul this renunciation of rights is a missional practice for the benefit of the spread of the gospel that is itself rooted in the gospel, specifically the gospel of Christ's love displayed on the cross. The text of 1 Corinthians 9:19 is an echo of Philippians 2:6-8:

[6]. . . though he [Christ] was in the form of God, did not regard equality with God as something to be exploited, [7]but emptied himself, taking the form of a slave, being born in human likeness. And being found in human form, [8]he humbled himself and became obedient to the point of death — even death on a cross.

The cruciform love of Christ has shaped Paul's life; in this sense, *he has become the gospel, and he is inviting the Corinthians to do the same:* "Be imitators of me, as I am of Christ" (1 Cor. 11:1). He wants their injustice to be transformed into cruciform justice by the power and example of Christ mediated through his own ministry.

Thus the Corinthians are also to become the gospel, and also for missional purposes — to ensure that none of the weak brothers and sisters are destroyed, cut off from Christ (1 Cor. 8:9-12).[73] Furthermore, looking outside the church, Paul also admonishes them, in the spirit of missional engagement with nonbelievers in their cultural context, regarding meals taken in the homes of nonmembers of the community. Paul directs them to eat any meat they are served in nonbelievers' homes unless the host reveals the source of the meat to be a pagan temple sacrifice (1 Cor. 10:27-33). Once again, for the good of the other (in this case the unbeliever), becoming the gospel of cruciform justice (that is, imitating Christ's death and Paul's life) may mean foregoing a right, a desire, even a perfectly acceptable habit (10:23-24). This, then, is also a missional practice for the benefit of the spread of the gospel that is itself rooted in the gospel. It is not apostolic preaching in the sense of in-

---

73. I once again use the word "missional" in the sense rightly advocated by Michael Barram, *Mission and Moral Reflection in Paul,* Studies in Biblical Literature 75 (New York: Peter Lang, 2006): as a descriptor of all of Paul's apostolic activity as he participates in the mission of God.

tentional evangelistic activity, but it is nonetheless missional living and hence the proclamation of the gospel. Paul wants the Corinthians to imitate him precisely in this way: "Give no offense to Jews or to Greeks or to the church of God, just as I try to please everyone in everything I do, not seeking my own advantage, but that of many, so that they may be saved" (1 Cor. 10:32-33).

It is, Paul would say to us, incumbent on all Christian individuals and communities to discern any culturally appropriate analogies to the phenomenon of meat sacrificed to idols and the effect of such activity on others, both within the church and outside it. This requires a kind of disciplined scriptural imagination and readiness to be transformed — made more fully into the likeness of Christ and the gospel. It is not something that can be mandated for permanent keeping. Becoming the gospel always requires a careful exegesis of one's own culture as well as a careful reading of the text of Scripture, leading to a conversion of the imagination and of daily existence.[74]

### 1 Corinthians 11:17-34/Injustice in the Subversion of the Lord's Supper

We return now to "the church of God" mentioned at the end of 1 Corinthians 10, and specifically to the Corinthian practice of the Lord's Supper (discussed in 1 Cor. 11:17-34), where Jesus is supposed to be both host and guest. For Paul the situation involving the Lord's Supper in Corinth is a very serious one that in several respects actually does harm rather than good (v. 17).

First, the Corinthians' assembling for the Lord's Supper perpetuates their predilection for divisions (v. 18). Second, the meal is no longer the Lord's Supper but a conglomeration of private meals (vv. 20-21a). Third, although Paul does not use a word from the *dikaio-* family, because this combination of factionalism and self-interest is a direct assault on those in the community "who have nothing" (v. 22; *tous mē echontas*), it is clearly another act of injustice (not to mention drunkenness — v. 21). This time, unlike the situation addressed in 6:1-11 but like that addressed in 8:1–11:1, it is definitely a matter of injustice against the weak and vulnerable. Paul's exasperation is palpable: "What! Do you not have homes to eat and drink in? Or do you show contempt for the church of God and humiliate those who have nothing? What should I say to you? Should I commend you? In this matter I do not commend you!" (v. 22).

---

74. For the term "scriptural imagination" and "conversion of the imagination" I am indebted to various scholarly and ecclesial works by Richard B. Hays.

Those being treated unequally and hence unjustly are, ironically, precisely the sorts of people with whom the host–Lord Jesus identified in the cross and whom God called in Corinth (1:18-31). Whereas "God chose what is weak in the world to shame [*kataischynē*] the strong" (1:27b), the Corinthian strong are now shaming *(kataischynete)* the weak (11:22), acting in ways antithetical to the justice of God. This meal cannot, therefore, be the Lord's Supper because its host would not, and does not, tolerate such injustice at his meal. The meal "no longer points to Christ's death"[75] for nobodies.

Therefore, Paul implies, the Lord — whose identity can never be separated from his death by crucifixion (1 Cor. 2:2) — is absent, for the Corinthians have essentially expelled the crucified Lord by their un-cruciform mistreatment of his guests and hence the subversion of his supper. Certain Corinthians think they have a corner on the Lord's presence and favor, but Paul says instead that they are under apostolic (11:22) and especially divine (11:27-31) judgment. As for the prophets, so also for Paul: God's judgment of the community is based on how they treat the poor and marginalized.

It is remarkable that Paul makes such strong statements about the way in which injustice, not only idolatry (10:1-22), is incompatible with communion (*koinōnia;* 10:16-21) with the Lord Jesus. Warnings in chapter 10 (10:1-14) about sharing in the fate of the people of God who committed idolatry and sexual immorality *(porneia)* in the wilderness have been transferred to those committing injustice toward the weak in Corinth. True communion with, or participation in, the one body of Christ broken in death (10:16) must express the reality of the church as the one body of Christ (10:17; 11:29), with its preferential option for the weak grounded in the cross of its Lord.

As in 2 Corinthians 9 (see discussion below), Paul sees inequality among believers both as an injustice and as an opportunity for the practice of justice. Despite, or perhaps because of, the gravity of the situation in Corinth, Paul offers hope to the Corinthians: if they change their ways and appropriately welcome the weak (11:33), thereby discerning the body (i.e., the body of Christ that should take care of its weaker members; v. 29; cf. 12:22-26), they will be spared final condemnation (vv. 32-34). In so honoring the weak, they will truly remember Jesus, participate in the new covenant his death inaugurated, and proclaim that death in both word and deed (vv. 24-26). The community will then be one that "repeats the Supper in its daily living

---

75. Hays, *First Corinthians,* p. 200.

and constitutes each time anew the fellowship of the saints which even now practises justice."[76]

Although Paul does not specifically mention outsiders or the possible negative missional impact of this activity at the (alleged) Lord's Supper, we know that at Corinth, and likely elsewhere, the communities sometimes had "visitors" (1 Cor. 14:16, 21-25). Internal injustice may have serious external consequences, harming the church's witness (as examples too numerous to count from recent history confirm). What is more, if a community can practice such injustice toward its own members — its own *family* members, no less — how much more likely are they to mis-embody the gospel in public? Paul's concern about not giving offense to anyone (1 Cor. 10:32) must surely have relevance here, too, if only by extension.

### 1 Corinthians 12/The Body of Christ as the Locus of Justice for the Weak

The well-known text on the church as Christ's body in 1 Corinthians 12 is often said to be about unity and diversity, or "diversity and interdependence."[77] But just as importantly for Paul, this passage both reiterates and underwrites the practices of justice that he has been describing and prescribing since chapter 1. In continuity with the prophets and with God's action in Christ, Paul elevates the "weaker . . . less honorable . . . less respectable" members to the status of being "indispensable" and receiving "greater honor . . . [and] respect," claiming simply that this is what "we do" (vv. 22-24a).

But of course for Paul this is what "we" do because this is what God has done: "God has so arranged the body, giving the greater honor to the inferior member" (v. 24b). The church participates in the cruciform justice of God, doing so inasmuch as it practices this justice through mutual care (vv. 25-26), with special attention to the most vulnerable, such as the suffering. Paul's cruciform justice and cruciform ecclesiology — the church as the locus of justice for the weak — are rooted ultimately, therefore, in his cruciform

---

76. Luise Schottroff, "Holiness and Justice: Exegetical Comments on 1 Corinthians 11.17-34," *Journal for the Study of the New Testament* 79 (2005): 51-60 (p. 60). R. Alan Street argues that for Paul (as well as Luke), the Supper is an anti-imperial meal in which the ideology and practices of Rome are challenged and principles and practices of God's kingdom promoted (*Subversive Meals: An Analysis of the Lord's Supper under Roman Domination during the First Century* [Eugene, OR: Pickwick, 2013]).

77. Hays, *First Corinthians*, p. 213.

theology proper — his doctrine of God.[78] Once again, Paul echoes Scripture's identification of God as the God of the weak, the God whose thoughts are not ours. Paul knows these divine thoughts as the mind of Christ.

For yet another time, Paul does not speak *explicitly* of the missional dimension of being the body of Christ. But if the body of Christ is not a metaphor but a reality — the identity of Christ in the world today — then there are inevitably missional consequences to being the body of Christ. As the body cares for itself and functions justly, or not, it does so as the ongoing presence of Christ in the world. And Christ is therefore interpreted by "outsiders" by watching how "insiders" treat one another. Paul would not hesitate to agree with the words of Jesus reported in the Fourth Gospel:

> [20]"I ask not only on behalf of these, but also on behalf of those who will believe in me through their word, [21]that they may all be one. As you, Father, are in me and I am in you, may they also be in us, so that the world may believe that you have sent me. [22]The glory that you have given me I have given them, so that they may be one, as we are one, [23]I in them and you in me, that they may become completely one, so that the world may know that you have sent me and have loved them even as you have loved me." (John 17:20-23)

We turn now to two passages from 2 Corinthians.

### 2 Corinthians 5:21/The Church as the Justice of God

If 1 Corinthians 12, in spite of its length as a sustained argument, is thought to be one of the clearest passages in Paul's letters, 2 Corinthians 5:21, in spite of its brevity, has been one of the most inscrutable for interpreters:

> For our sake he [God] made him [Christ] to be sin who knew no sin, so that in him we might become the justice [*dikaiosynē*; NRSV "righteousness"] of God.[79]

---

78. On this, see my *Inhabiting the Cruciform God*, esp. pp. 9-39, and *Cruciformity*, pp. 9-18.

79. None of the standard translations render *dikaiosynē* as "justice." Surprisingly, the NJB translates it "uprightness." For a longer treatment of this passage, see my "Paul's Corporate, Cruciform, Missional Theosis in Second Corinthians," in *"In Christ" in Paul: Explorations in Paul's Theology of Union and Participation*, ed. Kevin J. Vanhoozer, Constantine R. Campbell, and Michael J. Thate, WUNT 2 series (Tübingen: Mohr Siebeck, 2014). For additional interpretations that are harmonious with this brief exposition, see especially Grieb, "'So That in

The first thing to note about this text is that it is one of Paul's "interchange" texts, as Morna Hooker has described them.[80] Interchange texts in Paul convey the notion that "Christ is identified with the human condition in order that we might be identified with his."[81] For Hooker, interchange is not about substitution, but about Christ's representation and our participation. Interchange texts depict Christ becoming like us, sharing in our reality in incarnation and/or death, so that we might become like him and share in his reality.[82] The reality under consideration here is that Christ "became for us wisdom from God, and righteousness . . . ," or justice (*dikaiosynē*; 1 Cor. 1:30). Linking 1 Corinthians 1:30 to 2 Corinthians 5:21, we can conclude that God's saving justice was in Christ with the result that we, in him, can become — can participate in — that divine saving justice.

The interchange named in 2 Corinthians 5:21 should be understood as a reference to Christ's death, which is part of the larger narrative of reconciliation that includes the incarnation and the entire Christ event: "God was in Christ, reconciling the world . . ." (5:19 NRSV alt.). The "we" in 5:21 refers not merely to Paul and his colleagues, but to all the Corinthians and indeed all human beings of every place and time.[83] Accordingly, as an interchange

---

Him,'" and also Morna D. Hooker, "On Becoming the Righteousness of God: Another Look at 2 Corinthians 5:21," *Novum Testamentum* 50 (2008): 358-75.

80. Morna D. Hooker, "Interchange in Christ" and "Interchange and Atonement," in *From Adam to Christ: Essays on Paul* (Cambridge: Cambridge University Press, 1990), pp. 13-25 and 26-41; and "On Becoming the Righteousness of God."

81. Hooker, *From Adam to Christ*, p. 26.

82. See also Gal. 3:13a ("Christ redeemed us from the curse of the law by becoming a curse for us"); 2 Cor. 8:9 ("For you know the generous act of our Lord Jesus Christ, that though he was rich, yet for your sakes he became poor, so that by his poverty you might become rich"), discussed below; and Rom. 8:3-4 ("For God has done what the law, weakened by the flesh, could not do: by sending his own Son in the likeness of sinful flesh, and to deal with sin, he condemned sin in the flesh, so that the just requirement of the law might be fulfilled in us . . ."), which is quite parallel to 2 Cor. 5:21.

83. A few interpreters limit the scope of the "we" in 2 Cor. 5:21 to Paul and his colleagues, arguing that it does not include the whole body of Christ. (See N. T. Wright, "On Becoming the Righteousness of God: 2 Corinthians 5:21," in *Pauline Theology; Volume 2: 1 and 2 Corinthians*, ed. David M. Hay [Minneapolis: Fortress, 1993], pp. 200-208.) Although the "we/us" language in 2 Corinthians is quite tricky to interpret in some places, here it seems quite clearly to involve everyone, unless we could imagine Paul saying that Christ died just for the apostles, a new form of limited atonement(!): "For the sake of Peter, James, John, Titus, Timothy, Junia, me, and maybe a few others, God made him to be sin who knew no sin, so that in him we apostles might become the righteousness of God by spreading the gospel of God's justice." This is a highly unlikely sentiment for Paul to express. See, e.g., Frank J. Matera, *II Corinthians: A*

text, 2 Corinthians 5:21 — despite centuries of argument about its implicit doctrines of the atonement and of justification — is fundamentally a text about participation and transformation. The key words that underscore these two inseparable dimensions of the text are "in him" (*en autō;* participation) and "become" (*genōmetha;* transformation).

The theme of transformation is reinforced in context by the words "no longer" (v. 16) and "new creation" (v. 17):

> [16]From now on, therefore, we regard no one from a human point of view; even though we once knew Christ from a human point of view, we know him no longer in that way. [17]So if anyone is in Christ, there is a new creation: everything old has passed away; see, everything has become new! (2 Cor. 5:16-17)

Richard Hays is therefore absolutely right to make the following strong assertion about our text:

> [Paul] does not say "that we might *know about* the righteousness of God," nor "that we might *believe in* the righteousness of God," nor even "that we might *receive* the righteousness of God." Instead, the church is to *become* the righteousness of God: where the church embodies in its life together the world-reconciling love of Jesus Christ, the new creation is manifest. The church incarnates the righteousness of God.[84]

Accordingly, if 2 Corinthians 5:21 is about justification and atonement (as I think it is), then Paul's understanding of each "doctrine" is inclusive of both participation and transformation.

---

*Commentary,* New Testament Library (Louisville: Westminster John Knox, 2003), p. 144, for the view that Paul's "we" is wide in scope. Hooker ("On Becoming the Righteousness of God") thinks that although the first referent of the "we" here and often elsewhere in 2 Corinthians is to Paul and colleagues, the apostle's life and ministry are intended as a model for all Christians. See, e.g., p. 365: "The use of the first person plural throughout these chapters clearly applies to Paul in particular; he is describing his own experience. Yet what he says is true — or *ought to* be true! — of Christians in general. The pattern of the Gospel should be stamped on *all* their lives." Cf. p. 373, following a focus on Paul's ministry as embodying the righteousness of God: "Nevertheless, it is 'we' who become the righteousness of God, and that righteousness should therefore be revealed in the lives of *all* believers, not just those of the apostles."

84. Richard B. Hays, *The Moral Vision of the New Testament: Community, Cross, New Creation; A Contemporary Introduction to New Testament Ethics* (San Francisco: HarperCollins, 1996), p. 24.

The theme of participation is further reinforced by the narrative logic of the passage: God was in Christ, who became like us, and now we who are in Christ can become like God. Indeed, that was the purpose ("so that"; *hina*, v. 21) of God's reconciling action in Christ. God's participation in our humanity, in Christ, makes possible our participation in God's divinity — specifically God's *dikaiosynē*, God's justice — in Christ. (As noted in this book's introduction ["Invitation"], one way to characterize this participation in God's character is by using the term "theosis."[85]) As in Romans 5:1-11, language of reconciliation and language of *dikaio-* appear together, in parallel: God's not counting trespasses (v. 19) and God's transformative project (vv. 17, 21) are not two separate acts but one unified salvation. Here, as elsewhere in Paul, forensic and participatory language kiss; justification and justice embrace. And, most importantly for our purposes, participation and *mission* embrace, as Hooker also notes above. Or, to reintroduce a word from the opening pages of this book, theosis and mission embrace.

Paul's point is this, in Katherine Grieb's words: "The 'new creation/new creature' that God has accomplished in Christ belongs to a spiritually empowered reality that was previously as inconceivable as it was impossible: God's own covenant righteousness enacted in community — in Corinth."[86] In other words, the Corinthians can become the gospel they have embraced — or, better, that has embraced them. The greatest human privilege, Paul suggests, is to be part of this new creation, to participate in the very purpose of God for humanity: becoming the embodiment of God's saving, reconciling, restorative justice in the world.

But what does it mean to become the justice of God? That is a question with many possible answers, a question always in search of imaginative respondents. Paul does, however, provide one concrete, "on-the-ground" example of the church becoming God's justice in 2 Corinthians. Not surprisingly, that example is wrapped around another text about interchange, participation, and transformation (or theosis) — 2 Corinthians 8:9.

### 2 Corinthians 8–9/Gracious, Participatory Economic Justice

Chapters 8 and 9 of 2 Corinthians contain Paul's appeal to the believers in Corinth for their support of the collection for the Jerusalem church. Spe-

---

85. In the chapter on Romans, we will have more to say about the church's transformative participation in the life of God as sharing in God's divinity while, of course, remaining always the creature, not the creator.

86. Grieb, "'So That in Him,'" p. 66.

cifically, Paul is urging them to fulfill their previous commitment to that effort. The Greek language supplies Paul with yet another opportunity for a wordplay as he seeks to call the justified/justice-ized community at Corinth to practice justice. In 2 Corinthians 8–9 Paul uses the word *charis,* often translated "grace," ten times, with various but interconnected senses: benefaction, generosity, generous act, gratitude.[87]

Paul likely draws on both the scriptural sense of God's benefaction (expressed by the Hebrew word *hesed* and cognates) and the contemporary Greco-Roman usage of *charis,* which could refer to a generous disposition, a generous gift, and the response of gratitude and subsequent indebtedness to the giver.[88] In addition, Paul uses the cognate *eucharistia,* "thanksgiving," twice, and he quotes Psalm 112:9 (LXX 111:9) in 9:9, which refers to the manifestation of justice *(dikaiosynē)* in generosity to the poor. These chapters, then, reveal one instance of what Paul means by the church becoming the justice of God (5:21).

This eloquent piece of rhetoric is worth quoting at length; once again, I cite the NRSV but replace "righteousness" with "justice"; occurrences of it, "grace" (variously translated by the NRSV), and "thanksgiving" *(eucharistia)* are underlined:

> 8¹We want you to know, brothers and sisters, about the <u>grace</u> [*charin*] of God that has been granted to the churches of Macedonia; ²for during a severe ordeal of affliction, their abundant joy and their extreme poverty have overflowed in a wealth of generosity on their part. ³For, as I can testify, they voluntarily gave according to their means, and even beyond their means, ⁴begging us earnestly for the <u>privilege</u> [*charin*] of sharing [*koinōnia*] in this ministry to the saints — ⁵and this, not merely as we expected; they gave themselves first to the Lord and, by the will of God, to us, ⁶so that we might urge Titus that, as he had already made a beginning, so he should also complete this <u>generous undertaking</u> [*charin*]

---

87. 8:1, 4, 6, 7, 9, 16, 19; 9:8, 14, 15.

88. Thus English translations, unfortunately, do not always reveal all the linguistic and theological connections in the text. The cluster of occurrences of *charis* in these two chapters is rivaled only by Romans 5. For a rich theological exegesis of this section of 2 Corinthians, see Richard B. Hays, *Echoes of Scripture in the Letters of Paul* (New Haven: Yale University Press, 1989), pp. 87-91; and John M. G. Barclay, "Manna and the Circulation of Grace: A Study of 2 Corinthians 8:1-15," in *The Word Leaps the Gap: Essays on Theology and Scripture in Honor of Richard B. Hays,* ed. J. Ross Wagner, C. Kavin Rowe, and A. Katherine Grieb (Grand Rapids: Eerdmans, 2008), pp. 409-26.

among you. [7]Now as you excel in everything — in faith, in speech, in knowledge, in utmost eagerness, and in our love for you — so we want you to excel also in this generous undertaking [*chariti*]. [8]I do not say this as a command, but I am testing the genuineness of your love against the earnestness of others. [9]For you know the generous act [*charin*] of our Lord Jesus Christ, that though he was rich, yet for your sakes he became poor, so that by his poverty you might become rich. . . . [16]But thanks [*charis*] be to God who put in the heart of Titus the same eagerness for you that I myself have. . . . [19] . . . he has also been appointed by the churches to travel with us while we are administering this generous undertaking [*chariti*] for the glory of the Lord himself and to show our goodwill. . . . 9. . . . [8]And God is able to provide you with every blessing [*charin*] in abundance, so that by always having enough of everything, you may share abundantly in every good work. [9]As it is written, "He scatters abroad, he gives to the poor; his justice [*dikaiosynē*] endures forever." [10]He who supplies seed to the sower and bread for food will supply and multiply your seed for sowing and increase the harvest of your justice [*dikaiosynēs*]. [11]You will be enriched in every way for your great generosity, which will produce thanksgiving [*eucharistian*] to God through us; [12]for the rendering of this ministry not only supplies the needs of the saints but also overflows with many thanksgivings [*eucharistiōn*] to God. [13]Through the testing of this ministry you glorify God by your obedience to the confession of the gospel of Christ and by the generosity of your sharing with them and with all others [*eis pantas*], [14]while they long for you and pray for you because of the surpassing grace [*charin*] of God that he has given you. [15]Thanks [*charis*] be to God for his indescribable gift!

Laced with the word *charis* ("grace") and additional rich theological language, artfully mixed with the idiom of honor and shame, the appeal for generosity has as its goal something approximating equality (so CEB, NAB, NET, NIV in 8:13-14 for *isotēs*; NJB and NRSV: "fair balance"), or what we would describe as economic justice.[89]

89. So also Grieb, " 'So That in Him,' " p. 69 et passim. Gordon Zerbe (*Citizenship: Paul on Peace and Politics* [Winnipeg, MB: CMU Press, 2012], pp. 82-87) argues that "economic mutualism" was a consistent part of Paul's teaching in the various assemblies. Ancient ethicists such as Aristotle often discussed economic issues of equality or fairness in the context of justice. (For a selection of texts, see Craig S. Keener, *1-2 Corinthians*, New Cambridge Bible Commentary [Cambridge: Cambridge University Press, 2005], p. 206.)

Paul's appeal is grounded in what Katherine Grieb has labeled the "generous justice of God."[90] This phrase appropriately summarizes what Paul conveys through multiple occurrences of the word *charis* and related terms in conjunction with the two occurrences of *dikaiosynē* (9:9, 10), which echo 5:21. In 2 Corinthians 8–9 as a unit, Paul speaks of Christ both as the generous, "indescribable gift" of God (*dōrea;* 9:15) and as the gracious self-gift of Christ himself (*charis;* 8:9). The latter narrates Christ's self-emptying, or kenosis (as in Phil. 2:6-8), in metaphorical economic language. Paul calls the Corinthians, as beneficiaries of this greatest gift, to participate in it more fully and responsibly — yet freely, cheerfully, and without worry — by sharing in the grace of Christ, which is summarized in 8:9, and the justice of God, which is summarized in 9:9-10.

Paul wants the Corinthians' life in the Spirit to be marked not only by *charismata* (charismatic gifts; 1 Cor. 1:7; 1 Corinthians 12, 14) but also by Christlike *charis*; he wants their justification to be expressed in a "harvest of [their] justice" (9:10) — which is ultimately the justice of God (9:9). "The Corinthians," writes John Barclay, "are being invited not just to *imitate* God's dynamic of grace [and we should add justice] toward the world but to *embody* it, to continue and extend it in their own giving to meet the needs of others."[91] Indeed, what is remarkable is that Paul sees such a close relationship between grace and justice, first as the characteristic of God (including Christ and the Spirit) and then as the characteristic of God's people. The church participates in God's mission, and Paul indicates this by using the common Greek word for sharing, *koinōnia* (8:4; 9:13), giving it a theological twist.

Furthermore, Paul uses a common image — the sowing of seed — to make it clear that God is the ultimate source of generosity and justice for the poor, while the church participates in that generous justice. Paul invites believers to "sow" bountifully and cheerfully, knowing that God provides abundantly for the doing of good (9:6-11): "He who supplies seed to the sower and bread for food will supply and multiply your seed for sowing and increase the harvest of your justice" (9:10).

This point raises the question of the grammatical subject in 9:9, which quotes Psalm 112:9. Is the one who "scatters abroad" and "gives to the poor," whose "justice endures forever," God, or is it the just and faithful person? In Psalm 112 itself, the subject is the one who fears the Lord, but Paul's use is less

---

90. Grieb, " 'So That in Him,' " pp. 59, 74, et passim.
91. Barclay, "Manna and the Circulation of Grace," p. 420 (emphasis added).

clear; the subject may be God. In either case, however, God is the "supreme benefactor"[92] who provides and multiplies the seed, blessing the sower to bless others. Thomas Stegman suggests that Paul's thought reflects the flow of Psalms 111 and 112 (LXX 110 and 111): Psalm 111 describes the generous, merciful, and just God who feeds those who fear him, while Psalm 112 describes the one who fears and imitates that God by doing justice and giving to the poor.[93] Both are characterized by justice (*dikaiosynē* in LXX 110:3; 111:3, 9). Accordingly, for Paul, "those who give generously to the needy should know that their charitable act is a part of that larger righteousness of God by which they themselves live and in which they shall remain forever."[94] This is a text, in other words, about missional participation.

The overall participatory thrust of Paul's gentle but prophetic argument and the presence of *dikaiosynē* language suggest that it is no coincidence that we find in these chapters another "interchange" text, namely 8:9, following 5:21. Christ became sin so that we might become just(ice) (5:21), and he became poor so that we might become rich (8:9). His self-gift to us in our spiritual poverty translates into the gift of our material possessions to others in their material poverty.[95] Again, this is not a mere summons to imitation, but rather "the identification of *a divine momentum in which believers are caught up*, and by which they are empowered to be, in turn, richly self-sharing with others."[96] That is, both 5:21 and 8:9 are speaking of what we can call theosis, specifically missional theosis; that is the ultimate significance of these interchange texts and of the actual interchange to which they bear witness. Together the two interchange-theosis texts in 2 Corinthians suggest that Paul's addressees will be on their way to becoming the justice of God when they are conformed to the cruciform grace of Christ expressed in selfless generosity to the poor.[97] And in 2 Corinthians 9, at least, the poor to

---

92. Keener, *1-2 Corinthians*, pp. 213-14.

93. Thomas D. Stegman, *Second Corinthians*, Catholic Commentary on Sacred Scripture (Grand Rapids: Baker Academic, 2009), p. 214.

94. Victor Paul Furnish, *II Corinthians*, AB 32a (Garden City, NY: Doubleday, 1984), p. 449.

95. "The ultimate goal is not a reversal of fortunes through some kind of class warfare, but 'equality' through the establishment of new economic relationships under the sign of Messiah's economic divestment for the sake of the other" (Zerbe, *Citizenship*, pp. 81-82).

96. Barclay, "Manna and the Circulation of Grace," p. 421 (emphasis added). Barclay does not use the language of justice, but he does describe justice in characterizing Paul's vision of equality as the "redistribution of surplus" that is "bilateral" and "reciprocal" because all parties have different sorts of riches to give and needs to be met (p. 423).

97. "[J]ustice, as a healthy humanitarian social relationship, means the reversal of un-

be cared for are not only believers ("the saints"; 9:1, 12) but "all" (9:13; *pantas;* NRSV "all others") — meaning outsiders.[98]

It is significant that Paul refers to this generous justice as ministry (*diakonia;* 8:4; 9:1, 12, 13), the same word he uses in 2 Corinthians to describe his own ministry, that is, of embodied gospel proclamation (3:8-9; 4:1; 5:18; 6:3; 11:8). Moreover, he refers to his own ministry as a "ministry of justice" (*dikaiosynēs;* 3:9) and a "ministry of reconciliation" (5:18). More precisely, Paul participates in God's ministry of justice and reconciliation — and so do the Corinthians. As Morna Hooker writes,

> Paul's appeal to the Corinthians in chapters 8–9 can also be seen as a logical continuation from the conviction that Christians are agents of righteousness. . . . Since God's righteousness abides for ever, he will increase the yield of *their* righteousness (9:8-10): once again, we see the link between God's righteousness and that of Christians — and this righteousness is demonstrated in bringing assistance to those in need. It is certainly no accident that the key appeal in this section is made on the basis of another of Paul's "interchange" statements . . . (8:9). The Corinthians, too, must in their turn bring riches to others. By doing so, they will be sharing in Paul's ministry, and God's saving power will work through them.[99]

This is not to say that working for economic justice and evangelizing unbelievers are synonymous, but it is to say that each is a ministry, each embodies the gospel of God's powerful restorative justice and reconciliation, and each is appropriate for the church to do *as the church.*

## Paul and Justice in the World

Finally we come to the last connection between justification and justice in Paul: the church's presence in the world. We have just seen a glimpse of this

---

healthy economic relationships" (Bennett, "Justice, OT," p. 477, commenting on the Psalter and the prophets).

98. See Zerbe, *Citizenship,* p. 80; Bruce W. Longenecker, *Remember the Poor: Paul, Poverty, and the Greco-Roman World* (Grand Rapids: Eerdmans, 2010), pp. 291-94. "All," as we will see momentarily, is Paul's way of referring to, or including, those outside the church. Translations express this interpretation of 9:13 in various ways: CEB, NET, and Wright, *Kingdom New Testament:* "everyone"; NIV: "everyone else"; NKJV: "all men." The NLT has "all believers," which seems unlikely.

99. Hooker, "On Becoming the Righteousness of God," p. 374.

connection in 2 Corinthians 9:13. However, even interpreters who grant that Paul was concerned about justice in his churches usually hesitate at this point, suggesting that Paul did not have a social agenda or was not concerned about the fate of the world.

Yet it would seem strange indeed if the apostle who believed that in Christ God was reconciling the world did not care about the people in that world, or believed that the arrival of God's *shalom* (peace and justice) in his Messiah was not meant for the good of all humanity. To be sure, Paul did not have a social agenda in the modern sense of an autonomous program to overcome social ills, or to establish universal human rights.[100] We have already suggested in this chapter that Paul is concerned about the impact of the church's practices of injustice or justice on the outside world. This is, so to speak, the church's passive, or unintentional, witness to God's justice. But what is also crucial to grasp is that Paul did in fact expect his communities to be active agents of goodness, compassion, reconciliation, and justice in the world, not merely in the church. He expected them to practice the same kind of justice toward outsiders as toward believers.

The explicit evidence here is admittedly not vast, but what does exist is weighty; it revolves around the word "all" (Greek *pantas,* etc.) as either an inclusive term for all people or as a term to distinguish those outside the *ekklēsia* from those within. Here are three texts that we have not yet met in this chapter, though the second and third were discussed in the overview chapter on peace:

> So let us not grow weary in doing what is right [*to kalon*], for we will reap at harvest-time, if we do not give up. So then, whenever we have an opportunity, let us work for the good [*to agathon*] of all [*pros pantas*], and especially for those of the family of faith. (Gal. 6:9-10)

> And we urge you, beloved, to . . . encourage the faint-hearted, help the weak, be patient with all of them. See that none of you repays evil for evil, but always seek to do good to one another and to all [*pros pantas*]. (1 Thess. 5:14-15)

> Bless those who persecute you; bless and do not curse them. . . . Do not repay anyone evil for evil, but take thought for what is noble in the sight

100. For an attempt to put Paul in dialogue with the struggle for human rights, with each partner in the conversation gaining from the other, see Adrian Long, *Paul and Human Rights: A Dialogue with the Father of the Corinthian Community,* The Bible in the Modern World 26 (Sheffield: Sheffield Phoenix Press, 2009).

of all. If it is possible, so far as it depends on you, live peaceably with all [*meta pantōn*]. (Rom. 12:14, 17-18)

And then there is the text we have just considered from 2 Corinthians:

Through the testing of this ministry you glorify God by your obedience to the confession of the gospel of Christ and by the generosity of your sharing with them and with all others [*eis pantas*]. . . . (2 Cor. 9:13)

In each of these texts, the outside world is referred to with the term "all," and in each case the expectations of biblical justice — working for the good of others, having compassion for the weak, and rejecting retaliation and violence but making peace — are presented as mandates to the church for its life in the world of unbelievers. N. T. Wright says that such passages "may appropriately be read as a Christianizing of the command in Jer. 29[LXX 36].7 to 'seek the welfare of the city' where the exiles found themselves, though there is no obvious verbal echo."[101] They constitute, he says, "at least the beginnings of an outline sketch of a Christian responsibility in relation to the wider world, rather than an ethic which is concerned only for the ordering of the household of faith."[102]

Furthermore, in light of Romans 8:18-25, it does not require a great stretch of the imagination to think that Paul recognized the justice connections between human beings and the rest of creation that earlier prophets had also seen (e.g., Hosea 4:1-3; Isa. 65:17-25).[103] Paul was likely aware of Rome's imperial acts of ecological exploitation.[104] He may not have thought there was anything his churches could do about it, but that does not mean he had no opinion about such ecological injustice. He knew that to become

101. Wright, *Paul and the Faithfulness of God*, p. 380 n. 107. He is referring specifically to Gal. 6:10 but looking also beyond. Wright refers readers also to Bruce W. Winter, *Seek the Welfare of the City: Christians as Benefactors and Citizens* (Grand Rapids: Eerdmans, 1994). Winter does not deal with 2 Cor. 9:13.

102. Wright, *Paul and the Faithfulness of God*, p. 380.

103. See, e.g., David Horrell, "A New Perspective on Paul? Rereading Paul in an Age of Ecological Crisis," *Journal for the Study of the New Testament* 33 (2010): 3-30; David G. Horrell, Cherryl Hunt, and Christopher Southgate, eds., *Greening Paul* (Waco, TX: Baylor University Press, 2010); and Presian Smyers Burroughs, "Liberation in the Midst of Futility and Destruction: Romans 8 and the Christian Vocation of Nourishing Life" (Th.D. diss., Duke Divinity School, 2014). See also the brief comments in the chapter on Philippians.

104. See J. Donald Hughes, *Ecology in Ancient Civilizations* (Albuquerque: University of New Mexico Press, 1975), pp. 99-127.

the justice of God is to participate in a cosmic, not merely an ecclesial or even universal, divine mission (cf. Col. 1:15-20).

As we noted in the chapter on Philippians, to honor Jesus as Lord of all means to participate not only in the great commandment and the great commission, but also in what we called the "great challenge" that the crisis of the environment poses to humanity. Here, in Romans, we look at the same crisis from the perspective that is even larger than the human race: to suffer and groan with the entire created order (Rom. 8:18-25) means to live in sympathy and solidarity with the world that God created, continues to love, and will fully redeem. Christians cannot *effect* that redemption of the creation, but they can *affect* the creation in proto-redemptive ways. They can extend their justice in such a way that they live in participatory anticipation of the liberation and redemption of the creation. Once again, acts of scriptural imagination are needed for that justice to occur.

## Conclusion

We began with the question, Did Paul abandon the biblical, prophetic teaching on justice, especially in his theology of justification? We proposed a forceful "no" to this question and have now seen many and deep connections between justification and justice in Paul's letters. Justice for Paul is continuous with the concerns of the prophets but is also reshaped by his gospel of Christ crucified; justice is covenantal and cruciform. In Christ God was and is making peace with the world, and God was — and is — making a reconciled and justified people into the justice of God. We need to stress once again that this is not an argument for justice instead of spirituality, but rather a fully biblical spirituality that *includes* spiritual practices of justice. In Christ, as already in the Scriptures of Israel, love of God and love of neighbor coalesce.

Also in Christ, and now in and through the church by the power of the Spirit, the eschatological day of justice and peace has arrived, if only partially and proleptically, as I suggested at the start of the chapter. Indeed, as we have seen briefly at several points, justice is inseparable from peace.[105] Theologically, this makes sense for all sorts of reasons, chief among them being, in the words of Jonathan Wilson, that "[j]ustice and justification simply name

---

105. "Peace and justice are a biblical hendiadys [one word/idea expressed in two], in Paul and elsewhere" (Zerbe, *Citizenship*, p. 174).

the right alignment of the world with God through the redemption of the creation," and "*reconciliation* is God's act of aligning all things in their proper relationship to God through Christ's cross."[106]

We conclude our discussion of justification and justice with these final words. For Paul, God is the God of justice, and the church is a community of justice; justice is both a divine trait and an ecclesial practice. Accordingly, justice is not an optional supplement to the Pauline and Christian gospel; it is who God in Christ is, and what the church in Christ is, and what it is becoming. It is the church's name: "the justice of God." Justification that is not inclusive of justice is un-Jewish, un-Pauline, and ultimately un-Christian.

## Missional Justice Today

With many other theologians and Christian leaders, I welcome the many ways in which Christians of all sorts are taking the prophetic, Pauline, and evangelical vision of justice seriously. Time and space would fail me to begin cataloging this renewal. Nevertheless, I wish to highlight a few dimensions of this understanding of Christian mission, both positively and negatively. I will begin with the negative.

Not everything that calls itself "justice" embodies the spirit of Pauline participatory justice we have discussed. For example, in the 1970s and 1980s a major mainline Protestant denomination set up something called the "Choice Justice Fund." Its sole purpose was to fund abortions for women, mostly urban minority women, who could not afford them. Apart from a host of issues from the morality of abortion itself to the focus on urban African Americans, this nomenclature did not do justice to the words in its name. First, the women were offered no "choice" to keep and raise the children, no possibility of financial or other assistance to welcome new life rather than to end it, no support network to help them negotiate life as a mother (or a mother again) in poverty, no addressing of the core issues. The prophetic and Pauline vision of "justice," in which children and mothers experience security and have their needs met with a sense of equity, in which life is abundant and flourishing for all because of the self-giving action of some — this was not the result of the "Choice Justice" fund.

Much more choice and justice are to be found in the ministry of Mary's

---

106. Jonathan R. Wilson, *God's Good World: Reclaiming the Doctrine of Creation* (Grand Rapids: Baker Academic, 2013), p. 123.

Cradle in Bluefield, West Virginia.[107] Sponsored by five mainline Protestant (United Methodist) churches and housed in a simple but beautiful space in one of them, Mary's Cradle has the following mission statement: "It is our profound wish to honor and value each person who is served by Mary's Cradle and we strive to benefit all infants and children through our service to their parents and/or guardians." The services Mary's Cradle provides include assistance for pregnant women, infants, and toddlers in the form of furnishing clothing to women and children (up to size 4T — way beyond the infant phase), diapers, supplies, and even furniture. They also have a library with books about pregnancy, raising healthy children, and children with special needs, as well as children's books.

Mary's Cradle exists because of the generosity of Christians and others who are participating in the justice of God. The ministry cooperates with other Christian ministries, with the local WIC program, and with others of goodwill.

A similar kind of ministry of justice occurs in the West African country of Cameroon. Fr. Maurice Akwa, a Catholic priest and seminary professor, struggled to know how to address the cultural reality of the fate of widows and orphans in his country, and particularly in his city of Bertoua. Traditionally when husbands die in Cameroon, their property reverts to their families, often leaving their wives and children destitute. Fr. Maurice founded a ministry to orphans and widows and, working with some women who had become community leaders, helped to start a series of educational and entrepreneurial activities for women, so that widows and others could learn trades and other skills to support their families.

The same priest saw other needs that cried out for compassion and justice, among them the situation of patients at the local hospital, many of whom were without families, or without families nearby. Since the hospital does not provide food for its patients, Fr. Maurice organized an ecumenical network of churches to make meals for those without families. Despite their own poverty (as with the Philippians and other Macedonian believers), these Christians give of their time and treasure.

On a larger scale, whether regional, national, or global, other Christians are finding ways to participate in God's justice-making mission. Disabled in a swimming accident as a teenager, Joni Eareckson Tada now directs Joni and Friends International Disability Center, whose mission is one of "extending the love and message of Jesus Christ to people who are affected by disability

---

107. See http://www.maryscradle.com/.

around the world."[108] Joni and Friends provides connections to disability-friendly churches, retreats for families with disabled children, training in disability ministry, and wheelchairs for disabled people around the world.

Christians (and others of goodwill) have begun microloan programs around the globe, allowing entrepreneurs in developing countries to receive the startup capital they need for small businesses that will keep their families from poverty and death, and make a better life possible. As of this writing, the Christian relief agency World Vision alone has made more than 3.5 million loans since 1993 and currently has thousands in need of support.[109]

For several years now, some of these ministries have sponsored a "Justice Conference" to inform and inspire other Christians.[110] The vision of the conference is to "reach thousands of people through a networked national conference that educates, inspires and connects a generation of men and women around a shared concern for the vulnerable and oppressed." Its organizers describe it as "an annual pilgrimage for justice workers, students and learners from all over the world."

The simulcast conference has featured leading Christian voices, including scholars like N. T. Wright, Walter Brueggemann, Miroslav Volf, and Nicholas Wolterstorff; activist-ministers like Jim Wallis, John Perkins, and Bernice King (daughter of Martin Luther King); pastoral leaders such as Lynne Hybels; community organizers and activists like Shane Claiborne; and heads of relief organizations such as Rich Stearns (World Vision) and Stephen Bauman (World Relief). But perhaps most fascinating are speaker-participants like Rev. Eugene Cho.[111] Cho is the founder and lead pastor of Quest Church, an urban, multicultural, and multigenerational church in Seattle, Washington; founder and executive director of the Q Café, a nonprofit community café and music venue; and founder of One Day's Wages (ODW), a grassroots movement of people, stories, and actions to alleviate extreme global poverty. Within four years of its founding in 2009, ODW raised more than $1.3 million to promote awareness, encourage simpler living, and support sustainable relief through partnerships, especially with smaller organizations in developing regions.

I could go on and on, but that is not necessary. The point is that the church is hearing with renewed imagination the call to justice that comes from the prophets and Jesus — and from Paul. The Spirit's work continues.

108. See http://www.joniandfriends.org/.
109. See http://www.worldvisionmicro.org/.
110. See http://thejusticeconference.com/.
111. See http://eugenecho.com/.

# CHAPTER 8

# Becoming the Gospel of God's Justice/Righteousness and Glory: Missional Theosis in Romans

I suspect that, for many people, the approach to Romans taken in this chapter will be something they have not previously encountered. The typical themes associated with Paul's most significant letter — justification, the righteousness of God, Jew and Gentile, the obedience of faith — reappear here but in a new idiom, a new key. Other important themes in Romans that have received less attention, such as peace (see chapter five) and resurrection/immortality, also figure in the account of Romans offered in the following pages. What is new is the strong emphasis on participation, specifically participation in God's righteousness (or justice) and glory. What is also new, and what may be strange for some, at first, is the language of theosis.

The argument of this chapter is that a central theme of Romans is theosis — becoming like God by participating in the life of God — and that this theosis is inherently missional.[1] In a way, then, this chapter is *not* so new or strange. Not only was the language introduced in the book's Introduction ("Invitation"), but it has also appeared here and there throughout the book, most recently in the previous chapter. In the Introduction, in fact, I said that the thesis of this entire book is that theosis — Spirit-enabled transformative participation in the life and character of God revealed in the crucified and resurrected Messiah Jesus — is the starting point of mission and its proper theological framework. At the same time, however, as also noted in the Introduction, not everyone who finds participation to be central to Paul likes the word "theosis" and similar terms (such as "deification" and even "Christosis") or thinks it appropriate to use them of Paul. If readers of this chapter are willing to be patient, I think they will find its take on Romans to

---

1. This chapter is an expansion and revision of my article "Romans: The First Christian Treatise on Theosis," *Journal of Theological Interpretation* 5 (2011): 13-34.

be missionally significant, even if they ultimately do not choose to use the same idiom to describe it.

Finally, then, we come (again) to Romans.

## (Re-)Introducing Theosis

We begin with the following characterizations of Christ's mission to humanity:

- "Christ became what we are — *'adam* — in order that we might share in what he is — namely the true image of God."
- Christ "became like human beings, so that we would be like him."
- "Christ becomes what we are, that we through his death may become what he is."

This language, which is rather foreign to many Western Christians, is typical of many of the church fathers, particularly in the East, and it is still common language in the Orthodox Church. But these three quotations do not come from church fathers like Irenaeus or Athanasius; nor are they modern statements of the Orthodox understanding of salvation. Rather, each one is a summary of Paul's soteriology (understanding of salvation) from one of his great interpreters of the last century or so: Morna Hooker, Dietrich Bonhoeffer, and Wilhelm Wrede, respectively.[2] The quotation from Morna Hooker is specifically her summary of Romans 5–8. The traditional heart of Romans, in other words, is about what the Eastern church (especially) calls "theosis." Additionally, in *The Deliverance of God,* largely a study of Romans, with a particular emphasis on chapters 5–8, Douglas Campbell implies on two occasions that theosis may well describe Paul's soteriology.[3] And even

2. "Christ became what we are . . . image of God" is from Morna D. Hooker, *From Adam to Christ: Essays on Paul* (Cambridge: Cambridge University Press, 1990; repr. Eugene, OR: Wipf & Stock, 2008), p. 19. On the previous page (18), she writes in reference to Romans 8, "Christ became what we are, in order that (in him) we might become what he is." Hooker finds the same soteriological pattern throughout Paul, especially also in Galatians and 2 Corinthians. Christ "became like human beings . . . like him" is from Dietrich Bonhoeffer, *Discipleship,* Dietrich Bonhoeffer Works 4, trans. Barbara Green and Reinhard Krauss (Minneapolis: Augsburg Fortress, 2001), p. 285. "Christ becomes what we are . . . what he is" is from Wilhelm Wrede, *Paul,* trans. Edward Lummis (London: Green, 1907 [1904]), p. 110.

3. Douglas A. Campbell, *The Deliverance of God: An Apocalyptic Rereading of Justification in Paul* (Grand Rapids: Eerdmans, 2009), pp. 211, 265.

N. T. Wright, in his massive study of Paul, says that Paul's soteriology not only *can* be but *must* be described as theosis.[4]

For many Western Christians the term theosis is unknown or, if known, unwelcome or even suspect — perhaps bordering on heresy, especially when it is referred to as deification or divinization. Each of the words suggests transformation into the divine: humans becoming *theos* (Greek for "god") or *deus/divus* (Latin for "god"). Humans becoming gods, or even like God? May it never be! I have heard Protestant theologians in the Reformed tradition, for instance, react even to the mention of the word dismissively or, in (serious) jest, with a remark such as, "Sounds like something to be allergic to." One well-known biblical scholar said, at a scholarly conference, that theosis "scares the hell out of me, especially in the American context." Americans, he explained, do not need an even greater sense of superiority, power, and godlike status. And, as we noted in this book's Introduction, even some who are sympathetic to theosis have suggested that focusing on it inherently excludes a focus on mission.

But theosis will not go away so easily or quickly. And its connection to Romans and to mission will, I suggest, become quite clear as we proceed. It is the same kind of connection to mission for which we have been arguing throughout this book and with sharp focus in our discussion of 2 Corinthians.

In an essay published in 1990, Frances Young argued that Romans needs to be read in light of 2 Corinthians, for Romans develops some of the core themes of Paul's defense of his ministry sent to Corinth.[5] For those interested in theosis, this insight is particularly significant, because 2 Corinthians includes at least three explicitly "theotic" texts (3:18; 5:21; 8:9), two of which (5:21; 8:9) we examined in the previous chapter as examples of

4. N. T. Wright, *Paul and the Faithfulness of God,* vol. 4 of Christian Origins and the Question of God (Minneapolis: Fortress, 2013), p. 1021. The context is Wright's discussion of the church as the dwelling of God's Spirit. He says, "At this point a whole new theme opens up, which until recently would have been thought impossible for Paul, but which, in the light of the redefined election by the spirit, is not only possible but vital. If the spirit of the living God dwells within his people, constituting them as the renewed tabernacle (or the new temple . . .), then the work of this transforming spirit can and must be spoken of in terms, ultimately, of *theōsis,* 'divinization.'" (This is not to say that Wright, Campbell, I, and others all have the same understanding of theosis or its role in Paul's theology.) Perhaps one correction of this quotation is in order here: the tradition of speaking of Paul in terms of theosis is not recent but ancient, going back to the church fathers.

5. Frances M. Young, "Understanding Romans in the Light of 2 Corinthians," *Scottish Journal of Theology* 43 (1990): 433-46.

participatory righteousness/justice, briefly noting that this can properly be described as theosis.[6]

Second Corinthians 3:18 has been called "the most frankly theotic passage in Paul":[7] "And all of us, with unveiled faces, seeing the glory of the Lord as though reflected in a mirror, are being transformed into the same image from one degree of glory to another; for this comes from the Lord, the Spirit." Second Corinthians 5:21 — "For our sake he made him to be sin who knew no sin, so that in him we might become the righteousness [or justice] of God" — was identified by Morna Hooker as a key to Paul's soteriology of "interchange," which corresponds to the pattern of theosis as it has been historically understood in the Christian tradition.[8] This theotic text is also highly significant because it contains the language of both transformation ("so that . . . we might become," *hina hēmeis ginōmetha*) and justification (NRSV: "righteousness," *dikaiosynē*; perhaps better rendered "justice," as the previous chapter suggests), seamlessly interwoven. Another similar text is 2 Corinthians 8:9 ("For you know the generous act [*charin*; grace] of our Lord Jesus Christ, that though he was rich, yet for your sakes he became poor, so that by his poverty you might become rich"), which shows how practical this "doctrine" of interchange is for Paul, as he uses it to promote generosity and justice, specifically as a sign of Gentile-Jewish harmony (i.e., for the Jerusalem collection), at Corinth. We considered this in some detail in chapter seven.

In this chapter I will argue that Romans is about theosis. In fact, I would suggest that it is an early Christian *treatise* on theosis, a theological extension

6. In addition to the discussion in the previous chapter, see also my essay "Paul's Corporate, Cruciform, Missional Theosis in Second Corinthians," in *"In Christ" in Paul: Explorations in Paul's Theology of Union and Participation*, ed. Kevin J. Vanhoozer, Constantine R. Campbell, and Michael J. Thate, WUNT 2 series (Tübingen: Mohr Siebeck, 2015).

7. Stephen Finlan, "Can We Speak of *Theosis* in Paul?" in *Partakers of the Divine Nature: The History and Development of Deification in the Christian Traditions*, ed. Michael J. Christensen and Jeffery A. Wittung (Grand Rapids: Baker Academic, 2007), pp. 68-80 (p. 75).

8. I mean this in two senses: that interchange is the fundamental semantic and theological pattern of theosis, and that the resulting human transformation into the image of Christ ("Christosis") is transformation into the image of God ("theosis"). For more on these texts, see the discussion in the previous chapter, on justice. I am aware that N. T. Wright and others read the "we" of 5:21b as an apostolic reference, but that would almost require the impossible restriction of God's salvific action mentioned in 5:21a to Paul and colleagues. See N. T. Wright, "On Becoming the Righteousness of God: 2 Corinthians 5:21," in *Pauline Theology*, vol. 2, *1 & 2 Corinthians*, ed. David M. Hay (Minneapolis: Augsburg Fortress, 1992), pp. 200-208. As in the chapter on justice, the view proposed here is similar to that of A. Katherine Grieb, " 'So That in Him We Might Become the Righteousness of God' (2 Cor. 5:21): Some Theological Reflections on the Church Becoming Justice," *Ex Auditu* 22 (2006): 58-80.

of the theotic, or participationist and transformational, themes of justification and glorification found in 2 Corinthians. The subject of Romans is salvation *(sōtēria):* God's restoration of righteousness/justice *(dikaiosynē)* and glory *(doxa)* to unrighteous/unjust and glory-less humanity. Paul's soteriology of human *dikaiosynē* and *doxa* means participation in the divine *dikaiosynē* and *doxa* by participation in the death and resurrection of the Messiah Jesus, God's righteous and now glorified Son. Paul offers this interpretation of *sōtēria* explicitly as the fulfillment of Israel's hope for *sōtēria*, *dikaiosynē*, and *doxa* (salvation, righteousness/justice, and glory), extended now to the Gentiles. At the same time, at least implicitly, Paul holds out this message of *sōtēria* as the true gospel of God in contrast to the pseudo-gospel of Rome's *sōtēria*, *dikaiosynē*, and *doxa*. Romans, therefore, is an implicit invitation both to join in and to help spread the ultimate divine project: the fulfillment of God's promise to allow Israel and the nations to share in the justice/righteousness and glory of God. That is, theosis in Paul will have an inherent Christological, political, and missional character.

This argument extends the work of Wrede, Bonhoeffer, Hooker, Hays, and Campbell already noted, plus that of interpreters focused on Romans in particular, such as Ann Jervis.[9] Jervis argues that the purpose of discipleship in antiquity, for both Jews and Gentiles, was "to achieve likeness to God."[10] Richard Hays has said that the study of Paul's participationist soteriology needs to look East, in the direction of theosis, though he does not use that word.[11] In addition, there is great interest in Paul and theosis in emerging

---

9. L. Ann Jervis, "Becoming like God through Christ: Discipleship in Romans," in *Patterns of Discipleship in the New Testament,* ed. Richard N. Longenecker (Grand Rapids: Eerdmans, 1996), pp. 143-62. Neither Jervis nor the other scholars mentioned (except Campbell) use the term "theosis," but they all understand Paul's emphasis on participation and/or transformation in ways that are similar to at least some interpretations of theosis.

10. Jervis, "Becoming like God," p. 144. She shows how in Paul this desire for Godlikeness merges the " 'mystical' " (her term, meaning participationist) and the juridical dimensions of Paul's theology. Similar language, though less developed, can also be found in Udo Schnelle, *Theology of the New Testament,* trans. M. Eugene Boring (Grand Rapids: Baker Academic, 2009), pp. 261-62, 342-44.

11. Writes Richard Hays: "My own guess is that [E. P.] Sanders's insights [about participation in Paul] would be supported and clarified by careful study of participation motifs in patristic theology, particularly the thought of the Eastern Fathers" (*The Faith of Jesus Christ: The Narrative Substructure of Gal. 3:1–4:11,* 2nd ed. [Grand Rapids: Eerdmans, 2002 (orig. 1983)], p. xxxii). In the same context (p. xxix), Hays also expresses his attraction to the Eastern theological interest in "recapitulation" (starting with Irenaeus), over against most Western atonement theories.

scholars such as Ben Blackwell and David Litwa.[12] Blackwell, for instance, has written an essay, independently, with a thesis that is quite compatible with many of the claims of this chapter.[13]

In spite of such significant established and emerging voices, the claims of the chapter may concern certain readers, and that on three counts (apart from general concerns about theosis itself). First, some may say something like, "Romans is an occasional letter, not a theological treatise. This interpretation is backtracking several decades, if not centuries — perhaps to Melanchthon, who called Romans a 'compendium' of Christian teaching. 'Treatise' does not sound like much of an invitation to participation, much less to mission."

Second, others may say that, even if Romans is considered to be, in certain respects, a theological essay, how does one justify using the term "theosis" to characterize it? Why not justification or rectification by faith, salvation more generally, Gentile and Jewish harmony in Christ, the apocalyptic deliverance of God, hope, or resurrection? These all make sense and sound very Pauline. Others have argued that the theme of Romans is one or the other of these. But theosis? That sounds, at the very least, anachronistic, better used of a treatise by Irenaeus or Athanasius or the Ecumenical Patriarch.

Third, others may say that theosis, even if theologically and exegetically credible as an interpretation of Paul and of Romans in some sense, sounds hopelessly un-missional, perhaps even self-centered. And Romans, they will rightly add, is nothing if not a text about the gospel of salvation for all and the missional task of proclaiming the "obedience of faith" (Rom. 1:5; 16:26) and the Lordship of Jesus throughout the world (e.g., Romans 10).

Thus the title and the main contentions of this chapter that I have outlined may seem both inaccurate and anachronistic, with respect to the term "theosis," the notion of Romans as a "treatise" on anything, and the alleged

12. See, e.g., Ben C. Blackwell, "Immortal Glory and the Problem of Death in Romans 3.23," *Journal for the Study of the New Testament* 32 (2010): 285-308; and *Christosis: Pauline Soteriology in Light of Deification in Irenaeus and Cyril of Alexandria,* WUNT 2/314 (Tübingen: Mohr Siebeck, 2011); M. David Litwa, "2 Corinthians 3:18 and Its Implications for *Theosis,*" *Journal of Theological Interpretation* 2 (2008): 117-34; and *We Are Being Transformed: Deification in Paul's Soteriology,* BZNW 187 (Berlin: De Gruyter, 2012).

13. Ben C. Blackwell, "Righteousness and Glory: New Creation as Immortality in Romans" (delivered at the International SBL meeting, July 2, 2009). "The story of glory" is from ms. p. 12. In that paper, Blackwell argued that "glory" is only future (immortality) and that "the story of glory" ends in Romans 8. In his later *Christosis* (pp. 157-61), he has changed his mind and argues that glory begins in the present, and the theme continues into Romans 15.

connection between theosis and mission. We will begin by addressing the genre and theme of Romans. Concerns about theosis and mission will be handled once we turn to the text of Romans itself.

## Paul on Theosis: The Form of Romans and Its Master-Theme

Even an introductory treatment of the complex issues involved in identifying the interrelated subjects of the form and purpose, and thus also the theme, of Romans is beyond the scope of this chapter. Regarding the form of Romans, it must suffice to say that the overreaction to Melanchthon, Luther's assistant who called Romans a "compendium of Christian doctrine," has caused the pendulum to swing too far. Romans may not be a handbook of Christian doctrine, but neither is it your everyday letter, not even an everyday Pauline pastoral letter. After the formal address in 1:1-15, for eleven chapters there are few if any undisputed explicit references to the community/ies at Rome — a marked difference from every other Pauline letter. Thus Robert Jewett, in his commentary, keeps reminding us to make connections between each section of Romans and the overall purpose of the letter in light of the situation in Rome as he (Jewett) understands it.[14] Such strategies are needed because Paul himself does not make those explicit connections. And why not? In part, at least, because his letter — for whatever reason(s) — has the marks of a sustained treatise. Hans-Josef Klauck rightly notes that Romans "can be compared with the doctrinal letters of Epicurus or with the long pieces in the later books of Seneca's *Moral Epistles*. Yet over against these works Romans still remains more anchored to a particular situation. . . ."[15]

In other words, Romans is a peculiar kind of treatise. It is indeed a sustained, coherent treatment of a subject, both argumentative and narrative (with a plot and a variety of characters) in form. But ultimately, of course, the content of the treatise is intended for and applied to the Roman house churches. The question is, What is the subject matter of this "treatise"?

Some will surely respond, "We know what the theme of Romans is because Paul himself tells us, either in 1:16-17 (the gospel as the power of God for salvation, or the righteousness of God), or in 1:3-4 (Jesus the resurrected

14. Robert Jewett, *Romans,* Hermeneia (Minneapolis: Fortress, 2007), e.g., pp. 203-4, 218, 235.

15. Hans-Josef Klauck, *Ancient Letters and the New Testament: A Guide to Context and Exegesis* (Waco, TX: Baylor University Press, 2006), p. 304.

and royal Son of God), or, in bookend-fashion, in 1:5 and 16:26 (assuming this verse is part of the original letter[16]) — "the obedience of faith." Whichever of these is identified as the theme of Romans, one might argue, we do not need to import a foreign and anachronistic term such as "theosis" to replace Paul's own words.

I do not wish to discard any of the legitimately recognized themes of Romans, but I do wish to suggest that theosis needs to be added to the list of themes in the letter. Moreover, I want to argue that this theme is a kind of master-theme in the letter, encompassing (while not blotting out) certain other acknowledged themes.

We have already defined theosis (or deification, or divinization[17]) as, in brief, "becoming like God by participating in the life of God." It is imperative to note that the term and the reality it describes always maintain the creature-Creator distinction, even when a phrase like "becoming gods" is used to describe theosis, as has often been the case in the Christian tradition (due in part to the influence of Ps. 82:6; cf. John 10:34-36). Theosis, then, means taking on certain divine attributes, either in the present or in the age-to-come. The seventh-century Byzantine theologian Maximus the Confessor illustrated theosis by comparing it to the placing of an iron sword in a fire, such that it remains an iron sword but also takes on certain properties of the fire — light and heat — by "participating" in it.[18] Less metaphorically, but more famously, Irenaeus summarized the doctrine of theosis in his oft-quoted words: "He became what we are, so that we might become what he is."[19] Earlier we displayed quotations from various interpreters of Paul expressing this basic view.

16. See the commentaries for the issues and arguments.

17. Another term sometimes used is *theopoiesis*. The term is not restricted to Christian theology or experience. Within the Christian tradition, it is sometimes referred to as "Christification" or, more recently, "Christosis" (see Blackwell's book with that title). I am not here distinguishing, as some do, between theosis and divinization or deification, and I am not suggesting a difference between theosis and Christosis. Nor am I suggesting that we need to define these terms in precisely the same way that particular theologians and spiritual writers, past or present, have done. Instead, I am starting with a rather generic understanding of theosis and will then demonstrate its specifically Pauline formulation.

18. *Ambigua* 7; cf. opuscule 16.

19. This is something of a compilation of various specific quotes. In *Against Heresies* 5.Preface.1, Irenaeus says that the "Lord Jesus Christ . . . did, through his transcendent love, become what we are, that he might bring us to be even what he is himself." See also Athanasius, *Incarnation of the Word* 54. The two authors express the same basic theological conviction in various ways.

Three further brief points about theosis are needed, however, before we consider Romans.[20] First, there is debate about which divine attributes humans can take on, but it is generally agreed that these include holiness (i.e., God's moral character) and immortality. Theosis does not mean merely "ethical behavior" or "sanctification," but the present and future reality of becoming "participants [or 'partakers'] of the divine nature" (2 Pet. 1:4), which includes holiness but also eschatological transformation. Second, then, theosis is normally seen as a continuous process from earthly inception to eschatological completion, but it clearly has two stages, or dimensions, the temporal and the eschatological. Third, because Christians believe in the incarnation, theosis or deification cannot be separated from Christology. It means sharing in the likeness of the Son, who is the image of God. This is why deification/theosis can also be called Christification, or even Christosis. For Paul in particular, I have argued in *Inhabiting the Cruciform God*, theosis should be defined as follows:

> transformative participation in the kenotic [self-emptying], cruciform character of God through Spirit-enabled conformity to the incarnate, crucified, and resurrected/glorified Christ.[21]

Though "theosis" is not a specifically Pauline term, using it to describe this transformative participation is no less appropriate than using other "foreign" terms to describe Pauline theology, such as participatory, narrative,

---

20. For recent introductions to theosis, see Paul M. Collins, *Partaking in Divine Nature: Deification and Communion* (New York: T. & T. Clark, 2010); Norman Russell, *Fellow Workers with God: Orthodox Thinking on Theosis* (Crestwood, NY: St. Vladimir's Seminary Press, 2009); and Daniel A. Keating, *Deification and Grace* (Naples, FL: Sapientia, 2007). See also the following collections of essays: Michael J. Christensen and Jeffery A. Wittung, eds., *Partakers of the Divine Nature: The History and Development of Deification in the Christian Traditions* (Grand Rapids: Baker Academic, 2007); and Stephen Finlan and Vladimir Kharlamov, eds., *Theōsis: Deification in Christian Theology* (Eugene, OR: Pickwick, 2006). For works of Orthodox theology in which theosis is prominent in various ways, see John Behr, *The Mystery of Christ: Life in Death* (Crestwood, NY: St. Vladimir's Seminary Press, 2006); John D. Zizioulas, *Being as Communion: Studies in Personhood and the Church* (Crestwood, NY: St. Vladimir's Seminary Press, 1985); Panayiotis Nellas, *Deification in Christ: Orthodox Perspectives on the Nature of the Human Person*, trans. Norman Russell (Crestwood, NY: St. Vladimir's Seminary Press, 1987); and Vladimir Lossky, *The Mystical Theology of the Eastern Church* (Crestwood, NY: St. Vladimir's Seminary Press, 1976 [orig. in French, 1944]).

21. Michael J. Gorman, *Inhabiting the Cruciform God: Kenosis, Justification, and Theosis in Paul's Narrative Soteriology* (Grand Rapids: Eerdmans, 2009), pp. 7, 162.

or even apocalyptic. As the philosopher and literary critic Mikhail Bakhtin wisely said, "Semantic phenomena can exist in concealed form, potentially, and be revealed only in semantic cultural contexts of subsequent epochs that are favourable for such disclosure."[22]

"Theosis," then, should not be seen as anachronistic but as retrospectively appropriate. Now I would add that it should also be seen as retrospectively *accurate*.[23]

For the moment let us suppose that each of the texts named above (1:16-17; 1:3-4; ch. 10; 1:5 and 16:26), plus others we could summon, contributes to the theme of Romans, but let us also focus on the one that Paul seems to underscore by virtue of its place in the letter: at the beginning (1:5), and possibly also the end (16:26), of the letter: "the obedience of faith." Interpreters of Paul have differed significantly on the translation and meaning of this phrase. Does it signify the obedience that comes from faith, the obedience that is inseparable from faith, faithful obedience, believing fidelity or allegiance, or something else? No matter how we translate it, we must certainly recognize its connection to Christ, whom Paul characterizes as the *obedient* one (5:19) in contrast to disobedient Adam. And if, in addition, as I and others contend, there are phrases in Paul's letters that refer to the "faith" or the "faithfulness" of Jesus, then Paul also characterizes Christ as the *faithful* one, both here in Romans (3:22, 26) and elsewhere.[24] I would submit, therefore, that "the obedience of faith" is a soteriological term coined by Paul from his Christological convictions: life *in* Christ means fundamentally sharing in the obedience and faithfulness *of* Christ.

That is to say, "the obedience of faith" is, essentially, Christlikeness. Paul's mission was to bring about "the obedience of faith," resemblance to the obedient and faithful Son of God, among the nations. But as we will shortly see more fully, this Christlikeness is simultaneously Godlikeness. Thus enters, appropriately and accurately, the term "theosis." But of course for Paul (as I

---

22. Mikhail Bakhtin, *Speech Genres and Other Late Essays* (Austin: University of Texas Press, 1986).

23. Space does not permit a discussion of the broader theological question of concern to some, namely, the appropriateness of speaking of theosis at all, as noted above. I would contend that the solution for any legitimate concerns is to define and explain theosis properly, not to do away with the concept or term.

24. Gal. 2:16 (twice); 2:20; 3:22; Phil. 3:9. Cf. Eph. 3:12. That is, if the so-called subjective-genitive reading of *pistis Christou* ("faith of Christ" or "faith in Christ") and similar texts is right, which makes Christ the subject of faith: the "faith of Christ." See the discussions in earlier chapters.

have just noted) God, and thus theosis, can only be understood Christolog-ically; Paul's theosis is *cruciform* theosis, and it is corporate, or communal, because it is by common incorporation into Christ.

Thus we can describe Paul's mission by paraphrasing John Wesley's stated goal: to "spread scriptural holiness throughout the land." Paul's mission, I suggest, was to spread communal cruciform theosis, human participation in the divine *dikaiosynē* (justice/righteousness), and *doxa* (glory) throughout the world, meaning the Roman Empire.[25] It cannot be merely an accident that these two terms, *dikaiosynē* and *doxa*, were central to the empire's own identity and its own "gospel." Like many aspects of Roman ideology, Rome's claims to be the embodiment of justice and glory, and to offer justice and glory to its citizens, is at least implicitly challenged by Paul's letter to the Romans.[26] We will return to this below.

In the case of Rome itself, Paul's goal was to expand the presence of that *dikaiosynē* and *doxa* throughout the existing Roman house churches — right under the nose of the emperor, so to speak. The fullness of this salvation awaits the (imminent) arrival of Christ at the parousia, but it is realized partially and proleptically now in "righteoused" or "justice-ized"[27] communities of Gentiles and Jews who glorify God and practice cruciform faith, hope, and love together with a spirit of harmony in the midst of diversity. *They are communities of Spirit-enabled Christlike Godlikeness,* of righteousness and (cruciform) glory in anticipation of God's final glory and their participation in it. Thus my proposal about theosis in Romans is complementary to Beverly Gaventa's articulation of the mission of God according to Romans: God's work of "rescuing the world from the powers of Sin and Death so that a newly created humanity — Jew and Gentile — is released for the praise of God in community."[28]

25. Paul almost certainly saw his mission as part of the fulfillment of the prophetic promises that God's glory would one day be universally spread and recognized. Wesley, as we have noted in earlier chapters, defined salvation in theotic terms: "a recovery of the divine nature; the renewal of our souls after the image of God in righteousness and true holiness, in justice, mercy, and truth" (Gerald R. Cragg, ed., *The Works of John Wesley*, Vol. 11: *The Appeals to Men of Reason and Religion and Certain Related Open Letters* [Nashville: Abingdon, 1987], p. 106, para. 1.3).

26. On this aspect of Romans, see, among others, Wright, *Paul and the Faithfulness of God*, pp. 279-347, 1271-1319.

27. Although I do not like neologisms, and apologize for this one and its upcoming cognates, this approach is one way to keep the *dik-* family of words together in English *and* stress the moral or transformative side of the *dik-* language.

28. Beverly Roberts Gaventa, "The Mission of God in Paul's Letter to the Romans," in *Paul*

Finally, since we have already had a full chapter on justice/righteousness, a brief note on "glory" is also in order before we proceed to Romans itself. This is a relatively underexplored and yet contested area of Paul's theology. Ben Blackwell has surveyed various studies of glory in Paul and suggests that there are two related kinds, "social or relational status" ("honor"), part of Paul's honor-discourse; and "ontological experience," or "state of being," which is "related to the divine presence."[29] There has been significant and related debate about the background of Paul's glory-language: is it primarily Greco-Roman or Jewish? And if Jewish, to what specifically does it refer? It seems to be "something" that is both inherent to God and shareable with humanity. But does that mean splendor and radiance? Ethical perfection? Or perhaps immortality and thus, when shared with humans, the afterlife? Or is it the restoration of Adam's lost glory — perhaps meaning his dominion as God's steward (see Psalm 8)? Or perhaps it refers to the divine presence in the tabernacle/temple, or more specifically the return of God's presence to the temple in some way? Or the presence of God, and/or the reign of God, throughout the earth?[30]

While I would not discount the Greco-Roman influences on Paul, especially as he redefines honor and shame in the context of life in the crucified and resurrected Messiah, it seems clear that "glory" for him has primarily a set of Jewish connotations to which both scriptural and other Jewish texts bear witness.[31] In fact, it is quite possible that each of the Jewish nuances

---

as Missionary: Identity, Activity, Theology, and Practice, ed. Trevor J. Burke and Brian S. Rosner, Library of New Testament Studies 420 (London: T. & T. Clark, 2011), pp. 65-75 (here pp. 65-66).

29. Blackwell, "Righteousness and Glory," ms. p. 2. An important example of the former approach is Jewett, Romans.

30. Elements of all of these appear, for example, in Wright's Paul and the Faithfulness of God (see, e.g., p. 1075), though he especially stresses the rule of the creation by the renewed people of the Messiah (e.g., pp. 754, 843, 1091-92, 1116-17, 1126): "The point is that Israel's God justifies humans, puts them right, so that they can be people through whom the world is put right. That rule over the world, in both present and future, is what in Romans 8 Paul denotes by the language of 'glory'" (p. 1092). While I agree with Wright that glory is both present and future, I find his arguments for glorification as dominion to have little basis in Paul himself. Carey Newman summarizes these various understandings into four groups: theophany, including splendor and visibility; presence in the tabernacle/temple; eschatological hope; and kingly dominion (Carey C. Newman, Paul's Glory-Christology: Tradition and Rhetoric, NovTSup 69 [Leiden: Brill, 1992], p. 152).

31. I am indebted to the work of my student Daniel Jackson on glory, especially his (unpublished) paper "The 'Glory About to Be Revealed': Glory in Paul's Letter to the Romans" (St. Mary's Seminary & University, May 2013). He argues convincingly that the Jewish background is determinative for Paul's own understanding of glory.

regarding divine glory and its shareability with humans noted above impacts Paul in various places in Romans. The various understandings are not mutually exclusive.

Blackwell places special emphasis on the connection between divine and human glory as "denot[ing] the [human] experience of divine life," specifically as immortality.[32] Blackwell cites C. F. Evans in support of this claim: glory, according to Evans, is "an eschatological term which comes nearest to denoting the divine life itself," the foretaste of which, says Evans, is life in the Spirit.[33] While it seems to be the case that the primary reference to humans' sharing in God's glory is, for Paul in Romans, immortality, or eternal life, that eternal life is an *embodied* existence, as Romans, the Corinthian correspondence, and Philippians all make clear. (Apart from Romans, see especially 1 Cor. 15:35-57; 2 Cor. 5:1-4; Phil. 3:21.) This cannot be because God (the Father) has a body, but because Paul's understanding of glory has been Christologically reshaped. The crucified and resurrected Jesus is the image of God into which believers are being remade (cf. 2 Cor. 4:1-7). It is God's desire (according to the prophets), and thus Paul's desire, that this glory be known and experienced throughout the world.

The "glory" of God, then, refers to the eternal splendor and honor that God has by virtue of being God and that God has chosen to share with humanity. It is a central conviction of the Jewish and Christian Scriptures that God already shares this glory in various but limited ways with human beings, and in turn humans give glory (honor, praise) to God as their appropriate response to God's glory. At the same time, the eschatological hope of both Testaments is for humans to share in this divine glory in ways hitherto unexperienced and even unimagined, with a corollary increase in the glory rendered to God. Paul himself possesses this hope for the glory of both humanity and God. Indeed, this hope is central to his letter to the Romans.

## Rereading Romans as a Text on Cruciform, Missional Theosis

The bulk of the remainder of the chapter will offer a rereading of Romans from the perspective of theosis, specifically a cruciform, missional interpre-

---

32. Blackwell, "Righteousness and Glory," passim (quotation from ms. p. 2).

33. C. F. Evans, *Resurrection and the New Testament* (London: SCM, 1970), p. 160, cited in "Righteousness and Glory," ms. p. 4 n. 8. Evans says that "[T]he present possession of spirit, which is all there is, is a foretaste and promise of something further, which is the full life of 'glory.'"

tation of theosis, highlighting some parts of the letter more than others. Will this sound like an old perspective, a new perspective, or a fresh perspective? Yes — and no. Among other things, reading Paul with the question of theosis in mind will transcend, and perhaps even break down, certain categories.

## *The Human Condition: Lacking Righteousness and Glory (Rom. 1:18–3:20)*

Romans 1:18–3:20 is a creative rereading of Genesis 3, Wisdom 12–14, Exodus 32, Psalm 89 and several other psalms, plus additional texts, through the prism of salvation, righteousness, and glory in Christ. Despite the protestations of Douglas Campbell,[34] it constitutes Paul's depiction of the human condition outside of Christ, which is one of "frustration" or "futility" (*emataiōthēsan,* 1:21[35]) — not fulfilling the purpose God intended.[36] That purpose can be described, implicitly, as harmony and proper relations between humanity and God, within humanity itself, and between humanity and the rest of creation. The language of "image of God" is at least in the background (*homoiōmati eikonos,* 1:23; NRSV "images resembling [a mortal human being]").

More specifically, this section of Romans either asserts or infers that humans are to give thanks and glory/honor to God (1:21), do good (2:7) by acting justly and righteously toward their fellow humans, and not glorify the creature instead of the creator (1:23, 25). Furthermore, according to 2:7-10 humanity is intended ultimately for glory (*doxa,* twice), honor (*timē,* twice), peace, immortality, and eternal life, this being the intended and natural result of the normal human life of doing good (rather than unrighteousness/ injustice [*adikia*] and evil), that God intended. Thus *dikaiosynē* and *doxa,* meaning present righteousness/justice and future glory *(doxa),* including eternal life, are two key terms that summarize Paul's understanding of humanity's raison d'être.

---

34. In *The Deliverance of God* (esp. pp. 519-600), Campbell argues that the bulk of this section of Romans represents the perspective of Paul's opponent, the Teacher, not Paul. In *Deliverance* he refers to the text as "speech-in-character," whereas more recently he has used the language of "parody." See, e.g., his response to the criticisms of Robin Griffith-Jones in Chris Tilling, ed., *Beyond Old and New Perspectives on Paul: Reflections on the Work of Douglas Campbell* (Eugene, OR: Cascade, 2014), pp. 176-81.

35. A condition now shared by the rest of creation (8:20).

36. See James D. G. Dunn, *Romans 1–8,* WBC 38A (Dallas: Word, 1988), pp. 71, 470, 487-88.

Humanity is currently characterized, however, by the opposite of these divine intentions. Paul supplies us with numerous terms and phrases to describe this condition, some perhaps geared primarily toward Gentiles and others toward Jews. Among them are:

- 1:18: ungodliness and unrighteousness/injustice (*asebeia* and *adikia*, the latter mentioned twice[37]);
- 1:21: failing to glorify (*edoxasan*, from *doxazō*[38]) and thank God;
- 1:21-22: futile thinking, darkened minds, foolishness;
- 1:23, 25, 28: "exchang[ing] the glory *(doxan)* of the immortal God for images *(homoiōmati eikonos)* resembling a mortal human being" or animals; "exchange[ing] the truth about God for a lie and worship[ing] and serv[ing] the creature rather than the Creator"; not "acknowledg[ing] God";
- 1:24, 26: "impurity" and "degrading passions";
- 1:29-31: "every [kind of] unrighteousness/injustice (*adikia;* NRSV 'wickedness'), evil . . .";
- 1:32: the just divine decree (*dikaiōma;* NRSV, "decree") that practitioners of these things (all the forms of *asebeia* and *adikia*) deserve death;
- 2:23: "dishonor[ing] God by breaking the law";
- 3:3: faithless (cf. 1:31);
- 3:9: "under the power of sin";
- 3:10-11: " 'There is no one who is righteous [*dikaios*], not even one; there is no one who has understanding, there is no one who seeks God'"; and
- 3:23: "all have sinned and fall short of the glory *(doxēs)* of God."

Despite the frequent failure of the NRSV, especially in 1:18-32, to show the interconnections among key phrases and between those phrases and 1:17 *(dikaiosynē)*, Paul insists that the common human problem revolves around the referents of the words *dikaiosynē* and *doxa.*[39] *Adikia,* the opposite of *dikaiosynē,* leads not to *doxa,* to glorious life, but to death. Human beings

---

37. The NRSV, NIV, and NAB unfortunately obscure a key linguistic and theological link in Paul generally, and in Romans particularly, by translating *adikia* as "wickedness" rather than as "unrighteousness" or "injustice." See also the discussion of this problem in the chapter on justice.

38. The NRSV (though not the NIV or NAB) once again obscures an important linguistic and theological connection in Romans by translating the verb "glorify" as "honor."

39. As was the case for the Corinthian correspondence, the NJB does a better job than most English translations with Romans, using "injustice" in both 1:18 and 1:29.

have become something other than what they were intended to become, and their fate is something other than their intended *telos*. "Exchange" — of right relations with God, with one another, and with all creation — has become the order of the day (1:23, 25, 26).

In such a situation humans do not need merely a word of forgiveness with the chance for a new start, much less a legal fiction;[40] they need a powerful means of undoing the exchange, a powerful means of becoming the righteousness of God that God intended, a powerful means of attaining the glory they lack. Paul, of course, believes that this happens in Christ, for the gospel is "the power of God for salvation" (1:16). The West's fixation on sin and guilt has sometimes hampered us from seeing how central to Paul's anthropology and soteriology are the themes of glory, life, and immortality — both their absence in Adam and their restored presence in Christ.

Christopher Bryan writes that when Paul in Romans 3:23 says humanity falls short of the glory of God, he is speaking of "that very [divine] glory which, by being what it is, would also be our glory."[41] If we return to Romans 1, we learn more specifically what losing or lacking the glory of God now means. Humanity was created to glorify God and to live honorably with other human beings; instead, the human race has failed to glorify God, has descended into shame in relations with others, has expressed its enmity toward God and others in all sorts of creative ways, and has learned that death is the ultimate and natural consequence of this downward spiral (its "wages," according to 6:23). It is a story of sin and shame and death.[42]

The solution to the human predicament, as many Jews of Paul's day thought, is restoration to glory.[43] For Paul specifically, that will mean to reverse the headlong, sin-filled descent into death by means of something that liberates from both Sin and Death,[44] that restores humanity to a place of

40. The phrase "legal fiction" refers to certain interpretations of justification as God's "legal" pronouncement of human righteousness, because of Christ, which is made in spite of the reality of human unrighteousness and thus is, technically, a fiction.

41. Christopher Bryan, *A Preface to Romans: Notes on the Epistle in Its Literary and Cultural Setting* (New York: Oxford University Press, 2000), p. 84. Dunn suggests that Paul means that humans have both lost (because of Adam) and now fail to attain God's glory (*Romans 1–8*, p. 108).

42. See Blackwell, "Immortal Glory." Blackwell argues that in Romans "glory denotes not only elevated honour but also incorruption. Thus, the lack of glory in 3:23 refers to mortality and shame as the result of sin" (abstract, p. 285).

43. Dunn, *Romans 1–8*, p. 168.

44. I capitalize "Sin" and "Death" to indicate their being powers that can dominate human existence and from which humans need liberation.

glorifying God and honoring others, that creates a community of *pistis* and *dikaiosynē* rather than *apistia/asebeia* and *adikia*.[45] What humanity needs is a present godly and Godlike life free of Sin, and a future, eternal life free of Death. In other words, humanity needs to share in the divine *moral* character and the divine *eternal* character. That is, humans are in need of righteousness and immortality, the chief characteristics of God associated with theosis.

## The Divine Solution: The Gifts of Justice/Righteousness and Glory (Rom. 3:21–8:39)

For Paul the solution to the human condition of sin and death, of unrighteousness and unglory, is new and eternal life by participation in Christ. This participation provides the "space" for the Spirit-enabled ethical and eschatological transformation that human beings need. In Christ, humans begin sharing in the righteousness of God and even begin the process of sharing in God's glory. This is because God's righteousness and glory are found in Christ, and those who are in Christ are being transformed (12:1-2) and conformed into the image of Christ (8:29; cf. 2 Cor. 3:18), who is the true image of God (2 Cor. 4:4), both as divine Son and as last and true Adam. In Morna Hooker's words quoted earlier: "Christ became what we are — *'adam* — in order that we might share in what he is — namely the true image of God."[46]

### Faith and Participation (3:21–4:25)

In Romans 3:21-26 Paul explains that God has provided the solution to the human crisis of sin and death: forgiveness (3:25, expiation) and liberation (3:24, redemption) for those who share in the faith of Christ (3:26; cf. 3:22).[47] God's gracious gift is explicitly described as the "justifying" or "righteousing"

---

45. That is, faithfulness and justice (righteousness) rather than unfaithfulness (unbelief)/ ungodliness and injustice (unrighteousness).

46. Hooker, *From Adam to Christ*, p. 19, summarizing Romans 5–8.

47. In 3:22 and 3:26 there are variants of the *pistis Christou* phraseology discussed earlier in the chapter. Despite the common translation of "faith in Jesus [Christ]," the preferable rendering is "the faith of Jesus [Christ]," with the meaning that God's justice/righteousness is revealed in the faithfulness of Christ (3:22), and that the just/righteous God justifies those who have, or share, this faithfulness of Christ (3:26; cf. 4:16 for similar wording about sharing the faith/faithfulness of Abraham). The primary focus of 3:21-26 is sin; both sin and death receive attention in chapter 6.

of humans (3:24, 26), and implicitly described as well as their restoration to the glory they have lost (3:23). The human role in this is *pisteuein/pistis* (3:22, 26), traditionally translated "believe" and "faith," but Paul's notion of faith is much more participatory than is often thought. In fact, 3:21-26 should be read in connection with chapter 6, which does not describe a supplement to "justification by faith" but rather depicts baptism, the public expression of the event of justification, as a participatory experience of death and resurrection (see further below).

Romans 4, I want to suggest, offers Abraham as a prototype of this death and resurrection with Christ. If this is correct, then Abraham serves as an example of Paul's unique participatory understanding of justification by faith as co-crucifixion and co-resurrection with Christ (4:16-17).[48] The basic argument here is rather simple: because Abraham himself was functionally dead (4:19a) — along with his wife's womb (4:19b) — his faith was that God could bring life out of *his* death, could transform *his* deadness into life. In other words, his faith was completely self-involving and participatory. That he was justified by faith means not that he was fictitiously considered just or righteous, but that he was granted the gracious gift of new life out of death, which was concretely fulfilled in the birth of a descendant — a very Jewish notion of life and resurrection rooted in biblical stories like the one to which Paul appeals in Romans 4.[49] This resurrection life is actualized, not merely in the birth of Isaac, but in the subsequent reality of many descendants (4:16-18). This foreshadows and signals the reality of new and eternal resurrection life provided by God in the resurrection of Jesus, which took place for *our* justification (4:24-25), i.e., *our* resurrection to life. In retrospect, from Paul's own position of having died and been resurrected in Christ, Abraham's experience is prospectively analogous to what Paul says about all baptized believers in Romans 6: their justification by faith means a participatory experience of resurrection out of death, for God is the one who "gives life to the dead"

---

48. "Prototype" and "example" are not quite sufficient to describe Abraham's role; he is the parent, the source, but of course he is such without displacing Christ, God the Father, or the Spirit. For this understanding of justification as co-crucifixion and co-resurrection, see Gal. 2:15-21, Romans 6, and the discussion of both in my *Inhabiting the Cruciform God*, pp. 40-104.

49. See Kevin J. Madigan and Jon D. Levenson, *Resurrection: The Power of God for Christians and Jews* (New Haven: Yale University Press, 2008), pp. 107-20. They speak of the barren womb and the bereavement of progeny as the functional equivalent of death (p. 112), and birth and progeny as "the reversal of death" and thus "to a large degree the functional equivalent of resurrection (or afterlife in general)" (p. 113). "In these stories, it is not death but birth that is God's last word" (p. 113).

(4:17). Thus Abraham's righteousness and his eternal life — his glory, so to speak[50] — are inseparable.

### The Present and Future of Theosis (5:1-8:39)

Chapters 5 through 8 of Romans do not present a narrative sequence of the believer's life in Christ, as is often thought.[51] Rather, they present a set of various explanations of the meaning of participating in the narrative of Christ, that is, salvation as Christlike *dikaiosynē* and *doxa,* or cruciform theosis. Douglas Campbell rightly insists in *The Deliverance of God* that the material content of Romans 5–8 is transformation or sanctification or "ontological reconstitution," and that it is not supplemental to the gospel or to justification but constitutive of them.[52] And Richard Hays rightly argues that "[u]ltimately, *being united with Christ is salvific because to share his life is to share in the life of God."*[53] Following an overview in 5:1-11 that depicts salvation in its various interrelated dimensions (justification, peace, love, grace, reconciliation, hope, final glory), Paul presents new life in Christ in terms of three pairs of antitheses: 5:12-21; 6:1–7:6; and 7:7–8:39.[54]

In 5:12-21, the first antithesis, Paul contrasts the righteousness and life that come from Christ with the unrighteousness and death that proceed from Adam. In 5:18-19, he describes Christ's death as an act of obedience and righteousness that effects righteousness, justification, and life for all who are in him. This act is juxtaposed to that of Adam, an act of disobedience and unrighteousness that effected condemnation and death for all who are in him. Implicitly, the contrast is between those who do, and will, share in God's glory (righteousness and eternal life) noted in 5:2, and those who do not and will not share in it.

In 6:1–7:6, the second antithesis, Paul contrasts slavery to sin with slav-

---

50. Unlike humanity in Romans 1, Abraham "gave glory to God" (4:20), a sign, for Paul, of restoration to and participation in God's own glory. See the discussion of Romans 15 below.

51. The sequence is sometimes thought to run something like this: justification and new life → the beginnings of sanctification → struggles with sin → victory over sin by the work of the Spirit.

52. Campbell, *The Deliverance of God,* p. 185 (and elsewhere).

53. Hays, *The Faith of Jesus Christ,* p. xxxiii; emphasis added. For the narrative character of salvation and participation in Paul, see the entirety of Hays's *The Faith of Jesus Christ* and his article "Christ Died for the Ungodly: Narrative Soteriology in Paul?" *Horizons in Biblical Theology* 26 (2004): 48-69.

54. On the interpretation of Romans 5–8, see my *Apostle of the Crucified Lord: A Theological Introduction to Paul and His Letters* (Grand Rapids: Eerdmans, 2004), pp. 363-79.

ery to righteousness. He explains that participation in Christ's death (Christ's act of obedience and righteousness) and resurrection brings new life and therefore righteousness and obedience in the present, plus eternal life in the future. As I have argued at length elsewhere, this should be understood as justification/righteousness/life by means of co-crucifixion.[55] And as Daniel Kirk has persuasively argued, Paul sees new life in Christ as present participation in Christ's resurrection, with eternal life, obviously, as future participation in his resurrection.[56] We should therefore see present newness of life and future eternal life with more continuity than discontinuity; they are two dimensions of one participatory soteriological reality, theosis.

In the early part of Romans 6, Paul affirms that we are baptized into Christ's death and raised to new life. Three important things emerge here:

- Baptism is transfer into Christ.
- Baptism is participation in Christ's death, i.e., his act of obedience and righteousness (linking chapter 6 back to 5:12-21).
- Baptism is participation in Christ's resurrection, both now (as new life; 6:4, 6-7, 11) and later (as eternal life; 6:8).

In the rest of Romans 6, Paul describes more fully how this participation in Christ means taking on the qualities of Christ's death and resurrection, i.e., new life and eternal life. Believers are already "alive to God" (6:11) and will one day share in "eternal life" (6:22-23).

Thus in Romans 6 Paul presents the divine goal for humanity: that *in* Christ, we might become *like* Christ in embodying both his righteousness — "the obedience of faith" — and his resurrection life. Furthermore, since Christ embodied the righteousness and faithfulness of God, and since his life-out-of-death was effected by "the glory of the Father" (6:4) so too our current walking in newness of life is a proleptic and partial, but very real, participation in that divine glory, a sharing in the very life of God. It is glory *regained,* glorification *now.*[57] The hope of final and full glory is still precisely that — a hope. Moreover, as Paul will indicate especially in chapters 8 and 12–15, any present resurrection or glory is always and necessarily cruciform.

To this point in Romans there has been little that might be called "mis-

---

55. Gorman, *Inhabiting the Cruciform God,* pp. 40-104.

56. J. R. Daniel Kirk, *Unlocking Romans: Resurrection and the Justification of God* (Grand Rapids: Eerdmans, 2008), pp. 107-17. See also my *Inhabiting the Cruciform God,* pp. 40-104.

57. Similar is Paul's claim in 2 Cor. 5:17 that new creation is (partially and proleptically) *now.* See also 2 Cor. 3:18 for present and future glory.

sional" in the centrifugal sense of the community's outreach or presence in the world (centrifugal activity). But in chapter 6, the life Paul describes is an apocalyptic battle involving the presentation of believers' selves to God and to justice/righteousness (6:11-23), their members as "weapons" (*hopla*; 6:13, twice; cf. 13:12) in the battle, as we noted in the discussion of Romans and peace in chapter five. That is, the mission of God is to create a people who share in this battle by their new life in the world, as (once again) Romans 12–15 will make clear.

In 7:7–8:39, the third antithesis, Paul contrasts life in the flesh with life in Christ and the Spirit, the former characterized by sin and death, the latter by righteousness (8:4) and life (8:2, 6).[58] Paul summarizes this contrast nicely in 8:10, and then he indicates in 8:11 that the present and future dimensions of salvation are closely related as two aspects of participation in the life of the Spirit: "If the Spirit of him who raised Jesus from the dead dwells in you [present], he who raised Christ from the dead will give life to your mortal bodies also through his Spirit that dwells in you [future]."[59]

Indeed, Romans 8 as a whole concerns the present and future dimensions of salvation. Each has a cruciform shape. Present righteousness, which receives more attention early in the chapter, requires "put[ting] to death the deeds of the body" (8:13), while future co-glorification, the focus of the later part of the chapter, requires prior co-suffering (8:17).[60] The two dimensions of the narrative of salvation are still closely related, even in the second half of the chapter, as the phrase "we were saved in hope" (8:24) clearly demonstrates.

Paul in this context also tells us the ultimate *telos* of human existence: experiencing the "freedom of the glory *(doxa)* of the children of God" (8:21) and conformity to Christ the Son of God (8:29; *symmorphous tēs eikonos tou huiou autou*). But is the conformity mentioned in 8:29 — "those whom [God] foreknew he also predestined to be conformed to the image of his Son" — an ethical (present) or an eschatological conformity, or both? The emphasis here is probably on the eschatological, though the somewhat similar language of 2 Corinthians 3:18 (*metamorphoumetha*; NRSV "[all of us] are being transformed") and Romans 12:2 (*metamorphousthe*; NRSV "be

---

58. Sin: 7:8-9, 11, 13, 14, 17, 20, 23, 25; 8:2; death: 7:10, 11, 13, 24; 8:2, 6.

59. See also 8:12-13, which shows the same continuity, as well as its converse: the continuity between present life according to the flesh and future death.

60. Cf. Blackwell, "Righteousness and Glory," ms. p. 4: "In chapter 8 the death-life dialectic is central . . . , and my contention is that the glory-suffering dialectic in the second half of the chapter repeats that death-life contrast through different terms."

transformed") will not permit us to rule out an ethical transformation.[61] The question, however, really presents a false dichotomy; conformity to Christ is both present and future; it is both ethical and ontological. Romans 8:29 is the primarily ontological, primarily eschatological counterpart of 8:3-4: "For God has done what the law, weakened by the flesh, could not do: by sending his own Son in the likeness of sinful flesh, and to deal with sin, he condemned sin in the flesh, so that the just requirement of the law might be fulfilled in us, who walk not according to the flesh but according to the Spirit." This passage, in turn, is an echo of 2 Corinthians 5:21, that fundamental text of interchange or, as we have suggested, theosis.[62]

There is a sense, of course, in which ethical conformity precedes and is the prerequisite for eschatological, ontological conformity, but the two are related, indeed inseparable: two dimensions of the same reality, the same narrative, participatory salvation. Paul has already clearly indicated this inseparable connection in 8:17: "and if children, then heirs, heirs of God and joint heirs with Christ — if, in fact, we suffer with him so that we may also be glorified with him." The narrative pattern of Christ, from suffering to glory, from death to resurrection, becomes our pattern. In other words, Christlikeness now — faithful obedience even to the point of suffering and death — becomes Christlikeness later: glory. The process is seamless, and it may be termed "Christosis."[63]

But that term, though accurate, is insufficient. Paul avers that God's eternal plan is to create a family of siblings who resemble the firstborn and definitive Son, namely, Jesus. What Paul does not state explicitly is the obvious: that the Son is like the Father, and that the siblings will ultimately be like the Father because they are like the Son. Christosis, therefore, is ultimately theosis.[64]

All of this transformation takes place in and through the Spirit, who is mentioned nearly twenty times in Romans 8. Of course the Spirit is not working as a kind of independent contractor but is in a triadic relationship with the Father and the Son. But if we are to understand the mission of God in Christ fully for Paul, we cannot do so without giving proper place to the

61. So also, e.g., Jewett, *Romans*, pp. 528-30. Even if 2 Cor. 3:18 is referring only to apostolic transformation (which is unlikely), then Frances Young is right to say that in Romans Paul is "generalising his own sense of vocation" ("Understanding Romans," p. 438).

62. Young says that 2 Cor. 5:21 "surely explains" Rom. 8:3 ("Understanding Romans," p. 440).

63. See Blackwell, *Christosis*.

64. See Gorman, *Inhabiting the Cruciform God*, pp. 9-39.

work of the Spirit. It is the Spirit in whom believers live and who lives in believers (8:9); indeed the very purpose of the Spirit is to give life (8:10-13), making them know their status as children of God the Father and joint heirs with Christ (8:14-17). The second half of Romans 8 makes it clear that all this is true in spite of suffering. In fact, the main suffering to which Paul refers, at least with respect to himself, is what we might call "missional" suffering: suffering as a result of proclaiming the gospel (8:36). And such suffering is normal, even "required," for those in Christ because his own glorification was preceded by suffering (8:17). That is, the mission of God has a pattern of being accomplished in and through suffering, even though suffering is not the end of the story. Paul here is assisting his audience to accept the reality that the power of the gospel for salvation is also, often, powerfully opposed by those who are threatened by a divine purpose that challenges the world's status quo. The mission of God does not go forward without opposition.

The divine purpose for believers in this age of suffering prior to glory is indicated in 8:29: predestination to conformity to Christ, meaning ultimately to God the Father and by the working of the Spirit. This purpose is further elaborated in 8:30. In this verse a series of verbs, presented in stairstep fashion, narrates the saving activity of God: predestined, called, justified, glorified. This series is often taken as a reference to the *ordo salutis,* the order of God's saving acts toward the individual. But in context the last three verbs are more precisely an elaboration of what God has done to create a family of Christlike (which is to say Godlike) siblings. Paul's point is not to define an order so much as to stress the effectiveness and totality of God's saving action. More than a desire (predestination/election), more even than a summons (call), God's salvation means righteousification and restoration to right covenant relations (justification, or "justice-ification") and participation in the glory of God (glorification). The absence of "sanctification" between "justification" and "glorification" has sometimes puzzled interpreters. It now becomes clear why it is not there: *Paul does not conceive of sanctification as a stage of salvation between justification and glorification.* Rather, justification/righteousification and glorification, new life and eternal life, *dikaiosynē* and *doxa,* are two inseparable dimensions of God's overall salvation project.

This brings us to the use of the aorist (generally indicating the past tense) verb "glorified" in 8:30: "And those whom he predestined he also called; and those whom he called he also justified; and those whom he justified he also glorified." How can Paul speak of glory in this age of suffering?

Was not Christ glorified only *after* suffering? Many commentators argue that "glorified" does not refer literally to a past event or experience. They stand on an apparently firm foundation of texts such as 5:2 ("our hope of sharing the glory of God") and 8:17-18 ("so that we may also be glorified with him . . . the glory about to be revealed to us"). Thus they offer several different interpretations of the aorist:

- a proleptic, futuristic, or prophetic aorist: a future action is so certain that it may be narrated in the past tense;
- a properly theological use of the aorist: a future action is already complete from the timeless, eternal perspective of God;
- an ahistorical use of the aorist: like "predestined," "glorified" expresses a view of salvation events that occur outside of time as we know it, unlike "called" and "justified," which refer to events within time;
- a punctiliar/nontemporal aorist: an action is perceived and described with respect to its aspect (one-time or completed character), not its temporality; or
- a liturgical aorist: an act celebrated in baptism or worship, the language for which is borrowed by Paul but not representative of his theology.[65]

While each of these interpretations could make sense of the text in isolation, or in connection only with texts that clearly refer to the future experience of glory, there are at least five reasons to think that Paul believes that the glorification of humanity in Christ has already begun.[66]

First, this is the implicit argument of Romans to this point. Because resurrection and glory are inseparable, the partial and proleptic resurrection experience described in Romans 6 implies that believers already have a foretaste of the coming glory.

Second, and similarly, there exists in Romans 8 a "dialectic" of "present/hidden — future/revealed" that is articulated in terms of both "sonship [being 'children of God'; NRSV] and glory."[67] Because of the Spirit, being God's children is both a present reality (8:14-15) and a reality still to be revealed and expanded (8:19-21). The situation is the same with glory (8:18,

---

65. For example, Dunn (*Romans 1-8*, pp. 485-86) leans toward the first and the third; Leander Keck (*Romans*, Abingdon New Testament Commentary [Nashville: Abingdon, 2005], pp. 217-18) prefers the second. The terms for the types of aorists are partly my own.

66. So also, with some similar arguments, Jewett, *Romans*, p. 530.

67. Andrzej Gieniusz, *Romans 8:18-30: "Suffering Does Not Thwart the Future Glory"* (Atlanta: Scholars Press, 1999), p. 280.

21 versus 8:30). The certainty of future glorification is not only that Christ has been glorified, but also that *our* glorification has already been "set in motion."[68] And this is true for the missional community of the Messiah even in the midst of sharing in his sufferings.

Third, Paul will indicate in Romans 14 and 15 that the renewed, missional community of Gentiles and Jews in Christ embodies (or should embody) the glory of God, as we will see below.

Fourth, moving outside Romans, in 2 Corinthians 3:7-11, 18 we see Paul speaking of a present glory, though he does so, as in Romans 8, only in connection with cruciform existence (2 Cor. 4:8-12) and the future "eternal weight of glory beyond all measure" (2 Cor. 4:17).

Finally, looking behind Romans, indeed outside the New Testament, we note that Isaiah 55 describes the people's glorification, in the past tense (*edoxasen*), as follows:

> ³Incline your ear, and come to me; listen, so that you may live. I will make with you an everlasting covenant, my steadfast, sure love for David. . . . ⁵See, you shall call nations that you do not know, and nations that do not know you shall run to you, because of the LORD your God, the Holy One of Israel, *for he has glorified [edoxasen] you.* ⁶Seek the LORD while he may be found, call upon him while he is near; ⁷let the wicked forsake their way, and the unrighteous their thoughts; let them return to the LORD, that he may have mercy on them, and to our God, for he will abundantly pardon. (Isa. 55:3, 5-7, emphasis added)[69]

Here glorification is linked specifically to themes we see in Romans: God's love, witnessing to the nations, forgiveness of sin, and the transformation of the unrighteous. I would suggest that this text has influenced Paul's understanding of glory. *It is as the missional community, sought out for salvation by God and sharing that salvation with others, that the believers in Rome — and believers of all time — participate now in the glory of God.*

This present reality of glorification does not, of course, eliminate the future fullness of glory. Present, missional glory is partial, proleptic, and — paradoxically — cruciform. Glory is God's redemptive purpose for

---

68. The phrase is from the heading of Gieniusz's discussion (*Romans 8:18-30*, pp. 278-81).

69. Cf. also the universal summons to salvation and the promise of Israel's glorification in the context (Isa. 45:20-25) of a text (Isa. 45:23) that Paul uses in Rom. 14:11; Isa. 45:25 reads, "In the LORD all the offspring of Israel shall triumph and glory." See also Isa. 46:12-13.

humanity. As Dunn puts it, referring back to Romans 1: "It is a finely conceived reversal that the *doxazein* [glorifying] that man failed to give to his Creator in the beginning is finally resolved in God's *doxazein* [glorifying] of man."[70]

### Righteousness and Glory for Israel (Romans 9–11)

Critical to any recent interpretation of Romans is its understanding of the place of chapters 9–11 in the letter. What, then, does this section of Romans have to do with theosis and with mission?

The first thing to be said is that Paul does not substantially develop his view of the *content* of justice/righteousness and glory in these chapters. Rather, Paul argues primarily that God's irrevocable gift and promise to Israel (11:29) will mean their ultimate receipt of the justice/righteousness they currently lack (9:31; 10:3; cf. 11:31) and the glory that was their own heritage (9:4). That is, if we define theosis as sharing in God's justice/righteousness and glory, then that is precisely the focus of Romans 9–11. The divine mission includes Israel, and the promise to accomplish that mission is irrevocable (11:29).

This section of Romans begins with Paul's frustration, expressed in a lament about what he later characterizes as the unbelief/faithlessness (11:20, 23), disobedience (10:16, 21), and misguided zeal (10:2-4) of the majority of his fellow Jews:

> [4]They are Israelites, and to them belong the adoption, the glory, the covenants, the giving of the law, the worship, and the promises; [5]to them belong the patriarchs, and from them, according to the flesh, comes the Messiah, who is over all, God blessed forever. Amen. (Rom. 9:4-5)

Paul aches for his people (9:2-3; 10:1), and the deepest source of the apostle's pain is the tragic irony that God's glory — among other gifts and graces, including the Messiah himself — "belongs" to Israel, to his people. It appears that the "story of glory," at least with respect to (most of) Israel, has come to a screeching halt. Sharing in God's glory, both present and future, is for those "in" the Messiah (8:17-18, 21, 30); sharing in God's justice/righteousness is the experience of those who have been justified and made just/righteous by their sharing in the faithfulness of the Messiah, specifically in his death and

---

70. Dunn, *Romans 1–8*, p. 485.

resurrection (all implied in the phrase "the righteousness of God" in 10:3, which summarizes the entire first half of the letter). It looks as if Gentiles are nearly the only ones believing this good news, and that simply makes no theological sense.

Paul's long argument against the implications of what appears to be the case need not detain us at length. He affirms the existence of a believing Jewish remnant; he argues for the mysterious, missional providence of God in the outworking of belief and unbelief among both Jews and Gentiles. Most importantly, he affirms that God is in fact sharing his glory and his justice/righteousness with both Gentiles and Jews:

> [22]What if God, desiring to show his wrath and to make known his power, has endured with much patience the objects of wrath that are made for destruction; [23]and what if he has done so in order to make known the riches of his glory for the objects of mercy, which he has prepared beforehand for glory — [24]including us whom he has called, not from the Jews only but also from the Gentiles? (Rom. 9:22-24, focusing on glory)

> [8]But what does it say? "The word is near you, on your lips and in your heart" (that is, the word of faith that we proclaim); [9]because if you confess with your lips that Jesus is Lord and believe in your heart that God raised him from the dead, you will be saved. [10]For one believes with the heart and so is justified, and one confesses with the mouth and so is saved. [11]The scripture says, "No one who believes in him will be put to shame." [12]For there is no distinction between Jew and Greek; the same Lord is Lord of all and is generous to all who call on him. [13]For, "Everyone who calls on the name of the Lord shall be saved." (Rom. 10:8-13, focusing on justification and thus justice/righteousness)

It is this conviction that prompts Paul to argue for the necessity of mission (10:14-21). The hope of universal theosis (participation in God's justice/righteousness and glory) does not prompt apathy, even for someone like Paul with a keen sense of divine providence, indeed sovereignty. Rather, the hope of theosis impels Paul — and, by extension, the church — to mission. While it is true that Paul does not tell the Roman believers to organize door-to-door evangelistic events, he does imply that they are responsible for sending proclaimers of the gospel (10:14-15), and there is no reason to think that those proclaimers might not come from their own house churches.

Moreover, as we will see in the discussion of chapters 14 and 15, the very character of the house churches in Rome is to be a living proclamation of the gospel. If the gospel is for both Jews and Gentiles, meaning for people of all ethnicities, then the church must be a hospitable place for all if it is to be a faithful instantiation of the gospel.

But of course Paul does not simply say in Romans 9–11 that the gospel is for all. He returns to the promises with which he began. His knowledge of God's unshakeable faithfulness to Israel drives him to affirm that which only the eyes of faith can see: all Israel will be saved (11:26), all Israel will experience the glory and justice/righteousness that is God's gift to the chosen people and to the entire world in the Messiah Jesus. For this reason, Paul shares in this glory in the very appropriate human response of giving glory to the God of inscrutable, universal riches and mercy (11:33-36). This culminating act of praise anticipates the description of Gentiles and Jews united in Christ to glorify God that follows in chapters 12–15.

## Communities of Justice/Righteousness and Glory: Spirit-Enabled Christlike Godlikeness (Romans 12–15)

Theosis, we have said, means participating in the justice/righteousness and glory of God. Romans 12–15 answers the question, What does theosis look like in everyday life? What does the "Daybreak Ethos"[71] look like on the ground? What does it mean to be a community of *dikaiosynē* and *doxa* that participates in the life of the Father, Son, and Spirit whose activity has been narrated in chapters 5–8 and extended explicitly to both Jews and Gentiles in chapters 9–11?

The overarching answer is provided in the introductory exhortation of 12:1-2:

> [1]I appeal to you therefore, brothers and sisters, by the mercies of God, to present your bodies as a living sacrifice, holy and acceptable to God, which is your spiritual worship. [2]Do not be conformed to this world, but

---

71. Keck's eloquent characterization of Romans 12–15 (*Romans*, p. 289). On the "practices" of participation, see also Richard B. Hays, "What Is 'Real Participation in Christ'? A Dialogue with E. P. Sanders on Pauline Soteriology," in *Redefining First-Century Jewish and Christian Identities: Essays in Honor of Ed Parish Sanders*, ed. Fabian E. Udoh et al. (Notre Dame: University of Notre Dame Press, 2008), pp. 335-51, as well as the discussion in chapter one of this book.

be transformed by the renewing of your minds, so that you may discern what is the will of God — what is good and acceptable and perfect.

The echoes of Romans 1 ("bodies," *sōmata;* cf. 1:24; "worship," *latreian;* cf. 1:25, "worshiped," *elatreusan*) and Romans 6 ("present," *parastēsai;* cf. 6:13, 16, 19) reveal that Paul wants the Roman communities in Christ to become the antithesis of Adamic humanity depicted in chapters 1–3 and to embody concretely the en-Christed, righteoused humanity he says (in chapter 6) that they have become. The language of nonconformity *(mē syschēmatizesthe)* and transformation *(metamorphousthe)* are key aspects of theosis. Paul implies that there is a standard, a pattern, other than "this world" or (better) "this age" (so NAB; *aiōni*). Although Paul does not specifically name Christ, the use of the verb "conformed" *(syschēmatizesthe),* which is similar to "conformed *(symmorphous)* to the image of his Son" in 8:29, makes it clear that the transformation he has in mind is increasing conformity to Christ. The passive voice suggests that this is the work of God, probably specifically the Spirit, and is reminiscent of the several occurrences of the passive voice in chapter 6 (6:3-6), confirming the suspicion that this transformation is the result of the ongoing participation in Christ that begins at the moment of faith/baptism. The goal of the transformation, discerning and doing "the will of God," means that Spirit-enabled conformity to Christ is in fact the will of God. Since God's will must be in line with God's own character, Paul implies once again that conformity to Christ is conformity to God.

There are several ways that Paul wants "becoming like God/Christ" to be manifested in the Roman house churches.

- As "one body in Christ" (12:5) they manifest their confession that God is one (3:30).
- As practitioners of love and the good who show exorbitant honor to others (12:9-10), they embody the image of Christ the new Adam, reversing the consequences of life in Adam depicted in Romans 1–2.
- As those who are prayerful, hopeful, and patient in suffering (12:12), they re-narrate the pattern of Jesus, who suffered prior to glorification.
- Inasmuch as they are hospitable to strangers and strive to live in peace with all, without practicing evil or revenge (12:14-21), they express the character of the One who graciously loved and justified/righteoused us while we were still sinners and enemies of God (5:1-11), allowing us to participate in the peace (5:1; 14:17) of "the God of peace" (15:33).

- As those who practice humility in the service of unity, they put on the mind of Christ (12:16, echoing Phil. 2:1-5 and anticipating 15:1-5[72]).

There is of course more, all summarized in the great admonition to participation: to be clothed in the Lord Jesus Christ (13:14).[73] To "wear" Jesus is to become like the God of the gospel by the power of the Spirit.

### Missional Practices

Of particular importance for a missional reading of Paul is the stress he places on the treatment of outsiders in 12:13-21. We cannot know for sure if the word "strangers" (v. 13) includes outsiders, but it may well do so.[74] But we can be quite certain that the reference to persecutors does (v. 14). As with the Thessalonians and the Philippians, it is clear that the Roman believers have made an impact on their community, for they have serious opposition — harassers, at least. The Romans have evangelized others in some way, shape, or form. They have perhaps explained to their family members, associates, fellow slaves or masters, co-workers in the trade guilds, and so on why they no longer sacrifice to the deities that protect the Empire, including the emperor. Some may have even explained their new beliefs, behaviors, and community in terms of an alternative gospel, lifestyle, and family to that offered by Rome.[75]

We cannot know with certainty precisely what they said or did. But whatever words or practices they previously have shared with others, Paul makes it clear that they now need to speak and perform the gospel in its most demanding form: blessing, doing good to, and trying to live peaceably with enemies — and indeed with everyone else ("all" — v. 18). That is, they need to become the gospel in a radical way. This will be a witness to "all"

---

72. In all three passages a form of the phrase *to auto phronein* ("the same mind [of Christ]") appears: Rom. 12:16; 15:5; Phil. 2:2.

73. The one way believers are *not* to resemble God is in the practice of punishing evildoers, which is a divine, eschatological "reserved power" (12:19-21).

74. It is hard to know whether "strangers" is a further explication of "saints" (believers) or a different group, though I am inclined toward the latter.

75. It is quite possible that in the difficult and disputed text of 13:1-7 Paul wants to make sure that the believers in Rome are not tempted to oppose Rome in some violent or otherwise unacceptable way, such as not paying taxes — or worse. Furthermore, he may well want the Roman believers to be ready to explain to Roman authorities or whomever that their gospel may indeed challenge everything Roman but is not a direct attack on the government.

(v. 17), says Paul, for others will find such behavior "noble." Their role in the midst of such evil is not to seek vengeance but to do everything possible to do good — even offering food and drink (v. 20) — and thereby to be victorious over evil (v. 21). In the immediate context, such victory would seem to include the possibility that persecutors would stop persecuting, repent, and believe the gospel.

### Cruciform Hospitality, Harmony, Worship, and Humanity's Theosis

These various practices of participation,[76] of Christosis/theosis, come together in the issue to which Paul devotes the most attention at the end of Romans: harmony in the midst of diversity.[77] Certainly one (and perhaps the chief) pastoral and rhetorical goal of Romans comes to expression in chapters 14 and 15. James Miller argues persuasively that the purpose of Romans emerges in this context:

> [M]utual reception embodies the will of God for God's eschatological people (15:8-12). Paul's purpose, therefore, involves forming a "community of the new age." . . . Paul writes not only to shape a community of the eschatological people of God, but also to defend his understanding of the gospel. . . . I contend that shaping a community of the new age serves as Paul's best defense against the overtures of Paul's opponents.[78]

Miller adds that such a community of mutual love and recognition will not only be "his best defense against his opponents," but will also "preserve his [upcoming] Spanish mission."[79] While not disagreeing with this focused understanding of the missional significance of the church at Rome for Paul, we would want to expand this claim and say more broadly that the church is the best instantiation and therefore the best preservation of God's mission — period. That is, as Miller rightly concludes, "the church stands at the heart of his [Paul's] argument in the letter."[80]

76. See also Hays, "What Is 'Real Participation in Christ'?"

77. See especially Philip F. Esler, *Conflict and Identity in Romans: The Social Setting of Paul's Letter* (Minneapolis: Fortress, 2003).

78. James C. Miller, *The Obedience of Faith, the Eschatological People of God, and the Purpose of Romans*, Society of Biblical Literature Dissertation Series 177 (Atlanta: Society of Biblical Literature, 2000), p. 176. To be clear, Miller does not use the word "theosis" in his work.

79. Miller, *The Obedience of Faith*, p. 177.

80. Miller, *The Obedience of Faith*, p. 180.

Paul wants the Roman believers to share in Christ's love for the weak, which is simultaneously God's impartiality, love, and hospitality — all of which Paul has touched on briefly in the two preceding chapters.

A strong "therefore" *(dio)* indicates a rhetorical climax in 15:7-13:

> [7]Welcome one another, therefore *(dio)*, just as Christ has welcomed you, for the glory of God. [8]For I tell you that Christ has become a servant of the circumcised on behalf of the truth of God in order that he might confirm the promises given to the patriarchs, [9]and in order that the Gentiles might glorify God for his mercy. . . . [13]May the God of hope fill you with all joy and peace in believing, so that you may abound in hope by the power of the Holy Spirit. (Rom. 15:7-9, 13)

This admonition is, in turn, predicated on the story of Christ re-narrated in 15:1-6, which summons the strong to exhibit regard for the weak (vv. 1-4) as a theological and practical requirement for the fulfillment of God's purpose: that all live in harmony and glorify God with one voice (vv. 5-6). Paradoxically, because humans always remain creatures, they share in the glory of God only when they give glory to God.

This powerful embodiment of welcome and worship, this community of Gentiles and Jews in mutual hospitality and in common glorification of God, is said in effect to be the very mission of Christ as the agent of God (vv. 8-9). That is, what God wanted, Christ effected. At the same time, however, Paul implies that Christlike regard for others (v. 7; cf. v. 3) can be replicated in the churches (vv. 1-2, 5) only by the grace and action of God, so Paul makes that his prayer (vv. 5-6, 13). *In other words, what God wanted is what Christ did, and what Christ did is what God now does.* If we wish to confuse things still further, we can go back to Romans 8 and see that what God now does must somehow be related to what Christ does, which is what the Spirit does.

All of this is to say that the *Christological* imperative and paradigm of Romans 15 is ultimately a *theological* (divine) imperative and paradigm. The cruciform hospitality to which Paul summons the church is ultimately willed and effected by the Father who sent his Son into the world. To be like Christ is to be like God: to share God's desires and to do God's will.

This is neither theologically incoherent nor unexpected in Romans. For one thing, Paul can tell us that believers experience both the love of God (5:5, 8) and the love of Christ (8:35), and that these loves are in fact one divine love, "the love of God in Christ Jesus our Lord" (8:39), poured into our hearts in the presence of the Holy Spirit (5:5). For another, Christ is the Son of God, whose Sonship means his sharing in the royal character of the Father, which for Paul will mean also in God's justice — his restorative, reconciling action. Third, if we accept the subjective-genitive ("faith of Christ") reading of *pistis Christou* in Romans 3:21-26, then Paul associates the faithfulness of God with its manifestation in the faithfulness of Christ. That is, there is a close association in Romans between *God's* love, righteousness, and faithfulness and *Christ's* love, righteousness, and faithfulness.

Paul will not allow us to interpret the experience of this divine life individualistically.[81] What will make the Roman community truly the antithesis of Romans 1-2, and a credible example of what God intended for humanity, is the community's gathering together in unity, Gentiles and Jews, to glorify God. The result is the church's most powerful evangelistic "tool" — a community that has become, and is always becoming, the gospel.

## Theosis in Romans and the Politics of Empire

At several points in this chapter we have briefly noted the counter- or alter-imperial character of the church's gospel and life. Rome made certain claims that are clearly (even if only implicitly) challenged, and indeed made void, by the vision of theosis — salvation, righteousness, and glory — in Paul's letter:

1. that the Roman empire is the source of salvation and the locus of glory;
2. that emperors either are divine or can become divine by apotheosis, and that they are worthy of titles like Lord, Savior, and Son of God;
3. that the Roman value of seeking more and more honor for self is the most natural human pursuit; and
4. that Roman justice is true justice, indeed the justice of God.[82]

Paul may not address these claims head-on, but it is clear that anyone who accepts his gospel will be unable to affirm the Roman pseudo-gospel and its

---

81. So, too, e.g., Miller, *The Obedience of Faith*, who argues that "the obedience of faith" is in fact a corporate vocation.

82. See, among others, Wright, *Paul and the Faithfulness of God*, pp. 279-347, 1271-1319; Warren Carter, *The Roman Empire and the New Testament* (Nashville: Abingdon, 2006), esp. ch. 6, "Imperial Theology: A Clash of Theological and Societal Claims"); and Neil Elliott, *The Arrogance of Nations: Reading Romans in the Shadow of Empire*, Paul in Critical Contexts (Minneapolis: Fortress, 2008).

claims. It is also clear, I would suggest, that the Roman pseudo-gospel is not limited to first-century Rome.

What Kavin Rowe has said with respect to the book of Acts and the early Christians' consistent challenge to Roman culture and politics narrated in that book can also be said of Paul: *"New culture, yes — coup, no."*[83] Or, at more length:

> [I]n its attempts to form communities that witness to God's apocalypse [God's revelation in Jesus Christ], Luke's second volume is a highly charged and theologically sophisticated political document that aims at nothing less than the construction of an alternative total way of life — a comprehensive pattern of being — one that runs counter to the life-patterns of the Graeco-Roman world.[84]

So, too, Paul in Romans. Theosis is political. It is counter- and alter-cultural. It is missional. It means that God has a project for restoring humanity's lost *dikaiosynē* and *doxa,* its righteousness/justice and glory. And it could not be further from Rome's project, or from any intervening or contemporary imperial project in the course of human history.

## Conclusion

Our study suggests that the various themes and purposes of Romans that have been traditionally identified work together to serve a larger theological agenda: the desire of God in Christ to save and shape a Spirit-empowered Christlike/Godlike people, a multicultural people of *dikaiosynē* and *doxa.* "Justification is God's act of new creation."[85] Theosis, specifically cruciform communal theosis, constitutes the rhetorical, pastoral, and theological theme and purpose of Romans. Paul's deeply theocentric — but also thereby Christocentric and anthropocentric — goal is that the Roman community of diverse communities would become more like the impartial God who justifies ungodly Jews and Gentiles alike and forms them into one covenant people. Romans narrates what God has been up to in "salvation history" so that his

---

83. C. Kavin Rowe, *World Upside Down: Reading Acts in the Graeco-Roman Age* (New York: Oxford University Press, 2009), p. 91; see also p. 150.

84. Rowe, *World Upside Down,* p. 4.

85. Blackwell, "Righteousness and Glory," ms. p. 13.

Roman auditors will know what God is up to in Rome itself, the heart of the empire: the creation of a new humanity in Christ, empowered by the Spirit to treat others in Godlike ways and to glorify God together, with the hope that this will spread also now to Spain. Such a community, as part of the new humanity, is on its way to being restored to the original glory for which it was created but which has been lost for a very long time. That glory will be finally realized only at the parousia, but it is experienced partially and proleptically in communities that glorify God and love others as God has loved them.

## Cruciform Missional Theosis Today

As in previous chapters, I offer here merely a snapshot of participatory, Pauline mission on the ground, in this case a snapshot of theosis.

A few years ago I attended the dedication of Jubilee Arts Center, the most recent major endeavor of Newborn Holistic Ministries in the Sandtown area of Baltimore. Newborn has reclaimed its urban four-corner intersection from drug addicts, having first built a halfway house for women on one corner, then constructing long-term housing for them diagonally opposite, then renovating green space and a fountain at a third corner, and finally transforming a dilapidated building into a beautiful arts outreach center. After an hour of speeches, prayers, and enthusiastic renditions of "This Little Light of Mine" and "Amazing Grace," the culturally and racially diverse crowd of 200 or so toured the new facility on the fourth corner, symbolic perhaps of the gospel-justice of God reaching the four corners, not only of the 'hood or the city, but of the world.

As the final prayer ended, a woman said to me, "This is what the kingdom of God looks like." Paul would agree: a culturally diverse community of believers glorifying the triune God, caring for one another, anticipating the liberation of creation, and reaching out to strangers, for

> the kingdom of God is not food and drink but righteousness [*dikaiosynē*] and peace and joy in the Holy Spirit. The one who thus serves Christ is acceptable to God and has human approval. Let us then pursue what makes for peace and for mutual upbuilding. (Rom. 14:17-19)

A part of Sandtown has been transformed from Romans 1 to Romans 8 and 15. Theosis has been at work, a foretaste of the glory to come.

But the church as a whole has a lot of work to do in this regard. In the United States, it is still the case that "11 a.m." (i.e., the traditional time for church) is still the most segregated hour of the week. Prejudice against people of different cultures — the "other" — is still rampant in many places, including many churches. And Christian-on-Christian violence, on scales both small and large, is no stranger to the contemporary world. If the church is supposed to be the "microcosmos, a little world . . . the prototype of what [is] to come," then it has both a high calling and a long way to go.[86]

To be sure, there are signs of hope everywhere, Sandtown being just one of them. It is for this reason that the people who read Romans as Scripture can look around with something more than despair and can aim, with the Spirit's power, to be that which Paul envisions:

> A place of reconciliation between God and the world; a place where humans might be reconciled to one another; a microcosmos in which the world is contained in a nutshell as a sign of what God intends to do for the whole creation; a new sort of polis in which heaven and earth come together. . . .[87]

It is this sort of community that brings glory to the God who glorifies us by the Spirit in Christ. It is a community in which more and more people confess, in words and deeds (righteousness), that "Jesus Christ is Lord, to the glory of God the Father" (Phil. 2:11).

---

86. This is N. T. Wright's summary of the character of the church according to Paul (*Paul and the Faithfulness of God*, p. 1492).

87. Wright, *Paul and the Faithfulness of God*, p. 1492.

# Final Reflections: Becoming the Gospel (Reprise)

This book, as I noted in the opening "Invitation" (replacing the traditional Introduction), is the third in a sort of accidental trilogy, following *Cruciformity: Paul's Narrative Spirituality of the Cross* and *Inhabiting the Cruciform God.*[1] It has been an exercise in reading Paul missionally. The central claim, found in the title — *Becoming the Gospel: Paul, Participation, and Mission* — is that already in the first Christian century the apostle Paul wanted the communities he addressed not merely to *believe* the gospel but to *become* the gospel and thereby to *advance* the gospel. That is, they were to participate in the very life and mission of God, through proclamation, praxis, and even persecution. They were to become a living exegesis of the gospel. The corollary claim for us who read Paul's letters as Christian Scripture, as divine address, is that we too are invited, in analogous ways, to become the gospel in our own particular contexts. That is, we have been considering Paul's letters as documents that both reflect and foster participation in the *missio Dei,* the mission of God.

The phrase "corollary claim" should not, however, be taken to imply a subsidiary, or less important, claim. On the contrary, the actual burden of this book is a hermeneutical one: that Paul's letters speak to us, offering us the most appropriate starting point and theological framework for mission: Spirit-enabled transformative participation in the life and character of God revealed in the crucified and resurrected Messiah Jesus.

It is time now to take stock, briefly, of where we have been and what we have discovered. This is not so much a thoroughgoing summary, however, as it is a retrospective reflection.

---

1. *Cruciformity: Paul's Narrative Spirituality of the Cross* (Grand Rapids: Eerdmans, 2001); *Inhabiting the Cruciform God: Kenosis, Justification, and Theosis in Paul's Narrative Soteriology* (Grand Rapids: Eerdmans, 2009).

297

## The Gospel and the *Missio Dei*

A critical part of becoming the gospel is appropriately defining the gospel. A narrow, privatistic understanding of the gospel (such as, "Believe in Jesus as Savior and Lord so that you will have your sins forgiven and go to be with him when you die") may require the church to say a lot, but it will not require it to become much of anything other than a loud voice. It does not even have to be a very credible loud voice as long as it says what (it thinks) needs to be said.

A more robust understanding of the gospel, however, radically alters everything without losing the message of forgiveness and eternal life. It changes not only the message, deepening and broadening it, but also the bearers of the message. From Paul's perspective the gospel itself is a powerful word of transformation, its content being given voice not merely in words but also, and inseparably, in actions. This does not eliminate the need for, or the importance of, words, but it does imply that the words have meaning and power only in action. God did something in Christ; Christ did something in becoming human and giving himself for us; the Spirit does something to and through people who believe the good news of this divine activity.

Furthermore, the content of the gospel Paul preaches is so thoroughly rooted both in the peculiar Christological shape of this divine activity — the life and teaching, and especially the death and resurrection, of Jesus — and in the Scriptures of Israel, with their promises of the Spirit and of *shalom*, that people who believe such good news are ineluctably drawn into its strange Christ-shaped and Scripture-shaped reality. So if the gospel has to do with a faithful God, a Suffering Servant who inaugurates God's *shalom*, and a prophetically promised indwelling Spirit, then the individuals and communities who believe in *that* good news will be shaped in their minds and bodies, their thinking and their living, into Godlike, Christlike, Spirit-enabled people who in some real, if imperfect, way instantiate the message they believe. This is hard to do, to put it mildly. Paul's churches did not succeed perfectly, and neither do we. (On the other hand, if this kind of gospel is *difficult* to embody, I would suggest that a gospel of believing in Jesus so that you go to heaven when you die is *impossible* to embody.)

This is why our understanding of the gospel and our understanding of the *missio Dei* are so interconnected. A thin, lightweight view of the gospel entails a similar thin, lightweight understanding of salvation and the *missio Dei*. But a thick, robust understanding of the gospel involves an equally complex and comprehensive perspective on salvation and the *missio Dei*.

What God was and is up to in Christ is ultimately cosmic in scope, but in the present that future cosmic reality is anticipated in the formation of what Ephesians refers to as a new humanity. If the gospel of Christ crucified, raised, and exalted as Lord means anything for the human race, according to Paul, it means that transformation into the cruciform image of God is possible in the present. And that means that the message and the people, the gospel and the church, are inseparable; the witness to the reality of transformation through death and resurrection is the existence of a transformed and being-transformed people.

To be sure, this present transformation, what Paul even refers to as this present glorification, is only partial and proleptic, for the kingdom that the gospel promises is here, *really* here, but not *fully* here. Thus the church's transformative participation is anticipatory, not complete, and in fact its present glorification is, once again, cruciform. The church, therefore, cannot be triumphalistic, but neither should it be shy. The gospel of God is power, power unleashed in the world, in the church, and in the lives of individuals. Because the gospel is power, the church knows that its witness is not a faint whisper in the dark but participation in something beyond human imagination. And this power does not exist independently of God but, on the contrary, derives from the very life of God. The gospel of God is the power of God, and it therefore reflects the divine character. Paul's mission and our mission are nothing less, and nothing more, than participation in that power — that cruciform gospel power — at work in the world. From this gospel and this power come Paul's missional theology and praxis.

## Key Aspects of Paul's Missional Theology and Praxis

Throughout this book a few key words and phrases have appeared again and again, indicating what are, I have argued, key elements of Paul's missional theology and key dimensions of his missional spirituality and praxis. These terms include cruciform and cruciformity (cross-shaped existence), which further develop the key theme of book one in the trilogy *(Cruciformity)*. Also important in that first book are the words faith, hope, and love. In addition, the key themes of the church as a countercultural or alter-cultural community, as well as the likelihood of faithfulness leading to suffering, as it did for Jesus, all figure prominently in both *Cruciformity* and in this book.

An additional set of terms in the chapters we have just finished develops more explicitly the key theme of the trilogy's second volume *(Inhabiting the Cruciform God)*: participation, now often reformulated as *anticipatory participation*, and theosis, with significant attention paid as well to nonviolence, which was also a critical aspect of *Inhabiting*. Theosis, we have argued, is helpful language to describe the reality of participation in the life and mission of God, and thus becoming like God; Paul's notion of theosis, or transformative participation, is inherently missional. We have also suggested that less important than agreeing on the term "theosis" is agreeing that the realities that are central to Paul (justification, salvation, etc.) are inherently participatory, transformational, and missional.

Yet a third set of terms indicates aspects of Paul that were hinted at in the first two volumes but that were largely developed (in my thinking, not Paul's) after the publication of *Inhabiting*. These include specifically missiological terms such as *missio Dei* (which we have just briefly revisited), centripetal and centrifugal activity, and witness, as well as more general theological terms like *shalom*, peace and reconciliation, and justice (meaning saving, restorative justice). Of course this third set of terms is not unrelated to the previous two sets. At the heart of this book's entire discussion, therefore, has been the notion of transformation, of actually becoming the gospel in its manifold cruciform dimensions, which is itself a missional form of existence, an instantiation of and witness to the gospel.

A key argument of the book has been that the lack of specific Pauline exhortations to the churches about "spreading the gospel" means neither that Paul expected nothing of the sort from them nor that they failed to be public witnesses. Rather, we have argued, the letters (1) assume that the churches have been, or in some cases should be, living the gospel — its faithfulness, love, hope, peace, justice and so on — in the public square; (2) address the consequences of doing so, or not doing so; and (3) call on the churches to continue to do so despite whatever those consequences have been or might be. The churches, no less than Paul, are called to embody the master story of Christ found in Philippians 2:6-11, and thus to be Christ's ambassadors, participants in the divine mission, even if their specific roles differ from Paul and his colleagues. This conclusion means, at the very least, that Paul's missional theology and the praxis associated with it can speak in creative ways to the contemporary church's own missional theology and praxis for the church as a whole, not just for its ordained ministers or "missionaries."

Furthermore, at various points in the book we have noted the importance of the imagination, enlivened by the Spirit, in thinking and acting missionally in new situations but with Paul's claims and contributions in mind. We have offered a few examples of each dimension of the transformative participation we have considered, but we have also deliberately refrained from overloading the book with examples in order to allow readers to think creatively and contextually for themselves.

At the risk of reducing some carefully woven strands into a list of individual items, we might suggest, in summary, that the following have been key ingredients in the missional interpretation of Paul offered in this book:

- the *missio Dei* of salvation, understood in thick, robust terms;
- participation/anticipatory participation (see chapter one for this as the basic framework of our discussion);
- transformation;
- countercultural or alter-cultural existence, in contrast to "Empire";
- centripetal (community-directed) and centrifugal (outwardly directed) activity;
- witness in word and deed;
- cruciformity;
- faith as faithfulness, love, and hope (see especially chapter three on 1 Thessalonians);
- suffering (see especially chapter four on Philippians);
- *shalom* (see especially chapters five through seven);
- peaceableness, peacemaking, reconciliation (see especially chapters five and six, with treatments of Romans and Ephesians);
- cruciform, saving/restorative, generous justice (see especially chapter seven on 1 and 2 Corinthians); and
- theosis (see especially chapter eight on Romans).

Although we have found different emphases in the various Pauline letters, we have insisted that the church Paul seeks to form then and now is called not to embody one or two of these missional virtues and practices but all of them. This is what it means for the church to be the church — a high calling indeed.

## Paul in One (Modified) Sentence

When we try to synthesize these various dimensions of Paul's theology and praxis, which (I have been arguing) means also the contemporary church's theology and praxis, we might very well come up with a phrase or sentence to express the heart of the claims about Paul, participation, and mission being made.

In an earlier, small book on Paul (not part of this trilogy) called *Reading Paul,* I attempted to summarize what the apostle was up to in one sentence — one very long sentence.[2] Having thought even more explicitly about Paul from a missional perspective since that time, I have had to modify that long sentence. So what follows here is the original sentence plus the modification, which is set in bold type:

> Paul preached, and then explained in various pastoral, community-forming letters, a narrative, apocalyptic, theopolitical gospel (1) in continuity with the story of Israel and (2) in distinction to the imperial gospel of Rome (and analogous powers) that was centered on God's crucified and exalted Messiah Jesus, whose incarnation, life, and death by crucifixion were validated and vindicated by God in his resurrection and exaltation as Lord, which inaugurated the new age or new creation, in which all members of this diverse but consistently covenantally dysfunctional human race who respond in self-abandoning and self-committing faith thereby participate in Christ's death and resurrection and are (1) justified, or restored to right covenant relations with God and with others; (2) incorporated into a particular manifestation of Christ the Lord's body on earth, the church, which is an alternative community to the status-quo human communities committed to and governed by Caesar (and analogous rulers) and by values contrary to the gospel; and (3) infused both individually and corporately by the Spirit of God's Son so that they may lead "bifocal" lives, focused both back on Christ's first coming and ahead to his second, consisting of Christlike, cruciform (cross-shaped) (1) faith(fulness) and (2) hope toward God and (3) love toward both neighbors and enemies (a love marked by peaceableness and inclusion), **thereby bearing witness in word and deed to the one true God and the Lordship of Christ, and participating by the power of the Holy Spirit in God's mission of reconciliation and restorative justice in Christ, even at the risk of suffering and death,** all in joyful anticipation of (1) the return of Christ, (2) the resurrection of the dead to eternal life, and (3) the renewal of the entire creation.

What this modification to my original sentence is meant to suggest is that we cannot think about Paul's own purpose or mission without also thinking about the mission of God and the mission of the church. To practice "cruci-

2. *Reading Paul* (Eugene, OR: Cascade, 2008), p. 8.

formity," to "inhabit the cruciform God," to be in Christ, to be filled with the Spirit of this God and this Son of God is inherently a *missional* participation, an anticipatory participation in the coming kingdom of God's *shalom* that was promised by the prophets and inaugurated by God in his Messiah and by his Spirit.

## The Elimination of Binaries, the Preservation of Diversity, and the Integrity of the Church's Witness

If the church is not called to choose two or three items from the list above, like ordering from a Chinese menu, then one fundamental conclusion of this book also needs to be restated here: Paul's letters summon us to eliminate the standard binaries of Christian praxis that are too often found in the church. By "binaries of Christian praxis" I mean the phenomenon of some churches and Christian groups being known for one thing and others for an almost diametrically opposed other, a phenomenon in which complementary aspects of Christian praxis are misunderstood as competing, or even mutually exclusive, categories. These inappropriate binaries, or false either-or's, include the following:

- spirituality versus social justice;
- evangelism versus peacemaking;
- pastoral care versus missional work;
- worship (or Christian education) versus outreach;
- the "vertical" dimension of salvation versus the "horizontal" dimension of salvation;
- and so on.

The error of this bifurcation was already stressed by Jürgen Moltmann in *The Crucified God*:

> In many Christian churches . . . polarizations have come into being between those who see the essence of the church in evangelization and the salvation of souls, and those who see it in social action for the salvation and liberation of real life. But in Christian terms evangelization and humanization are not alternatives. . . . Nor are the "vertical dimension" of faith and the "horizontal dimension" of love for one's neighbor and political change. Nor are "Jesuology" [sic] and christology, the humanity and

the divinity of Jesus. Both coincide in his death on the cross. Anyone who makes a distinction here, enforces alternatives and calls for a parting of the ways, in dividing the unity of God and man in the person, the imitation and the future of Christ.

These alternatives are equally absurd from the point of view of practice. Evangelization would lead either to a crisis of relevance or to an inevitable involvement in the social and political problems of society. Beginning with preaching, one is then faced with questions of community organization, the education of children and the work for the sick and poor. The humanization of social circumstances leads either to a crisis of identity, or inevitably to evangelization or pastoral care.[3]

This does not mean, however, that all churches will be missionally identical. Each church, each Christian community, must discern its particular calling. The practice of missional hermeneutics stresses the significance of context. My point, however, is that because the gospel of God is inclusive of all the realities implied in the list of (false) binaries, every Christian community should be open to where and how God is leading it into a diversity of missional practices that reflects the breadth of the gospel and the comprehensive nature of what participating in the life of the God revealed in that gospel means.

Ultimately, the integrity and the impact of all Christian witness depend on the integration of message and mission. When the church, or an individual Christian, preaches the gospel but does not live the gospel, or deliberately lives only a slice of it, perhaps even publicly criticizing those who focus on other slices, the witness is likely to have no effect — or the wrong kind of effect. However, as the church, by the power of the Spirit, becomes the gospel in its fullness by participating fully in the life of God manifested in Christ, the church offers an appropriate and credible witness to the gospel. This does not in any way guarantee "success," at least as success is typically measured by humans, but it does increase the likelihood that those who both hear and see this embodiment of the gospel will have had an encounter with the living God.

3. Jürgen Moltmann in *The Crucified God: The Cross as the Foundation and Criticism of Christian Theology*, trans. Margaret Kohl (Minneapolis: Fortress, 1993 [1974]), p. 22. As seen here, Moltmann connects this mistake to the error of choosing between the divine and the human Christ and thus missing the fact that "both coincide on the cross." I would add (and think that Moltmann would concur) that both of the members of all the pairs (false binaries) listed above coincide on the cross, too.

## Mission and the Sanctified Imagination: Invitation and Promise

At various points throughout these chapters we have stressed that becoming the gospel is not a matter of merely imitating Paul and the churches to which he wrote, but of having our imaginations ignited by the letters he penned and the churches that lived by them, or at least were called to do so.[4] It is the task of the Spirit to spark and sanctify the Christian imagination, so that together believers may discern what it means for them, in their particular contexts, to become the gospel in ways analogous to the praxis of the churches in Thessalonica, Philippi, and elsewhere. It is also the task of the Spirit to sharpen the Christian vision so that contemporary believers may perceive where they may be mis-embodying the gospel in ways analogous to certain practices in Corinth, Rome, and elsewhere.

This book began with an "Invitation" instead of a traditional "Introduction." It now closes with a prayer that is an invitation as well, but also something more like a promise. It is, of course, a prayer from a Pauline letter, perhaps a kind of circular letter addressed to both first-century and twenty-first-century believers. It is therefore a prayer for all Christians and for all seasons, a prayer about participation in the God of the gospel, a prayer about the transformation of our missional imaginations and our missional communities in Christ:

> [14]For this reason I bow my knees before the Father, [15]from whom every family in heaven and on earth takes its name. [16]I pray that, according to the riches of his glory, he may grant that you [plural, here and throughout] may be strengthened in your inner being with power through his Spirit, [17]and that Christ may dwell in your hearts through faith, as you are being rooted and grounded in love. [18]I pray that you may have the power to comprehend, with all the saints, what is the breadth and length and height and depth, [19]and to know the love of Christ that surpasses knowledge, so that you may be filled with all the fullness of God. [20]Now to him who by the power at work within us is able to accomplish abundantly far more than all we can ask or imagine, [21]to him be glory in the church and in Christ Jesus to all generations, forever and ever. Amen. (Eph. 3:14-21)

This is the prayer of the church that wants to become the gospel.

---

4. The juxtaposition of some of the terms in this sentence is inspired by Andy Johnson, "The Sanctification of the Imagination," in *Holiness and Ecclesiology in the New Testament*, ed. Kent E. Brower and Andy Johnson (Grand Rapids: Eerdmans, 2007), pp. 275-92.

# Bibliography

Allen, John L., Jr. *The Global War on Christians: Dispatches from the Front Lines of Anti-Christian Persecution.* New York: Image/Random House, 2013.

Ascough, Richard S. "Redescribing the Thessalonians' 'Mission' in Light of Graeco-Roman Associations," *New Testament Studies* 60 (2014): 61-82.

Bakhtin, Mikhail. *Speech Genres and Other Late Essays.* Austin: University of Texas Press, 1986.

Barclay, John M. G. "Manna and the Circulation of Grace: A Study of 2 Corinthians 8:1-15." In *The Word Leaps the Gap: Essays on Theology and Scripture in Honor of Richard B. Hays,* ed. J. Ross Wagner, C. Kavin Rowe, and A. Katherine Grieb, pp. 409-26. Grand Rapids: Eerdmans, 2008.

Barram, Michael. "The Bible, Mission, and Social Location: Toward a Missional Hermeneutic," *Interpretation* 61 (2007): 42-58.

———. *Mission and Moral Reflection in Paul.* Studies in Biblical Literature 75. New York: Peter Lang, 2006.

———. "Pauline Mission as Salvific Intentionality: Fostering a Missional Consciousness in 1 Corinthians 9:19-23 and 10:31–11:1." In *Paul as Missionary: Identity, Activity, Theology, and Practice,* ed. Trevor J. Burke and Brian S. Rosner, pp. 234-46. Library of New Testament Studies 420. London: T. & T. Clark, 2011.

———. "Reflections on the Practice of Missional Hermeneutics: 'Streaming' Philippians 1:20-30." Paper presented at the Gospel and Our Culture Network Forum on Missional Hermeneutics at the annual meeting of the Society of Biblical Literature. New Orleans, LA, November 21, 2009.

Barrett, Lois Y, et al. *Treasure in Clay Jars: Patterns in Missional Faithfulness.* Grand Rapids: Eerdmans, 2004.

Barth, Markus. *Ephesians: Introduction, Translation, and Commentary on Chapters 1–3.* Anchor Bible 34. Garden City, NY: Doubleday, 1974.

———. "Jews and Gentiles: The Social Character of Justification in Paul," *Ecumenical Studies* 5 (1968): 241-67.

Bassler, Jouette M. "Peace in All Ways: Theology in the Thessalonian Letters. A Response to R. Jewett, E. Krentz, and E. Richard." In *Pauline Theology*. Vol. 1: *Thessalonians, Philippians, Galatians, Philemon*, ed. Jouette Bassler, pp. 71-85. Minneapolis: Fortress, 1991.

Bauckham, Richard. *The Bible and Mission: Christian Witness in a Postmodern World*. Grand Rapids: Baker Academic, 2003.

―――. *Jesus and the God of Israel: God Crucified and Other Studies on the New Testament's Christology of Divine Identity*. Grand Rapids: Eerdmans, 2009.

―――. "Mission as Hermeneutic for Scriptural Interpretation." Lecture presented at Cambridge University, Cambridge, 1999. Cited 31 July 2014. Online: http://richardbauckham.co.uk/uploads/Accessible/Mission%20as%20Hermeneutic.pdf.

Behr, John. *The Mystery of Christ: Life in Death*. Crestwood, NY: St. Vladimir's Seminary Press, 2006.

Beker, J. Christiaan. *Paul the Apostle: The Triumph of God in Life and Thought*. Philadelphia: Fortress, 1980.

Bennett, Harold V. "Justice, OT." In vol. 3 of *The New Interpreter's Dictionary of the Bible*, ed. Katherine Doob Sakenfeld, pp. 476-77. 5 vols. Nashville: Abingdon, 2008.

Berlatsky, Noah. "Bend Your Knee." No pages. Cited 11 December 2013. Online: http://www.hoodedutilitarian.com/2012/04/bend-your-knee.

Birch, Bruce C. "Reclaiming Prophetic Leadership." *Ex Auditu* 22 (2006): 10-25.

Blackwell, Ben C. *Christosis: Pauline Soteriology in Light of Deification in Irenaeus and Cyril of Alexandria*. Wissenschaftliche Untersuchungen zum Neuen Testament 2/314. Tübingen: Mohr Siebeck, 2011.

―――. "Immortal Glory and the Problem of Death in Romans 3.23." *Journal for the Study of the New Testament* 32 (2010): 285-308.

―――. "Righteousness and Glory: New Creation as Immortality in Romans." Paper presented at the international meeting of the Society of Biblical Literature. Rome, July 2, 2009.

Bloomquist, L. Gregory. *The Function of Suffering in Philippians*. Journal for the Study of the New Testament: Supplement Series 78. Sheffield: Journal for the Study of the New Testament, 1993.

Bockmuehl, Markus. *The Epistle to the Philippians*. Black's New Testament Commentary. Peabody, MA: Hendrickson, 1998.

Boesak, Allan Aubrey, and Curtiss Paul DeYoung. *Radical Reconciliation: Beyond Political Pietism and Christian Quietism*. Maryknoll, NY: Orbis, 2012.

Bonhoeffer, Dietrich. *Discipleship*. Dietrich Bonhoeffer Works 4. Translated by Barbara Green and Reinhard Krauss. Minneapolis: Augsburg Fortress, 2001.

Braaten, Laurie J. "All Creation Groans: Romans 8:22 in Light of the Biblical Sources." *Horizons in Biblical Theology* 28 (2006): 131-59.

Brenneman, Laura L., and Brad D. Schantz, eds. *Struggles for Shalom: Peace and Violence Across the Testaments*. Eugene, OR: Pickwick, 2014.

Bridges, Matthew. "Song of the Seraphs." In *The Passion of Jesus*. London: Richardson & Son, 1852.

Brown, Raymond E. *An Introduction to the New Testament.* Anchor Yale Bible Reference Library. New York: Doubleday, 1998.

Brownson, James V. "A Response at SBL to Hunsberger's 'Proposals . . .' Essay." Paper presented at the Gospel and Our Culture Network Forum on Missional Hermeneutics at the annual meeting of the Society of Biblical Literature. Boston, MA, November 22, 2008. Cited: 31 July 2014. Online: http://www.gocn.org/resources/articles/response-sbl-hunsbergers-proposals-essay.

————. *Speaking the Truth in Love: New Testament Resources for a Missional Hermeneutic.* Harrisburg, PA: Trinity Press International, 1998.

Brueggemann, Walter. *Biblical Perspectives on Evangelism: Living in a Three-Storied Universe.* Nashville: Abingdon, 2003.

————. *Isaiah 1–39.* Westminster Bible Companion. Louisville: Westminster John Knox, 1998.

————. *Theology of the Old Testament: Testimony, Dispute, Advocacy.* Minneapolis: Fortress, 1997.

Bruland, Esther Byle, and Stephen C. Mott. *A Passion for Jesus, A Passion for Justice.* Valley Forge, PA: Judson, 1983.

Brunner, Emil. *The Word and the World.* London: SCM, 1931.

Bryan, Christopher. *A Preface to Romans: Notes on the Epistle in Its Literary and Cultural Setting.* New York: Oxford University Press, 2000.

Burke, Trevor J., and Brian S. Rosner, eds. *Paul as Missionary: Identity, Activity, Theology, and Practice.* Library of New Testament Studies 420. London: T. & T. Clark, 2011.

Burroughs, Presian Smyers. "Liberation in the Midst of Futility and Destruction: Romans 8 and the Christian Vocation of Nourishing Life." Th.D. diss., Duke Divinity School, 2014.

Campbell, Constantine R. *Paul and Union with Christ: An Exegetical and Theological Study.* Grand Rapids: Zondervan, 2012.

Campbell, Douglas A. *The Deliverance of God: An Apocalyptic Rereading of Justification in Paul.* Grand Rapids: Eerdmans, 2009.

————. *The Quest for Paul's Gospel: A Suggested Strategy.* London: T. & T. Clark, 2005.

Carter, Warren. *The Roman Empire and the New Testament.* Nashville: Abingdon, 2006.

Cavanaugh, William T. *Torture and Eucharist: Theology, Politics, and the Body of Christ.* Malden, MA: Blackwell, 1998.

Chester, Stephen J. *Conversion at Corinth: Perspectives on Conversion in Paul's Theology and the Corinthian Church.* Studies of the New Testament and Its World. London: T. & T. Clark, 2003.

Chilcote, Paul, and Laceye Warner, eds. *The Study of Evangelism: Exploring a Missional Practice of the Church.* Grand Rapids: Eerdmans, 2008.

Christensen, Michael J., and Jeffery A. Wittung, eds. *Partakers of the Divine Nature:*

*The History and Development of Deification in the Christian Traditions*. Grand Rapids: Baker Academic, 2007.

Collins, Paul M. *Partaking in Divine Nature: Deification and Communion*. New York: T. & T. Clark, 2010.

Colwell, John E. *Living the Christian Story: The Distinctiveness of Christian Ethics*. New York: T. & T. Clark, 2001.

Congdon, David W. Review of Michael J. Gorman, *Inhabiting the Cruciform God: Kenosis, Justification, and Theosis in Paul's Narrative Soteriology*. *Koinonia* 21 (2009): 125-28.

———. "Why I Think Missional Theology Is the Future of Theology, or, Why I Think Theology Must Become Missional or Perish," 1-9. Cited 31 July 2014. Online: http://theologyandpraxis.files.wordpress.com/2008/08/why-i-think-missional -theology5.pdf.

Cragg, Gerald R., ed. *The Works of John Wesley*, Vol. 11: *The Appeals to Men of Reason and Religion and Certain Related Open Letters*. Nashville: Abingdon, 1987.

Cummins, S. A. "Divine Life and Corporate Christology: God, Messiah Jesus, and the Covenant Community in Paul." In *The Messiah in the Old and New Testaments*, ed. Stanley E. Porter, pp. 190-209. Grand Rapids: Eerdmans, 2007.

Curran, Shannon. "Become God's Justice (2 Cor. 5:21), Become Known by God (1 Cor. 8:3): How Paul Guides Corinth to Prefer Weakness and to Be Transformed through God's Justice." M.A. thesis, St. Mary's Seminary & University, 2013.

Desjardins, Michael. *Peace, Violence and the New Testament*. Sheffield: Sheffield Academic Press, 1991.

Dickson, John P. *Mission Commitment in Ancient Judaism and in the Pauline Communities*. Wissenschaftliche Untersuchungen zum Neuen Testament 2/159. Tübingen: Mohr Siebeck, 2003.

Dunn, James D. G. "ΕΚ ΠΙΣΤΕΩΣ: A Key to the Meaning of ΠΙΣΤΙΣ ΧΡΙΣΤΟΥ." In *The Word Leaps the Gap: Essays on Scripture and Theology in Honor of Richard B. Hays*, ed. J. Ross Wagner, C. Kavin Rowe, and A. Katherine Grieb, pp. 351-66. Grand Rapids: Eerdmans, 2008.

———. "The Justice of God: A Renewed Perspective on Justification by Faith," *Journal of Theological Studies* new series 43 (1992): 1-21.

———. *Romans 1–8*. Word Biblical Commentary 38A. Dallas: Word, 1988.

———. *The Theology of Paul the Apostle*. Grand Rapids: Eerdmans, 1998.

Dunn, James D. G., and Alan M. Suggate. *The Justice of God: A Fresh Look at the Old Doctrine of Justification by Faith*. Carlisle, UK: Paternoster, 1993. Repr., Grand Rapids: Eerdmans, 1994.

Dunne, John Anthony. "Suffering in Vain: A Study of the Interpretation of ΠΑΣΧΩ in *Galatians* 3.4," *Journal for the Study of the New Testament* 36 (2013): 3-16.

Elliott, Neil. *The Arrogance of Nations: Reading Romans in the Shadow of Empire*. Paul in Critical Contexts. Minneapolis: Fortress, 2008.

Esler, Philip F. *Conflict and Identity in Romans: The Social Setting of Paul's Letter.* Minneapolis: Fortress, 2003.

Evans, C. F. *Resurrection and the New Testament.* London: SCM, 1970.

Fee, Gordon D. *Paul's Letter to the Philippians.* New International Commentary on the New Testament. Grand Rapids: Eerdmans, 1995.

Feldmeier, Reinhard, and Hermann Spieckermann. *God of the Living: A Biblical Theology.* Translated by Mark E. Biddle. Waco, TX: Baylor University Press, 2011.

Finlan, Stephen. "Can We Speak of *Theosis* in Paul?" In *Partakers of the Divine Nature: The History and Development of Deification in the Christian Traditions,* ed. Michael J. Christensen and Jeffery A. Wittung, pp. 68-80. Grand Rapids: Baker Academic, 2007.

Finlan, Stephen, and Vladimir Kharlamov, eds. *Theōsis: Deification in Christian Theology.* Eugene, OR: Pickwick, 2006.

Flemming, Dean. "Exploring a Missional Reading of Scripture: Philippians as a Case Study," *Evangelical Quarterly* 83 (2011): 3-18.

———. *Philippians: A Commentary in the Wesleyan Tradition.* New Beacon Bible Commentary. Kansas City, MO: Beacon Hill, 2009.

———. *Recovering the Full Mission of God: A Biblical Perspective on Being, Doing, and Telling.* Downers Grove, IL: InterVarsity, 2013.

———. "Revelation and the *Missio Dei:* Toward a Missional Reading of the Apocalypse," *Journal of Theological Interpretation* 6 (2012): 161-78.

———. *Why Mission? A New Testament Exploration.* Nashville: Abingdon, forthcoming.

Forum on Missional Hermeneutics of the Gospel and Our Culture Network. Review of Michael J. Gorman, *Becoming the Gospel: Paul, Participation, and Mission.* Forthcoming.

Foster, Paul. "Who Wrote 2 Thessalonians? A Fresh Look at an Old Problem," *Journal for the Study of the New Testament* 35 (2012): 150-75.

Fowl, Stephen E. "Christology and Ethics in Philippians 2:5-11." In *Where Christology Began: Essays on Philippians 2,* ed. Ralph P. Martin and Brian J. Dodd, pp. 140-53. Louisville: Westminster John Knox, 1998.

———. *Ephesians: A Commentary.* The New Testament Library. Louisville: Westminster John Knox, 2012.

———. *God's Beautiful City: Christian Mission after Christendom.* The Ekklesia Project Pamphlet #4. Eugene, OR: Wipf & Stock, 2011.

———. *Philippians.* Two Horizons New Testament Commentary. Grand Rapids: Eerdmans, 2005.

———. *The Story of Christ in the Ethics of Paul.* Journal for the Study of the New Testament: Supplement Series 36. Sheffield: Sheffield Academic Press, 1990.

Fowler, James S. *Stages of Faith: The Psychology of Human Development and the Quest for Meaning.* San Francisco: HarperSanFrancisco, 1982.

Furnish, Victor Paul. *II Corinthians*. Anchor Bible 32a. Garden City, NY: Doubleday, 1984.

Gabrielson, Jeremy. *Paul's Non-Violent Gospel: The Theological Politics of Peace in Paul's Life and Letters*. Eugene, OR: Pickwick, 2013.

Gallagher, Robert L., and Paul Hertig. "Introduction: Background to Acts." In *Mission in Acts: Ancient Narratives in Contemporary Context*, ed. Robert L. Gallagher and Paul Hertig, pp. 2-17. American Society of Missiology Series 34. Maryknoll, NY: Orbis, 2004.

Gaventa, Beverly Roberts. "The Mission of God in Paul's Letter to the Romans." In *Paul as Missionary: Identity, Activity, Theology, and Practice*, ed. Trevor J. Burke and Brian S. Rosner, pp. 65-75. Library of New Testament Studies 420. London: T. & T. Clark, 2011.

————, ed. *Apocalyptic Paul: Cosmos and Anthropos in Romans 5–8*. Waco, TX: Baylor University Press, 2013.

Gibbs, Eddie. *The Rebirth of the Church: Applying Paul's Vision for Ministry in Our Post-Christian World*. Grand Rapids: Baker Academic, 2013.

Gieniusz, Andrzej. *Romans 8:18-30: "Suffering Does Not Thwart the Future Glory."* Atlanta: Scholars Press, 1999.

Goheen, Michael W. *A Light to the Nations: The Missional Church and the Biblical Story*. Grand Rapids: Baker Academic, 2011.

Gombis, Timothy G. *The Drama of Ephesians: Participating in the Triumph of God*. Downers Grove, IL: InterVarsity, 2010.

————. "The Triumph of God in Christ: Divine Warfare in the Argument of Ephesians." Ph.D. diss., University of St. Andrews, 2005. Cited 31 July 2014. Online: http://research-repository.st-andrews.ac.uk/bitstream/10023/2321/6/Timothy-GombisPhDthesis.pdf.

Goodwin, Mark J. *Paul: Apostle of the Living God*. Harrisburg, PA: Trinity, 2001.

Gorman, Michael J. " 'Although/Because He Was in the Form of God': The Theological Significance of Paul's Master Story (Philippians 2:6-11)," *Journal of Theological Interpretation* 1 (2007): 147-69.

————. *Apostle of the Crucified Lord: A Theological Introduction to Paul and His Letters*. Grand Rapids: Eerdmans, 2004.

————. *Cruciformity: Paul's Narrative Spirituality of the Cross*. Grand Rapids: Eerdmans, 2001.

————. *The Death of the Messiah and the Birth of the New Covenant: A (Not So) New Model of the Atonement*. Eugene, OR: Cascade, 2014.

————. *Elements of Biblical Exegesis: A Basic Guide for Students and Ministers*. Rev. and exp. ed. Grand Rapids: Baker Academic, 2009.

————. *Inhabiting the Cruciform God: Kenosis, Justification, and Theosis in Paul's Narrative Soteriology*. Grand Rapids: Eerdmans, 2009.

————. "Justification and Justice in Paul, with Special Reference to the Corinthians," *Journal for the Study of Paul and His Letters* 1 (2011): 23-40.

————. "The Lord of Peace: Christ Our Peace in Pauline Theology," *Journal for the Study of Paul and His Letters* 3 (2013): 219-53.

————. "Missional Musings on Paul," *Catalyst* (Spring 2011). No pages. Cited: 31 July 2014. Online: http://www.catalystresources.org/missional-musings-on-paul.

————. "Paul and the Cruciform Way of God in Christ," *Journal of Moral Theology* 2 (2013): 64-83.

————. "Paul's Corporate, Cruciform, Missional Theosis in Second Corinthians." In *"In Christ" in Paul: Explorations in Paul's Theology of Union and Participation,* ed. Kevin J. Vanhoozer, Constantine R. Campbell, and Michael J. Thate. Wissenschaftliche Untersuchungen zum Neuen Testament 2. Tübingen: Mohr Siebeck, 2014.

————. *Reading Paul.* Eugene, OR: Cascade, 2008.

————. *Reading Revelation Responsibly: Uncivil Worship and Witness; Following the Lamb into the New Creation.* Eugene, OR: Cascade, 2011.

————. "Romans: The First Christian Treatise on Theosis," *Journal of Theological Interpretation* 5 (2011): 13-34.

————. "The This-Worldliness of the New Testament's Other-Worldly Spirituality." In *The Bible and Spirituality: Exploratory Essays in Reading Scripture Spiritually,* ed. Andrew T. Lincoln, J. Gordon McConville, and Lloyd K. Pietersen, pp. 151-70. Eugene, OR: Cascade, 2013.

Gorman, Michael J., and David W. Congdon. "Theosis and Mission: The Conversation Continues." No pages. Cited 16 August 2009. Online: http://www .michaeljgorman .net/2009/08/16/theosis -and -mission -the -conversation -continues.

Gorman, Michael J., and Richard Middleton. "Salvation." In vol. 5 of *New Interpreter's Dictionary of the Bible,* ed. Katherine Doob Sakenfeld, pp. 45-61. 5 vols. Nashville: Abingdon, 2009.

Graham, Billy. *Peace with God: The Secret of Happiness.* Garden City, NY: Doubleday, 1953. Rev. ed. Nashville: Thomas Nelson, 1984.

Grieb, A. Katherine. " 'So That in Him We Might Become the Righteousness of God' (2 Cor. 5:21): Some Theological Reflections on the Church Becoming Justice," *Ex Auditu* 22 (2006): 58-80.

Guder, Darrell L., ed. *Missional Church: A Vision for the Sending of the Church in North America.* Grand Rapids: Eerdmans, 1998.

Gupta, Nijay K. *Colossians.* Smyth & Helwys Bible Commentary. Macon, GA: Smyth & Helwys, 2013.

Haacker, Klaus. "Der Römerbrief als Friedensmemorandum," *New Testament Studies* 36 (1990): 25-41.

————. *The Theology of Paul's Letter to the Romans.* Cambridge: Cambridge University Press, 2003.

Habel, Norman C. "The Third Mission of the Church: Good News for the Earth," *Trinity Occasional Papers* 16 (1998): 31-43.

Harink, Douglas. *Paul among the Postliberals: Pauline Theology beyond Christendom and Modernity.* Grand Rapids: Brazos, 2003.

———. "Setting It Right: Doing Justice to Justification," *Christian Century* (June 14, 2005): 20-25.

Hastings, Ross. *Missional God, Missional Church: Hope for Re-evangelizing the West.* Downers Grove, IL: InterVarsity, 2012.

Hauerwas, Stanley. *War and the American Difference: Theological Reflections on Violence and National Identity.* Grand Rapids: Baker Academic, 2011.

Hays, Richard B. "Christ Died for the Ungodly: Narrative Soteriology in Paul?" *Horizons in Biblical Theology* 26 (2004): 48-69.

———. *Echoes of Scripture in the Letters of Paul.* New Haven: Yale University Press, 1989.

———. *The Faith of Jesus Christ: The Narrative Substructure of Gal. 3:1–4:11.* 2nd ed. Grand Rapids: Eerdmans, 2002.

———. *First Corinthians.* Interpretation. Louisville: Westminster John Knox, 1997.

———. *The Moral Vision of the New Testament: Community, Cross, New Creation; A Contemporary Introduction to New Testament Ethics.* San Francisco: HarperCollins, 1996.

———. "Reading the Bible with Eyes of Faith: The Practice of Theological Exegesis," *Journal of Theological Interpretation* 1 (2007): 5-21.

———. "What Is 'Real Participation in Christ'? A Dialogue with E. P. Sanders on Pauline Soteriology." In *Redefining First-Century Jewish and Christian Identities: Essays in Honor of Ed Parish Sanders,* ed. Fabian E. Udoh et al., pp. 335-51. Notre Dame: University of Notre Dame Press, 2008.

Hellerman, Joseph H. *Reconstructing Honor in Roman Philippi: Carmen Christi as Cursus Pudorum.* Society for New Testament Studies Monograph Series 132. Cambridge: Cambridge University Press, 2005.

Heschel, Abraham J. *Between God and Man: An Interpretation of Judaism.* New York: Harper & Row, 1959. Repr., New York: Free Press, 1997.

———. *The Prophets.* Perennial Classics. New York: Harper & Row, 1962. Repr., New York: HarperCollins, 2001.

Holmes, Stephen R. "Trinitarian Missiology: Towards a Theology of God as Missionary," *International Journal of Systematic Theology* 8 (2006): 72-90.

Hooker, Morna D. *From Adam to Christ: Essays on Paul.* Cambridge: Cambridge University Press, 1990. Repr., Eugene, OR: Wipf & Stock, 2008.

———. "On Becoming the Righteousness of God: Another Look at 2 Cor. 5:21," *Novum Testamentum* 50 (2008): 358-75.

Hooker, Morna D., and Frances M. Young. *Holiness and Mission: Learning from the Early Church about Mission in the City.* London: SCM, 2010.

Horrell, David. "A New Perspective on Paul? Rereading Paul in an Age of Ecological Crisis," *Journal for the Study of the New Testament* 33 (2010): 3-30.

Horrell, David, Cherryl Hunt, and Christopher Southgate, eds. *Greening Paul: Read-*

ing the Apostle in a Time of Ecological Crisis. Waco, TX: Baylor University Press, 2010.

Hughes, J. Donald. Ecology in Ancient Civilizations. Albuquerque: University of New Mexico Press, 1975.

Hultgren, Arland J. Christ and His Benefits: Christology and Redemption in the New Testament. Philadelphia: Fortress, 1987.

Hunsberger, George R. "Proposals for a Missional Hermeneutic: Mapping a Conversation," Missiology: An International Review 39 (2011): 309-21.

———. "Starting Points, Trajectories, and Outcomes in Proposals for a Missional Hermeneutic: Mapping the Conversation." Paper presented at the annual meeting of the Society of Biblical Literature. Boston, MA, November 22, 2008. Cited 31 July 2014. Online: http://www.gocn.org/resources/articles/proposals-missional-hermeneutic-mapping-conversation.

Hunsberger, George R., and Craig Van Gelder, eds. The Church between Gospel and Culture: The Emerging Mission in North America. Grand Rapids: Eerdmans, 1997.

Hunsinger, George. How to Read Karl Barth: The Shape of His Theology. New York: Oxford University Press, 1991.

Jackson, Daniel. "The 'Glory About to Be Revealed': Glory in Paul's Letter to the Romans." St. Mary's Seminary & University, Baltimore, MD, May 2013.

Jervis, L. Ann. "Becoming like God through Christ: Discipleship in Romans." In Patterns of Discipleship in the New Testament, ed. Richard N. Longenecker, pp. 143-62. Grand Rapids: Eerdmans, 1996.

Jewett, Robert. Romans: A Commentary. Hermeneia. Minneapolis: Fortress, 2007.

Johnson, Andy. 1-2 Thessalonians. Two Horizons New Testament Commentary. Grand Rapids: Eerdmans, forthcoming.

———. "The Sanctification of the Imagination." In Holiness and Ecclesiology in the New Testament, ed. Kent E. Brower and Andy Johnson, pp. 275-92. Grand Rapids: Eerdmans, 2007.

Jones, Scott J. The Evangelistic Love of God and Neighbor: A Theology of Witness and Discipleship. Nashville: Abingdon, 2003.

Kallenberg, Brad J. Live to Tell: Evangelism for a Postmodern Age. Grand Rapids: Brazos, 2002.

Keating, Daniel A. Deification and Grace. Naples, FL: Sapientia, 2007.

Keck, Leander. Romans. Abingdon New Testament Commentary. Nashville: Abingdon, 2005.

Keener, Craig S. 1-2 Corinthians. New Cambridge Bible Commentary. Cambridge: Cambridge University Press, 2005.

———. Romans. New Covenant Commentary Series. Eugene, OR: Cascade, 2009.

Keown, Mark J. Congregational Evangelism in Philippians: The Centrality of an Appeal for Gospel Proclamation to the Fabric of Philippians. Milton Keynes, UK: Paternoster, 2008. Repr., Eugene, OR: Cascade, 2009.

Kim, Yung Suk. *Christ's Body in Corinth: The Politics of a Metaphor.* Minneapolis: Fortress, 2008.

Kirk, J. R. Daniel. *Unlocking Romans: Resurrection and the Justification of God.* Grand Rapids: Eerdmans, 2008.

Klassen, William. "The God of Peace: New Testament Perspectives on God." In *Towards a Theology of Peace: A Symposium,* ed. Stephen Tunnicliffe, pp. 121-30. London: European Nuclear Disarmament, 1989.

————. "Pursue Peace: A Concrete Ethical Mandate (Romans 12:18-21)." In *Ja und Nein: Christliche Theologie im Angesicht Israels: Festschrift zum 70. Geburtstag von Wolfgang Schrage,* ed. Klaus Wengst and Gerhard Saß, pp. 195-207. Neukirchen-Vluyn: Neukirchener, 1998.

Klauck, Hans-Josef. *Ancient Letters and the New Testament: A Guide to Context and Exegesis.* Waco, TX: Baylor University Press, 2006.

Kraybill, Donald B., Steven M. Nolt, and David L. Weaver-Zercher. *Amish Grace: How Forgiveness Transcended Tragedy.* San Francisco: Jossey-Bass, 2007.

Lewis, C. S. *Mere Christianity.* New York: HarperCollins, 2001 [orig. 1952].

Lincoln, Andrew T. *Ephesians.* Word Biblical Commentary 42. Dallas: Word, 1990.

————. "The Letter to the Colossians: Introduction, Commentary, and Reflections." In vol. 11 of *The New Interpreter's Bible,* ed. Leander E. Keck, pp. 551-669. Nashville: Abingdon, 2000.

Litwa, M. David. "2 Corinthians 3:18 and Its Implications for *Theosis,*" *Journal of Theological Interpretation* 2 (2008): 117-34.

————. *We Are Being Transformed: Deification in Paul's Soteriology.* Beihefte zur Zeitschrift für die neutestamentliche Wissenschaft 187. Berlin: De Gruyter, 2012.

Long, Adrian. *Paul and Human Rights: A Dialogue with the Father of the Corinthian Community.* The Bible in the Modern World 26. Sheffield: Sheffield Phoenix Press, 2009.

Longenecker, Bruce W. *Remember the Poor: Paul, Poverty, and the Greco-Roman World.* Grand Rapids: Eerdmans, 2010.

Lossky, Vladimir. *The Mystical Theology of the Eastern Church.* Crestwood, NY: St. Vladimir's Seminary Press, 1976. Reprint of *The Mystical Theology of the Eastern Church.* London: James Clarke, 1957. Translation of *Essai sur la théologie mystique de l'Église d'Orient.* Paris: Éditions Montaigne, 1944.

Maddox, Randy L. "John Wesley and Eastern Orthodoxy: Influences, Convergences, and Differences," *Asbury Journal* 45 (1990): 29-53.

Madigan, Kevin J., and Jon D. Levenson. *Resurrection: The Power of God for Christians and Jews.* New Haven: Yale University Press, 2008.

Malchow, Bruce V. *Social Justice in the Hebrew Bible.* Collegeville, MN: Liturgical, 1996.

Malherbe, Abraham J. *The Letters to the Thessalonians.* Anchor Bible 32b. New York: Doubleday, 2000.

Marshall, Christopher. "'Making Every Effort': Peacemaking and Ecclesiology in

Ephesians 4:1-6." In *Struggles for Shalom: Peace and Violence Across the Testaments,* ed. Laura L. Brenneman and Brad D. Schantz, pp. 256-66. Eugene, OR: Pickwick, 2013.

Martin, Ralph, and Peter Williamson, eds. *John Paul II and the New Evangelization: How You Can Bring Good News to Others.* Cincinnati: Servant Books, 2006.

Martin, Ralph P. *Reconciliation: A Study of Paul's Theology.* Atlanta: John Knox, 1981.

Martin, Ralph P., and Brian J. Dodd, eds. *Where Christology Began: Essays on Philippians 2.* Louisville: Westminster John Knox, 1998.

Martin, Ralph P., and Gerald F. Hawthorne. *Philippians.* Word Biblical Commentary 43. Rev. ed. Nashville: Thomas Nelson, 2004.

Matera, Frank J. *II Corinthians: A Commentary.* New Testament Library. Louisville: Westminster John Knox, 2003.

Mauser, Ulrich. *The Gospel of Peace: A Scriptural Message for Today's World.* Studies in Peace and Scripture 1. Louisville: Westminster John Knox, 1992.

Míguez, Nestor O. *The Practice of Hope: Ideology and Intention in 1 Thessalonians.* Translated by Aquíles Martínez. Paul in Critical Contexts. Minneapolis: Fortress, 2012.

Miller, James C. *The Obedience of Faith, the Eschatological People of God, and the Purpose of Romans.* Society of Biblical Literature Dissertation Series 177. Atlanta: Society of Biblical Literature, 2000.

———. *Reading Scripture Missionally.* Eugene, OR: Cascade, forthcoming.

Moltmann, Jürgen. *The Crucified God: The Cross as the Foundation and Criticism of Christian Theology.* Translated by Margaret Kohl. London: SCM, 1974. Repr., Minneapolis: Fortress, 1993.

Moo, Douglas J. "Justification in Galatians." In *Understanding the Times: New Testament Studies in the 21st Century; Essays in Honor of D. A. Carson on the Occasion of His 65th Birthday,* ed. Andreas J. Köstenberger and Robert W. Yarbrough, pp. 160-95. Wheaton, IL: Crossway, 2011.

Morales, Rodrigo. "A Liturgical Conversion of the Imagination: Worship and Ethics in 1 Corinthians," *Letter and Spirit* 5 (2009): 103-24.

Munck, Johannes. *Paul and the Salvation of Mankind.* Translated by Frank Clarke. London: SCM, 1959.

Murphy-O'Connor, Jerome. *Paul: A Critical Life.* New York: Oxford University Press, 1996.

Myers, Ched, and Elaine Enns. *Ambassadors of Reconciliation,* Vol. 1: *New Testament Reflections on Restorative Justice and Peacemaking.* Maryknoll, NY: Orbis, 2009.

———. *Ambassadors of Reconciliation,* Vol. 2: *Diverse Christian Practices of Restorative Justice and Peacemaking.* Maryknoll, NY: Orbis, 2009.

Nellas, Panayiotis. *Deification in Christ: Orthodox Perspectives on the Nature of the Human Person.* Translated by Norman Russell. Crestwood, NY: St. Vladimir's Seminary Press, 1987.

Newbigin, Lesslie. *The Gospel in a Pluralist Society.* Grand Rapids: Eerdmans, 1989.

————. *The Open Secret: An Introduction to the Theology of Mission.* Rev. ed. Grand Rapids: Eerdmans, 1995.

Newman, Carey C. *Paul's Glory-Christology: Tradition and Rhetoric.* Novum Testamentum Supplements 69. Leiden: Brill, 1992.

Oakes, Peter. *Philippians: From People to Letter.* Society for New Testament Studies Monograph Series 110. Cambridge: Cambridge University Press, 2001.

O'Brien, P. T. *Gospel and Mission in the Writings of Paul: An Exegetical and Theological Analysis.* Grand Rapids: Baker, 1995.

Perkins, Pheme. "Justice, NT." In vol. 3 of *The New Interpreter's Dictionary of the Bible,* ed. Katherine Doob Sakenfeld, pp. 475-76. 5 vols. Nashville: Abingdon, 2008.

Peterson, Brian K. "Being the Church in Philippi," *Horizons in Biblical Theology* 30 (2008): 163-78.

Plummer, Robert L. *Paul's Understanding of the Church's Mission: Did the Apostle Paul Expect the Early Christian Communities to Evangelize?* Paternoster Biblical Monographs. Milton Keynes, UK: Paternoster, 2006.

Porter, Stanley E. "Reconciliation as the Heart of Paul's Missionary Theology." In *Paul as Missionary: Identity, Activity, Theology, and Practice,* ed. Trevor J. Burke and Brian S. Rosner, pp. 169-79. Library of New Testament Studies 420. London: T. & T. Clark, 2011.

Powers, Daniel G. *Salvation through Participation: An Examination of the Notion of the Believers' Corporate Unity with Christ in Early Christian Soteriology.* Contributions to Biblical Exegesis and Theology 29. Leuven: Peeters, 2001.

Prokhorov, Alexander V. "Taking the Jews out of the Equation: Galatians 6.12-17 as a Summons to Cease Evading Persecution," *Journal for the Study of the New Testament* 36 (2013): 172-88.

Purves, David R. "Relating Kenosis to Soteriology: Implications for Christian Ministry amongst Homeless People," *Horizons in Biblical Theology* 35 (2013): 70-90.

Rauschenbusch, Walter. *A Theology for the Social Gospel.* New York: Macmillan, 1917. Repr., Louisville: Westminster John Knox, 1997.

Reasoner, Mark. *Roman Imperial Texts: A Sourcebook.* Minneapolis: Fortress, 2013.

Reumann, John. "Justification and Justice in the New Testament," *Horizons in Biblical Theology* 21 (1999): 26-45.

————. *Philippians.* Anchor Bible 33b. New Haven: Yale University Press, 2008.

Rowe, C. Kavin. *World Upside Down: Reading Acts in the Graeco-Roman Age.* New York: Oxford University Press, 2009.

Russell, Norman. *Fellow Workers with God: Orthodox Thinking on Theosis.* Crestwood, NY: St. Vladimir's Seminary Press, 2009.

Rutba House, ed. *School(s) for Conversion: 12 Marks of a New Monasticism.* Eugene, OR: Wipf & Stock, 2005.

Rynkiewich, Michael A. "Mission, Hermeneutics, and the Local Church," *Journal of Theological Interpretation* 1 (2007): 47-60.

Sanders, E. P. *Paul and Palestinian Judaism.* Philadelphia: Fortress, 1977.

Schnabel, Eckhard J. *Paul the Missionary: Realities, Strategies and Methods.* Downers Grove, IL: InterVarsity, 2008.

Schnelle, Udo. *Theology of the New Testament.* Translated by M. Eugene Boring. Grand Rapids: Baker Academic, 2009.

Schottroff, Luise. "Holiness and Justice: Exegetical Comments on 1 Corinthians 11.17-34," *Journal for the Study of the New Testament* 79 (2005): 51-60.

Shortt, Rupert. *Christianophobia: A Faith Under Attack.* Grand Rapids: Eerdmans, 2012.

Sider, Ronald J. *Nonviolent Action: What Christian Ethics Demands but Most Christians Have Never Really Tried.* Grand Rapids: Baker Academic, 2015.

Sider, Ronald J., Philip N. Olson, and Heidi Rolland Unruh. *Churches That Make a Difference: Reaching Your Community with Good News and Good Works.* Grand Rapids: Baker, 2002.

Smith-Christopher, Daniel L. "Peace in the OT." In vol. 4 of *The New Interpreter's Dictionary of the Bible,* ed. Katherine Doob Sakenfeld, pp. 423-25. 5 vols. Nashville: Abingdon, 2009.

Stegman, Thomas D. "'Run That You May Obtain the Prize' (1 Cor. 9:24): St. Paul and the Spiritual Exercises," *Studies in the Spirituality of the Jesuits* 44 (2012): 16-19.

———. *Second Corinthians.* Catholic Commentary on Sacred Scripture. Grand Rapids: Baker Academic, 2009.

Still, Todd D. *Conflict at Thessalonica: A Pauline Church and Its Neighbours.* Journal for the Study of the New Testament: Supplement Series 183. Sheffield: Sheffield University Press, 1999.

———. "Paul's Thessalonian Mission," *Southwestern Journal of Theology* 42 (1999): 4-16.

Stone, Bryan P. *Evangelism after Christendom: The Theology and Practice of Christian Witness.* Grand Rapids: Brazos, 2006.

Street, R. Alan. *Subversive Meals: An Analysis of the Lord's Supper under Roman Domination during the First Century.* Eugene, OR: Pickwick, 2013.

Stubbs, David L. "The Shape of Soteriology and the *Pistis Christou* Debate," *Scottish Journal of Theology* 61 (2008): 137-57.

Sunquist, Scott W. *Understanding Christian Mission: Participation in Suffering and Glory.* Grand Rapids: Baker Academic, 2013.

Swartley, Willard M. *Covenant of Peace: The Missing Peace in New Testament Theology and Ethics.* Grand Rapids: Eerdmans, 2006.

———. "Peace and Violence in the New Testament: Definition and Methodology." In *Struggles for Shalom: Peace and Violence Across the Testaments,* ed. Laura L. Brenneman and Brad D. Schantz, pp. 141-54. Eugene, OR: Pickwick, 2014.

———. "Peace in the NT." In vol. 4 of *The New Interpreter's Dictionary of the Bible,* ed. Katherine Doob Sakenfeld, pp. 422-23. 5 vols. Nashville: Abingdon, 2009.

———. "The Relation of Justice/Righteousness to *Shalom/Eirēnē,*" *Ex Auditu* 22 (2006): 29-53.

————. *Send Forth Your Light: A Vision for Peace, Mission, and Worship.* Scottdale, PA: Herald Press, 2007.

Talmon, Shemaryahu. "The Signification of שלום and Its Semantic Field in the Hebrew Bible." In *The Quest for Context and Meaning: Studies in Biblical Intertextuality in Honor of James A. Sanders,* ed. Craig A. Evans and Shemaryahu Talmon, pp. 75-115. Leiden: Brill, 1997.

Tamez, Elsa. *The Amnesty of Grace: Justification by Faith from a Latin American Perspective.* Translated by Sharon H. Ringe. Nashville: Abingdon, 1993.

Tannehill, Robert C. "Participation in Christ." In *The Shape of the Gospel: New Testament Essays,* pp. 223-37. Eugene, OR: Cascade, 2007.

Thompson, James W. *The Church according to Paul: Rediscovering the Community Conformed to Christ.* Grand Rapids: Baker Academic, 2014.

————. *Moral Formation according to Paul: The Context and Coherence of Pauline Ethics.* Grand Rapids: Baker Academic, 2011.

————. *Pastoral Ministry according to Paul: A Biblical Vision.* Grand Rapids: Baker Academic, 2006.

Thompson, Marianne Meye. *Colossians & Philemon.* Two Horizons New Testament Commentary. Grand Rapids: Eerdmans, 2005.

Tilling, Chris, ed. *Beyond Old and New Perspectives on Paul: Reflections on the Work of Douglas Campbell.* Eugene, OR: Cascade, 2014.

Torrance, T. F. *Theology in Reconstruction.* Grand Rapids: Eerdmans, 1965. Repr., Eugene, OR: Wipf & Stock, 1996.

United States Conference of Catholic Bishops. "Called to Be Disciples: The New Evangelization." Washington, DC: United States Conference of Catholic Bishops, 2012.

Van Gelder, Craig, and Dwight J. Zscheile. *The Missional Church in Perspective: Mapping Trends and Shaping the Conversation.* Grand Rapids: Baker Academic, 2011.

Vanhoozer, Kevin J., Constantine R. Campbell, and Michael J. Thate, eds. *'In Christ' in Paul: Explorations in Paul's Theology of Union and Participation.* Wissenschaftliche Untersuchungen zum Neuen Testament 2. Tübingen: Mohr Siebeck, 2014.

Villiers, Pieter G. R. de. "Peace in the Pauline Letters: A Perspective on Biblical Spirituality," *Neotestamentica* 43 (2009): 1-26.

Volf, Miroslav. "The Social Meaning of Reconciliation," *Interpretation* 54 (2002): 158-72.

Waaler, Erik. "Israel's Scripture in Phil. 2:5-11." Paper presented at the annual meeting of the Society of Biblical Literature. New Orleans, LA, November 23, 2009.

Wagner, J. Ross. "Working Out Salvation: Holiness and Community in Philippians." In *Holiness and Ecclesiology in the New Testament,* ed. Kent E. Brower and Andy Johnson, pp. 257-74. Grand Rapids: Eerdmans, 2007.

Ware, James P. *Paul and the Mission of the Church: Philippians in Ancient Jewish Context.* Grand Rapids: Baker Academic, 2011.

Weima, Jeffrey A. D. "'Peace and security' (1 Thess. 5.3): Prophetic Warning or Political Propaganda?" *New Testament Studies* 58 (2012): 331-59.

Wengst, Klaus. *Pax Romana and the Peace of Jesus Christ.* Translated by John Bowden. Philadelphia: Fortress, 1987.

Wesley, John and Charles. *Hymns on the Lord's Supper.* Bristol: Farley, 1745. Repr., London: Paramore, 1786. Cited: 31 July 2014. Online: http://divinity.duke.edu/initiatives-centers/cswt/wesley-texts/charles-wesley.

Williamson, Peter S. *Ephesians.* Catholic Commentary on Sacred Scripture. Grand Rapids: Baker, 2009.

Wilson, Jonathan R. *God's Good World: Reclaiming the Doctrine of Creation.* Grand Rapids: Baker Academic, 2013.

Wilson-Hartgrove, Jonathan. *The Awakening of Hope: Why We Practice a Common Faith.* Grand Rapids: Zondervan, 2012.

———. *New Monasticism: What It Has to Say to Today's Church.* Grand Rapids: Brazos, 2008.

———. "Rutba House: Family Economics in the Household of God." No pages. Cited 31 July 2014. Online: http://emerging-communities.com/tag/rutba-house.

———. *Strangers at My Door: A True Story of Finding Jesus in Unexpected Guests.* New York: Convergent/Random House, 2013.

———. *The Wisdom of Stability: Rooting Faith in a Mobile Culture.* Brewster, MA: Paraclete, 2010.

Winter, Bruce W. *Seek the Welfare of the City: Christians as Benefactors and Citizens.* Grand Rapids: Eerdmans, 1994.

Witherington, Ben, III. *1 and 2 Thessalonians: A Socio-Rhetorical Commentary.* Grand Rapids: Eerdmans, 2006.

———. *Paul's Letter to the Philippians: A Socio-Rhetorical Commentary.* Grand Rapids: Eerdmans, 2011.

Witherup, Ronald D. *Saint Paul and the New Evangelization.* Collegeville, MN: Liturgical, 2013.

Wrede, Wilhelm. *Paul.* Translated by Edward Lummis. London: Green, 1907. Translation of *Paulus.* Halle: Gebauer-Schwetschke, 1904.

Wright, Christopher J. H. *The Mission of God: Unlocking the Bible's Grand Narrative.* Downers Grove, IL: InterVarsity, 2006.

———. *Old Testament Ethics for the People of God.* Downers Grove, IL: InterVarsity, 2004.

Wright, N. T. *The Case for the Psalms: Why They Are Essential.* New York: HarperCollins, 2013.

———. *Justification: God's Plan and Paul's Vision.* Downers Grove, IL: InterVarsity, 2009.

———. *Kingdom New Testament: A Contemporary Translation.* New York: HarperOne, 2011.

———. "New Perspectives on Paul." In *Justification in Perspective: Historical Devel-*

*opments and Contemporary Challenges,* ed. Bruce L. McCormack, pp. 243-64. Grand Rapids: Baker Academic, 2006.

―――. "On Becoming the Righteousness of God: 2 Corinthians 5:21." In *Pauline Theology.* Vol. 2: *1 and 2 Corinthians,* ed. David M. Hay, pp. 200-208. Minneapolis: Fortress, 1993.

―――. *Paul and the Faithfulness of God.* Vol. 4 of Christian Origins and the Question of God. Minneapolis: Fortress, 2013.

―――. *Paul: In Fresh Perspective.* Minneapolis: Fortress, 2005.

―――. *What Saint Paul Really Said: Was Paul of Tarsus the Real Founder of Christianity?* Grand Rapids: Eerdmans, 1997.

Yoder, John Howard. *He Came Preaching Peace.* Scottdale, PA: Herald Press, 1985. Repr., Eugene, OR: Wipf & Stock, 1998.

―――. *The Politics of Jesus: Behold the Man! Our Victorious Lamb.* 2nd ed. Grand Rapids: Eerdmans, 1994.

Yoder, Perry B. *Shalom: The Bible's Word for Salvation, Justice, and Peace.* Nappanee, IN: Evangel, 1987.

Young, Frances M. "Understanding Romans in the Light of 2 Corinthians," *Scottish Journal of Theology* 43 (1990): 433-46.

Zerbe, Gordon Mark. *Citizenship: Paul on Peace and Politics.* Winnipeg, MB: CMU Press, 2012.

―――. "Paul's Ethic of Nonretaliation and Peace." In *The Love of Enemy and Nonretaliation in the New Testament,* ed. Willard M. Swartley, pp. 177-222. Louisville: Westminster John Knox, 1992.

Zizioulas, John D. *Being as Communion: Studies in Personhood and the Church.* Crestwood, NY: St. Vladimir's Seminary Press, 1985.

# Index of Subjects and Names

# Index of Scripture and Other Ancient Sources